LINCOLN

LINCOLN IN 1858

*From an ambrotype, said to have been made by T. P. Pearson,
in Macomb, Illinois*

ABRAHAM LINCOLN

The Full Life Story of
Our Martyred President

BY

EMIL LUDWIG

Translated by
EDEN and CEDAR PAUL

ILLUSTRATED

2166

NEW YORK
LIVERIGHT PUBLISHING CORPORATION

BLACK *and* GOLD EDITION

JANUARY, 1949

*

Copyright 1929, 1930

By EMIL LUDWIG

*

Dedicated

to

THOMAS A. EDISON

who, in 1860, as a newsboy of thirteen, sold Lincoln's campaign picture on railroad trains, and brought down to us Lincoln's spirit of humanity

PREFACE

The art of portraying human characters cannot be achieved by merely studying historical documents: it is practiced and learned in a never-ending study of living men and women. But we want the inspiring light of a great character to make documents breathe with the vividness and veracity of to-day.

I am sure that my American friends are not expecting me to give them a new Lincoln, or to open up fresh and undiscovered material, but rather to present Lincoln in a new historical method.

Consequently, I have made no effort to cover the history of slavery and of the great Civil War, but only to paint a picture of Abraham Lincoln. Excepting the English, Europeans, even intelligent and scholarly men and women, know far less about American history than Americans about the story of Europe, so I consider it one of the happiest privileges of my career to be able to present this greatest of American characters to the Old World.

In the New World, a number of American specialists, particularly Miss Ida M. Tarbell and Mr. Frazier Hunt, have earned my thanks by their advice and coöperation. I have no doubt, however, that many of my American readers will find faults in my story, and I can only beg them to consider the portrait as a whole and not to be too critical of minute parts. Lincoln's career, more than that of any other man in history, is so grandly conceived by Fate that the first act is illuminated by the last, and every scene is bound together by dramatic destiny.

I see him like one of Shakespeare's characters, absolutely original, comparable to none, immemorably unique. He has fascinated me for years, and if some good may be found in this effort of mine, it has sprung from a personal sympathy which I have never felt so strongly for any other great man of history.

E. L.

Table of Contents

List of Plates

From photographs in the collection of Frederick H. Meserve, New York

BOOK ONE
WAGE EARNER

I

The wintry blast howls round the cabin. As the storm sweeps over the clearing, the giant trees, still standing, groan beneath its buffetings. But these settlers within the cabin are used to the storm and sleep soundly, deaf to the tumult. Parents and children alike are tired out after the long labors of the day.

All but one of them. A little boy, four years old, has just been awakened by a stone blown from the chimney, that rattles down the rough, hand-split shingles and thumps against the log sides. It strikes the very spot where he and his sister are lying on a bed of sacks filled with dried leaves. He sees her little hand, one of her ears, and her rumpled, dark hair. Cuddling up against her for warmth, he can feel her toes with his. It's a good thing there is still a glimmer from the fire. He can amuse himself by looking around the room.

He sees something close at hand, glimmering with a golden sheen — Mother says that heaven is aglow with gold like that. It is the water in the great wooden bucket which she fills at the brook every evening. There's something else that glints in the firelight, hanging on the wall: Father's ax. The children are not allowed to touch it, for it is frightfully sharp, and will chop off a finger before you know where you are. Father is sound asleep there, under the ax, beside Mother. He's snoring again!

The little boy's thoughts, in their wandering course, come now to the sleeping mother. A sense of deprivation steals over him as he recalls how he used to lie beside her. His earliest memories are of lying close to Mother's warm body. The thought of the lost warmth makes him feel colder than ever. He would like to call to Mother for help, but Father has told him not to. It will be all right soon. He manages to pull some of the coverlet away from Sarah. It's warmer now. — In a trice, he is asleep once more.

When he wakes, the fire is burning brightly, its warmth and color driving out the gray daylight that blinks through the crannies. Sarah is still asleep, but Mother is standing by the fire, pouring some hot water into the milk — because one of the three cows has just died. The youngster knows that, for he is sharp of sight and hearing, takes note of all that goes on around him. No doubt Father is out in the barn now. Yet when he asks, Mother makes no answer; she is too busy.

Deliberately, as if in play, he puts on his breeches, jacket, and shoes; all made of buckskin. Father skinned the deer and tanned the hide; Mother stitched the things together; nobody wears anything but buckskin.

"When will it be Sunday?" he asks Mother, snuggling down beside the fire. She laughs, for she knows what he has in mind — the biscuits she always bakes on Saturdays. From the shelf which is out of the children's reach she takes down the last loaf, and with the big bread-knife she cuts him a substantial slice. As he squats on the floor, dipping the bread in the milk before he eats it, suddenly she stoops, gives him a hug, and kisses him. He sits quite still, arms outstretched, tin cup of milk in one hand and slice of bread in the other, waiting till she has finished and he can go on eating. Then, glancing up at her, he wonders why she looks so sad; he does not ask, for she can't bear to be asked that.

Now she stands at the table. The table top is a rough-hewn slab, with the bark still coating the under surface; it is smoother above, but even there a little boy must be careful about touching it or he will get a splinter in his finger, which will make him cry, and then Father will scold.

They are frontier folk, living in Kentucky, at a time when half the New World is still virgin forest — as the Old World was two thousand years ago. This is a barren region; it is even called "the Wilderness." Before a man can be a farmer and grow Indian corn, he needs must fell the great trees and clear the ground and win most of his food with his long-barreled rifle.

There he comes back, the hunter! Towards noon, the children hear the dog barking. Undoing the thong with which the door is fastened, they tumble out into the open to meet their father, who comes, musket on shoulder, carrying a fine, big hare. Tall, dark, and bearded, he is clad in skins made from the game of his own shooting. He prefers a hunter's life to a carpenter's, though really he is a carpenter by trade; when he works at his bench he makes tables and chairs for the neighbors. As the man lounges now by the fire, and, sharp-set, falls to upon the food his wife has served on the earthenware platter, the boy, looking at them both, thinks to himself that his mother has a harder time of it than his father.

II

When the boy is five, his restless father moves with his family eleven miles to the north. Here are fine woods and rich soil. The new cabin stands above a running brooklet. In summer, life is easy; it is no longer cold at night, and there's plenty to eat, for the woods are full of game. Not far from the log cabin runs the high road. Such a lot to see there, for it connects two towns. As the boy grows older, he learns their names, Louisville and Nashville. Wagons pass by, sometimes several of them in one day, carrying grown-ups and children with their belongings, always in the direction of the setting sun. Men ride towards the town, taking sacks of corn along with them. Others bring back boxes filled with all sorts of wonders. Soldiers go by too, from time to time; Father says they are on their way home from the war. Once there comes a man in such splendid clothes — Mother says they are made of wool. He talks to Father about the rich soil of the Far West, and how cheap land is out there.

The children are not allowed to play in the road for as long as they would like. Their mother calls them home, sets them to weeding the garden, to gathering berries and picking mushrooms. These she dries and stores up for the winter. When the boy is six or seven, his father takes him into the fields, not to play, but to do his share of the labor. Up and down, up and down! It's tiring work, sawing, but one must learn to do it well. At home, Sarah helps her mother to milk the cows, and she spins of an evening.

But on Sundays they sit in front of the cabin, and their mother, who has a lovely voice, though not a very strong one, sings to them. Sometimes she tells them Bible tales, for she has the wonderful memory of an illiterate. Throughout life the lad's speech will smack of the Scriptural phraseology which becomes so familiar to him in early youth. Father sits by, smoking as he listens. Comparing the two, the boy cannot but be drawn more to his mother. She is gentler, younger; and, though quite as tall as her husband, she seems more winsome. He studies her shrewdly but unobtrusively; notes the sallow tint of her skin, sees that her features are pinched; looks into her sad, gray eyes. His heart is touched, and he understands why she is inclined to sing slow and mournful songs.

One Sunday, however, when they all go to visit friends in the village, he is surprised to see her among the merriest in the company. She outdances the rest as if nothing could tire her. This is his first acquaintance with alternations of mood from sad to gay and back again. Something stirs dimly in the depths within him, where he feels, with a budding alarm, that his mother, too, must have hidden depths in her nature.

Now and again, he goes with her to a neighboring farm, where she sits and sews. These folk have a big house. The kitchen alone is larger than the whole cabin at home. Upstairs are two rooms in which there are real beds — Father made them. Why should Father and Mother work for other people? Because the carpentry and the needlework bring in money, which will buy a new horse. Why have the others more money? Because they are rich. Why? No answer.

The boy's wonderment grows as he studies these and other neighbors. An uncle and an aunt have come to live near by. He is especially fond of Auntie Sparrow. She is a lively woman, brisk in her movements, clever, solidly built, gray-headed, in better health than his mother. She has fine things to tell the children, for in youth she traveled far afield, and saw some of the happenings in the great war when the Americans gave the English a thrashing. She can read the Bible and even write as easily and as freely as if she had never had to help in the fields and garden.

The children sometimes ask Father and Mother what they did when they were young. Their mother says her forbears came from Virginia, a long way off. But when the little boy asks about her mother, and where Auntie came from, she gives evasive answers.

Their father is more communicative. Fond as he is of riding, he is even fonder of telling the children about earlier days. This time he has a story about the Indians. A good while back his folk had come here from Virginia; really, like Mother's, they had sprung from the North, and had no truck with the South. When he was a little boy, no bigger than Sonny now (Sonny listens with all his ears, staring at his father and pursing his lips), the Indians were on the warpath against the white men. One day he was in the forest with his father and his brother, near the cabin, when a shot rang out. Father fell; Brother ran home for help; he was left alone, for Father did not stir after the redskins shot him. Father was dead. The redskins came out from among the trees, and started to carry off the youngster, who cried and struggled. Brother came back with a musket and killed one of the braves. Then there was shooting all over the place and the child ran back to the log hut.

The little boy has listened breathlessly to his father's tale. If Grandfather, after whom he was called Abraham, was killed by the Indians, the same thing might happen to Father any day! The father laughs, saying that new times have come now.

How beautifully Father tells a story, think the children. But he cannot read, and he laughs at Mother when she says that learning to read is a good thing. He can make cupboards and window frames, can shoot, can fell trees; what does he want with book learning?

"Still, I should like to be able to read," thinks the little boy — "and write too, like Aunt!" He goes to school now, four miles there and back, and when it rains he might just as well go barefoot, for all his moccasins do to keep his feet dry. The school is a log hut, scarcely larger than the cabin at home, with a dirt floor, but with windows, and a big hearth. Teacher is a local Irishman. A book is passed from hand to hand, the teacher shows them the letters, makes them spell out the words, over and over and over again.

So that's reading, is it? Letters and words, letters and words; nothing like a story as yet. As for writing like Aunt Sparrow, they have not even begun to learn it.

But this year brings other events; his father has been appointed road surveyor. The little boy, going to town sometimes with Father, hears talk of Indiana, a wonderfully fertile land, north of Kentucky; and of the Ohio, the great river which flows between the two States. As road surveyor, or supervisor, Father sometimes has constabulary duties to perform; and, having a taste for any kind of occupation rather than carpentering at home, he gets about a good deal — made welcome everywhere because he is a good story-teller. The boy is quick to notice when a story is a little different at a second telling!

When Father meets a Negro he asks the man to show his papers — a permit entitling him to travel. "Why?" asks the boy. "You can't understand that yet."

Once some prisoners are put in his father's charge. What are prisoners? Bad men, in irons. The child is horrified at the fierce faces of these bad men, who scowl at the supervisor as, with a huge, rusty key, he opens the door of the dark little lockup, and motions them in. There they remain, behind a barred door. Bad men? The boy's heart goes out to them, all the same. So there are some folk who put iron chains on other folk's feet? That's even worse than that there should be rich people for whom Father must make chairs and Mother sew before they can buy meal and salt.

A lot more to see and to think about this summer! Father fells some of the tallest trees. With the ax, sharpened from time to time with the whetstone tied to his belt, he cuts into the old giants close above the roots. "Why? We've got a house already!" "That's going to be a raft." "What is a raft?" "A big, flat sort of ship which can float down river to the sea." "Where is the sea?" "'Way down south." The boy can hold the cords now, can help a little in the making of the raft; can think he is helping to push the raft off from the shore of Knob Creek, which runs into Salt River, as Salt River runs into the great Ohio. His father rolls ten barrels down to the creek and loads them on to the raft. They are full of

whisky. Mother is always sighing, these days, and at length the
children learn why. Dad has sold their cabin and the farm. He is
going to move to Indiana, where the land is much richer. To work
little and earn easily is what he likes. The sale has brought in the
ten barrels of whisky and twenty dollars in cash. Who knows
what good fortune may be waiting for them up there in the
north?

At last everything is ready. They stand on the bank, waving
farewells. Father pushes off, steers with a long, newly made oar,
floating downstream, and is soon lost in the distance. Ere long,
however, he is back again, with much to tell them about his journey.
He is in a laughing humor, claps his wife heartily on the back, and
declares that Indiana is a paradise. Autumn comes; rainy weather.
They pack up their belongings; pots and pans, tools, coverlets,
clothing; all are loaded on two horses. Mother and Sis climb on
top of one load; Father takes the little boy in front of him on the
other. Off they go, in the direction in which they have watched
so many others go before them. The journey takes five days. At
night, Father keeps watch while Mother and the two children sleep
on a bed of branches and leaves. There are still wild beasts in these
parts, and wild men to fear.

III

Their new home in Pigeon Creek is to be larger and better lighted
than was the cabin in Kentucky. They have all set to work together to build it, the father and his relatives, camping meanwhile
as best they can in the pole shed run up near at hand. Uncle, Aunt,
and a cousin have all come to the newly settled region, under spell of
the old lure. The boy is glad when he sees his father cutting larger
trees and making the cabin bigger, and also he is happy that it has
a loft beneath the roof. Father is always cheerful now. Luck has
turned, and he's going to get rich. There is fine hunting here;
the land is full of game. The new farm is on a little hill, surrounded by swampy thickets. The spring is rather far off, however.
Nearly a mile for the children to fetch water, and they must be
careful not to spill it on the way back. The boy, who is eight

now, sleeps in the loft, clambering up by rungs which Father has nailed to the wall. That is easy, and great fun; but it is pitch-dark in the loft, for there is no window, or firelight.

More life and movement here than at the old home. Mother's parents, the old Sparrows, have come to Indiana, bringing along their adopted son, Dennis Hanks, a youth of eighteen. They are not so very old, the grandparents, and they make much of little Abraham.

They have to live pretty close together, these relatives. The country is much wilder; there are bears in the woods, and a man was killed by them not long ago. A fire is kept burning day and night in front of the pole shed where they live until the cabins are finished, partly to scare away the beasts, and partly to make things warmer and drier. The region is marshy; horses and cattle sicken, and men are struck down with fever; the children have to take Peruvian bark, to keep off malaria. Maybe it's of some use, but it makes them low-spirited. A strange dread of the open country has driven these folks into the woods and thickets, where they have to make clearings and grub up stumps, before they can plow and plant corn. The young people must lend a hand, especially a strong lad like Abe, sowing in springtime, harvesting in August. At all seasons he must help his mother, and soon take her place, beating the corn into meal with the flat of an ax, feeding the pigs, milking the cows, fetching wood and water. Thus does life run its round from day to day, from year to year. In the winter they can rarely wash; often they huddle for days around the fire; then comes a neighbor and they all, even the women folk, drink, smoke, chew snuff and spit; and tell weird stories.

Then comes an October, two years after the arrival at the new home, when a malignant fever breaks out, striking down beast and man. Have the cattle eaten something unwholesome? Is it because the soil is too damp? Who can tell? The horses cannot get up; the sheep writhe on the ground; the milk has to be poured away; men, women, and children take the infection, and lie groaning on their beds. Send for the doctor? The nearest doctor lives thirty-five miles away, and has his hands full in his own district.

The inertia of grave illness and the desperate longing to do what is best for oneself and one's housemates get the upper hand by turns. Inertia has the best of it. No one to care for those of the children who have not yet fallen sick; no one to cook; no one to work in the fields; no one to tend the cattle; no one to swing an ax. No one! No one! Mother lies sick; all are ailing together; some are at the point of death.

Neighbors die. Grandfather and Grandmother die on their leaf beds in the pole shed. Then comes Mother's turn. She has a lean, ill-nourished frame, inclining to consumption, apparently lacking in the will-to-live, and the illness has its way with her. The boy, nearly ten now, stands by the pallid woman's couch, and cannot help her or himself. He watches his father's tears falling thick and fast, drenching the unkempt beard. During the early days of the epidemic the child's mood has been one of mingled alarm and curiosity. Since the first death has occurred among the neighbors, most of Father's time has been spent in making coffins, roughly timbered. The sound of the hammering, when the boards were being joined together — with whittled wooden pegs — is nerve-racking to the sick and a menace to those still afoot.

He watches furtively as his father takes the measure of the dead mother's body; tall, she is, he thinks, and will need a long coffin. While the father is making it, the boy has to help, fetching and carrying. That takes his mind momentarily off his sorrow.

When his mother has been laid in the coffin and the coffin has been put away under the sod, when he comes back to look at the empty couch, the thoughtful boy is overwhelmed with a sense of loneliness. His father is no longer dear to him. If, as happens sometimes, Father gives him a rough word or a slap, he recalls that his mother has always been gentle to him. In her melancholy moods she had sometimes looked steadfastly at him, as if thinking that he was growing up to resemble her. The sense that there had been a secret sympathy between them (a sympathy which had perhaps existed only in his imagination) springs up in his mind, and becomes intensified by his sorrow. It is to last all his life. The proneness of reflective and serious natures to long for the unattainable and the irrevocable makes him cherish the memory of his mother, and increases his spells of melancholy.

A year later the father sets out on a journey; says he is off to town and will not be back for some time. Maybe he tells the children he is going to bring them a new mother, or perhaps the cousin has overheard some discussion. Certainly the thoughtful boy, eleven years old now, spends an uneasy fortnight, for he has heard plenty of stories about stepmothers.

Then comes the evening in December when the father returns. Four horses draw the wagon that brings him back from Kentucky, well-fed horses and a smart wagon. The children's hearts are fluttering with anxiety. What will *she* be like? A strong, bright-looking, rather talkative woman gets out; she has curly hair and a friendly countenance. But who are those others? No less troubled than the two children peeping out of the farmhouse are the three children peeping from under the cover of the wagon; and perhaps the father is the most embarrassed of them all. However, he brings the strange youngsters in, and introduces them as John, Sarah, and Matilda. Another Sarah! Abe and his Sarah have little time to think about this at the moment. Their father is unloading boxes and baskets, unwrapping furniture, producing a polished wardrobe, and real beds!

In a few days, those who had made acquaintance so shyly are playing together in friendly fashion. Abe and Sarah learn that their new mother likewise is named Sarah. This third Sarah gets to work promptly, setting matters to rights. The cracks between the logs must be filled up with clay; the table must be planed; and soon Abraham, still sleeping in the loft, does so on a sure-enough bedstead, with John Johnston beside him.

Johnston had been his father's name, says the stepbrother; dead only last autumn. Then Father must have known my new mother a good while back, thinks the youngster, puzzling matters out for himself.

Although there is no evidence that the second Mrs. Lincoln can read, she values book-learning, and is set upon it that all the children shall go to school together. This endears her to the boy, for he has long been eager to win the power of mining the treasures that must lie buried in books. Especially has he felt this desire burn within him when listening to the conversation of the parson, the land surveyor, or the lawyer who sometimes passes by on circuit. His father is still determined that Abe shall be a carpenter and nothing more. He has got on famously himself without book-learning, he says, and laughs at the new mother when she speaks of its advantages. Tom Lincoln is of sanguine temperament, prone to look upon the world, and upon his own life, through colored glasses.

They go to church on Sundays. It is a bald, bare-looking place. Often one of the congregation addresses the rest, but the children find it hard to understand. At school, however, Abe makes good progress, and soon learns to write as well as to read. In later years his cousin remembers that the boy had been quicker at his books than the others.

What a pity that paper is so scarce and so dear. He makes a preliminary sketch of what he wants to write in charcoal on the top of a box, and only when he is satisfied with the first script does he transfer it to the precious paper. Thus early does he acquire the art of thinking out essentials and expressing his thoughts concisely. That is how Abraham Lincoln learns to write.

His fingers are rather stiff and clumsy, since up to now he has used them for nothing but hard manual work. In winter, too, it is so cold that the children carry hot potatoes with them on the way to school, to keep their hands warm. If money is scarce, or if his father needs his help on the farm, he has to stay away from school. Wood for the stove is more important than schooling; a calf is worth six dollars, whereas a book is worth nothing at all; for a farmer's son in the west, the ax is mightier than the pen.

He can swing an ax now, being tall and strong for his age, a boy on whom the father has come to depend. Father and son go out shooting together. Abe must learn how to use a gun. Wild turkeys! A fine fellow, close at hand! Aim and fire! He does so, and the bird lies on the ground. He steps up to his victim. Suddenly the boy takes fright. He has, for the first time in his life, realized the formidable power which one living creature can arrogate over another. No longer does he think with anticipatory delight of the flavor of the Sunday roast. Horror-stricken, he hands the weapon back to his father, who is surprised, but keeps his own counsel. Still, he is probably annoyed when his boy, who has the makings of a good shot, refuses henceforward to shoulder a firearm. What! — to live in the West, to be big and strong, and yet refuse to be a hunter?

Is the youth thinking about the prisoners? Is he comparing one creature's lot with another's? Is he vainly seeking light in the darkness? Never again did Abraham Lincoln fire a shot at a living thing.

IV

The most fun of all is to ride off to the mill. Such a lot of folk are there, and all of them with plenty of time on their hands, waiting their turn. The horses take turns too, harnessed to the beam that drives the mill. General conversation goes on, and a boy can learn a lot.

Abe is always happy to hear his father spin yarns. He often watches his father unnoticed and takes heed of Tom Lincoln's sayings and doings. Is Father kind to Mother? Is he fond of work? In truth the boy and his father do not care much for one another. The father evidently prefers his easy-going stepson, John, to Abe. Sometimes his father rides to the law court. On returning, Lincoln is full of angry declamations against a neighbor; and against the government, which is demanding money for the land he has settled on. Has he not worked on the land for years, cleared it, and made it cultivable? Yet the State wants money from him, as well as work. Is he a slave, then? The son does not think very much of his father's abilities; yet it seems natural enough to the son, in this place where there is nothing to stimulate ambition, that his father should be fonder of spinning a yarn than of putting a shoulder to the wheel. What if Father and not Mother is right about book-learning?

The boy learns that his father's brothers have all got on in the world, are prosperous men with large farms — and have no interest in poor relations. He hears strange things from his cousin Dennis, and ponders them deeply when he is in bed in the loft. Dennis tells him that Father has married his employer's niece. Then Father must once have been a laborer. And he says that Father had wanted Sarah Bush first of all for his wife, but she had married Johnston because Johnston was better off. Then Father had married Abe's real mother, and Tom Lincoln and Sarah Johnston had only come together when first wife and first husband were dead.

Queer thoughts buzz in the boy's developing brain. His own mother, it seems, had been the wrong wife for Father. Was that why she had been so melancholy? Yet Abe loves his new mother, who shows no favor among the children, is, indeed, equally kind to all. Meditating these things, he at length falls asleep beside "Brother" John, with whom he is not connected by any tie of blood.

It must often occur to him that there are too many of them to provide for. Once, when they sit down to dinner, and his father asks a blessing, Abe, seeing that there is nothing to eat but potatoes, interjects: "Those are mighty poor blessings!" He is beginning to make his own characteristic comments on daily happenings. At Gordon's mill one day he is mounted on the revolving pole, driving his mare to turn the mill. At each revolution he gives the beast a cut with the whip, saying "Get up, you old hussy!" Tired of these lashings, the mare flings up her unshod heels and kicks him on the forehead. He falls to the ground, bleeding and insensible, and has to be carted home, not to recover consciousness till next morning. Then his first words are "you old hussy!" — the latter half of the exclamation he had been uttering when struck down. He was fond of telling the story, being throughout life interested in self-examination, and keen on applying its lessons.

He is always a keen learner, though not in search of vast erudition. He wants manifold experiences; he wishes to understand human nature, and especially his own. He reads everything he can get hold of: very little, it is true; and besides, he lacks time for reading in the daylight hours, and light for reading after nightfall. In summer, when the evenings are long drawn out, he squats beneath the lean-to roof of the outhouse, knees drawn up, poring over the pages; at night he does the same thing, crouching by the fire, blowing it thriftily to a flame from time to time — for the candles his stepmother makes (soap and candles are homemade) are reserved for Sundays and holidays. What books does this lanky youth devour when he lies prone to read, propping himself on his elbows?

Whatever chance brings to him, out here in the West, opens large fields of knowledge to him, like the peep through a half-opened door. "The Pilgrim's Progress" gives the impetus to his first thoroughgoing self-examination. "Robinson Crusoe" is an intensified description of his own frontier life; the Bible ever and again comes back to him, an eternal melody from earliest childhood. Other books are brought to the house by passing visitors. "Aesop's Fables" is one of them, his first introduction to genial satire of human weaknesses; it sharpens his wits, and at the same time quickens his sympathies. Weems' "Life of Washington", and also his life of Franklin, with its numerous stories of the War of Independence, furnish Abe with an abundance of anecdotal material such as hitherto he has had only from his father's story-telling. At times a parcel comes from town wrapped in an old newspaper, this wrapper supplying him with information on current topics and the small change of everyday life.

Sometimes when he goes over to Gentryville he will pick up the newspaper in the store, will read about the elections, and will learn that there is hope of Andrew Jackson, a plain man of the people, being chosen President, in defiance of the rich dandies who wear ruffled shirts.

Unceasingly, in the conversations to which he listens, in the scraps of newspaper he glances at, comes up the topic of the slave-holding South; and in the little church that is built not far from his home at Pigeon Creek when he is fourteen years old, much is said about slavery. He cannot understand it all yet, cannot see his way clear; but he sits for hours, brooding, and doing his best to puzzle things out.

In the church, a log house like the others, the minister reads the Scriptures, by firelight in winter; and the congregation sings psalms and hymns. At home, too, there is much saying of prayers. Yet these religious exercises seem to have less influence upon him than do his own chance explorations of the human mind. A man of wide experience, a man of insight, meeting him at this stage, would be inclined to regard him as a budding poet, or an imaginative writer in the making. And that he is. He makes verses and reads them to his friend. He ponders deeply over the things he reads.

Year by year the range of his experience widens, though socially it is narrow. He goes down sometimes to the Ohio, where there is much traffic. Pioneers are going westward in flatboats, keel boats, rafts, every imaginable sort of craft. Then there are the boats and barges, manned by lively crews, laden with hogs and flour. Steamboats too, occasionally; newfangled craft that are always catching fire, or breaking down, so that their machinery must be tinkered with till they can get under way again. The keel boats and the flatboats interest young Abraham more than the uncanny steam-driven contraptions; he knows all about woodworking, how to hollow a tree trunk into a boat, and how to make a raft by binding logs together.

Most of the boats go downstream, far down to the sea, where the great Mississippi ends. Southward go the traders when they want to sell their produce; there is a brisk demand for produce in the South, and plenty of money, for cotton is king there — cotton grown by slave labor. Continually his thoughts turn towards the South. He notices how much the river folk talk of the South; some with a sort of dread, it seems, and some with uneasy consciences. He grows aware of these things as he waits on the bank of the river, ready to turn a hand at anything, questioning all and sundry.

V

At sixteen, he is so strong that he is spoken of as the best axman in the district. At seventeen, he is six feet four inches tall. In a third school, which he now has a chance of attending for a few months, he has some more training of the old-fashioned kind — in the three R's, readin', 'ritin' and 'rithmetic — and yet, taken all together, his total days at school do not amount to a full year. Though he has learned to write fluently, his hands are calloused, being less used to handling the pen than saw or plane, plow or ax — especially the last. When there is a giant of the forest to be laid low, it is Abe Lincoln people send for. He is a powerful boy, so his father hires him out for a wage of twenty-five cents a day, the father pocketing the money.

He devotes more and more time to meditation as the years go by, half reclining against the wall with his knees drawn up. Sitting or lying stretched out suit him better than walking or riding. His daily work means tough exertion and he does not care much for it. Malaria and spare diet have left him very lean, a lanky giant with a narrow but well-rounded chest. His shoulders droop forward; and, as a heritage from his mother, his face is dry and sallow and early wrinkled, and coarse of feature. The girls, likely enough, don't think much of Abraham's looks. They are not impressed by the heroic structure of his head, the virile strength of his great nose; nor do they understand the mute earnestness of his narrow lips, the taciturn eloquence of his questioning gray eyes. They see nothing but that he is gawky and odd; and they can appreciate Tom Lincoln's description of Abe in images drawn from the carpenter's handicraft. "He looked as if he had been rough-hewn with an ax and needed smoothing with a jackplane."

He is eccentric in his ways, and soon comes to be regarded as a queer fellow. When he is at work in the fields he will suddenly drop his spade or hoe, take a book out of his pocket, and begin to read with lower lip outthrust, as is his habit when reading to himself; but now he reads aloud, as if for the benefit of his companions. Sometimes, indeed, urging them to knock off work too, he will sit down on a railing or on a stone and begin to talk to them. The others are surprised at first; soon they realize that he has something fresh to tell them about the river, the elections, or days of old. Yet they cannot help laughing at him for the queer way he has of putting all that he says in the form of a story, a trick he has caught from his father, and perhaps from Aesop as well. On one of these occasions his father happens along, knocks him off the fence, and curses him for a lazybones.

Once when he had seen some of his schoolfellows torturing a mud-turtle — they had lighted a fire on its back — he had raged against them, and, on getting home, had written an essay against cruelty to animals. Probably this was his first literary effort; at about the same time, he penned a screed against drunkenness. This strange lad wants to help both man and beast. He saves a dog from drowning amid the ice floes on the river; comes to the aid of a man who is getting the worst of it in a wrestling bout. All dread him as an adversary, for, with his long limbs and great strength, he can outrun and outfight the lot of them. Because of that strength of his, he is in request as country butcher; and the young man who will not go out shooting, and is loath to hurt a rabbit, knocks a steer on the head, killing it deftly, skins it, cleans and quarters it as if trained for the work. The neighbors think much of him for his skill; and the only thing that puzzles them is that, when they want a letter written and addressed, he can do that job for them just as well.

Another strange thing about him is that now and again his thoughts will wander from what he is doing, and he will laugh for no apparent reason, or for a reason which is apparent to no one but his stepmother. According to her report, he never told a falsehood. Because at seventeen he has suffered many an injustice, or has often felt the injustice of a poor boy's lot, he is ready to turn his bodily powers to account when he can ward off injustice from another. Since his mind is thus attuned, he is an attentive member of the audience when a court is held in the neighboring village. Will they sentence the accused to be hanged, for having killed an Indian? Unwittingly, his sympathy has gone out to the Indians, for they have been driven off the lands of their fathers, they are an oppressed people. He feels, however, that he ought to use his head and examine what his heart prompts; ought to weigh carefully the testimony that he hears; so he borrows a statute book, "The Revised Laws of Indiana", and gets his first glimpse into the world of jurisprudence. On once hearing a noted lawyer plead, he even makes up his mind to rival this great man's eloquence some day.

In order to earn a little extra money that may give him a measure of freedom, he must use the strength of his arm, not the cunning of the writer's hand. It takes a strong arm to row two travelers with a lot of baggage halfway across the Ohio that they may catch a steamer. Each throws him a piece of silver. Two half dollars! Young Lincoln has never dreamed of getting so much pay for so brief a spell of work. These strangers have been liberal. It is an experience he will not forget.

When he is seventeen and Sarah nineteen, his sister is to be married. Perhaps he sees the papers relating to the affair. A point they cannot but bring to his notice has probably arrested his attention earlier. With his passion for inquiries and comparisons, he can hardly have failed, ere this, to discuss with his cousin the history of their family for a couple of generations. He must have lighted on the inexplicable fact that, whereas his maternal grandparents had been called Sparrow, his mother, before marrying Tom Lincoln, had been known by the name of Nancy Hanks. He must have detected Aunt Sparrow's embarrassment when he questioned her about this, and his curiosity may well have been quickened by a hint from his cousin. In the end, indubitably, the youth learned what had been hidden from the child. "Granny" had in truth been his mother's aunt. His real grandmother was Aunt Sparrow herself, the vigorous old woman who had such a bold handwriting. Why had a mystery been made of this? What lay behind? He was now told the amazing truth.

His mother, whose memory he revered, was the natural daughter of Lucy Hanks. Lucy's parents, rigid moralists, had refused to have anything more to do with her after her slip, but had adopted the illegitimate child. Lucy's sister, Elizabeth Hanks, married to a man named Thomas Sparrow, had no children, and had brought up little Nancy as her own. These had been Abe's ostensible "grandparents." In due course Lucy Hanks had married Thomas Sparrow's brother Henry, and had borne him nine children.

Who, then, had his grandfather been? He learned that "Aunt Sparrow", his grandmother, the sometime Lucy Hanks, had lived in Virginia as a girl, during the years when the War of Independence was drawing to a close. From his study of the "Life of Washington" Abraham had learned how in those days the South was full of soldiers and adventurers. That a girl of strong passions should find herself with a child was easy enough to understand. He had known of such things before. A slip of the kind would be covered up by the marriage of the pair, and the scandal would speedily be forgotten.

This was a very different matter. When Abe had learned all that he was permitted to know about the change of grandmothers, he naturally came to the conclusion that his maternal grandfather must have been a Southerner. An officer? Likely enough. A gentleman? Probably. Perhaps a slave owner!

The young man's brain simmers with the problems thus awakened. He will never cease turning them over in his mind; and after many years will confide to a friend that he ascribes his peculiarities and his gifts to inheritance from the unknown Virginian grandfather. For the nonce, however, all he feels is that the ground is rocking beneath his feet. His temperamental melancholy is intensified into depression, and there is an enhancement of the sense of loss and loneliness from which he has long suffered. His stepmother is very good to him, but she is not his mother; "Granny" had not been his grandmother; his father's first wife had not been the woman Tom Lincoln had coveted. Now, when his sister weds Aaron Grigsby, and he writes the wedding song, Abe notices that the Grigsby parents, who are well-to-do and think themselves fine folk, look down upon their daughter-in-law.

Next year his sister Sarah dies in childbed. It is current talk that she dies because her strength has been sapped by overwork. Enough, this, to concentrate the young man's ire. His mother is dead, his sister is dead, his father is not prospering, his relatives have been put in a false position by a lie. Wherefore? Because there are rich, those who grind the faces of the poor, make others sew garments and hew wood for them, compel their daughter-in-law to work as a servingmaid, and (when the fancy takes them) seduce a white girl with no more compunction than if she were a Negress.

He notices, too, that they had set the young wife to hard work very soon after the wedding. Then, when two more of the young Grigsbys, Reuben and Charles, are married, their parents inflict a public slight on Abraham by not inviting him to the "infare", as the wedding feast was called in those parts. For the first time in his life young Lincoln is inspired with a wish to retaliate, and he does so in a characteristic manner: he arranges a rural comedy by bribing a neighbor to exchange the bridal beds of the two couples. At the conclusion of the "infare", in accordance with the old-fashioned custom, the brides are formally put to bed. This had been done, the bridesmaids had been dismissed, and (while all heads were jingling with wine) the double consummation was at hand. At this juncture the young men's mother, in great perturbation, ran back into one of the bedrooms, exclaiming, "Oh, Lord, Reuben, you are in bed with the wrong wife!"

This incident is made by Lincoln the theme of a satire entitled "The First Chronicles of Reuben." He lets a copy of the manuscript drop at the door of the Grigsbys' cabin, and sees to its becoming known elsewhere in the community. It is couched in Biblical style, is free from lubricity, and so amusing that it has a great vogue. The story of the comedy of errors, thus embodied, spreads far and wide, coupled with the name of the author, so that for years, people said, this chronicle was better known in Indiana than the Bible.

The feelings that led to this satire might have given birth to a longing for vengeance, to an impulse towards revolt. Lincoln, however, is of the reflective type, is more inclined to study men than to lead them, is a teller of tales rather than a reformer; so the bitter experiences of his youth, though developing his irony, serve but to broaden his sympathies. He finds it more congenial to help the oppressed than to punish the oppressor; and all that he learns, in the world of thought and in the world of action, will (thanks to this appreciation of human rights and human worth) make of him one who always compares a neighbor's humiliations and sorrows with his own.

VI

One day a glimpse into a distant vista was granted him. A wagon broke down near by. A lady and her two daughters were in it. Tom Lincoln had to repair the damage, and the strangers entered the log house and made themselves at home. The passengers must have stayed some days. Abraham Lincoln told a friend about the matter long afterwards:

"While they were fixing up, they cooked in our kitchen. The woman had books and read us stories, and they were the first I had ever heard. I took a great fancy to one of the girls; and when they were gone I thought of her a great deal, and one day when I was sitting out in the sun by the house I wrote out a story in my mind. I thought I took my father's horse and followed the wagon, and finally I found it, and they were surprised to see me. I talked with the girl and persuaded her to elope with me; and that night I put her on my horse, and we started off across the prairie. After several hours we came to a camp; and when we rode up we found it was the one we had left a few hours before, and we went in. The next night we tried again, and the same thing happened — the horse came back to the same place; and then we concluded that we ought not to elope. I stayed until I had persuaded her father to give her to me. I always meant to write that story out and publish it; but I concluded that it was not much of a story."

This little tale reveals the poesy of Lincoln's nature, his inclination to make a parable out of chance happenings; and it gives us a deep insight into the youth's own spiritual life. Though stronger and taller than all the young fellows round about, he was shy of women. When he had become famous, every farmer in the neighborhood had anecdotes to tell about him, but none concerning girls. Did they seem too hoydenish for his taste? Maybe. One of his stepsisters, still half a child, followed him into a lonely wood, and suddenly jumped on his back in a playful way, cutting her foot as she did so on the ax that hung at his waist. Abe bound up the wound as best he could and sent the girl home.

These two trifling adventures appear to have been the sum and substance of the vigorous young farmer's love life during a long period of years. He was genuinely shy of girls, and yet he liked to tell racy stories. Never having had any intimate experiences of his own, he told these stories so decently that no one took offense — not even when he read aloud anecdotes from a rather unsavory jest book.

The outside world was booming on its course; soon its call would sound for youth a-waiting. Young Lincoln had proved his strength and skill on the river, and now a rich farmer hired him to take produce to New Orleans. Here was a chance to get away from the forest and its tiny villages, to see the Mississippi, and perhaps even the sea. Abe is ready and willing. He and the farmer's son make a flatboat; on his broad shoulders he carries pork, flour, bacon, and corn down to the river to sell to the South and in return intends to bring back cotton, tobacco, and sugar.

When they reach Cairo, where the Ohio ends, the Father of Rivers, yellow, turbid, incredibly wide, opens to their sight. New men and a new landscape, new trees and new birds, greet them on their southward voyage; then come storms and other perils, sandbanks and rapids, and an unexpected way of making acquaintance with the Negroes. They have tied up one night at a sugar plantation, and are sound asleep, when seven nocturnal marauders raid their flatboat, intending to steal the cargo. Lincoln goes for them with a crabapple-tree club, and, alarmed by his stature and the fight he puts up, they quickly flee to land. Abe and his companion are now fighting mad, and chase the would-be thieves far afield. Abe gets back to the raft with a gash over the right eye. Such is his first encounter with men of color.

Wider and wider grows the Mississippi, hotter the days, steamier the nights, and perhaps the poet's mind of the young steersman ponders: "Is this life?" He certainly for the first time has a picture of life's unceasing movement spread before his gaze when they reach the end of their journey. Here is New Orleans but no sea is in sight. A thousand rafts seem to block the way seaward, and ocean-going vessels, such as he has never seen on the Ohio; sacks of flour from the North, barrels of pork piled mountain high on the wharves; smoke and clamor; hustle and bustle. What are those bales, lying on the quays and stored in sheds, thousands upon thousands of them? Some of them are torn, and the white, downy contents protrude. The Northerner recognizes it as cotton, which is making so much commotion all over the States. For some time, now, Lincoln has been wearing jean trousers; he has a cotton coat too, to don in the town.

He and his companion have landed their freight, and tread the streets of the great city. Whites, blacks, and mulattoes swarm everywhere. Europeans in strange costumes drive past; gayly dressed women laugh and fan themselves. They all seem merry, hopeful, independent, enjoying life to the full. But the blacks? A placarded advertisement catches his eye: "I will at all times pay the highest cash prices for negroes of every description, and will also attend to the sale of negroes on commission, having a jail and yard fitted up expressly for boarding them." At the next corner, another: "One hundred dollars reward for return of a bright mulatto man slave, named Sam; light sandy hair, blue eyes, ruddy complexion, — is so white as very easily to pass for a free white man."

So these are the disinherited, thinks the youthful traveler. Hunted like stray dogs, auctioned like horses, prisoned like criminals. The things he has heard his father talking about at home, has had attested by the minister, has read of in the newspapers, — these things now take living shape before him.

A few days later he returns upstream. When he gets home after three months' absence, he is richer by an unrivaled experience, and by twenty-four dollars.

VII

At home, things are astir. Relatives who live farther west, in Illinois, have brought news of a real paradise. The soil is fertile, and all in all it is a place where a man can soon make his fortune. Perhaps they have told a flattering tale in order to better their own lot by promoting an influx of neighbors! If so, they gain their end, for many of the disappointed Indiana settlers lend a ready ear, and several families migrate simultaneously, making for new homes near Decatur.

Thomas Lincoln has relations over there, and, restless man that he is, eager for novelty, always hoping for better luck next time, he pays no heed to warnings that fever is troublesome in Illinois. He sells his farm for one hundred twenty-five dollars; and his wife, who had inherited a farm in Kentucky when her first husband died, disposes of that for one hundred twenty-three dollars. And now, with all their possessions packed in wagons, and with fourteen head of farming stock trailing behind, they start on their great journey. Abraham, on whose strength and skill they all count, is to drive one of the teams. Abe, now showing a practical turn, goes to the local shop before starting and invests his savings (more than thirty dollars) in "notions" to peddle on the way. He buys pins and needles, buttons, suspenders, and so on, the most expensive item being a set of knives and forks.

At length they reach Decatur, and four miles beyond they are hospitably welcomed by their kin. Abraham is in high fettle, having peddled his stock for more than double what it cost him. Folks are livelier here, it seems; there is an atmosphere of hope, and as soon as a log house can be built all will go well.

Look at our twenty-one-year-old giant as he stands felling trees for the new home. In the evening he yokes the oxen to them and drags them off to the cabin site. With mighty strokes he splits some of them into rails for fencing, his strength now greatly exceeding his father's. Who, that watches him at work, would ever dream that such a to-do will one day be made about these rails split by Abraham Lincoln? No one in the world, least of all the young rail-splitter himself. He is thinking only of the work, of building the cabin and fencing the land. When the house is finished, mainly by his efforts, he resumes a farming life like that in Indiana. He and his cousin John Hanks break up ten acres of ground and fence it in.

Home? How was he, who four times in twenty years had left land and cabin behind, to have a home-sense; he to whom Kentucky, Indiana, and Illinois were naught but fleeting pictures? Lincoln's home was America.

He can earn more here than he could in Indiana, soon being in much demand among the settlers on account of his strength. In the first weeks of his stay he has won a victory in wrestling with the local champion, stabilizing his fame.   One day when the Sangamon River is in flood, two men in a canoe are upset and only save themselves from drowning by clinging to a half-submerged tree.   Lincoln gets out to them on a log and rescues both of them.   The fame of this and like exploits spreads through the settlement, where everything is still fresh and new, where as yet there are no traditions, where no one is distinguished for wealth or greatness.

One of the neighbors, an old major who got his title in the War for Independence, employs him to split rails for a fence; he has "to split four hundred rails for every yard of brown jeans dyed with white-walnut juice that would be necessary to make him a pair of trousers."   The old army man has books, which Abraham borrows. Another time, during this bitterly cold winter, crossing the Sangamon in a flatboat, he is wrecked, has a long swim, and then a long walk, before, with frozen feet, he reaches shelter at the house of a farmer who had at one time been a judge.   Here he stays a fortnight, helping with the chores, fetching wood and water.   At odd times, during this visit, he is able to read "The Statutes of Illinois", the second lawbook to fall into his hands.

A shrewd man, reading newspaper reports of debates in Congress, scanning leaflets, attending trials when the judge comes on circuit, and comparing what he learns in this way with the legal principles garnered from the two lawbooks, he has the pieces of the puzzle in his hands, and can soon fit them together.   Since earliest childhood he has been trained to help himself, self-taught, learning more from his mistakes than from any set instruction.   From the study of his own position, that of his father and his mother and his sister, he has realized the curse of dependence.   In this new land of self-help, from such chance encounters, theory and practice together, he constructs a picture of the world of law.   Has he not for years been animated by a longing for greater justice, saddened as a boy by the sight of the torments inflicted on man and beast?   Now he becomes acquainted with the protective laws of the State and speedily understands them.

Need we be surprised that he, with a leaning toward story-telling, should soon begin to make speeches to his neighbors? One of the farmers is opposed to the river improvement works which the State legislature is planning. Lincoln knows r vers. He has been wrecked in them, has saved lives on them, has traveled on them a thousand miles down to the sea. He is well aware that they must be kept under control; so one evening, when there is an informal meeting of the farmers to discuss the question, a cousin urges him to take the floor against the objector. Jumping on to the box, he makes short work of the opposing arguments. The *raconteur* is gradually becoming an orator — but to the end of his days he will remain a story-teller.

At present, however, he is famous for brawn rather than for brains. A neighboring trader has had proof of his helpfulness when there is trouble, of his strength and skill, and has doubtless heard of Lincoln's successful trip to New Orleans. Now this man, Offutt by name, sends him South in command of a large flatboat. He is to have sixteen dollars a month. He sets off in a flatboat of his own building, clad in jeans of blue homespun, jacket, vest, and pantaloons, the latter tucked into the tops of his rawhide boots. Thus attired, he waves good-by and slips away from the home he has helped to build, never again to settle down under his father's roof, never again to dwell in a log cabin.

Spring has come and he is twenty-two years old. Lincoln has done with life as a farmer.

VIII

It takes some weeks before the boat, loaded with Offutt's goods, leaves for the South, and almost at the start it narrowly escapes being wrecked. When rounding a great curve of the Sangamon River, it is stranded on a milldam. The flatboat hangs on the dam, nose in air and stern half under water; the cargo is in danger of sliding off. The people of the adjoining village flock to the scene of the impending disaster, shout advice, but can give no effective aid. Lincoln finds a way out of the difficulty. He manages to get another boat alongside and unloads the sacks and boxes into it;

then he rolls the barrels into the bow, thus transferring forward the weight in the now lightened craft; he bores a hole in the stern of her, to let the water run out; the stern rises, and the flatboat can easily be slid over the dam. The story of the tall skipper's device is in every one's mouth, and loses nothing in the telling, so that he acquires a sort of legendary fame in this village called New Salem. Unaware of this, and with no shadow of a thought that it will influence his subsequent career, he carefully navigates his rescued vessel southward, to pay his second visit to New Orleans. This time he makes a longer stay, a whole month.

The first thing he sees, or at least the most impressing experience he has, is the slave market.

In front of him stands the slave dealer, dressed in startling clothes, noisy and swaggering. He holds a small whip, with which he points to one or another of the half-naked Negroes, as they slowly file around the hall. All wear shackles on their legs, and if one of them stops moving, or moves too quickly, he is berated by the dealer or an assistant, or given a cut with the whip. Among them is a mulatto girl, slender, delicately built, and obviously a virgin. Her appearance pleases the gentlemen mightily. At a sign from the dealer, she too, shackled and all but naked, steps out of the rank; he displays this treasure to the customers, makes her move to and fro that she may exhibit her girlish charm. Then he calls out: "The gentleman who buys her will get good value for his money!" All the possible customers have the same secret thoughts and bid briskly against one another for the prize morsel.

The tall stranger from Indiana trembles. As a young and vigorous man, he cannot contemplate this charming nudity without having his senses stirred; as a Northerner, he cannot but be enraged at the spectacle. In addition, however, he is keenly imaginative, and is a girlishly shy lad who has never known woman. In a word, he is Abraham Lincoln, and is shaken to the core. Memories of his straitened upbringing, musings as to his father's lot and his mother's, wrestle in his mind with speculations concerning the personality of his unknown grandfather. That progenitor may have been just such a man as these! His heart is racked. All his sympathies go out to the fettered, half-naked slaves; possibly wrath against the buyers, richly clad freemen, surges up within him. Sorrowfully he turns to leave the auction mart.

By the straightforwardness and reserve of his nature, by the incorruptibility of a character steeled by poverty and hard work, by the lack of money and position, by the frugality of an almost homeless boyhood, he is safeguarded against the temptations that might have assailed a youth in this strange, alluring city. Unwavering recognition of the weaknesses of his fellow mortals, poignant memories of the ignominious sale of the mulatto girl — brain and heart combine to prompt him to a dispassionate study of the slaves and their masters.

The first thing that must have struck him was that in this part of the world there were no white servants, and very few whites engaged in any kind of servile occupation. The "black man" (who was not always black, being sometimes of a shade of brown hard to distinguish from the sun-tanned whites) had been subjugated and did not revolt against his servile lot. Who among the masters could be expected to renounce the advantages of a commanding position, simply on moral grounds? Had not the men of God excellent reasons with which to justify the enslavement of the Negroes? The sons of Esau, they said, must pay for their father's greed. Esau had sold his birthright, and now a few million Africans in America must atone for the weakness of a Jewish herdsman in Palestine, who had lusted after a mess of pottage.

Besides, were not the Negroes better off than if they had been free? Our "peculiar institution" (that is what some of the Southerners called it, those who were mealy-mouthed about the ominous word "slavery") is natural. For Negroes, freedom would be unnatural, would be a complicated affair. How can these Northerners, who are "poor whites" anyhow, men of the plowtail, shopkeepers, clerks toiling in an office, rail-splitters, hunters — how can they understand that which has come down to us from our forefathers through the centuries, that which we are developing for the general welfare? What would happen to the United States if our slaves were to stop planting and picking cotton? What would the

moralists of New England say if we gave up sending them raw
materials for their factories? Would these indignant and Chris-
tianly people like to stand under a southern sun from morning till
night? Working here under intelligent guidance, those who are
diligent can earn finer chains than ever their fathers dreamed of in
the African forests; food and clothing and a little whisky as well;
and, to conclude, the blessings of church, so that they can hope
to inherit eternal life.

Lincoln learns more about slavery as he rides to and fro among
the plantations. If, in conversation with a parson, a school-teacher,
or a magistrate, he makes any allusion to the "institution", the
ready answer is always couched in the same terms. These colored
folk (so it runs) are sprung from a race which is engaged in a war of
all against all. In the primeval forest, they slaughter their brethren
as ruthlessly as the monkeys. Here, we save their lives, take good
care of them, provide for them in sickness and in old age, teach
them to be moral — whereas those that have been set free commit
the most abominable crimes. Of course we have to flog them now
and again. When we used to lock them up for stealing, we found
that it only ministered to their natural sloth. Nor had the Northerners all been enamored at the idea of freedom for Negroes. When
some of the northern States had decreed the gradual abolition of
slavery, had not many of the northern slave owners sent their slaves
to be sold in the southern market? Besides, the slaves themselves
laugh at the idea of being freed. If we want to rid ourselves of an
old Negro, and propose to set him free, he comes whimpering to us,
begs to be kept as a slave that he may be sure of his victuals — for
salt meat and fish, rum and molasses, are not to be sneezed at.

Lincoln is amazed the first time he listens to these defenders of
the South. He can only suppose that the apologists are dependents
of the wealthy slave owners. Well, he must see for himself how
the slaves live.

When, profoundly moved, the young man from the North returns
to the harbor, he may, glancing through the window of a saloon,
see two flushed faces over a game of faro; and the doorkeeper, in
an undertone, will perhaps tell him how the day before one of the

wealthier slave owners had gambled away two of his own half-caste sons. Hanks, Lincoln's companion on one of the New Orleans trips, reports: "His heart bled; he said nothing much; was silent; looked bad. . . . It run its iron in him then and there. He said to me, 'I would not be a slave, but neither would I be a slave owner.'"

IX

Lincoln works his way back up the Mississippi as fireman. When, on the hot June evenings, he sees the passengers drinking and laughing, we may well suppose that he is deeply stirred, that he ponders and draws comparisons, meditates upon class privileges and slavery.

Offutt, greatly impressed by the talents of his flatboat man, engages him for the new store he intends to open in New Salem, sends him on in advance, and after a short visit, Lincoln quits his paternal house for ever. He has neither horse nor boat, so he walks mile after mile through the high prairie grass, towards his new home.

In New Salem he finds no Offutt and no store, so for a while there is nothing for him to do. But he soon makes friends and as the elections are coming off and the election clerk has left, Lincoln writes out the polling list, and so is at once introduced into local politics. When at last Offutt arrives, Lincoln helps as a carpenter with the building, makes the shelves and counters, and does a hundred and one odd jobs. Finally the stock of goods arrives, and is displayed, and at last the painted sign, "Denton Offutt", is nailed over the door. Now the young giant stands behind the counter, measuring cloth, weighing out coffee and nails to the farmer customers.

Every one in the district soon knows him, for Offutt blows his trumpet about the storekeeper — much as the slave dealer had vaunted the charms of the mulatto girl. "He can outrun, outlift, outwrestle, and throw any man, even Jack Armstrong!" Promptly a match is arranged; for, in a new settlement like this, wrestling bouts and drinking matches are the standard amusements. Lincoln has seen the famous Armstrong before, a powerful, thickset fellow, and an experienced wrestler. Strength and skill are unavailing, however, and the newcomer soon lays the local champion low. There is applause; but there are murmurs as well. Armstrong's friends declare that Lincoln has not fought fair. But the vanquished wrestler, getting up from the ground, shakes hands with his adversary, and declares himself honestly beaten. Henceforward the two men are fast friends, and in years to come destiny will bring the two together at a moment when Lincoln's shrewdness and eloquence will save the life of Armstrong's son.

Days in the store pass pleasantly enough. The place is clean and well lighted. The stock on the shelves, in the cases, and in the tubs is kept in tolerably good shape. It consists of what is required for a pioneer's simple needs: hardware, shoes and stockings, groceries, and piece goods. Lincoln has a cot to sleep on, at the back of the store. True, he must share it with his assistant, but in the wild West a century ago, few had the luxury of a bed to themselves. The sales are nothing to boast of, for the whole population of the new settlement is little more than a hundred. That is Mr. Offutt's concern, anyhow, and is not likely to disturb the young storekeeper, who is happy because at length he has plenty of time for reading. He piles up a bolt of calico print for a pillow and lies down at full length on the counter, book in hand. Since he always reads aloud to himself (in order, as he says, to heighten the effect by taking in the matter through ear as well as eye), he must make a comical impression upon incoming customers. But they know young Lincoln and his ways, and merely smile indulgently as he rolls off the counter and stands to order behind it. Should the purchaser, however, take too long in finding what he wants, the salesman is likely to leave him to his own devices. He will see and hear Lincoln at the book once more.

No one grumbles, however. Who is likely to complain of a man strong enough to lift single-handed a barrel of whisky from floor to counter, and capable of tricks showing skill as well as strength. Besides, he is never out of humor when customers arrive, and is always willing to have a friendly chat, or ready to spin a yarn. Offutt thinks himself lucky in his store clerk. Does he not attract customers by his willingness to oblige in the way of writing letters for those unable to wield the pen? He neither smokes, nor chews, nor drinks; is never quarrelsome, despite his overwhelming strength; is happiest when playing with children, letting them scramble over him as he lies on the ground, laughing when they tease him and pull him about. Above all, people prize him for his sterling honesty; he can always be trusted, and soon he becomes known as "Honest Abe."

From time to time he is taciturn and melancholy, but no one minds. He does not try to force his dark moods on others, being inclined rather to show people the sunny side. They laugh at him, now and again, as when they catch sight of him strolling along with an open book in his hand, and then stopping short because he has come to a specially interesting passage which he must read over to himself out loud. The laughter is friendly, and even appreciative when they repeat his quaint phrases, such as: "I don't feel easy till I have turned my thoughts all round, north, south, east, and west."

One day a customer brings him tidings of an English grammar, at a farm six miles away. He walks over to borrow the book, and for the first time becomes acquainted with the systematization of his own language. An acquaintance lends him a volume of Gibbon; from the minister he gets another history book; he learns much from talks with the schoolmaster, and from questioning things and people.

It is natural that, at the village meetings, and at the local literary and debating society, the long-limbed student should be expected to hold forth. He speaks quite informally: about the roads; about the chance of a railway coming to those parts; but best about the river, and how its flow must be brought under control up there at the milldam. The river is one of his favorite topics, and one on which he has expert knowledge. He proves so successful as a speaker that ere long one of his hearers suggests that he should run for the Illinois legislature, seeing that, in this new country, there are so few capable men. He is dubious; and, while he still hesitates, circumstances give him a push.

The man who puts the thought of a political career into Abraham Lincoln's mind is named James Rutledge; one of the earliest settlers,

he helped to found New Salem, and is owner of the mill, which he
now leases to the enterprising Offutt.   Rutledge also keeps a tavern
where the young store clerk comes of an evening.   There he finds,
bent over her needlework, a slim daughter, good-looking, with a
delicate complexion and auburn hair.   Unfortunately eighteen-
year-old Ann is not free; but it may well be that this barrier, this
perilous freedom from risk, is the very thing required to stimulate
the imagination of a young man who is shy with girls, of one used
to wandering in a dreamland of fancy.

There is no chance for a poor lover against a rich betrothed, to
say nothing of the fact that old Rutledge is well-to-do and will never
give away his daughter for nothing.   Young McNeil is rich.   Coming from New York, he has made money in the West and has bought
land from his prospective father-in-law, to the tune of twelve thousand dollars, it is said.   Maybe the queer lamp-post of a fellow,
with a taste for reading and his own company, and a dread of girls,
would have been content to go on casting sheep's eyes at the pretty
young woman, would never have made any further advances, had
not Offutt proved a broken reed, and had not life among these
pioneers been so full of vicissitudes.

Next year, less than a twelvemonth after the founding of the
store, Offutt goes bankrupt, and Herndon, owner of a rival establishment, buys shop and stock at a low figure.   Since Herndon,
likewise, is not financially stable, it is just as well that at this time
the first steamboat comes up the river, and Lincoln is hired as pilot
to steer it through the dangerous rapids.   For the up-and-down
voyage he gets a fee of forty dollars, which helps him to keep his
head above water.

Once more he is at a loose end and can choose between the careers
of pilot, store clerk, politician, and soldier.

For the moment he chooses that of politician.   His humble origin
has its advantages and its drawbacks here.   Everybody knows
him, and many grin with pleasurable anticipation directly they
catch sight of him, sure that he will tickle them with one of his
whimsical anecdotes.   How can he win general respect, how can he
acquire a reputation for knowledge and solid ability?   Elections

are still a simple matter in these days, and the young man of three-and-twenty must be his own election agent and canvasser. As he goes from farm to farm and lends a hand in the work, he does it so naturally and in so friendly a fashion that neither he nor any of the voters can feel that he is merely trying to worm his way into people's good graces. In the evening all go together to the inn; there are wrestling matches and drinking bouts; then the candidate mounts one of the tables to speak.

How can he fail to please? The fact that, despite his immense strength, he never willingly harms man or beast, means more to these level-headed farmers than it would to sophisticated townsmen. They think it a strange contradiction, of course, ascribing it to his better education, which will make him fit for the legislature. They have seen for themselves that he spends much of his time reading; they have heard for themselves how good he is at spinning a yarn. They are confident that he will be able to make a speech. No doubt he's a queer-looking figure. His trouser legs are several inches too short; the sleeves of the gray check coat are only halfway down to his wrists and the swallow-tails are too short.

As long as he stands still, thinking, with his hands behind him, his roughly chiseled features, befitting a man much older than he, make him look as if carved out of wood; but now he begins to move, his long arms rising and falling to punctuate the periods, and when he moves forward toward the edge of the table, some of the audience, more eager to watch than to listen, lose the thread of his discourse for a moment. His voice is not altogether pleasing, for it is high-pitched and rather strident, but it improves as he goes on and forgets himself in the rush of oratory. Then, as an interlude, comes one of the anecdotes which every one has been awaiting; for he uses this popular method of expression in order to assist the molding of his thought. Here we see Lincoln the born story-teller, as the born *raconteur*, brilliant rather than a man likely to become a public speaker. He wants to share his information with others, not to instruct them; to convince his hearers, not to overpersuade them, wielding more influence in this way than the platform orator.

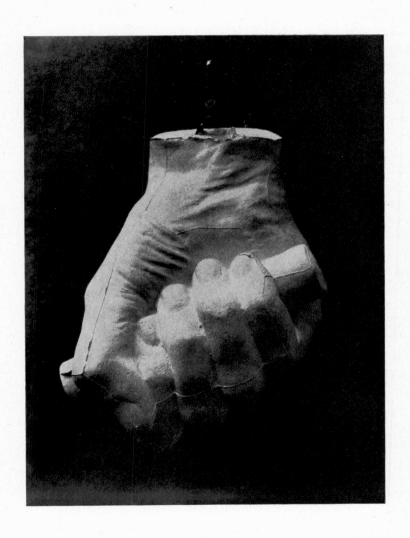

LINCOLN'S RIGHT HAND

From a cast by Volk, 1860

He ignores high politics, though people are ready enough to discuss them even in these western taverns, and confines himself to what he understands, to that which directly touches the lives of his neighbors: river control and road improvement. Thus he never quits the sphere of the things amid which he has grown up. All the time he is speaking, he is watching his audience keenly. So once, when a bully attacks one of his friends in the hall, he leaps from the rostrum, seizes the offender by belt and collar, and hurls him a dozen feet away; then, quietly smoothing his ruffled clothes, he regains the platform and takes up his parable once more.

What party he joins does not matter very much. Up to his twentieth year he has called himself a Democrat, like his father and cousin, but the brilliancy of Henry Clay's speeches, Webster's logic and pathos make him a Whig.

Lincoln is already what he will remain throughout life — conservative. Always, therefore, he speaks with well-nigh religious veneration of the fathers of his country, of those who established liberty and order, of those who so ably compacted a number of raw and youthful States into an organic whole.

To-day at the age of twenty-three he ends his first extremely guarded speech with the laconic words: "My politics are short and sweet, like the old woman's dance. I am in favor of a national bank. I am in favor of the internal-improvements system and a high protective tariff. These are my sentiments and political principles. If elected, I shall be thankful; if not, it will be all the same." Thus he speaks, then gets down from the table and returns to his seat among the audience. Does any one there, does he himself, perceive the singularity of this peroration? It expresses the second elemental trait of Lincoln's character, showing that in his youthful renunciation he is safeguarded against the perils of ambition. Things, rather than the urges of egoism, spur him to action. A splendid objectivity combines in his nature with a sense of fatality, both being outcomes of his simple and toilsome upbringing, and in their union incorruptible.

The concluding sentiments do not express the mood of a fleeting moment. When his hearers look at the printed circular that is now distributed (it is of Lincoln's own composition, but, since his spelling is not yet to be relied on, has been edited by a somewhat more lettered acquaintance), they read :

"I was born, and have ever remained, in the most humble walks of life. I have no wealthy or popular relations or friends to recommend me. My case is thrown exclusively upon the independent voters of the county; and, if elected, they will have conferred a favor upon me for which I shall be unremitting in my labors to compensate. But if the good people in their wisdom shall see fit to keep me in the background, I have been too familiar with disappointments to be very much chagrined."

Here the tone of renunciation is tinged with humor, and the declaration of a lowly origin is made with obvious pride. The man who has written this electoral manifesto is already feeling that a rough-and-tumble youth on the edge of things has been worth while in this country, and he stresses the dignity of the poor pioneer who owes all his advantages to himself.

X

Black Hawk, the famous Indian chief, is at war with the whites because he wishes to reclaim the land he sold to the government thirty years before. He is raiding the frontier country and this news alarms people, even at New Salem, a good way from the seat of trouble. The store has petered out, a new job has not yet been found, no one can tell how the election will turn; and if Lincoln potters about through the summer, and is defeated at the polls, he will miss the chance of soldiering. Besides, the campaign is not likely to be a long one, and should it end before election day his laurels as an Indian fighter will help to win votes. Lincoln, therefore, becomes one of a volunteer force which forms part of an army of sixteen hundred, and his company chooses him as its captain. He never forgets this first popular election. Badly provisioned and poorly equipped, they march northwestward across the open prairies, wading the creeks and rivers. He is familiar with hardships in the frontier country, and they do not trouble him. Little is seen of the enemy, and after a month his company disbands. Meanwhile a remarkable new experience has come to him, that of being worsted in single combat. He has early learned to renounce; he demands nothing and expects little; but he has always been sustained by the consciousness of his own bodily strength. Now he is thrown by a man named Thompson, a private from another company. This is a public defeat, the first; well, a young man must learn not to pitch his anticipations too high! He challenges the victor and now gains two victories over Thompson. Shortly after this match he is reënlisted by a lieutenant named Anderson. Thirty years later these two will be brought together by destiny.

What has Lincoln to do with war? He does not care for hunting or for fighting, does not even like to kill an animal; and when, after the disbanding of his company, he reënlists for another three weeks, it may be more from a sense of duty than from a lust of adventure, and perhaps from the lack of anything better to do. Certainly he has no special talent for military command. Once he is marching in company front across a field and comes to a gateway through which they must pass. For the life of him, he cannot recall the proper word of command to get his company "endwise", so at length he shouts: "This company is dismissed for two minutes, when it will fall in again on the other side of the gate!"

Another time, coming to a forsaken camp of white scouts, they find five scalped corpses. Lincoln describes the scene years afterwards, with an artist's vivid insight. He speaks of the little hill, in the light of the morning sun. "They lay heads towards us on the ground. Every man had a round red spot on the top of his head about as big as a dollar, where the redskins had taken his scalp. It was frightful, but it was grotesque; and the red sunlight seemed to paint everything all over." Then, after a pause: "I remember that one man had buckskin breeches on." The report of an observer with vision; of one used since early childhood to see things clearly and to see them quickly in a comprehensive glance.

He has not had a chance of proving himself a hero. His most notable deed is the saving of an old Indian who has strayed into

camp one day, and whom his men want to butcher in spite of a safe-
conduct pass. Lincoln does not kill a single enemy, but he saves a
foe from the clutches of his own friends; such is the only warrior
exploit of this friend of humanity.

On his way home his horse is stolen, and he has to walk; then
goes some distance by water in a canoe and at last afoot again to
his village, where no triumphal arches or garlands welcome the
returning man of war. Nay, the other side has been making headway while he has been absent; nor is the new Whig party popular,
so he is unsuccessful in his first attempt to enter political life.
Locally, however, in the New Salem precinct, he has secured a
triumph, for of three hundred votes he gets two hundred and seventy-
seven — though the sentiment of the region is predominantly Democratic. Lincoln's acquaintances have voted for Lincoln. He can
go to bed happy that night, though defeated in the election.

Well, he must gain a livelihood somehow or other, so he takes a
partner, borrows money, buys what had been Offutt's store and also
Herndon's (for Herndon, likewise, has failed meanwhile), paints a
new sign, and is now partner in the firm of "Berry and Lincoln."
Neither is an efficient business man and Berry is a hard drinker, so
most of the work falls on Lincoln's shoulders.

But Lincoln is more interested in his customers' conversation than
in their ability to pay, and when "Honest Abe" — in blue shirt,
brown coat, and trousers — as ever much too short for his long legs —
stands behind the counter, one can always reckon on being served,
even if one cannot pay. The only trouble is that the store is so
often closed, the senior partner being in his cups, and the junior,
who has now become postmaster, being otherwise engaged.

The postmastership seems to have become his main source of
income; he holds it four years and finds it advantageous in many
ways. He is appointed because people trust him, and because he
can write and read so well; now he can enjoy a first reading of all
the newspapers brought by the post-coach. That is an old privilege
of western postmasters, and the subscriber is apt to expect, when
he receives his journal, that the postmaster will be so obliging as
to give him an abstract of the contents. The recipient of a letter,

too, generally gets the postmaster to read it aloud to him; or, if he is one of the lucky ones who can read, he will not be such a curmudgeon as to keep all the news to himself. This is very agreeable to our anecdotalist and student of human nature; and as he goes his rounds, carrying all the undelivered letters in his hat, he gets to know folk more intimately.

All this brings him day after day into touch with the varied thoughts of the people. He learns about classes, temperaments, grades of life, types of character; and during the next few years, in this remote settlement, he gains by direct observation such treasures of human experience as no formal process of education on the grand scale could ever have supplied.

Still, he remains an omnivorous reader. All is grist that comes to his mill: besides the newspapers which pass through his hands as postmaster, he gets books from wayfarers, some of them light reading. When by a lucky chance an emigrant in a covered wagon wants to get rid of a barrel full of rubbish, Lincoln good-naturedly buys it. A few days later, emptying his new acquisition, he finds amid the plunder the four volumes of a famous work, Blackstone's "Commentaries on the Laws of England", the most notable law book of the day. This supplies him with a hundred important ideas and teaches him where to look for additions to his knowledge. He borrows more books from judges and lawyers and immerses himself in study, withdrawing for a time from his comrades.

But he soon gets acquainted with a vagabond of artistic temperament, an inspired loafer who spends most of his time on the river bank with rod and line and knows by heart long passages of Shakespeare and Burns. He quotes them feelingly to Lincoln, and lends him the originals, thus opening new worlds to his friend. Lincoln, however, is most eager to get hold of history books. In them he discovers that the fathers of his country were more or less opposed to slavery; that Washington and Adams, Jefferson and Madison, Franklin and Hamilton — in their various ways the best men in the land, and some of them slave owners — wanted to check the spread of the system. Ever ready to store up anecdotes in his mind, he cannot fail to note and to remember that Washington would not have a runaway Negress hunted and recaptured, but left it to her free choice whether she would stay away or return.

However, the reading of books and desultory conversations do not provide a living. The store, naturally, does not flourish, and the day comes when store and contents are seized by creditors. Berry decamps, and Lincoln has to shoulder the whole burden of debt, eleven hundred dollars in all. Daily bread can be earned readily enough, and in addition to such casual earnings he has his salary as postmaster. Enough for current expenses; but how on earth is he to free himself from the crushing load of his debts?

A friend of his, a land surveyor in the rising town of Springfield, twenty miles away, has often told Lincoln that at this occupation a man of his intelligence can earn thrice as much with his wits as he can earn with his hands, and so, with the aid of the schoolmaster, he picks up the elements of mathematics, and learns the use of the necessary instruments. Six weeks later he is appointed deputy land surveyor at New Salem. This gives him plenty to do, for land is constantly changing owners; a day's work in planning a road brings him in three dollars, with fifty cents extra for drawing the map. Besides, one hand can wash the other: when he is on a surveying job he can deliver the mail in the same quarter. Doubtless he has not forgotten that Washington in youth had also been a surveyor — and (eighty years earlier!) had earned fees thrice as large. Oh, well, we are not all of us Washingtons, thinks the modest young man, and whistles to the wind.

What a happy life his would be, but for those infernal debts. Implacable creditors get judgments, seize his horse, without which he cannot get about the country; take away his saddle, his bridle, his surveying instruments. Friends club together and buy back these indispensable possessions. Well, he is very poor in these days, but when things are at their worst he can always hike over to Armstrong's, help at the woodpile and in the garden, rock the baby's cradle, tell the older children stories and get his meals and a shakedown.

Among those who are continually asking the postmaster for letters is Ann Rutledge. Her betrothed is away, has gone to New

York on business, and will return for the marriage. But his letters grow fewer and fewer; and when he does write he is shifty, says that his father's death will delay his return, will keep him in the East for an indefinite time. Local gossips begin to prophesy that rich John McNeil will jilt poor Ann. Then it is noised abroad that she is likely to console herself by taking up with another man; for there is a second suitor waiting for pretty Ann — Lincoln's good friend, Sam Hill.

Lincoln's emotions are deeply stirred, his mind is in a turmoil. At this time his shyness of women has become so great that he has been reluctant to serve them in the store. When a lady with three daughters comes to stay a few weeks at Rutledge's inn, he shuns their company and will not sit down at meals with them. Some of his forbears were said to have been afraid of marrying. While in his case this may have been the outcome of an inborn trend towards melancholy, growing with the years, that trend, in its turn, reacted by increasing his aloofness from women. So much so that a friend of those days records Lincoln as having said: "I may seem to enjoy life rapturously, when I am in company. But when I am alone, I am so often overcome by mental depression that I never dare carry a pocketknife."

Lonely and sad at heart, burdened with anxieties, full of secret yearnings, he becomes utterly distraught when he learns that the girl he loves is at length free. Can he seriously wish her to marry him? Will he not risk reliving his mother's evil fate, that of being a poor substitute for one loved and lost? Will he not be happier if she remains unattainable? Yet how can he allow himself to be cut out by Hill, whose only advantage is that of being better off? The upshot of these conflicting meditations is that Lincoln goes to board in the Rutledge tavern. Now he is at close quarters with the maiden who has caught his elusive fancy.

Yet he makes no further move to win her. Nay, when the story runs that McNeil has been passing under an alias, is really called McNamar and is a bad lot, Lincoln comes to the defense of his absent rival. Before McNamar left he had bought land under another name because of some family quarrel. Lincoln has kept the information to himself, but when the story is divulged, and used to cast a slur on McNamar, he explains the true state of affairs to Ann. Poor Ann does not know what to make of it all. She hesitates to complete the breach with the sometime lover in New York, for her father, James Rutledge, has been losing money, is now McNamar's tenant, and would naturally like McNamar to become his son-in-law. Ann, meanwhile, must serve at table in the tavern, and, basket on arm, must carry dinner for the men working at the mill, often attended by her two suitors: the well-to-do Hill, who glibly plies his wooing, and the poor, taciturn Lincoln.

XI

Election time has returned, for the elections to the Illinois legislature are held every two years, and Lincoln runs once more. Puritans say he is an atheist, but whatever may be his creed he is always charitable and kind, fond of children and animals, and so he is elected and reëlected again and again, serving as a member of the State Assembly of Illinois for eight years continuously, from the age of twenty-five to the age of thirty-two. In those days he learned little of the artifices and intrigues of party life, but much of the great problems which form the moral and spiritual basis of partisan disputes. His leader was Clay; his exemplar, Jefferson.

Henry Clay was the most prominent statesman of that epoch. Lincoln, with his fondness for drawing comparisons and with his dispassionate temperament, could not but venerate Clay as one who thought it better to reconcile oppositions, rather than let them rage unchecked, until the safety of the whole was imperiled. Clay, now verging on sixty, had looked the fathers of the country in the face, and he seemed to Lincoln the natural guardian of their great traditions. Born the year after the Declaration of Independence, and one of those who had negotiated the second peace with England, Clay was an ardent supporter of all things that seemed to him likely to guarantee enduring freedom. To that end he favored a high tariff, in order to safeguard the United States against British competition; advocated public works; promoted industry and commerce; and subordinated everything, including the slavery question, to the need for maintaining the Union. For him, as for its founders, the Union was the primary source of liberty, the pledge of independence, in face of a monarchical Europe that seemed already to be anticipating the collapse of the young republic. He became a disciple of Jefferson, the National Republican; and Lincoln, who was approaching manhood when the tidings of Jefferson's death spread sorrow throughout the land, followed in Clay's footsteps.

For it was Jefferson, and not Washington, to whom Lincoln was most strongly drawn, both by temperament and by understanding. Jefferson had eschewed the heroic pose. Possessed of broad social sympathies, he had hoped to improve men and their interrelations from within; had been a skilled mechanic rather than a great designing engineer, better acquainted with the heart of the people than with the world situation, a democrat in the Greek sense of the term. Lincoln was fond of quoting Jefferson, and had of course long been familiar with the famous passage: "We hold these truths to be self-evident: that all men are created equal; that they are endowed by their Creator with certain unalienable rights; that among these are life, liberty, and the pursuit of happiness. That to secure these rights, governments are instituted among men, deriving their just powers from the consent of the governed."

Is it surprising that Jefferson, setting out from these propositions and arguing with incontrovertible logic, should have voiced a prophetic utterance regarding slavery? Himself a slave owner, he wrote:

"The whole commerce between master and slave is a perpetual exercise of the most boisterous passions, the most unremitting despotism on the one part, and degrading submissions on the other. . . . And with what execrations should the statesman be loaded, who, permitting one half the citizens thus to trample on the rights of the other, transforms those into despots and these into enemies, destroys the morals of the one part, and the *amor patriae* of the other. . . . With the morals of a people, their industry also is destroyed. For in a warm climate, no man will labor for himself

who can make another labor for him. . . . Indeed I tremble for
my country when I reflect that God is just."

It was growing plainer day by day that this question of slavery
was intertwined with the vital problem of the maintenance of the
Union. Again and again, ever more boldly, the South was threatening to secede from the North, if slavery, its most vital need, were
tampered with. Lincoln has read the history of slavery's beginnings in his country. He knows that simultaneously with the
arrival of the *Mayflower* at the shore of what was to be New England, a ship with nineteen Negro slaves on board had reached the
coast of what afterwards became Carolina; that good fortune and
bad, hope and despair, had crossed the North Atlantic in the same
year, to eventuate centuries later in a dangerous conflict between
the descendants of the men of those days. He knows that when
the Constitution was drafted, the original plan had been to
include a clause recognizing slavery; that in the end this had
been discountenanced; and that the wording finally adopted
in the Constitution had been designedly ambiguous. "Representatives and direct Taxes shall be apportioned among the several
States which may be included within this Union, according to their
respective Numbers, which shall be determined by adding to the
whole Number of free Persons . . . three-fifths of all other persons." The "other persons" were slaves; and, thanks to this
way of allotting representation, the slave owners could send a dis-
proportionate number of representatives to Congress. In a word,
the South at first was enabled to outvote the North. But, by the
Ordinance of July 13, 1787, for the government of the territory of
the United States northwest of the Ohio River, slavery was forbidden in that area forever.

When the Union was founded, there had been six slave States;
there were now fourteen!

The increase had come about in this way: after the Louisiana
Purchase in 1803, when a vast region west of the Mississippi was
added to the Union and had to be divided into new States, the
latent conflict over the extension of slavery became actual. Civil
war loomed in the distance, and Jefferson said: "This momentous

WAGE EARNER

question, like a fire bell in the night, awakened and filled me with
terror." Then Henry Clay, to save the Union from disintegration,
negotiated the Missouri compromise. In the area of the Louisiana
Purchase, slavery was forbidden north of latitude 36° 30′ (the southern boundary of the State of Missouri, now in process of formation),
except within the limits of the State of Missouri. In plain terms,
Missouri came into the Union as a new slave State. This took
place in 1820–1821.

The fifteen years that had elapsed since that date had served only
to make the question more critical. Reinforced in Congress by the
new West, the North enacted a high tariff on imports, thus arousing
a storm in the southern States. In the Nullification Ordinance of
1832, South Carolina categorically declared that the Acts of Congress to levy import duties were "null and void, and no law, nor
binding upon this State, its officers or citizens." It was ready for
armed revolt — but old Andrew Jackson had doggedly determined
to hold the Union fast. And in the end the tariff was modified
in such a way as to effect a compromise with the recalcitrant State.

Vandalia, the capital of Illinois, is buzzing with all this and
other slave talk, and in this little town the State Assembly sits,
eighty-one members in all, divided into two Chambers. They
meet in a small building with wooden desks and paneled walls.
Lincoln, who has borrowed some cash for new clothes, sits in his
blue suit as a member of the primitive parliament, and holds his
peace. For each sitting he receives a fee of three dollars, also
pens, ink, and writing paper. What is he thinking? Do these
politicians, many of them lawyers, impress him favorably? Have
they read more and seen more than the land surveyor and postmaster of twenty-five, who has made two trips southward to the
Gulf, and who for several years has been mastering all the books
he can get hold of? Their speeches are not remarkable, and there
are few men of conspicuous ability among them; little to stimulate
his ambition here. He is taciturn in the House and not until they
all get back to the inn, and his fellow legislators have laid aside
their pretentious airs, does he open his mouth and tell anecdotes.

Thus he soon becomes known as a story-teller. They call him

the Sangamon Chief, and a good many of them must regard his observant silence with mixed feelings; but no one can overlook the queer figure. Above all, one man who sits in the same row contemplates him with unostentatious attention; a great contrast to Lincoln in many respects, short and thickset, with a barrel chest and broad shoulders, wide-browed, full of life and energy, busily going to and fro to make himself acquainted with everything, an official from the East, a Democrat, almost as poor, but a few years younger. His name is Stephen A. Douglas. Sprung from the class of intellectuals, pliable, approachable, and smooth-tongued, he is the very antipodes of that rough-hewn, silent, eccentric, ironical giant, an antithesis which might have been invented by a dramatist for the stage. For the moment they do not clash. Lincoln seems scarcely to heed Douglas. But Douglas takes note of every one with whom he comes in contact, for his ruling passion is ambition, he is fired with a determination to achieve rapid advancement, and has his eye fixed on the highest office in the land. Every other politician is a possible rival. He reckons up their strength, one and all, and surely feels quite safe about this lonely fellow: Lincoln will do no harm.

XII

The Easterner, McNamar, with the double name, apparently has gone forever. When Lincoln gets back from Vandalia to New Salem, he finds the Rutledges in impoverished circumstances. The first settler in the region has had to give up the tavern and has moved back to a farm which also belongs to the vanished McNamar. Pretty Ann is cured of her fondness for the latter. She has drawn comparisons between him and the two local wooers. Moreover, Hill's wooing is also now a thing of the past. But here is one who has loved her faithfully for three years; one who in wedded life would rather have tranquillity and poverty than the pride of wealth; one who would fain make his way by his own exertions, without being beholden to another's help. For this man of silent dignity and self-denying heart, Ann is now in a position that overrules his hesitations. The two become engaged.

Spring has come; Lincoln often rides over to the Rutledge farm. He is six-and-twenty, she is four years younger. These months of betrothal seem to have been the happiest in his life. For this melancholy man, the idyll is but a brief halt on the shore of happiness, and speedily the river will sweep him along once more on its dark bosom.

For, that summer, malaria is prevalent in the neighborhood of New Salem, and just as fever had struck down his relatives and finally his mother in Indiana, so now it grips him, one of his friends, and his affianced. His strong constitution wrestles successfully with the disease. The friend dies, and at last Lincoln sees his loved one die. His sanity trembles in the balance. After a toilsome and joyless youth, he has ventured to set his heart upon a dream of happiness. He has hoped that to him, likewise, will come the delights by which so many of his more cheerful companions have been enthralled. From the treasure of fantasy he has conjured up an entrancing melody and has tried to make it audible to himself and others; but suddenly the melody stops and all his expectations of a lonely existence, full of unsatisfied yearnings, are confirmed. Can we be surprised that a week after the burial he is found rambling in the woods beside the Sangamon River, murmuring incoherencies? Or that another time he speeds seven miles afoot, to throw himself down in misery upon her grave? On the advice of a physician who is much attached to him, he is sent to the home of friends where he takes part in the harvesting, and at night holds the carded wool for the women's spinning. But once, in a thunderstorm, they suddenly hear him call out, "I can't bear to think of her lying out there alone. The rain and the storm sha'n't beat on her grave!"

The man whose melancholy makes him fear to carry a pocketknife is, for a time, reduced to utter despair.

XIII

And yet, life pursues its course; and one who refrains from suicide has to go on living somehow or other. The special laws which develop character become fixed in early youth; and even one of so restless a disposition, devoid of ambition, without any fixed aim in life, lacking the spur of necessity, will tend to continue moving in the customary orbit until what seem to be chance happenings expose the inner logic of events. Besides, Lincoln's nature is too fundamentally healthy to remain long dominated by a paralyzing gloom. The nervous crisis is severe but fleeting, and a man of imaginative temperament, accustomed to renounce concrete joys and to take refuge in the land of dreams, can for that very reason more speedily find his way back to chill reality.

For him, now that he is twenty-seven, the years of desultory reading are over. He has to study along specific lines; a sound knowledge of law and history has become indispensable; and a friendly teacher has also explained the laws of grammar to the youth. The basis of his casual education is growing solid. Transactions in land are going on more briskly than ever; and now, when Lincoln comes to survey with his instruments, he is expected to talk politics; as the *raconteur*, to oblige with an anecdote; judge of a wrestling match, or arbitrate in a dispute. In this way a natural growth in the ties between him and his constituents takes place, and there can be little doubt of his reëlection.

His second electoral campaign is, however, differently conducted from the first. He has become a politician, has noted many of his colleagues' electioneering arts, has learned how to write carefully composed letters and how to make set speeches. His self-confidence has grown, so that his methods are more dexterous and his demeanor more challenging than they had been two years earlier. He has even developed a program of his own, as his party notes askance; and he responds to a request of a local newspaper that candidates should "show their hands", as follows:

"I go for all sharing the privileges of the government who assist in bearing its burdens. Consequently, I go for admitting all whites to the right of suffrage who pay taxes or bear arms (by no means excluding females). If elected, I shall consider the whole people of Sangamon my constituents, as well those that oppose as those that support me. While acting as their representative, I shall be governed by their will on all subjects upon which I have the means of knowing what their will is; and upon all others I shall do what my own judgment teaches me will best advance their interests. Whether elected or not, I go for distributing the proceeds of the sales of the public lands to the several States, to enable our State, in common with others, to dig canals and construct railroads without borrowing money and paying the interest on it."

He had not used so firm a tone at the first election, but now he hits back when one of the other side publicly attacks him. The man was a local dignitary who, to the general astonishment, has just had the first lightning conductor in Springfield set up over his house. After answering the speaker's argument, Lincoln concludes by saying:

"The previous speaker commenced his speech by announcing that the young man would have to be taken down. It is for you, fellow citizens, not for me, to say whether I am up or down. The gentleman has seen fit to allude to my being a young man; but he forgets that I am older in years than I am in the tricks and trades of politicians. I desire to live, and I desire place and distinction; but I would rather die now than, like the gentleman, live to see the day that I would change my politics for an office worth $3,000 a year, and then feel compelled to erect a lightning-rod to protect a guilty conscience from an offended God."

The lust of battle seems to have awakened in him; and his irony, hitherto used only in jest, has become a rapier. His sense of personal dignity grows during these years of warfare, and manifests itself as a healthy pride when it is hurt. Some one had ordered newspapers but delayed payment; now he demands a receipt. "And I am surprised," says Lincoln, the postmaster. "The law requires newspaper postage to be paid in advance, and now that I have waited a full year, you choose to wound my feelings by intimating that unless you get a receipt I will probably make you pay again."

When one of the Democratic candidates has been spreading defamatory insinuations about Lincoln, he receives this letter:

"I am told that during my absence last week you stated publicly that you were in possession of a fact or facts which, if known to the public, would entirely destroy the prospects of N. W. Edwards and myself at the ensuing election; but that through favor to us you would forbear to divulge them. No one has needed favors more than I, and generally few have been less unwilling to accept them; but in this case favor to me would be injustice to the public, and therefore I must beg your pardon for declining it. That I once had the confidence of the people of Sangamon County is sufficiently evident; and if I have done anything, either by design or misadventure, which if known would subject me to a forfeiture of that confidence, he that knows of that thing and conceals it is a traitor to his country's interest. I find myself wholly unable to form any conjecture of what fact or facts, real or supposed, you spoke; but my opinion of your veracity will not permit me for a moment to doubt that you at least believed what you said. I am flattered with the personal regard you manifested for me; but I do hope that on mature reflection you will view the public interest as a paramount consideration, and therefore let the worst come.

"I assure you that the candid statement of facts on your part, however low it may sink me, shall never break the ties of personal friendship between us.

"I wish an answer to this, and you are at liberty to publish both if you choose."

Here we have Lincoln's first masterpiece as a stylist. He is absolutely sure of his ground, not having been nicknamed Honest Abraham for naught; and it is equally plain that he sees through his adversary's wiles. What, then, prevents him from answering in an outburst of defiance? Consideration for a sometime friend, and the tact of a politician. By feigning the truth of the offense, he can disclose his zeal for the public welfare, to which he sacrifices his own. By admitting that, in general, he is glad to accept favors, he unassumingly draws attention to his own modesty; and he knows that the recipient of his letter, after biting his lips at its veiled sarcasms, will be brought up with a jar by the concluding "I wish an answer." The bungling attack cannot but be welcome to him in the full tide of his electoral campaign, for if his opponent should refrain from publishing the letter, Lincoln will take steps to make its tenor generally known, and will gain public confidence because the other has not dared to follow up the original onslaught. Thus does he show himself a master of fence when his honor is assailed.

But when an adversary has shown real friendliness, giving Lincoln a "lift" to a meeting, Lincoln says to the assembled farmers, "I am too poor to own a carriage, but my friend has generously invited me to ride with him. I want you to vote for me if you will; but, if not, then vote for my opponent, for he is a fine man."

With his reëlection, the Whigs for the first time enter as victors with a group called the Long Nine (they average six feet in height and more than two hundred pounds in weight) who advocate bold financial schemes. Lincoln in his turn is industriously working, by compromising and bargaining, to collect votes for the transfer of the capital to Springfield. As his personal career has shown, he has not the temperament requisite for a financial expert — nor yet the temperament that would enable him to feather his own nest in parliamentary life. On one occasion he speaks frankly in the House of "the work of politicians; a set of men who have interests aside from the interests of the people, and who, to say the most of them, are, taken as a mass, at least one long step removed from honest men. I say this with the greater freedom because, being a politician myself, none can regard it as personal." The concluding admission is purely formal. It is the language of a man who feels himself essentially different from his colleagues. This is not arrogance but the knowledge that his own motives are untainted, for he is aware that almost all the others among whom he sits are hiding personal aims behind flourishes of speech; he himself has none.

Of course he knows the world of poverty, and the value of money, and when elected he is aware, as a realist, of his advantage; yet never for the sake of his own advantage will he vote for or support that which is false. Incorruptibility is made easy for him by the basic traits of his own character; would be forced upon him, did he not already possess it. Having a Socratic capacity for seeing both sides of every question, it comes natural to him to weigh conflicting wishes, one against the other. Feeling no need to defend such a compromise before his inner tribunal, he is not constrained to excuse his actions (either to himself or to others) by a parade of fictitious motives. Here is an instance :

Lincoln and the Long Nine are working for the removal of the seat of State government from Vandalia to the rising town of Springfield. Trade, communications, convenience of legal procedure, the whole course of development in Illinois, point to the step. Lincoln has a personal interest, too : he feels that for him the days of village life are over ; and he looks forward to activities on a larger stage, activities that can be combined with his political career. Others have private reasons for wishing Vandalia to remain the State capital. A third group, upon whose support the chance of inaugurating the Springfield scheme seems to depend, is willing to vote for it — on terms. Eventually, by clever trading, these terms are met and it is voted to move the State capital to Springfield. It is a great victory for Lincoln.

XIV

"Lincoln had a high conception of woman, and I can testify that during our long acquaintanceship I never heard him say an evil word about any one of them, nor utter one of those coarse sayings about the other sex which are common in most men's mouths. . . . He had a strong, if not terrible passion for women. He could hardly keep his hands off a woman, and yet, much to his credit, he lived a pure and virtuous life. His idea was that a woman had as much right to violate the marriage vow as a man — no more and no less. His sense of right, his sense of justice, his honor, forbade his violating his marriage vow. . . . I have seen Lincoln tempted, and I have seen him reject the approach of woman."

These cautiously worded observations, made by one of Lincoln's intimates, throw light on **part of** the dilemma in which he found himself when faced by women. Lonely, and having a poet's nature, he felt the need of women ; and yet an inborn delicacy, coupled with constitutional shyness where the female sex was concerned, held him in check. As he was by nature slow of action, he was always exposed to the onslaughts of the resolute type of women who were prepared to exchange the rôles of the sexes and make advances to this eccentric male. Once the gentle voice of a girl had touched his heart, but he had made no approach even to her until, after a year of waiting, she had felt freed from her betrothal to another, and was to Lincoln doubly attractive because she was both forlorn and poor. Now she was dead. A year had elapsed, and another woman crossed his path.

In intervals between sessions of the legislature, Lincoln visited New Salem, spending some of his time at the house of a young married woman of his acquaintance, who often spoke of her sister. He had met her there three years before, and half in jest, half in earnest, he agreed to wed this sister if she should return to New Salem.

"I, of course, accepted the proposal, for you know I could not have done otherwise, had I really been averse to it. I had seen the said sister some three years before, thought her intelligent and agreeable, and saw no good objection to plodding through life hand in hand with her."

Such was the beginning of the affair, two women putting their heads together to arrange the marriage of a man who was remaining a bachelor too long. For she was a year older than he, better educated, and better off in this world's possessions. As for him, he had "no good objection."

Mary Owens arrives in due course — and Lincoln grows uneasy. "Time passed on, the lady took her journey sure enough. This stomached me a little; for it appeared to me that her coming so readily showed that she was a trifle too willing; but, on reflection, it occurred to me that she might have been prevailed on by her married sister to come, without anything concerning me ever having been mentioned to her; and so I concluded that, if no other objection presented itself, I would consent to waive this. . . . In a few days we had an interview; and, although I had seen her before, she did not look as my imagination had pictured her. I knew she was oversize, but she now appeared a fair match for Falstaff. I knew she was called an 'old maid'. . . . Through life I have been in no such bondage, either real or imaginary, from the thralldom of which I so much desired to be free. After my return home, I saw nothing to change my opinions of her in any particular. She was the same, and so was I. I now spent my time in planning how I might get along through life after my contemplated change of circumstances should have taken place, and how I might procrastinate the evil day for a time, which I really dreaded as much, perhaps more than an Irishman does the halter."

He begins to displease her in various little matters. To this meticulous spinster he seems untidy in his ways; and he does not pay her the little attentions a well-bred young lady expects from a gentleman. Once when they are riding across country with others, and the men squire their dames in the fording of a difficult creek, Lincoln does not offer to help her. When she complains of his remissness, he calls back over his shoulder, "You're plenty smart enough to take care of yourself." Yet he once spoiled his best suit getting a casual hog loose from the mire. This seems to her sentimental; and when he refuses to help a woman carrying her baby uphill, she calls him rude. Such disharmonies multiply, and on one occasion, when he returns after a week's absence on a land-surveying job, she refuses at first to see him.

At length comes a fresh stir in the current of his life. After five years of stagnation the legislature moves to Springfield. He has put the measure through, and now he ventures on a step for which he has long been preparing. He will set up as a lawyer in Springfield. No examination is required, nothing but a formal license to practice; and from his borrowed law books Lincoln has learned more than many a local celebrity knows. Besides, he is convinced that acquaintance with men and things, the experiences of practical life, will stand him in better stead than dry-as-dust learning. Practice will fill up the gaps in his theoretical knowledge, and his partner will help him out when necessary. Is he not already well known far and near? As postmaster and land surveyor, as store clerk and rail-splitter, as candidate for the legislature, he has come in contact with half the population of the county. His experience in public speaking, the knowledge of the locality he has gained in his professional life, and above all his growing self-confidence, drive him to this venture. Should it fail, the failure will only be one more in a long series!

He is as poor as ever; yet he is in no mood to win fortune by marrying money. At twenty-eight, Lincoln rides forth to begin a new life, mounted on a borrowed nag, seven dollars in his pocket, with debts totaling more than a thousand dollars, and engaged (more or less) to a woman for whom he does not care.

BOOK TWO

CITIZEN

I

Ninety years ago, Springfield, Illinois, was already a town of some importance, with its fifteen hundred inhabitants and its four inns; its only genuine rival was Chicago and, being the seat of the legislature, the town could still look down upon the new city on the lake. As the political center of the State, the young community felt all the pride of authority, and, indeed, some of the airs of Washington itself seemed to have blown down its unpaved thoroughfares. And it was becoming quite a social center too. The richer people had built themselves brick houses. Many of them were of Southern origin, and here in the North tried to live, more or less, the life of a master class, even if they could not keep slaves.

Still, it is not possible to make the place into a thoroughly well-bred city at such short notice. More than a municipal law is needed to keep a sturdy pioneer from driving his hogs down the main street. In fact, the Town Council has to modify a prohibition which has been enacted at the request of the wealthy immigrants from the South, so the revised version reads: "No hog may be led through the streets of Springfield without a ring in its nose."

One of the opening social events following the removal of the capital was a great ball, at which Lincoln was a member of the reception committee. He had no inkling of what effect this first contact with society was going to have upon his life.

Being almost penniless, Lincoln on arrival looked up an old companion-in-arms, a storekeeper, to ask whether he could buy a bed and pay for it later. Speed was a kindly fellow, whose rather feminine type of countenance contrasted strongly with the harsh and weather-beaten features of most of the members of this circle — and his face looked all the stranger because it was fringed by a thick blond beard. Though in many respects a dreamer like Lincoln, inclined to shun the realities of life, he was somewhat spoiled, coming as he did from a well-to-do family of means. Speed lacked both the bodily powers and the mental talents which gave Lincoln dignity and insured him a position.

Being a good fellow, however, he made the impecunious comrade hospitably welcome, and let him share his own bed in the room over the store, where soon four young men would be sleeping in close quarters. Lincoln took his saddlebags upstairs, and, coming back, said, "Well, Speed, I'm moved."

For the time being he takes his meals with Bill Butler, who says there need be no hurry about settling accounts for board. He has, of course, abandoned his jobs as surveyor and postmaster in New Salem and is still faced with a heavy load of debt. He has, therefore, to find a new source of income, and so, after three weeks, he enters into partnership with a local lawyer. Stuart, the man who had formerly lent him law books to read, is running for Congress, and, if elected, will need to leave a partner at home. He knows that he can count upon Lincoln's good sense and eloquence, even if his knowledge of the law may still be elementary. Matters are soon arranged. A new sign reading "Stuart and Lincoln" is affixed on the first floor of the courthouse building in Springfield. It remained unaltered for four years.

The room is a small one, with a few rough bookshelves, a table, a couple of chairs, papers, and plenty of dust. Here our long, lean fellow, who has been used to an open-air life and to frequent changes of occupation, who has generally been able to dispose of his time pretty much as he pleases, this man who has been poor though independent, is now (being in truth half secretary, half lawyer) put to a hard test. He has to write legal documents, must turn up punctually at the sessions of the court, must sue for recovery of debts. One who has been half a gypsy must learn to become a full-fledged business man. What happens? He in part adapts himself to his profession, and in part adapts his profession to his own tastes.

At first it is easy and rather tedious, for Stuart, the man of experience and the chief, naturally keeps the most interesting cases for himself and leaves only the small change for his partner. Thus Lincoln has to handle the affairs of people who have quarreled over a deal in land, such things as any surveyor can manage; or who have differences about a yoke of oxen, or a cooking stove. Ere long, however, there comes a suit which makes the young lawyer known, after his own peculiar fashion. Lincoln never acquires the typical lawyer's fondness for the intricacies of legal logic, for the word-chopping of the codes. What interests him in his new profession is a sense of justice, the opportunities it gives him to help the oppressed. In political life he has already shown his detestation of corruption, and he now transfers this passion to his new career.

A widow had come to claim a legacy from her late husband — ten acres of land. When she arrived, she found that a certain old general had claimed the plot of land, which, he said, had been assigned to him by the deceased in payment of a debt. Stuart and Lincoln, who took up the case, discovered that the general had falsified a document. An immigrant from the East, in search of office, he wanted to secure election as justice of the peace. Realizing that the disclosure of the fraud would tell against his chances, he declared that the questionable document had been maliciously introduced among his papers. Lincoln was furious. A few days before the election he had a leaflet circulated, unsigned, which detailed the affair, and concluded with the following words:

"I have only made these statements because I am known by many to be one of the individuals against whom the charge of forging the assignment and slipping it into the general's papers has been made; and because our silence might be construed into a confession of the truth. I shall not subscribe my name; but hereby authorize the editor of the 'Journal' to give it up to any one who may call for it." The general is none the less elected and, Lincoln's name as writer of the leaflet having been disclosed, a wordy warfare ensues. Commenting on the general's defense in the newspaper, Lincoln writes:

"Let it be remembered that when he first came to this country he attempted to impose himself upon the community as a lawyer, and actually carried the attempt so far as to induce a man who was under a charge of murder to entrust the defense of his life in his hands, and finally took his money and got him hanged."

As to some other statements by the general, Lincoln says, "All this is false as hell," adding, "In conclusion I will only say that I have a character to defend as well as General Adams, but I disdain to whine about it as he does." Lincoln's final remark in the newspaper controversy is: "Farewell, General. I will see you again at court, if not before — when and where we will settle the question whether you or the widow shall have the land." Lincoln wins his case, becomes generally popular on that account, and is thenceforward a terror to Pharisees.

Soon this young man of twenty-eight has all he can want except money, and this he does not miss. He has been lucky in many respects. He is leader of his party in the legislature; partner of an able lawyer; contributor to the local newspaper; a favorite in the little town, because every one knows that he has been mainly instrumental in securing the transference of the seat of the legislature from Vandalia to Springfield; now in a position where he can study new and interesting circumstances; a local champion in wrestling and other sports; and the anecdotalist to whom all like to listen.

What he loves best is to sit in Speed's shop and discuss problems. There is clever Browning, the worldly Baker, also Stuart when he is in town and has time to spare, and Thomas, the minister, sprawled on the boxes or the counter, all sitting around Speed, who is the only one busy. Sometimes Douglas, the smooth-tongued Democrat, turns up, and is ready to agree or argue with both parties to a dispute. All these young fellows have more time and energy than the little town can utilize; they read the newspapers eagerly, and opine that they could make a much better job of things than the legislators in Washington. Lincoln finds it more amusing to talk politics and philosophy and to tell stories than to pore over tedious legal documents. The company becomes a sort of informal debating society; women do not intrude; friendship can only live amongst men. They read essays to one another. Lincoln produces his first, one on the virtue of women, and he also writes a poem on the seduction of women, which ends with the stanza:

" Whatever spiteful fools may say,
Each jealous ranting yelper,
No woman ever went astray,
Without a man to help her."

This expresses the mood of one who will find it more congenial to play the legal adviser to actors than to land speculators. So he espouses the cause of a traveling show which the puritans have forbidden in the town. He pleads for these clients without fee, and when the case comes into court he shows so much humor (carrying his allusions back to the days of Thespis' cart) that the prohibition of the performance is rescinded. The line he has taken in this case makes the godly begin to speak of him as "unchristian."

At this time Lincoln delivers his first great speech before the Young Men's Lyceum of Springfield, on "The Perpetuation of our Political Institutions." It has been very carefully prepared. He says that the United States need fear no danger from without.

"All the armies of Europe, Asia, and Africa combined, . . . with a Bonaparte for a commander, could not by force take a drink from the Ohio or make a track on the Blue Ridge in a trial of a thousand years." If danger were ever to threaten the United States, it would come from within. "As a nation of freemen we must live through all time, or die by suicide." He goes on to speak of something that omened ill. "I mean the increasing disregard for law which pervades the country." He alludes to the lynching of a mulatto in St. Louis, and continues as follows:

"Such are the effects of mob law, and such are the scenes becoming more and more frequent in this land so lately famed for love of law and order. . . . How shall we fortify against it? The answer is simple. Let every American, every lover of liberty, every well-wisher to his posterity, swear by the blood of the revolution never to violate in the least particular the laws of the country, and never to tolerate their violation by others. As the patriots of '76 did to the support of the Declaration of Independence, so to the support of the Constitution and laws let every American pledge his life, his property, and his sacred honor. Many great and good men, sufficiently qualified for any task they should undertake, may ever be found whose ambition would aspire to nothing beyond a seat in Congress, a gubernatorial or a presidential chair; but such belong not to the family of the lion, or the tribe of the eagle.   What! Think you these places would satisfy an Alexander, a Caesar, or a Napoleon?   Never!   Towering genius disdains a beaten path. . . . Passion has helped us, but can do so no more.   It will in future be our enemy.   Reason — cold, calculating, unimpassioned reason — must furnish all the materials for our future support and defence."

A decorative, sumptuous tone — a new tone in Lincoln's mouth. In this dimly lighted little room, before an audience of young people, a man is uplifting his voice, and, with the aid of careful notes, is delivering a formal oration such as the head of a State would deliver in a time of great danger — and perhaps in days to come, as the head of the State, he will have to deliver such a momentous address. But no one, least of all the orator, now foresees this.   He is merely trying his voice, which sounds like a great organ confined within a narrow space.   Sometimes, however, bold images flash through the speech, bearing witness to an ambitious imagination, the imagination of young genius looking back to the heroes of the past, imagination that dwells upon the conflict between tyranny and the public welfare, between reason and autocracy.   In its youthful glow, the oration opens for us glimpses into the secret recesses of his soul, which, when he is merely anecdotal, are hidden from himself and others.

And yet, not without good cause, he dwells upon reason in his peroration.   The hardships of his youth, the difficulties of his education, the slowness of his advancement, his recognition of the inertia of the human heart — all these combine to make him strive, not so much toward the best, as toward what he knows to be practicable.

Lincoln sees that the out-and-out abolitionists in New England (with whom he is sentimentally in sympathy) are advocating a dangerous policy and he cannot make common cause with those who demand from the government a simple and straightforward declaration that in the Union, henceforward, no one shall be born a slave. His moderation upon this matter is plainly disclosed by a protest formulated by him for his party :

"The undersigned . . . believe that the institution of slavery is founded on both injustice and bad policy, but that the promulgation of abolition doctrines tends rather to increase than abate its evils.

"They believe that the Congress of the United States has no power under the Constitution to interfere with the institution of slavery in the different States.

"They believe that the Congress of the United States has the power, under the Constitution, to abolish slavery in the District of Columbia, but that the power ought not to be exercised, unless at the request of the people of the District."

This halfway position, which he is led to take up by his Southern experiences, by his study of history, and by his knowledge of extant forces, is in conformity with what his master Jefferson had written half a century before :

"Nobody wishes more than I to see such proofs as you exhibit that nature has given to our black brethren talents equal to those of the other colors of men, and that the appearance of a want of them is owing merely to the degraded condition of their existence both in Africa and America. I can add with truth, that nobody wishes more ardently to see a good system commenced for raising the condition both of their body and mind to what it ought to be, as fast as the imbecility of their present existence and other circumstances which cannot be neglected will admit."

The moderation of Lincoln's phrasing was shown by the approval of the South, for, after the publication of the protest, some of the Southerners declared that in Illinois the adherents of Clay were quite reasonable. How shrewd they were, and how dangerous they could become, was to be disclosed by the subsequent experience of the South, which found that these same moderates were their most dangerous enemies.

Discussions on slavery and on other political topics are frequent in the church and in the courthouse, which is thrown open for public meetings in the evenings.

On one occasion, Lincoln imitated Thomas, the preacher, in such a way that the audience laughed uproariously, while the preacher began to weep. For this mimicking of Thomas, Lincoln afterwards excused himself, but decades later he spoke these bitter words: "If all the good things I have ever done had lingered in men's memories as vividly as this bad turn, I could congratulate myself." For Lincoln, too, was very sensitive. He found it depressing to speak in an almost empty hall and once when he had been defeated in debate by Douglas, the elegant opponent whom he could not help considering his rival, he was extremely distressed and did not recover his spirits until he had had another try at Douglas, and had come off this time with flying colors.

II

His heart is lonely during his first stay in Springfield, even lonelier than before. What can this new society offer him? He prefers, as of old, to visit tried and trusted friends, where he peers into the woodshed, saws some wood for them, and then slips away. Or he will borrow some law books from a fellow lawyer. One of his acquaintances reports: "Lincoln was the most uncouth-looking young man I ever saw. He seemed to have but little to say, seemed to feel timid, with a tinge of sadness visible in the countenance; but when he did talk all this disappeared for the time, and he demonstrated that he was both strong and acute. He surprised us more and more at every visit."

Difficulties occur in connection with Mary Owens, for she often comes to visit her kindred in Springfield. They spend the evening together, and he sees her home. Sometimes, too, he rides out to New Salem. Thus they have plenty of opportunity for convincing themselves how little they are suited to each other. Nevertheless, matters still hang in the wind. The man feels himself bound by his word; the girl appears to be waiting for a proposal; neither takes a clear line, but they exchange analytical letters. Here is one of Lincoln's:

"Friend Mary: I have commenced two letters to send you before this, both of which displeased me before I got half done, and so I tore them up. The first I thought was not serious enough, and the second was on the other extreme. I shall send this, turn out as it may.

"This thing of living in Springfield is rather a dull business, after all; at least it is so to me. I am quite as lonesome here as I ever was anywhere in my life. I have been spoken to by but one woman since I have been here, and should not have been by her if she could have avoided it. I've never been to church yet, and probably shall not be soon. I stay away because I am conscious I should not know how to behave myself.

"I am often thinking of what we said about your coming to live at Springfield. I am afraid you would not be satisfied. There is a great deal of flourishing about in carriages here, which it would be your doom to see without sharing it. You would have to be poor, without the means of hiding your poverty. Do you believe you could bear that patiently? Whatever woman may cast her lot with mine, should any ever do so, it is my intention to do all in my power to make her happy and contented; and there is nothing I can imagine that would make me more unhappy than to fail in the effort. I know I should be much happier with you than the way I am, provided I saw no signs of discontent in you. What you have said to me may have been in the way of jest, or I may have misunderstood it. If so, then let it be forgotten; if otherwise, I much wish you would think seriously before you decide. What I have said I will most positively abide by, provided you wish it. My opinion is that you had better not do it. You have not been accustomed to hardship, and it may be more severe than you now imagine. I know you are capable of thinking correctly on any subject, and if you deliberate maturely upon this before you decide, then I am willing to abide your decision.

"You must write me a good long letter after you get this. You have nothing else to do, and though it might not seem interesting to you after you had written it, it would be a good deal of company to me in this 'busy wilderness.' Tell your sister I do not want to hear any more about selling out and moving. That gives me the 'hypo' whenever I think of it. Yours, etc., Lincoln."

Another masterpiece! That is how a man writes who is engaged to be married, would like to break it off, but is prevented from doing so by his native kindliness of heart and by his inborn resignation. After his perfectly true remarks about his poverty, would he not do well to take the initiative, and say he considers this a sufficient reason against their marriage? Has he ever given the girl a formal pledge? Should not the obdurate unconcern with which, for a year or more, she has been contemplating his reluctance, be enough to warn him, and to set him free? No, he leaves the decision to her, throws a few grains of courtliness into this thorny thicket, and yet can write all the time in a style which might have seemed impossible to a man who only six years before had been a rail-splitter and a Mississippi raftsman. Yet he displays all the uneasiness of the ingrained bachelor and Bohemian in the hope he expresses that Mary Owens' sister will not sell out and move from New Salem; for he is much concerned when he contemplates the possibility that he will no longer find there a hospitable room and a welcome.

Thus the affair runs on: visits, a parting without a farewell, a renewed meeting. At length, trying to give things a shove, he writes:

"You will no doubt think it rather strange that I should write you a letter on the same day on which we parted, and I can only account for it by supposing that seeing you lately makes me think of you more than usual; while at our late meeting, we had but few expressions of thoughts. You must know that I cannot see you or think of you with entire indifference; and yet it may be that you are mistaken in regard to what my real feelings toward you are. If I knew you were not, I should not have troubled you with this letter. Perhaps any other man would know enough without further information; but I consider it my peculiar right to plead ignorance, and your bounden duty to allow the plea. I want in all cases to do right, and most particularly so in all cases with women. I want at this particular time, more than anything else, to do right with you; and if I knew it would be doing right, as I rather suspect it would, to let you alone, I would do it. And for the purpose of making the matter as plain as possible, I now say that you can now drop the subject, dismiss your thoughts (if you ever had any) from me forever, and leave this letter unanswered, without calling forth one accusing murmur from me. And I will even go further, and say that if it will add anything to your comfort or peace of mind to do so, it is my sincere wish that you should. Do not understand by this that I wish to cut your acquaintance. I mean no such thing. What I do wish is that our further acquaintance shall depend upon yourself. If such further acquaintance would contribute nothing to your happiness, I am sure it would not to mine. If you feel yourself in any degree bound to me, I am now willing to release you, provided you wish it; while, on the other hand, I am willing and even anxious to bind you faster, if I can be convinced that it will, in any considerable degree, add to your happiness. This, indeed, is the whole question with me. Nothing would make me more miserable than to believe you miserable — nothing more happy than to know you were so. . . . If it suits you best not to answer this, farewell. A long life and a merry one attend you. But if you conclude to write back, speak as plainly as I do. . . . Your friend, Lincoln."

He has written more candidly; and if he signs himself "your friend" instead of "yours, etc.", this only makes his aloofness plainer. She must have noticed it, and have made up her mind. But Lincoln had nothing to reproach himself with, and no one else has any right to reproach him. It is difficult to say whether we are more inclined to admire the nobleman in the rail-splitter, or the diplomat in the lawyer who could show so much literary adroitness in the composition of his notes to an alien power at a time of crisis. We do not know her answer. All we know is that Lincoln at length made up his mind to propose to her. What was the result? Something he had almost ceased to hope for. She refused.

"At first I supposed she did it through an affectation of modesty, which I thought but ill became her under the peculiar circumstances of her case; but on my renewal of the charge, I found she repelled it with greater firmness than before. I tried it again and again, but with the same success, or rather with the same want of success.

"I finally was forced to give it up; at which I very unexpectedly

found myself mortified almost beyond endurance.   I was mortified,
it seemed to me, in a hundred different ways.   My vanity was
deeply wounded by the reflection that I had been too stupid to discover her intentions, and at the same time never doubting that I
understood them perfectly; and also that she, whom I had taught
myself to believe nobody else would have, had actually rejected
me with all my fancied greatness.   And, to cap the whole, I then
for the first time began to suspect that I was really a little in love
with her.   But let it all go.   I'll try and outlive it.   Others have
been made fools of by the girls; but this can never with truth be
said of me.   I most emphatically, in this instance, made a fool of
myself.   I have now come to the conclusion never again to think
of marrying, and for this reason : I can never be satisfied with any
one who would be blockhead enough to have me.   When you receive
this, write me a long yarn about something to amuse me."

In the closing sentence of this detailed report to a lady friend,
Lincoln's humor for the first time gleams from under the depression
which he has vainly tried to overcome.   He has achieved what he
has so long desired, has recovered his freedom, but his nervous
temperament always takes alarm at a sudden fulfillment of a wish.
Though he has made fun of Mary Owen's corpulence, it suddenly
occurs to him that perhaps he has been in love with her after all,
and he reproaches himself for vanity instead of congratulating himself on a diplomatic victory.   Thus remote are Lincoln's thoughts
from reality, when reality has intruded into the domain of his
imagination, into the delicate regions of freedom and of love; so
little is he fitted to outmatch reality that he turns pale when reality
invades the realm of his constructions.   After the tragedy of his
first betrothal, and after the comedy of his second, no one can expect
that a man so timid will ever play the active rôle in a third love
affair.

III

"Mr. Lincoln . . . has . . . a sort of assumed clownishness
in his manner which does not become him, and which does not
truly belong to him. . . . He will sometimes make his language

correspond with this clownish manner, and he can thus frequently
raise a loud laugh among his Whig hearers; but this entire game of
buffoonery convinces the mind of no man, and is utterly lost on the
majority of his audience."

This criticism of his method of public speaking at the age of
thirty, published in one of the local papers, is one of the first indications that he is becoming a person of importance. For at this
very time, when the rotund Mary has given him his *congé*, he has
for the third time been elected a member of the legislature. As
one of the local leaders of his party he has almost acquired the
position of leader of the "Clay men" in Illinois. The following
year, when the country is in the throes of a presidential election,
when political passion is rife, Lincoln, who has hitherto had to content himself with audiences of two or three hundred, finds that the
number of his hearers has swelled to thousands, and he has to learn
how to rivet the attention of so vast an assembly. He begins to improve his natural talents as an orator, to make a deliberate use of
what has been no more than youthful improvisation. He learns
how to vary his style to fit the occasion and to suit the mentality
of his audience. He has become able to use all the registers.

Here is an example of a somewhat overladen style foreign to his
disposition, pulling out the emotional stops:

"I know that the great volcano in Washington . . . is belching
forth the lava of political corruption in a current broad and deep,
which is sweeping with frightful velocity over the whole length and
breadth of the land, bidding fair to leave unscathed no green spot
or living thing. . . . Broken by it I too may be; bow to it I never
will. . . . If ever I feel the soul within me elevate and expand to
those dimensions not wholly unworthy of its almighty Architect,
it is when I contemplate the cause of my country deserted by all the
world beside, and I standing up boldly and alone and hurling defiance at her victorious oppressors. Here, without contemplating
consequences, before high heaven and in the face of the world, I
swear eternal fidelity to the just cause, as I deem it, of the land of
my life, my liberty, and my love. And who that thinks with me
will not fearlessly adopt the oath that I take? . . . But if, after

all, we shall fail, be it so. We still shall have the proud consolation of saying to our consciences, and to the departed shade of our country's freedom, that the cause approved of our judgment, and adored of our hearts, in disaster, in chains, in torture, in death, we never faltered in defending."

Another time he employs a more popular kind of metaphor. While displaying all the knowledge of detail that is requisite to guide him throughout a thirty-four-page speech upon financial topics, he lightens the exposition by drawing instances from every-day life, trying, as always, to keep in touch with the generality of things, in the interpretation of which the political genius has stood side by side with the poet. He breaks off the tale of figures to say :

"How is it that we know anything — that any event will occur, that any combination of circumstances will produce a certain result — except by the analogies of past experience? What has once happened will invariably happen again when the same circumstances which combined to produce it shall again combine in the same way. We all feel that we know that a blast of wind would extinguish the flame of the candle that stands by me. How do we know it? We have never seen this flame thus extinguished. We know it because we have seen through all our lives that a blast of wind extinguishes the flame of a candle whenever it is thrown fully upon it. Again, we all know that we have to die. How? We have never died yet. . . . The fair analogy of past experience fully proves that the sub-treasury would be a less safe depository of the public money than a national bank."

Wishing to remind his hearers how prone people are to forget, he bitterly draws their attention to the unwelcome truth : "Great distance in either time or space has wonderful power to lull and render quiescent the human mind. Pleasures to be enjoyed or pains to be endured, after we shall be dead and gone, are but little regarded even in our own cases, and much less in the cases of others."

Speedily, too, he acquires the methods of the agitator, and is able to turn the story of his own penurious youth to account. When the Whigs are attacked by the Democrats for being elegant folk who wear fine clothes while pleading the cause of the common people, he, standing on the platform, slyly pulls at his adversary's tightly buttoned coat, which opens to disclose a ruffled silk shirt, and a watch-chain with gold seals. Amid laughter Lincoln proceeds:

"I was a poor boy hired on a flatboat at eight dollars a month, and had only one pair of breeches to my back, and they were buckskin. Now, if you know the nature of buckskin when wet and dried by the sun, it will shrink; and my breeches kept shrinking until they left several inches of my legs bare between the tops of my socks and the lower part of my breeches; and while I was growing taller they were becoming shorter, and so much tighter that they left a blue streak around my legs that can be seen to this day. If you call this aristocracy, I plead guilty to the charge."

Thus does Lincoln at the age of thirty know how to play upon the feelings of his audience by the description of earlier privations or by allusions to the mutability of all things; thus does he fetter their attention, move them to laughter, make them reflective, or arouse salvos of applause, now by examples familiar to their understanding, and now by appealing to their patriotic emotions. That year all Illinois assembles in Springfield to hold a monster demonstration on the occasion of the presidential election. The party groups bring along symbolic log cabins and make a tremendous noise with divers sorts of music. Chicago, instead of a log cabin, has brought a symbolical ship loaded on a wagon. An eyewitness describes Lincoln's participation in this tumultuous affair:

"He stood in a wagon, from which he addressed the mass of people that surrounded it. The meeting was one of unusual interest because of him who was to make the principal address. It was at the time of his greatest physical strength. He was tall, and perhaps a little more slender than in later life, and more homely than after he became stouter in person. He was then only thirty-one years of age, and yet he was regarded as one of the ablest of the Whig speakers in that campaign. There was that in him that attracted and held public attention. Even then he was the subject of popular regard because of his candid and simple mode of discussing and illustrating political questions. At times he was intensely logical, and was always most convincing in his arguments. The questions involved in that canvass had relation to the tariff, internal public improvements by the Federal Government, the distribution of the proceeds of the sales of public lands among the several States, and other questions that divided the political parties of that day. They were not such questions as enlisted and engaged his best thoughts; they did not take hold of his great nature, and had no tendency to develop it. At times he discussed the questions of the hour in a logical way, but much time was devoted to telling stories to illustrate some phase of his argument, though more often the telling of these stories was resorted to for the purpose of rendering his opponents ridiculous. That was a style of speaking much appreciated at that early day. . . . One story he told on that occasion was full of salient points, and well illustrated the argument he was making. It was not an impure story, yet it was not one it would be seemly to publish; but rendered, as it was, in his inimitable way, it contained nothing that was offensive to a refined taste."

Many of these speeches were carefully prepared. In his private letters of identical dates, we find portions of them repeated word for word to his friends. He regards them as important, for he urges his correspondents to read these speeches in the newspaper, or to read the newspaper reports aloud one to another. Sometimes his political associates are annoyed with him because, as so often happens with people of nervous temperament, he has been inert at a meeting, as though stricken with palsy; or because he has been rough and uncouth in his intervention; or, perhaps, because he has not been sufficiently radical for their taste. At times his wide tolerance makes it impossible for him to display the fire wanted in the political struggle. For that reason, he shows to best advantage when he is facing one whom he regards as his enemy.

Such an enemy is Douglas. Is this Democrat perpetually going to follow him about? At the time the two had begun their careers in Vandalia, Douglas had been a candidate for the office of State attorney. On the selfsame day, five years later, they had been admitted to legal practice before the Supreme Court; and now, in the same constituency, each is advocating the cause of the President of his choice. The presence of Douglas acts as a spur to Lincoln. Does he recognize in this man a predestincd opponent, one who possesses what he himself lacks — elegance of speech and mind? Is the small, elastic frame distasteful to him because it contrasts so strikingly with his own?

However that may be, when Douglas defends the extravagant expenditure of Van Buren as an administrator, Lincoln rejoins, "This list of excuses I will rapidly examine, and show, as I think, that the few of them which are true prove nothing, and that the majority of them are wholly untrue in fact." He heaps figures upon figures in proof of the assertion, reiterating that Douglas' excuses are "utterly false." At length he concludes by saying:

"Those who heard Mr. Douglas, recollect that he indulged himself in a contemptuous expression of pity for me. 'Now he's got me,' thought I. But when he went on to say that five millions of the expenditure of 1838 were payments of the French indemnities, which I knew to be untrue; . . . that ten millions had been for the Maine boundary war, which I not only knew to be untrue, but supremely ridiculous also; and when I saw that he was stupid enough to hope that I would permit such groundless and audacious assertions to go unexposed — I readily consented that, on the score both of veracity and sagacity, the audience should judge whether he or I were the more deserving of the world's contempt. . . . I will relate an anecdote which seems too strikingly in point to be omitted. A witty Irish soldier . . ."

So harsh can this kindly fellow Lincoln become, so fierce can this man ɔf mild disposition be, not because the other is a Democrat, but because Douglas is the predestined adversary of one who by temperament is slow-moving, straightforward and transparent — one whose mind fits the face and form God has given him.

IV

Over the way in a fine garden stands a large mansion with wooden pillars and a long veranda. It belongs to Ninian W. Edwards, one of the richest men in Springfield. Lincoln and Douglas often meet there, for Springfield political society does not split itself into separate parties but models itself in this matter upon the great world in Washington.

Mrs. Edwards had come from an aristocratic home. The Todds of Kentucky, of Scottish extraction, had distinguished themselves in the War of Independence. Mrs. Edwards' great-grandfather had been a general, and another relative had been State governor. Mrs. Edwards' father, Robert Smith Todd, had been a captain in the War of 1812, was president of the Bank of Kentucky in Lexington, and lived the wealthy and honored life of a patrician. He kept fine horses, had an abundance of cattle, and also a few slaves. In his town house, whose walls were hung with portraits of his famous ancestors, his children had been as carefully educated as those belonging to noble families in Europe.

Yet six of the Todd children left this house one after another, because, after the death of their mother, a stepmother ruled there, a stepmother who had borne their father children to whom the preference was given. Among the fugitives was Mary Todd, ambitious, inspired with a great aim; she was in search of a wider life, and she had made up her mind to look for it in Springfield where (she heard from her sister) a society was developing. So she got into her own traveling carriage and drove north to the home of her sister and her brother-in-law.

When Lincoln and Douglas were introduced to the newcomer, they saw a buxom and yet supplely formed girl, with a smooth, soft skin and artificially curled hair, wearing a dress with a low-cut bodice and a ballooned skirt: a young lady from the great world, a brilliant talker, well informed, able to intersperse French phrases here and there, and even to quote from the French classics. Though she was vivacious when speaking, when she was silent her lips showed a harsh line, and at a word of criticism her steel-blue eyes would freeze the offender with a chilly glance.

At her first ball she made a sensation, for she was an admirable dancer. All the young men vied with one another for the favor of being this clever and pretty girl's partner. But young Herndon, whom Lincoln had recently taken into his office, said the wrong thing in telling her that she had waltzed like a serpent! The comparison was not unkindly meant, but affronted the young lady's dignity. Her eyes flashed at him as she bowed and moved away, and an enmity which endured throughout life began with this glance. Nor did most of the other young men present on this occasion charm the girl, for she was not impressed either by a handsome face, elegance, family, or money — and her indifference to these matters seemed remarkable in one whose education had chiefly aimed at emphasizing class distinction. She appeared to revolt against guidance by ordinary feminine instincts. No, Mary had only one thought: Who had the best prospects of a great career? She had made up her mind to be neither more nor less than wife of a future President! With unerring discernment she was prompt to pick out from among her new acquaintances at Springfield the two most promising men, though they were both of them poor, both of lowly origin — one very short and one very tall: Douglas and Lincoln.

Douglas was as quick to recognize the young lady's abilities as she had been to recognize his, for the two were both dominated by ambition; and if, in her dreams, Mary went to live at the White House, she would be sure to meet the dreaming Douglas there, for Douglas had his thoughts also perpetually fixed on the highest office in the land and his whole life was directed toward the attainment of the presidential chair. Lincoln, ambitious but pessimistic, hardly gave a thought to the possibility of becoming President, and when he did so, it was probably in a way peculiar to himself. Douglas expected the office as his right; Lincoln may occasionally have thought that he might one day be worthy of it, but was never likely to attain it: Douglas had too much confidence in himself; Lincoln had too little in the world. Need we be surprised, then, that Douglas was prompt to show his admiration of Mary Todd, whereas Lincoln's attitude was one of reserve? The strange thing is that Mary none the less turned her eyes toward Lincoln.

He is impressed by her ere long, dazzled by her abilities. She has an art of which he knows nothing, the art of easy conversation, a pleasant flow of questions and utterances, pointless, aimless, the very opposite of Lincoln's *raconteur* style. He sits in silence, aston-

ished by a skill which is new to him in a woman, and which among
men he has hitherto seen only in Douglas. Indeed, all her gifts, all
her ways, her very appearance, cannot fail to remind him of Douglas.
Besides, his heart is no longer wholly his own. For some time he
has been paying court to Sarah Rickard, a girl of sixteen; has taken
her to the theater, has gone out walking with her, has jested with
her about their Biblical names, reminding her of what Sarah had
been to Abraham. But little Sarah Rickard has made Abraham
Lincoln keep his distance, saying afterwards: "His peculiar manner and general deportment would not be likely to fascinate a young
lady entering the society world."

Studying Mary Todd as a connoisseur of his fellow mortals, he
can easily read her character; he sees that she is subject to quick
changes of mood, being radiantly cheerful one moment and blazing
with wrath the next, varying from pale to red and red to pale, often
afflicted by headaches, terrified by thunderstorms; and he sees that
the tears come to her eyes when she is in the least wounded. Finding that she judges people by their table manners, he must feel, not
without amusement, that she despises him for his; but when he
watches her standing opposite her sister receiving guests, he is
amazed at her cleverness and grace, at her faculty for always picking up the latest news; and, when games are played, at her eagerness
to win the prize. Perhaps he has already heard how, when still
little more than a child, she had fashioned for herself a crinoline out
of willow withes, in order to cut a figure among her schoolfellows
— thus displaying a vanity which a generation later was to lead her
to the borderland of insanity.

All this causes him much astonishment, but he does not know
how to bring it into any sort of relation to himself. What he is
looking for in his partner is unselfishness, kindliness, fondness,
such as he experienced at the hands of the dear girl in New Salem;
he is not looking for knowledge and understanding; of that he has
enough himself. Still, perhaps his analytical powers enable him
to discern that this woman is competent to supply the impetus
he lacks. Maybe in her presence he becomes more plainly aware
that his own talents are of a comparatively passive order; that her

creative impatience might mingle effectively with his patience, and supplement it. She is swift and elastic, but essentially weak; whereas he is slow and cumbrous, but strong.

We may be sure that she realized these things, and one strong indication of Mary Todd's intelligence was the firmness with which she clung to Lincoln, being animated in this, not by feminine instinct, but by ambition. Yes, she was quick, and she was right in her forecast of the future. There was little in Lincoln's favor, as far as she was concerned, since he was poor, generally regarded as uncouth, ugly, and not apparently ambitious; and he was not, even at that date, regarded as a coming man. In all these things he contrasted markedly with Douglas, for whom a notable future was already being predicted, and who courted the girl in the belief that she would be a great help to him in his struggle for power.

But Mary stuck to her calculations. She ignored Lincoln's short trousers, his rough manners, his bad dancing, for she alone perceived an invisible coronal on his long bony forehead, and she wanted to share the distinction. With firm hands she spun the circle round the man of her choice. She did so in spite of her distaste for the Lincoln and the Hanks families, concerning whose position she was now informed; and she disregarded the wishes and the advice of her sister and her brother-in-law, who did not think that Lincoln was refined enough, and who told Mary she would be throwing herself away upon him. The opposition served only to stimulate her resolve. She said at a later date: "Mr. Lincoln is to be President of the United States some day; if I had not thought so, I would not have married him, for you can see he is not pretty."

When the situation between the young people becomes critical, Lincoln writes a letter to Mary Todd and shows it to Speed, who reads that Lincoln, considering the whole situation, has come to the conclusion that he does not love her enough. He seems to have made up his mind to avoid a repetition of the torments he had endured in his courtship of Mary Owens. Speed refuses to deliver the letter, saying, "Words may be forgotten, but letters remain." Having burned it, he says, "If you have the courage of manhood, go see Mary yourself; tell her you do not love her, tell her so, tell her you will not marry her." In this matter the storekeeper played the diplomatist, but showed himself a bad psychologist.

For Mary Todd knows perfectly well how a reluctant lover of the Lincoln type can be snared. After Lincoln returns that evening at eleven o'clock, he informs Speed in his tragic-comical way, "When I told Mary I did not love her, she burst into tears, and, almost springing from her chair and wringing her hands as if in agony, said something about the deceiver being himself deceived. It was too much for me. I found the tears trickling down my own cheeks. I caught her in my arms and kissed her." Speed told him that he had made a fool of himself, but Lincoln replied, "Well, if I'm in again, so be it. It's done, and I shall abide by it." Almost the same words of passive resignation with which, three years earlier, he had let himself become engaged to the first Mary.

The period of betrothal is one of mingled jealousies and fears. She wants to rule him, and he is used to being independent; quarrels are frequent. She annoys him by walking arm-in-arm with Douglas in the open street, and he seems inclined to console himself with her sister-in-law, pretty Matilda, who is also staying with the Edwards', and who, since accommodation is scanty, must share the jealous Mary's bed. Matilda's visit does not last long, but when she has gone Mary declares that Lincoln is paying too much attention to little Sarah Rickard. Well, perhaps with some reason; for what could be more natural than that such a man as Lincoln, on the eve of a marriage against which an inner voice warns him, should seek refuge from lonely and unpleasant thoughts? The restlessness of the previous year has returned and is more troublesome than ever, for this time his betrothed is close at hand and is not to be satisfied with off-and-on letters. In her home he can watch the preparations from day to day; the marriage day approaches him like a threat.

They have fixed the first of January. The New Year is to ring in the new life. A ceremonial and dinner proper to the marriage of a young lady in good society are prepared. But while the bride and her kin are interested in the wedding dress, slippers and gloves, in the wedding breakfast, plans for speeches and the like, the bridegroom's mood has become one of feverish excitement.

A man of lonely temperament, with a passion for freedom; whose way it has been to seek women and then flee from them; who has loved but once in his life, loved a girl whose affections he had won slowly to lose her all too soon; who had then become affianced to an unpleasing old maid, and had only freed himself from the engagement to her with difficulty; now feels himself snared, and his whole nature is at bay. Being of a hesitant disposition, disliking to resolve anything for a long time ahead, having the bachelor's love of independence, detesting formalities, careless of money and position, pledged to nobody — he now compares the energetic and domineering woman he is to marry with a gentle maiden who would let herself be loved. The upshot of all this is a sense of bodily anxiety which finds expression as insufficiency. Call it dread, morbid fear, insanity, if you like; the name matters little.

There are conflicting accounts as to what happened on the critical day; whether the bride was ready in all her splendor, and whether the guests were assembled; or whether there had been a violent scene the day before. Was all prepared, as the most trustworthy witnesses assure us, down to the cake? Did Lincoln openly exclaim that he hated Mary, as her sister declares — though that was certainly not his true feeling, "but only a folly?" This much, at least, is certain; that Lincoln did not turn up for the wedding. He spent the whole day in the legislature, obviously because he would be hard to get at there; at the wedding hour he was introducing a license bill; and during the next few days, likewise, he was busied fulfilling his duties as representative. Then for a week he was absent from the Assembly, being in the hands of his doctor.

V

For Lincoln is ill. The conflicting passions of the last few weeks have been too much for him, for his otherwise healthy nature; and he is now suffering from anxiety which no one would ever have expected in the rail-splitter. His doctor advises him to consult a nerve specialist in Cincinnati, and he does so by letter, but the expert replies that nothing can be done without a personal interview.

Lincoln clings to the Springfield doctor, and is in a panic lest he shall be deprived of his services. During this period he writes several impassioned letters to his partner Stuart, in Washington; letters which have not been published in full.

"I am now the most miserable man living. If what I feel were equally distributed to the whole human family, there would not be one cheerful face on earth. Whether I shall ever be better, I cannot tell. I awfully forebode I shall not. To remain as I am is impossible. I must die or be better, as it appears to me. . . . I fear I shall be unable to attend any business here, and a change of scene might help me. If I could be myself, I would rather remain at home. . . I can write no more."

In this same letter he begs Stuart to do all that is possible to secure the appointment of Doctor Henry as postmaster in Springfield:

"I have within the last few days been making a most discreditable exhibition of myself in the way of hypochondriasm, and thereby got an impression that Dr. Henry is necessary to my existence. Unless he gets that place he leaves Springfield. . . . My heart is very much set upon it."

Never before or afterwards did Lincoln, the solitary, declare any person to be necessary to his existence. What must he have been going through, this man who had always been so independent, who had never wanted a doctor or a change of scene? But now the frenzied Orestes finds a friendly Pylades, for on the same "fatal New Year's day" Speed sells his shop, moves to his mother's fine old farm in Kentucky, and invites Lincoln to come to see him in his native State.

The afflicted soul feels enchanted. In a large country house, where broad steps lead to a lordly hall, a slave brings his breakfast to his bedside; he can ride and drive out as often as he likes; the gentle manners of Speed's mother, the charm of a younger sister, the cheerfulness of wealthy country people, games, fun, flirtations, assuage the tormented heart. Once in his life Lincoln lives as a Southern gentleman; the friend of the black man has his coat brushed and stirrup held by a black; and his wounded heart for moments goes out to his friend's sister. Speed in the meantime courts the niece of a neighbor. Lincoln must keep up conversations with the uncle, and while the two are talking politics, his friend makes love to Fanny.

When, at length, he takes up his pen, what does he write? An essay on suicide, such as may well be penned by a man who wishes by means of an analysis to ward off a danger he has just escaped.

"I have done nothing to make any human being remember that I have lived. Yet what I wish to live for is to connect my name with the events of my day and generation, to link my name with something which will be of interest to my fellow men."

These words indicate that the crisis is passing; that ambition and hope have revived in the young man of thirty-two, and that his gaze is turning toward the wider interests of mankind.

The nature alike of the former depression and of the passing excitement are disclosed in letters written by Lincoln to Speed, a year after the critical New Year's Day, at a time when Lincoln had long since been back at home, tranquilized, and when Speed, himself about to be married, was troubled with qualms similar to those which had tormented his friend.

"I do not place what I am going to say on paper because I can say it better that way than I could by word of mouth; but, were I to say it orally before we part, most likely you would forget it at the very time when it might do you some good. As I think it reasonable that you will feel very badly some time between this and the final consummation of your purpose, it is intended that you shall read this just at such a time. Why I say it is reasonable that you will feel very badly yet, is because of three special causes added to the general one which I shall mention.

"The general cause is that you are naturally of a nervous temperament; and this I say from what I have seen of you personally, and what you have told me concerning your mother at various times, and concerning your brother William at the time his wife died. The first special cause is your exposure to bad weather on your journey, which my experience clearly proves to be very severe on defective nerves. The second is the absence of all business and conversation of friends, which might divert your mind, give it occasional rest from the intensity of thought, which will sometimes wear the sweetest idea threadbare and turn it to the bitterness of death. The third is the rapid and near approach of that crisis on which all your thoughts and feelings concentrate.

"If from all these causes you shall escape and go through triumphantly, without another 'twinge of the soul', I shall be most happily but most egregiously deceived. If, on the contrary, you shall, as I expect you will at some time, be agonized and distressed, let me, who have some reason to speak with judgment on such a subject, beseech you to ascribe it to the causes I have mentioned, and not to some false and ruinous suggestion of the devil.

"'But,' you will say, 'do not your causes apply to every one engaged in a like undertaking?' By no means. The particular causes, to a greater or less extent, perhaps do apply in all cases; but the general one — nervous debility, which is the key and conductor of all the particular ones, and without which they would be utterly harmless — though it does pertain to you, does not pertain to one in a thousand. It is out of this that the painful difference between you and the mass of the world springs."

Lincoln then attempts to remove the doubts Speed may entertain as to whether he and his bride are well matched.

"How came you to court her? Was it because you thought she deserved it, and that you had given her reason to expect it? . . . There was nothing at that time for reason to work upon. . . .

"Say candidly, were not those heavenly black eyes the whole basis of all your early reasoning on the subject? . . . I shall be so anxious about you that I shall want you to write by every mail."

When, shortly before the wedding, Speed's fiancée falls sick, and his mental agitation increases, his friend shows him that this very agitation is a proof of his fondness, of which he is still in doubt:

"Why, Speed, if you did not love her, although you might not wish her death, you would almost certainly be resigned to it. Perhaps this point is no longer a question with you, and my pertinacious dwelling upon it is a rude intrusion upon your feelings. If so, you must pardon me. You know the hell I have suffered on that point, and how tender I am upon it. I have been quite clear of 'hypo' since you left, even better than I was along in the fall. I have seen Sarah but once. She seemed very cheerful, and so I said nothing to her about what we spoke of."

With a full flow of his imagination, Lincoln participates at his friend's wedding, like a poet, just as young Goethe once did in a similar case:

"When this shall reach you, you will have been Fanny's husband several days. . . . You will hereafter be on ground that I have never occupied. . . . I do fondly hope . . . that you will never again need any comfort from abroad. But should I be mistaken in this, should excessive pleasure still be accompanied with a painful counterpart at times, still let me urge you, as I have ever done, to remember, in the depth and even agony of despondency, that very shortly you are to feel well again. I am now fully convinced that you love her as ardently as you are capable of loving. . . . I incline to think it probable that your nerves will fail you occasionally for a while; but once you get them firmly guarded now, that trouble is over forever. . . . If you went through the ceremony calmly, or even with sufficient composure not to excite alarm in any present, you are safe beyond question, and in two or three months, to say the most, will be the happiest of men. . . . P.S. I have been quite a man since you left."

But when Speed reports fresh anxieties, the friend who has hitherto been so consistently encouraging ceases to breathe consolation, and writes in a straightforward tone of renouncement:

"I now have no doubt that it is the peculiar misfortune of both you and me to dream dreams of Elysium far exceeding all that anything earthly can realize. Far short of your dreams as you may be, no woman could do more to realize them than that same black-eyed Fanny. If you could but contemplate her through my imagination, it would appear ridiculous to you that any one should for a moment think of being unhappy with her. My old father used to have a saying that 'if you make a bad bargain, hug it all the tighter.'"

In none of the abundant documents available do Lincoln's innermost character traits come more plainly to light. These letters are a veritable self-revelation. First, we see his desire for perfect clarity as to all his feelings and a skill in mental analysis like that which the psychiatrist shares, above with the poet and below with the lawyer, a power of deducing the minor motives from a main incentive. Not only is he aware of the influence exercised on the nerves by weather, traveling, and laziness; he is also psychologist enough to draw attention to family trends as shown in a mother and a brother — thinking doubtless the while, as he must often do, of those unknown ancestors of his on the maternal side. At the same time, while showing his brotherly interest in his friend, he also manifests the urge that moves the artist to identify himself with another, to penetrate the mystery of another's feelings and another's situation.

Above all, however, the letters give us a valuable clue as to his own inward unrest and how he explains it to himself. A year after the crisis, when his circumstances, outwardly considered, are perfectly tranquil, he is talking of despair, bitterness of death, hell. Whence do such thoughts derive? From a nervous temperament which distinguishes himself and his friend from the rest of the world, and exposes both of them to manifold terrors and anxieties to which only one or two in a thousand are prone. For "it is the peculiar misfortune of both you and me to dream dreams of Elysium far exceeding all that anything earthly can realize." Here is the fundamental cause of Lincoln's melancholy. Notwithstanding his robust energies, notwithstanding his shrewdness, experience, and success, this man with the poet's nature will again and again be disillusioned in the course of his struggle with the world.

Such is the core of tragedy in Lincoln, revealed to us by the sadness of his countenance.

VI

Speed's marriage has troubled Lincoln's nerves, has revived his memories, has intensified his loneliness. "If we have no friends, we have no pleasure; and if we have them, we are sure to lose them, and be doubly pained by the loss. I did hope she and you would make your home here; but I own I have no right to insist." When

Speed has written to say that he and his wife are now really "one flesh", and when Lincoln feels almost as if he had secured a personal triumph, the tension has been relieved; and when Speed writes details about his farm, his friend replies that he is much more interested in the other question "to hear you say you are 'far happier than you ever expected to be.'" He has now a tender feeling for the young wife, who knows nothing of the former letters, and it sounds like an extract from "The Sorrows of Werther" when he writes: "The sweet violet you enclosed came safely to hand, but it was so dry, and mashed so flat, that it crumbled to dust at the first attempt to handle it. The juice that mashed out of it stained a place in the letter, which I mean to preserve and cherish for the sake of her who procured it to be sent."

In this frame of mind, he once more seeks contact with some of the young women in Springfield. In several letters he alludes to having seen Sarah Rickard again; but he is more strongly attracted to Mary, though the sight of her must arouse disturbing memories.

"It seems to me I should have been entirely happy, but for the never-absent idea that there is one still unhappy whom I have contributed to make so. That still kills my soul. I cannot but reproach myself for even wishing to be happy while she is otherwise. She accompanied a large party on the railroad cars to Jacksonville last Monday, and on her return spoke, so that I heard of it, of having enjoyed the trip exceedingly. God be praised for that."

He seems to have had intimations that, despite what has happened, Mary has not completely given him up.

The young woman's spirit had not been broken by the terrible blow inflicted on her pride. Had she not been even more defiant than proud, she would assuredly have left Springfield forever after she, well-to-do and of good birth, had been slighted so publicly by an insignificant lawyer of lowly origin. Lincoln must have discussed these matters in correspondence with his friend Speed, for the next summer he writes:

"True, that subject is painful to me; but it is not your silence, or the silence of all the world, that can make me forget it. I acknowledge the correctness of your advice too; but before I resolve to do the one thing or the other, I must gain my confidence in my own ability to keep my resolves when they are made. In that ability you know I once prided myself as the only or chief gem of my character; that gem I lost — how and where you know too well. I have not yet regained it; and until I do, I cannot trust myself in any matter of much importance. I believe now that had you understood my case at the time as well as I understand yours afterward, by the aid you would have given me I should have sailed through clear. . . . I do not think I can come to Kentucky this season. I am so poor and make so little headway in the world, that I drop back in a month of idleness as much as I gain in a year's sowing."

So greatly has the whole affair shaken his sense of duty, the main source of his energy — his confidence in himself and in the uprightness of his own motives — that we find him tormented by doubts a year and a half after that New Year's Day. He feels that it behooves him to right the wrong, and this would seem to be his only motive for making new advances to Mary Todd, as there are no signs of any strong personal affection for her! But there she is, back in Springfield. Without any necessity she shows him and the others by her return that, despite all, she has no dislike for him. If fate is determined to bring these two together, means will be found. Inevitably in this little town they meet. They are invited by an editor and his wife who wants to play providence. Thus do they encounter one another again, astonished and embarrassed.

They come together from time to time in a lively circle where all are entertained by Lincoln's shrewd humor, and where political lampoons are sometimes hatched. A distrust of Democratic finance was widespread, and in this connection there was general amusement because Shields, the State auditor of accounts, had issued an order that paper money should not be accepted by the State government for taxes. Shields had been an adventurer, sailor, and law student; was a Democrat, and a man of affected manners; but now he is fulfilling his public duties. To this man Lincoln has three letters written by an imaginary backwoodswoman. Rebecca. They are full of his own memories of that sphere, splendid in their naturalistic style; crammed with mischievous fun which makes the whole town laugh. The assailed takes no notice. But now Mary Todd and Julia Jayne, the editor's wife, concoct a fourth letter, much coarser and full of provocations, in which Rebecca proposes to marry Shields, and even produces the wedding song. Shields takes umbrage and demands the name of the author. Lincoln, as a politician, would have done well to refrain from making himself responsible for the last letter.

He might have pleaded concern for the welfare of his party, and a man who was cultivating a reputation for style might well have hesitated to assume the authorship of some extremely bad verses. But Mary Todd was involved in the affair, was in truth the begetter of it, and Lincoln felt impelled to shield a lady to whom he owed amends. When the victim of the lampoon insisted on challenging the author, Lincoln, instead of disavowing the last letter and the verses, and though he was a declared opponent of dueling, consented to fight. Since dueling was prohibited in the State of Illinois, a place was chosen outside. Discountenanced though they were by the law, duels had become fashionable in the New World, and a large crowd assembled to see this one. Cavalry sabers were to be used. Lincoln had only learned to handle an ax, but that was not one of the regulation weapons. Pending the final arrangements, the long fellow sat on a log.

His face was serious, says a witness. "I never knew him to go so long before without making a joke. . . . He reached over and picked up one of the swords, which he drew from its scabbard. Then he felt along the edge of the weapon with his thumb, like a barber feels the edge of his razor, raised himself to his full height, stretched out his long arms, and clipped off a twig from above his head with the sword. There wasn't another man of us who could have reached anywhere near that twig, and the absurdity of that long-reaching fellow fighting with cavalry sabers with Shields, who could walk under his arm, came pretty near making me howl with laughter. After Lincoln had cut off the twig, he returned the sword to the scabbard with a sigh, and sat down, but I detected the gleam

in his eye which was always the forerunner of one of his inimitable
yarns, and fully expected him to tell a side-splitter, there in the
shadow of the grave — Shields' grave."

In the meantime, however, the seconds had come to an arrangement, the two parties exchanged assurances which were mutually
satisfactory, and went quietly home together.

The life of such a man as Lincoln is full of tragi-comedies, but
none can be finer than this one. The opponent of the chase and of
war, he who as a boy was unwilling to shoot a hare and who as a
soldier had rescued an enemy and never killed any, as tall as Goliath
and as good as David, sits there on a log, constrained by sentimental complications, waiting to kill one of his fellow men, unless
he is himself to die, since he is going for the first time to try
his hand at wielding a saber; but instead of practising the accepted thrusts and parries, what does he do? The woodcutter
awakens in him, and instinctively he uses the sharp steel in his
hand to lop off a branch as during the old days in Indiana. Then
a good story comes into his head; his eyes twinkle and he is
about to tell it. But the retreat sounds, tragedy retires, and comedy
is dominant.

Yet there is a serious side. Though neither party's life is endangered at this duel, the proposed duel decides the subsequent
course of Lincoln's life. His chivalry has reconciled the girl, she
can now tell her friends that Lincoln is her cavalier. The two are
in close touch once more; people smile to see them together, and
soon offer congratulations. For when Lincoln realizes that Mary
wants him to marry her after all, he does not hesitate. "He knew
he did not love her, but he had promised to marry her," says Herndon, who was living with Lincoln at the time. To a second friend,
who was his best man, Lincoln confessed: "Jimmy, I shall have to
marry that girl." On the day of the Shields' lampoons he had
written out in exceptionally large letters a register of the votes he
and others had received during the last years, with the aim of
showing his increasing popularity. He had this paper endorsed
in legal style and tied up with red tape — presumably to show Mary
that he was a man of some importance.

Before leaping into the water he shivers on the brink, for he writes the following extraordinary question to Speed:

"But I began this letter, not for what I have been writing, but to say something on that subject which you know to be of such infinite solicitude to me. The immense sufferings you endured from the first days of September to the middle of February you never tried to conceal from me, and I well understood. You have now been the husband of a lovely woman nearly eight months. That you are happier now than the day you married her I well know, for without you could not be living. . . . But I want to ask a close question: 'are you now in feeling as well as judgment glad that you are married as you are?' From anybody but me this would be an impudent question not to be tolerated; but I know you will pardon it in me. Please answer it quickly, as I am impatient to know."

Such is the nervous anxiety of a man who is afraid of losing his freedom, who is loath to enter into a position in which he will have to account for or explain his actions and his moods. And why? That he may marry a woman whose nature is foreign to him, who has hardly any charms but many faults in his eyes, and from whom he had unceremoniously fled in anguish only two years earlier! On her side, now, she wants a speedy marriage, with as little ceremony as possible, nothing but the essential religious service. So one morning Lincoln comes into a friend's bedroom and says, "I am going to be married to-day."

As they stand together at the altar this November day, the giant of thirty-three and the little woman of twenty-four, his look is not a happy one, and he is said to have blurted out some desperately humorous things afterwards. At the wedding breakfast, a small affair, he is said to have been cheerful, and to have told anecdotes. It was a Friday, however, and both husband and wife were superstitious. A business letter, penned five days after the wedding, closes with the words:

"Nothing new here, except my marrying, which, to me, is a matter of profound wonder."

VII

Soon after this, Lincoln enters into a' final partnership, with Herndon, the lively young abolitionist, who, acting on Lincoln's advice, has become a lawyer and soon is his most ardent admirer. Lincoln gives his full confidence to his new partner, and the friendship between the two men lasts throughout life. Intelligence and efficiency unite them in their daily work, a common idealism in political questions, humor, and irony. Herndon being almost ten years younger, Lincoln, now in the middle thirties, assumes a somewhat fatherly attitude toward his young partner, and for the first time enters into a position in which he is the leader.

Logan, who had replaced Stuart as his partner three years before Lincoln's marriage to Mary Todd, had been senior partner. Learned in the law, Logan had needed an orator to assist him, but had found it difficult, in the long run, to tolerate Lincoln's disorderly ways. Logan had been neat, scrupulous, particular, and precise, possessed of virtues which Lincoln lacked. All the better for Lincoln, who acquired a good deal of knowledge at Logan's hands, and for the first time in his life was able to earn a fair amount of money, which was helpful when he married. Logan's fame as a lawyer, Lincoln's political reputation, and the growth of Springfield (which had now built its own Capitol) had combined to give the firm a good standing. Maybe the partners would have been able to rub along together to their mutual advantage had they not been rivals in the political field, and quarreled for this reason.

After the break with Logan, a sign was put up on which Lincoln's name stood first — "Lincoln and Herndon." It was hung out somewhere on the second floor at the entrance to a medium-sized room, with two green tables in "T" form, an escritoire with pigeonholes, a bookcase, and a rickety leather-covered sofa which, though fairly long, was too short for Lincoln. Once when seed had arrived from the party headquarters for the farmers, some of the seeds, broken loose amid the general disorder, sprouted in the dirt on the floor.

Lincoln's trustworthiness had become proverbial. No one, least of all his partner Herndon, ever thought of expecting formal accounts from him. "There you are, that is your half," he would say, when a fee came in, dividing the banknotes. His generosity grew with success, instead of decreasing, as so often happens; and as for his honesty, that often got the better of his business interest. To a client whose chances of success were good, he said: "I can win your case, and get the six hundred dollars for you. But if I did so, I should bring misfortune upon an honest family, and I can't see my way to it. I would rather get along without your case and your fee. I will give you a piece of advice without charging you for it. Go home and try to think of some honester way of earning six hundred dollars."

Such Solomonic verdicts contrasted with the rough and tough practice of those days, and served when he was thirty-five to intensify the reputation he had already acquired at twenty-five of being an eccentric. He did not care for studying law books or to con the decisions of the higher courts, but was content as a rule with extemporizing his arguments to fit the occasion, trusting in the justice of the cause he represented, in the healthy understanding of the court, and in his own invincible sense of right which had developed in the course of his arduous youth and as a characteristic of his slow-moving temperament. Nor was he concerned as to the details of the business, leaving his junior partner to attend to the collection of fees. Yet when, on one occasion, after the lapse of many years, a man came to claim seventeen dollars from the sometime postmaster, Lincoln promptly opened a box and produced a little bag in which the sum had been kept ready all the time.

In the courts, too, his friends thought him eccentric and singular. "He had no system, no order; he did not keep a clerk; he had neither library, nor index, nor cash book. When he made notes, he would throw them into a drawer, put them into his vest pocket, or into his hat. . . . But in the inner man, symmetry and method prevailed. He did not need an orderly office, did not need pen and ink, because his workshop was inside his head."

Soon Lincoln's hat, in which he kept letters and checks, became famous; and when a legal colleague in another town complained of his failure to answer a letter promptly, Lincoln replied, apologetically: "First, I have been very busy in the United States court; second, when I received the letter I put it in my old hat and, buying a new one the next day, the old one was set aside, and so the letter was lost sight of for a time."

Besides the hat, he had an envelope to hold loose papers lying on the top of his desk, docketed, "When you can't find it anywhere else, look in this."

A man with such salient characteristics naturally found it easier to get on with a junior. He called his partner Herndon "Bill", and the latter said "Mr. Lincoln." But Lincoln never pretended to be better informed than he was. For instance, one day he came into the office asking, "Bill, what's the meaning of antithesis?" As an "original", he took his ease in this law office, would lie on the sofa in the morning, reading the newspaper aloud to himself; tell anecdotes to those who came to consult him on law business, once repeating the same good story to three of them on a single day; and during two whole days he refused to look at any law papers because he was trying, surrounded by drawings, lists of figures, compasses, and rulers, to square the circle.

It came natural to every one to trust him. The minister to whom he mortgaged his house asked for no receipt and wanted no registration. Two farmers who had a dispute as to the boundary between their farms entered into a mutual undertaking to submit the matter to Lincoln and to abide by his decision; they were content with a lawyer who did not pose as a learned man up in the clouds above them, but was one who seemed a farmer like themselves, stood on their level, and used their own familiar locutions.

Does he not look like a farmer in disguise? True, as a newly married man, he wears boots of tanned leather, a "boiled" shirt with a necktie, and a black stovepipe hat which makes him look taller than ever. But his clothes hang on him loosely, his waistcoat is rumpled, his trousers are baggy at the knees, his collar is too large, and his necktie usually askew.

So he stands with sloping shoulders, his arms hanging loose, his head lurching forward and lowered; and when he looks at people out of his large gray eyes, he either seems to be thinking of something else, or else he is boring into their very hearts.

VIII

Mary brought some advantages to Lincoln, for though she had little interest in his legal practice, she was much concerned with politics. From the very beginning she watched the career on which she had put all her hopes. Being colder-blooded than her husband, and less trustful, she was more skeptical as to people's motives, was readier than he to discover what those motives really were, and, having a definite aim in life, was naturally shrewder in mundane affairs than a man of contemplative nature like her husband. For her, every fellow creature she met was a possible competitor, whereas he looked upon every competitor primarily as a fellow creature, each of them projecting personal feelings into the minds of others. The result was that she acted as a stimulus upon his procrastinating nature, and thus, in his political life, was a help to him.

At home, he was ready to yield to her as a rule, laughed genially when she was out of humor, and, if her spell of temper lasted too long, went for a walk. He was indulgent to her weaknesses; hurried home to calm her fears when there was a thunderstorm; tried to reason her out of her dread of burglars. They were both of them superstitious; but in this matter it was characteristic that she, in feminine fashion, should believe in signs, whereas he, man-like, believed in dreams.

In the early days of their married life she had a hard time, for it did not come easy to a spoiled member of the Todd family to board at an inn in two rooms for four dollars a week; and when, as a reason for economy, he reminded her that he still had debts to pay, she must sometimes have wondered whether she would not have done more wisely to have given her hand to a richer man. The goal was so far off, the difficulties of getting there were so great, the means were so exiguous, that she must often have despaired.

It is a good thing that she soon becomes a mother, and that she has a chance of showing her family pride in the choice of a name.

She refuses to have a son of hers called Joshua, after her husband's friend Speed, and insists upon Robert, her father's name. Bearing four sons, only in the case of the last does she agree that it shall be named after Tom Lincoln, who has recently died. During ten years, this ambitious woman gives birth to sons only, as Macbeth said was proper to women of undaunted mettle.

She knows how to keep Lincoln's friends at arm's length, and especially their wives. His "love to Fanny" soon becomes "regards to Mrs. Speed." She has detested Herndon, her husband's daily companion, since their first waltz in Springfield; she has vainly endeavored to prevent the formation of the new firm, and for years, when she comes to the office, she passes the young man without a greeting, drawing her skirts aside as she goes by. Lincoln, being more a man of the world, does not follow Speed's example and write openly about his married life. Two months after the marriage he tells Speed ambiguously: "I will let you know when we meet how my marriage is going on." Alluding to his wife's condition, he seems to take his prospective fatherhood prosaically: "I reckon it will scarcely be in our power to visit Kentucky this year. Besides poverty and the necessity of attending to business, those 'coming events' I suspect would be somewhat in the way."

Soon, with the aid of Mary's income and by raising money on a mortgage, they are enabled to have a house of their own, a small place, which she keeps in perfect order. She is thrifty, does her own sewing. Then, when their income is larger, and when he (differing in this from most men who have risen in the world) is generous in donations and subscriptions, she always cuts down his proposed contributions by half — until he introduces an old political trick into his connubial relations and makes it his way to mention the double of what he proposes to give.

How could such a pair get on well together? He prefers to sit at a table in his shirt sleeves, and goes to open the door when there is a ring at the bell. These trifles annoy her; she loves to have things done "just so." How can a precise and orderly minded society woman be expected to get on with a husband who is as unpunctual as he is good-natured, as forgetful as he is gentle and humorous? Does not he like to stretch himself at full length on the carpet in the sitting room, lying there to read, so that one must make a wide circuit to avoid tumbling over his long legs? He sits on the floor, playing with the children; or says, in company, that he can eat corn cakes as fast as two women can make them. Since he keeps a cow, and his neighbor, the shoemaker, has one too, why should they not both milk their own beasts if they have time? He ought not to do it because he is a lawyer and has a seat in the legislature? For all she can say, he goes out to the barn in shirt and trousers, the trousers "fastened with one suspender"; and comes back, carrying the milk pail, his loose slippers shuffling as he walks.

But now, as she has little humor, her sense of breeding is outraged and she is on the verge of nervous collapse when he opens the front door to two fine ladies and says to them, "Come in, my wife will be down as soon as she gets her trotting harness on!" To her way of thinking, it is better to rule than to be witty; and going out for a drive with a friend just after she has had a wrangle with the maid, she says angrily, "Well, one thing is certain; if Mr. Lincoln should happen to die, his spirit will never find me living outside the boundaries of a slave State!" A grand epigram, throwing light upon a hundred conversations, for the joking utterance contains a kernel of tragic truth; if this dictatorial woman would rather have black slaves than white servants, it is the outcome of the Southern traditions in which she grew up, though she has forsaken them to marry a man whose whole nature is at war with the Southern slaveholders.

In his slow and quiet way he deals with the children as seems best to him, regardless of Mary's wishes. He wants them to learn goodness, rather than good manners, and his outlook on the nursery is always a humorous one.

"We have another boy, born the 10th of March. He is very much such a child as Bob was at his age, rather of a longer order. Bob is 'short and low', and I expect always will be. . . . He is quite smart enough. I sometimes fear that he is one of the little 'rare-ripe' sort that are smarter at about five years than ever after.

He has a great deal of that sort of mischief that is the offspring of such animal spirits. Since I began this letter, a messenger came to tell me Bob was lost; but by the time I reached the house his mother had found him and had whipped him — and by now, very likely, he is run away again."

This is full both of gentle sarcasm and of a profound knowledge of human nature. We can read much between the lines; above all, renunciation.

For, from the time of his marriage, the melancholy note increases in Lincoln's utterances. Whom does he love? His friends are estranged from him by his wife's jealousy; he is almost out of touch with his brother; to his father he sometimes sends money; but once, when there is talk of a visit from his parents, Mary puts a spoke in the wheel. His friends often see him sitting with his chair pushed against the wall of his office, his legs drawn up, his hat still on and pulled down over his eyes, his hands clasping his knees. There he broods for hours, staring into nothingness with dim eyes, no one venturing to speak to him. If, as now and again happens, he writes verses and sends them to his friends, they are full of pain and disillusionment.

Once, on a political tour, he visits Indiana, his second home, "where my mother and only sister were buried and from which I had been absent about fifteen years. That part of the country is, within itself, as unpoetical as any spot of the earth; but still, seeing it and its objects and inhabitants aroused feelings in me which were certainly poetry; though whether my expression of those feelings is poetry is quite another question. When I got to writing, the change of subject divided the thing into four little divisions or cantos."

One runs:

> Near twenty years have passed away
>   Since here I bid farewell
> To woods and fields, and scenes of play,
>   And playmates loved so well.
>
> Where many were, but few remain
>   Of old familiar things;

But seeing them to mind again
  The lost and absent brings.

The friends I left that parting day,
  How changed, as time has sped!
Young childhood grown, strong manhood gray,
  And half of all are dead.

I hear the loved survivors tell
  How naught from death could save,
Till every sound appears a knell,
  And every spot a grave.

I range the fields with pensive tread,
  And pace the hollow rooms,
And feel (companion of the dead)
  I'm living in the tombs.

IX

After working for eight years in the local legislature, Lincoln set his thoughts on Washington. Instead of seeking reëlection, he aspired to a seat in Congress. Since this resolve dates from the first year of his married life, we may assume that the impetus came from his wife. In accordance with an unwritten understanding, the leaders of the party decided to support one another in turn at the congressional elections. Since there were three nominees, and Baker was first chosen as candidate, Lincoln was disappointed, for he considered that his position in the party and his talents entitled him to nomination. "In getting Baker the nomination, I shall be fixed a good deal like a fellow who is made groomsman to a man that has cut him out, and is marrying his own dear gal." At the ensuing convention, however, neither Baker nor Lincoln was nominated, but a third member of the party, and then, two years afterwards, Baker was chosen — so Lincoln had to wait four years more before he was nominated for Congress. He thus missed the years between thirty-three and thirty-seven, when a man is most inclined for vigorous activity, and when his friends' mistakes annoy him more than defeats inflicted on him by his foes; a time in which his ambitious wife must have been continually urging him onward.

Year after year, the conflicts arising out of the slavery problem had become more menacing. Texas was the question of the hour. Was Texas to come into the Union, and was it to be a slave State? People took sides as annexationists on the one hand and pacifists on the other. Clay represented half the nation when he declared : "I regard the annexation of Texas at this hour without Mexico's consent as a measure injurious to our national character, and as one which would certainly involve us in a war, not only with Mexico, but also with other powers. I look upon it as dangerous to the integrity of the Union, as extremely undesirable in view of our present financial situation, and as not demanded by public opinion." Most of the army officers, though military men as a rule are in favor of war, were opposed to war on this occasion.

Polk, however, Clay's Democratic rival, promised the nation a short and victorious war, the annexation of Texas with its fertile lands, and was therefore supported by all the southern States. Slavery again raised its head. If Texas could be acquired and made a slave State, it would give the planters of the South new lands to develop and more territory to stamp with their "peculiar institution", therefore Lincoln was supporting Clay at the presidential election, not only for party reasons, but under the spur of strong feeling. What he said in his campaign speeches was the expression of convictions that had been ripening for many years ; not merely as to what was best for the welfare of his country, but also as to what would tend to promote the general happiness, would make for justice.

"I never could see much good to come of annexation, inasmuch as they were already a free republican people on our own model. On the other hand, I never could very clearly see how the annexation would augment the evil of slavery. . . . I hold it to be a paramount duty of us in the free States, due to the Union of the States, and perhaps to liberty itself (paradox though it may seem), to let the slavery of the other States alone ; while, on the other hand, I hold it to be equally clear that we should never knowingly lend ourselves, directly or indirectly, to prevent that slavery from dying a natural death — to find new places for it to live in, when it can no longer exist in the old."

Among his notes made at that epoch, obviously destined for use in speeches, we find striking arguments, popular in their phrasing, Socratic in their reasoning.

"If A can prove, however conclusively, that he may, of right, enslave B, why may not B snatch the same argument, even prove equally, that he may enslave A?

" You say A is white and B is black. — It is *color*, then ; the lighter having the right to enslave the darker? Take care — By this rule, you are to be slave to the first man you meet, with a fairer skin than your own.

" You do not mean *color* exactly? You mean the whites are *intellectually* the superior of the blacks, and, therefore, have the right to enslave them? Take care again — By this rule, you are to be slave to the first man you meet, with an intellect superior to your own.

" But, say you, it is a question of *interest;* and, if you can make it your *interest*, you have the right to enslave another — Very well — and if he can make it his interest, he has the right to enslave you."

These aspirations on behalf of the Negroes arise from his feeling for the oppressed whites. Lincoln's social sentiments have originated out of the bitterness and disillusionment of youth, and have been intensified by his study of the society in which he lives.

"There is no permanent class of hired laborers amongst us. Twenty-five years ago, I was a hired laborer. The hired laborer of yesterday labors on his own account to-day, and will hire the labor of others to-morrow. . . . As labor is the common burden of our race, so the effort of some to shift their share of the burden onto the shoulders of others is the great durable curse of the race. . . . And inasmuch as most good things are produced by labor, it follows that all such things of right belong to those whose labor has produced them. But it has so happened, in all ages of the world, that some have labored and others, without labor, enjoyed a large proportion of the fruits. This is wrong, and should not continue. To secure to each laborer the whole product of his labor, or as nearly as possible, is a worthy object of any good government."

When Clay was beaten, Lincoln took the matter humorously.

"Despite all my hopes for Clay's victory, and all my dislike of the manœuvres of the Democrats, my main feeling to begin with was a terrible anxiety as to how I should acquit myself as an orator. I had six weeks' campaign before me, and had to make a dozen speeches every day. I was quite sure of my own convictions, but, not being a Douglas, I could not be certain that I could speak again and again on the same topic without getting giddy. . . . Poor Clay was hopelessly beaten by Polk. I soon got over my vexation, but when I was alone once more I continually fancied that I was hearing my trumpet sound from the platform or from a tree stump."

X

Lincoln was ripe for Washington — after eight years in the State legislature. He had reluctantly made way for Hardin and for Baker; and even now, when he had waited four years, the party management was still inclined to give this obliging colleague the go-by. Had not his wife got to work behind the scenes, he would probably have failed. The way in which he puts aside his legal practice to devote himself exclusively to the elections, and the way in which he writes to friends and strangers to ask for their vote and influence, seem new in him. Although, at the age of thirty-seven he is in the prime of his powers, we may assume that the energy which animates him comes from the Todd inspiration. The ambition that pushes him forward during the next few years is obviously Mary's.

"You perhaps know," he writes to a man of influence, "that General Hardin and I have a contest for the Whig nomination for Congress for this district. He has had a turn, and my argument is 'turn about is fair play.' I shall be pleased if this strikes you as a sufficient argument."

To a friend, at about the same date, he admits that he might postpone pushing his claim.

"But to yield to Hardin under present circumstances seems to me as nothing else than yielding to one who would gladly sacrifice me altogether. This I would rather not submit to. That Hardin is talented, energetic, usually generous and magnanimous, I have before this affirmed to you and do not deny. You know that my only argument is that 'turn about is fair play.' This he, practically at least, denies.

"If it would not be taxing you too much, I wish you would write me, telling the aspect of things in your county, or rather your district; and also send the names of some of your Whig neighbors, to whom I might, with propriety, write. Unless I can get some one to do this, Hardin, with his old franking list, will have the advantage of me."

Thus is a retiring, self-effacing man driven into the struggles of party life, when self-confidence and ambition stir him. He writes: "If you should hear any one say that Lincoln don't want to go to Congress, I wish you, as a personal friend of mine, would tell him that you have reason to believe him mistaken. The truth is, I would like to go very much."

Ultimately he is nominated by the convention at Petersburg, a small but growing place, where he had worked as land surveyor a decade before and was well known. Now the fever of the contest attacks him, and he throws himself eagerly into the campaign.

"Nathan also said that some man, whom he could not remember, had said lately that Menard County was going to decide the contest and that made the contest very doubtful. Do you know who that was? Don't fail to write me instantly on receiving this, telling me all — particularly the names of those who are going strong against me."

His opponent in this election was Peter Cartwright, the famous Methodist circuit rider, known to half the State for his fiery speeches, a formidable adversary. Cartwright's religious connections gave him great influence, and he secured many supporters by his Jacksonian leanings. Not being able to find anything else to Lincoln's disadvantage, he took occasion to say that his Whig opponent was an unbeliever. In actual fact, Lincoln was not a member of any particular congregation, so Cartwright could say what he pleased in this respect. Once, in a church, Lincoln had made some slighting allusions to the insincerity of many professing Christians, who were ready enough to condemn drunkards and other sinners, instead of trying to save them. After this, Cartwright resorted to a trick.

Lincoln had gone to a religious meeting where Cartwright preached. In due course Cartwright said, "All who desire to lead a new life, to give their hearts to God, and go to heaven, will stand." Many stood and the preacher went on, "All who do not wish to go to hell will stand." The rest of the congregation, Lincoln excepted, rose. Cartwright said in solemn tones, "May I inquire of you, Mr. Lincoln, where you are going?" Lincoln stood up, at length, and answered, "I came here as a respectful listener. I did not know that I was to be singled out by Brother Cartwright. I believe in treating religious matters with due solemnity. Brother Cartwright asks me directly where I am going. I desire to reply with equal directness: I am going to Congress."

With this splendid answer, he brings a considerable part of the congregation over to his side and wins new votes. In like manner, he scores when charged with belonging to the aristocracy, on the ground that he is connected by marriage with the Todd family!

"It would astonish, if not amuse, the older citizens to learn that I (a strange, friendless, uneducated, penniless boy, working on a flatboat at ten dollars a month) have been put down here as the candidate of pride, wealth, and aristocratic family distinction." In the full tide of the electoral campaign, he is not afraid to say that he remembered but one relative "who ever came to see me, and while he was in town he was accused of stealing a jew's-harp."

As the issue of the war against Mexico was still uncertain, Lincoln, in a great speech, urged his fellow citizens, now that the country was in danger, to fight on its behalf, no matter what they thought about the origin of the war, and no matter who the leader might be. All the Whigs, many of them Lincoln's personal friends, went to the front or sent their sons thither. Even in this apparent contradiction, of condemning the war before it had been begun, and supporting it while it was in progress, we discern his capacity for seeing both sides of an issue, and we recognize his freedom from fanaticism. Later we shall see him taking a courageous step against the same war.

His prophecy comes true, and when the election is over people are astonished at the size of his majority. Never before, in Illinois, has a Whig received so many votes; not even Clay. For the campaign the party had handed him $200 for expenses. After the election he returned $199.25, saying, "I did not need the money. I made the canvass on my own horse; my entertainment, being at the houses of friends, cost me nothing; and my only outlay was seventy-five cents for a barrel of cider, which some farm hands insisted I should treat to."

Lincoln has attained his end, and he writes to Speed: "Being elected to Congress, though I am very grateful to our friends for having done it, has not pleased me as much as I expected."

Such is the usual experience of men for whom life in the imagination is more vivid than life in the real and whose expectations are superior to reality. Through this confession sounds those other words confided to the same friend about the dreams of Elysium which exceed all that anything earthly can realize. It happens to him with women, and with power, with love and with ambition, and so it will remain, a poet's destiny.

XI

Mary was happy. She could wander through the streets of Washington by the side of her husband, chosen of the people; could enter the Capitol, could look down from the gallery at her husband's seat and at length see in the flesh all the celebrated men whose names had, since earliest girlhood, aroused her to mingled awe and envy. She could critically scan the wives of the foreign diplomats from Europe, driving by proudly in their carriages. She could go to the White House.

There it was, plain and unadorned, not hidden by any walls; and far simpler than she had dreamed of. So near and so real: here the President's room, the office, the anteroom. And there was the great reception hall, in which lucky Mrs. Polk, as the first lady in the land, would receive her guests, all of whom must bow before her in reverence. Was she not as great as any of those queens in Europe who were said to rule by God's grace? If you wear a fine dress and a costly chain, you do not need a crown. Was she not even more than a queen, since the whole nation had confirmed her choice of a gifted husband? Mary dreamed of herself as mistress here.

But when she got back to the little boarding house, the modest quarters which were all they could afford, and when she had to pass her days there, little noticed, as wife of a newcomer (a man unknown in Washington), she may well have gone through periods of doubt and gloom. In Springfield she had been a person of some importance, but here in Washington, one among hundreds, she counted for little. "Who is that long, thin fellow?" — "Oh, a lawyer from the West."

And here is Douglas too, Lincoln's shadow, the short agile man, simultaneously entering the Capitol. He has been elected to the Senate, and, since a senator ranks far above a congressman, she may well have her thoughts. But the Whigs are at length on the upgrade and for the first time they have a majority in the House. With mixed feelings, Mary returns to Springfield. Lincoln stays behind in the capital city, occupying himself there as paterfamilias, trying to buy stockings she wants for the children, advising her to get a servant girl, and ending as usual with: "Kiss the children for me." Husband and wife seem to have been on exceptionally good terms at this time, for even Herndon, her adversary, reports her as saying, "Lincoln is not much to look at, but people don't know that his heart is as great as his arms are long."

After a few weeks Lincoln becomes recognized as "the champion story-teller of the Capitol." In the House of Representatives cloak rooms, where Congressmen meet to chat and laugh, he at first keeps to himself, watching and listening; but soon he begins to take part. In the boarding house, when he is about to break into the conversation, he lays down knife and fork, places his elbows on the table, props his face on his hands, and usually begins with the words: "That reminds me of a story." Should there be a dispute during dinner, he uses this anecdotal faculty of his to smooth matters down, and thus he speedily acquires a reputation for kindliness, which is apt to attach to humorists and to men of a melancholy turn. Near the boarding house is a bowling alley to which he goes sometimes. With his long limbs, he is not very good at bowling, but he takes his beatings with equanimity, quizzing himself on his own awkwardness; and at table, he speaks quite frankly of the way in which he and his hearers had behaved the day before when he had made his first speech in Congress. He writes to Herndon:

"As to speech-making — by way of getting the hang of the House, I made a little speech two or three days ago on a post-office question of no general interest. I find speaking here and elsewhere about the same thing. I was about as badly scared, and no worse, as I am when I speak in court. I expect to make one within a week or two in which I hope to succeed well enough to wish you to see it."

Equanimity and cheerfulness breathe through this report. He obviously is not overawed by Congress, and we gather that he is a trifle amused by his friends' confidence in him.

Within a few weeks he does actually make his first long speech in Washington. The war was pretty well at an end even before the elections; Vera Cruz was in the hands of the United States army; General Taylor had conquered a considerable part of Mexico, and the pacifist opposition to the campaign had collapsed. But Lincoln was not the man to be carried away by success, and was not one to be stampeded into a policy of which he fundamentally disapproved. Nay, at the very time when the army was marching from victory to victory, he declared the war to be an unjust one. Thus he made enemies in both camps, for the radical Whigs were discontented because he favored a vigorous support of the army, and was prepared to vote the sinews of war, and on the other hand, the Democrats were furious with him because he openly accused the President of being responsible for this war, with all the human sacrifices it entailed. Discussing the ticklish problem of whether the war had been a war of offense, whether, that is to say, the United States or Mexico had begun the fighting, he put a question to Mr. Polk.

"Let the President answer . . . fully, fairly, and candidly. Let him answer with facts and not with arguments. Let him remember he sits where Washington sat, and, so remembering, let him answer as Washington would answer. As a nation should not, and the Almighty will not, be evaded, so let him attempt no evasion — no equivocation. And if, so answering, he can show that the soil was ours where the first blood of the war was shed, . . . then I am with him for his justification. . . . But if he can not or will not do this — if on any pretence or no pretence he shall refuse or omit it — than I shall be fully convinced of what I more than suspect already — that he is deeply conscious of being in the wrong; that he feels the blood of this war, like the blood of Abel, is crying to heaven against him; that, originally having some strong motive . . . to involve the two countries in a war, and trusting to escape scrutiny by fixing the public gaze upon the exceeding brightness of military glory (that attractive rainbow that rises in showers of blood, that serpent's eye that charms to destroy), he plunged into it, and has swept on and on till, disappointed in his calculation of the ease with which Mexico might be subdued, he now finds himself he knows not where. . . .

" He is a bewildered, confounded, and miserably perplexed man. God grant he may be able to show there is not something about his conscience more painful than all his mental perplexity."

With such splendid impetus, such courage and candor, does Lincoln make his first public appearance before the whole nation, justice his only concern. Do not the very successes of the President support his contention? Did not every one, as well as the speaker, foresee more or less what was to happen during the next few weeks: a brilliant victory, the ceding of the disputed territory by Mexico, in return for a formal payment of fifteen millions, and the candidature of the victorious General Taylor at the next presidential election? Of course, there is a large admixture of party politics in Lincoln's speech, for one who has been opposed to a war which has ended in victory can find no other grounds than moral ones to justify his opposition.

The President could not be forced to answer Lincoln's questions,

being commander in chief, and safeguarded by the Constitution.
Yet none of these political considerations diminish the gravity of
Lincoln's attack.   Considered in historical perspective, it even gains
in tragical intensity when we bear in mind similar attacks which,
a dozen years later, were to be thundered from this same rostrum
against the same orator.

No one, however, understands Lincoln's holy zeal — not even
his friends.   Writing to Herndon (who has been critical), Lincoln
says:

"That vote affirms that the war was unnecessarily and uncon-
stitutionally commenced by the President; and I will stake my
life that if you had been in my place you would have voted just as
I did.   Would you have voted what you felt and knew to be a lie?
I know you would not.   Would you have gone out of the House,
skulked the vote? . . . You are compelled to speak; and your
only alternative is to tell the truth or a lie. . . . The provision
of the Constitution giving the war-making power to Congress was
dictated, as I understand it, by the following reasons: kings had
always been involving and impoverishing their people in wars,
pretending generally, if not always, that the good of the people
was the object.   This our convention understood to be the most
oppressive of all kingly oppressions, and they resolved to so frame
the Constitution that no one man should hold the power of bringing
this oppression upon us.   But your view destroys the whole matter,
and places our President where kings have always stood. . . .
After you get over your scare, read my speech again, sentence by
sentence, and tell me honestly what you think of it."

But his friends in Springfield shake their heads and Herndon
may have written something about youth and age, which could
never understand one another, for Lincoln rejoins:

"The subject of your letter is exceedingly painful to me, and I
cannot but think there is some mistake in your impression of the
motives of the old men.   I suppose I am now one of the old men.
. . . Do you suppose that I should ever have got into notice if
I had waited to be hunted up and pushed forward by older men?
You young men get together and form a 'Rough-and-Ready Club',

and have regular meetings and speeches. . . . As you go along, gather up all the shrewd wild boys about town, whether just of age or a little under age."

He remains solitary, even here among his fellow congressmen. What other representative in the political arena is likely to have written home such a letter as this: "Mr. Stephens, of Georgia, a little, slim, pale-faced consumptive man, with a voice like Logan's, has just concluded the very best speech of an hour's length I ever heard. My old withered dry eyes are full of tears yet."

Who can foresee at what fatal hour he and Stephens are to meet again — tears turned to wrath? For the time being, he and Stephens become friends.

Thus does an observer write who sits apart at his own desk, preserving perfect objectivity in a hall full of persons busied about their own concerns. What about his voters? Must not the electors cavil at a representative who refuses to help his party friends to appointments? What was he elected for, then, if he will not give a lift to his own people? "Honest Abraham" is a fine appellation — but one who will not howl with the wolves will be eaten by them!

There is current in Springfield the story of a voter whom Lincoln has refused to recommend for an appointment, and to whom he has subsequently written:

"From the beginning of our acquaintance, I had felt the greatest kindness for you, and had supposed it was reciprocated on your part. Last summer, under circumstances which I mentioned to you, I was painfully constrained to withhold a recommendation which you desired, and shortly afterwards I learned, in such a way as to believe it, that you were indulging in open abuse of me. Of course, my feelings were wounded. On receiving your last letter the question occurred whether you were attempting to use me at the same time you would injure me, or whether you might not have been misrepresented to me. If the former, I ought not to answer you; if the latter, I ought, and so I have remained in suspense. I now enclose the letter, which you may use if you see fit."

What an extraordinary fellow we have sent to Congress this

time! He is incorruptible, beyond question; he will not recommend any unfit person for a post, since he regards the State as more important than party ties. All the same, he is too good-natured to refuse, so in the end he sends a recommendation, coupled with an expression of mistrust which seems to revoke it. You can make neither head nor tail of a man like that. Better not reëlect him!

XII

At the foot of the Capitol, which was designed to safeguard liberty, within sight of its windows, was "a sort of negro stable where gangs of negroes were sold, and sometimes kept in store for a time pending transport to the southern market, just like horses." Such was the description given by Lincoln at a later date. Here in the capital, on the border, the moral paradox involved in slavery was even more unexplainable than in the South, and, for this reason, Lincoln conceived the plan of directing hence his first blow against slavery. He drafted a Bill to Abolish Slavery in the District of Columbia. There should be no slavery within the District — with the reservation that officers of the government of the United States might temporarily bring slaves into the district for their personal service. A temporary system was to prevail during the transition, and for the education of the children of slave mothers born within the District. Compensation was provided for the owners of the slaves who would be set free by the bill. The return of fugitive slaves to the slave States was arranged for. The law was to be enacted by a referendum to the electors of the District.

In this draft, as in Lincoln's own character, we see moderation linked with justice. Nothing is to be broken, everything is to be molded. A system of transitional measures is to obviate a sudden breach with the past. To a man of Lincoln's reasonable temperament, the maintenance of the Union seems fundamental. He says now, just as he had said a decade ago: "Inasmuch as the fathers of the country did not abolish slavery, we must not do so either; but we must make laws for the new States, which the fathers could not foresee." At that moment the youthful California, in which gold and other treasures had been discovered, was being brought into the Union. The southern States, however, opposed this, seeing that the Union now consisted of fifteen slave States and fifteen non-slave States, while the new State whither adventurers had flocked from all over the world was opposed to slavery. Texas too, which was about to enter the Union in sequel to the annexation, had been a non-slave region under the Mexican government, and Wilmot, a Democrat, was advocating his famous formula which would practically prohibit slavery there.

What happened to Lincoln's own Bill for the District of Columbia? Washington had no interest in it. A luxury-loving society, Europeans who set the tone, and who could, here in free America, gratify their love of playing the master more fully than at home, thousands of persons who felt that they had a share in the government, and who were far more inclined to adopt the forms of aristocracy than their simple-minded grandfathers could have dreamed; the influence of the Southern gentry, who came here as senators and members of the House of Representatives, bringing with them their horses and their slaves, and showing by their mode of life that enjoyment and power were their main objects: all this was an atmosphere in which Lincoln's scheme could not flourish. He does not belong to Washington and he will never belong to it. The commissioner of Washington, who had spontaneously approved the proposal, was forced by the pressure of public opinion to recant; those who pulled the strings in Congress, being anxious to avoid inconvenient discussions, managed to get the introduction of the Bill postponed until it was too late for the present session; and they hoped that the man who had been so ill-advised as to propose it would not return to Congress next year. Actually, it was twelve years before Lincoln was back in Washington, but when he did come he was armed with power and was to see that cautious proposal replaced by a comprehensive law.

Justice and logic are always the motive forces of his political activities. This is no less plain in sober questions of administration than where the problem of human enfranchisement is at issue.

Speaking in the House of Representatives concerning the centralization of administration, he says:

"The navy . . . is the most general in its benefits of all this class of objects; and yet even the navy is of some peculiar advantage to Charleston, Baltimore, Philadelphia, New York, and Boston, beyond what it is to the interior towns of Illinois. . . . There is something of local advantage in the most general objects. But the converse is also true. Nothing is so local as not to be of some general benefit. . . . The just conclusion from all this is that if the nation refuse to make improvements of the more general kind because their benefits may be somewhat local, a State may for the same reason refuse to make an improvement of a local kind because its benefits may be somewhat general. A State may well say to the nation, 'If you will do nothing for me, I will do nothing for you.' Thus it is seen that if this argument of 'inequality' is sufficient anywhere, it is sufficient everywhere, and puts an end to improvements altogether. . . . But suppose, after all, there should be some degree of inequality. Inequality is certainly never to be embraced for its own sake; but is every good thing to be discarded which may be inseparably connected with some degree of it? If so, we must discard all government. This Capitol is built at the public expense, for the public benefit; but does any one doubt that it is of some peculiar local advantage to the property-holders and business people of Washington? Shall we remove it for this reason?"

In every example, in every comparison, the speaker's sense of justice is luminous; yet side by side with it there shines the shrewdness of a practical man, who never tries to combine opposing interests on the slender support of one single idea, but wants a reasonable compromise, such as is dictated by the imperfection of human institutions.

Yet of a sudden this shrewd and practical mediator changes his tone, becoming sarcastic:

"I make no allusion to the present President when I say there are a few stronger cases in this world of 'burden to the many and benefit to the few', of 'inequality', than the presidency itself is by some thought to be. An honest laborer digs coal at about seventy cents a day, while the President digs abstractions at about seventy dollars a day. The coal is clearly worth more than the abstractions, and yet what a monstrous inequality in the prices! Does the President, for this reason, propose to abolish the presidency? He does not and he ought not. The true rule, in determining to embrace or reject anything, is not whether it have any evil in it, but whether it have more of evil than of good. There are few things wholly evil or wholly good. Almost everything, especially of government policy, is an inseparable compound of the two, so that our best judgment of the preponderance between them is continually demanded."

Seldom can so characteristically Socratic a demonstration, such incisive reasoning, have been heard from this rostrum. Where did the rail-splitter learn the art of dancing amid up-pointed knife blades without gashing himself? He is self-taught, and has learned more in this way than he could ever learn in a school; has learned from the perennial need for self-preservation, from persistent observation of those among whom he has lived. Here he developed his gift for making comparisons; the continual need for renunciation, nay, the impulse toward renunciation, underlies his judgment concerning his own and others' positions; and a wide but ironical tolerance is the outcome. Only a man of melancholy mood, only a poet, can speak so gently about human weaknesses.

But there are other tones which never fail to sound in his melodies. Here is the great humorist who, when the elections draw near and the floor of Congress is misused as platform for the politicians, lets himself go against the Democratic candidates. At that time the tangle of affairs had resulted in a paradoxical situation. The Whigs, opponents of the war, wanted the victorious General Taylor as President, a slave owner, but one who had never made a public utterance upon the slave question, whereas the Democrats were putting forward the less popular General Cass, and, with a certain amount of reason, were making fun of the Whigs, whom they charged with taking shelter under a military coat tail. This grotesque metaphor stirred Lincoln's risibilities, and gave him an image which he could turn against his adversaries.

LINCOLN IN 1848

From a daguerreotype made when Lincoln was a representative in Congress

CITIZEN 117

"Yes, sir, that coat-tail was used, not only for General Jackson himself, but has been clung to, with the grip of death, by every Democratic candidate since. You have never ventured, and dare not now venture, from under it. . . . A fellow once advertised that he had made a discovery by which he could make a new man out of an old one, and have enough of the stuff left to make a little yellow dog. Just such a discovery has General Jackson's popularity been to you. You not only twice made President of him out of it, but you have had enough of the stuff left to make presidents of several comparatively small men since. . . . Mr. Speaker, . . . military coat-tails, or tails of any sort, are not figures of speech such as I would be the first to introduce into discussions here; but as the gentleman from Georgia has thought fit to introduce them, he and you are welcome to all you have made or can make by them. If you have . . . any more tails, just cock them and come at us. I repeat, I would not introduce this mode of discussion here; but I wish gentlemen on the other side to understand that the use of degrading figures is a game at which they may not find themselves able to take all the winnings. . . .

"By the way, Mr. Speaker, did you know I am a military hero? Yes, sir; in the days of the Black Hawk War, I fought, bled, and came away. Speaking of General Cass's career reminds me of my own. I was not at Stillman's defeat, but I was about as near it as Cass was to Hull's surrender; and, like him, I saw the place very soon afterward. It is quite certain I did not break my sword, for I had none to break; but I bent a musket pretty badly on one occasion. If Cass broke his sword, the idea is he broke it in desperation; I bent the musket by accident. If General Cass went in advance of me in picking huckleberries, I guess I surpassed him in charges upon the wild onions. If he saw any live, fighting Indians, it was more than I did; but I had a good many bloody struggles with the mosquitoes, and although I never fainted from the loss of blood, I can truly say I was often very hungry. Mr. Speaker, if I should ever conclude to doff whatever our Democratic friends may suppose there is of black-cockade federalism about me, and therefore they shall take me up as their candidate for the presidency,

I protest they shall not make fun of me, as they have of General Cass, by attempting to write me into a military hero."

With what adroitness does he avoid any arrogant note in his criticism! While amusing himself by retailing his own prowess as a warrior, he not merely pricks the bubble of Cass' military reputation, but guards against producing the impression that he is animated by malicious jealousy. Lincoln is inexhaustible in the tones he can utilize. If humorous parallels be his third tone, a humorous use of statistics is the fourth, and with this he can cut the ground from under his opponent's feet.

"Mr. Speaker, I adopt the suggestion of a friend that General Cass is a general of splendidly successful charges — charges, to be sure, not upon the public enemy, but upon the public treasury. He was governor of Michigan Territory and ex-officio superintendent of Indian affairs, from the 9th of October, 1813, to the 31st of July, 1831 — a period of seventeen years, nine months, and twenty-two days. During this period he received from the United States treasury, for personal services and personal expenses, the aggregate sum of ninety-six thousand and twenty-eight dollars, being an average of fourteen dollars and seventy-nine cents per day for every day of the time. This large sum was reached by assuming that he was doing service at several different places, and in several different capacities in the same place, all at the same time."

Then come annihilating details concerning seven official positions, in connection with which General Cass had never kept a clerk, or even used any extra amount of fuel, etc. Lincoln continues:

"But I have introduced General Cass's accounts here chiefly to show the wonderful physical capacities of the man. They show that he not only did the labor of several men at the same time, but that he often did it at several places, many hundreds of miles apart, at the same time. And at eating, too, his capacities are shown to be quite as wonderful. From October, 1821, to May, 1822, he ate ten rations a day in Michigan, ten rations a day here in Washington, and near five dollars' worth a day on the road between the two places! And then there is an important discovery in his example — the art of being paid for what one eats, instead of having to pay for it. Hereafter, if any nice young man should owe a bill which he cannot pay in any other way, he can just board it out.

"Mr. Speaker, we have all heard of the animal standing in doubt between two stacks of hay and starving to death. The like of that would never happen to General Cass. Place the stacks a thousand miles apart, he would stand stock-still midway between them, and eat them both at once, and the green grass along the line would be apt to suffer some too, at the same time. By all means make him President, gentlemen. He will feed you bounteously — if — if there is any left after he shall have helped himself."

By making this slashing onslaught in the gentle tone of one who is telling a fairy tale, while sure of his statistical ground, he achieves his end. He knows that every farmer throughout the country will laugh as heartily as his hearers laugh to-day, and that he will have made Cass impossible as President. A newspaper describes him thus:

"Mr. Lincoln's method and style were so remarkable that for the last half hour of his speech the House rocked with laughter. He began in one of the passages, gesticulated while making his way to the rostrum, which he reached as he came to the end of a sentence. Then he went back to his place, began again, wandered to and fro while he was speaking."

Yet this very description shows us that the orator keeps away from all tricky methods, and we see that his gestures are spontaneous, not calculated.

XIII

Soon, Mary had hopeful hours. She rejoiced at the honors paid to him in Chicago and saw the desired future loom nearer. But she heard how, at the beginning of a speech, he would take off his cuffs, would turn back his sleeves as if he were in for a wrestling match; and she learned, too, how in the New England States, where he was little known, it was difficult for him at first to get audiences. She did not however accompany him on his journeys to win votes for Taylor, a campaign he fought on a larger scale and with more success than four years earlier on behalf of Clay.

Here, too, his chief success rested on his slashing criticism of the Democrats. For the first time he heard the cultured oratory of Eastern politicians, the pathos of the abolitionists, and he learned new aspects of his problems. He was deeply impressed by an orator in Boston, Seward by name, who a dozen years later was to become intimately connected with his destiny. At a banquet for Taylor, Lincoln heard the name of another orator, who spoke before him, Jefferson Davis.

He now saw with his own eyes the great factories of the East, and could study at first hand what had long been known to him on paper, the differences between North and South. He visited Niagara Falls and wrote of them:

"The geologists can prove, by the wearing back of the Niagara plunge, that the world is at least fourteen thousand years old; how Niagara calls up the past. When Columbus first sought this continent — when Christ suffered on the cross — when Moses led Israel through the Red Sea — nay, even when Adam first came from the hand of his Maker; then, as now, Niagara was roaring here."

Such romantic thoughts aroused in him by the sight of this wonder of nature may have long persisted in his mind. But when his friend Herndon wants to talk the matter over with him, wishing to probe his secret feelings, he at once draws into his shell and replies banteringly, to fend off the questioner: "The thing that struck me most forcibly when I saw the Falls was, where in the world did all the water come from?"

The session of Congress comes to an end, and Lincoln is not at present destined to return to Washington. His remarkable position between peace and war, his refusals to place hunters, the curious history of his Bill to Abolish Slavery in the District of Columbia, had alienated a good many supporters.

Taylor has been elected President, although he can barely read or write correctly, but Lincoln, now rather unwillingly, must quit the center of political life. Although he has no fondness for party intrigues, he has learned here a great deal about the nature of the Union, and would like to know more. His adversaries flourish.

Shields has become Senator and Douglas' influence is growing. Has Washington been nothing but a brief interlude? What will bring him thither a second time from Springfield? And yet, what is there to lure him back to the Springfield nest? A house where, under reproachful glances, he has to lead an orderly existence; an office in which he has to adjust uninteresting legal disputes; a newspaper in which he has to voice the views of his party? At most, the children — but will there be no disputes about their education? Mary, likewise, is depressed when she sees how quickly they fall back into the old rut. She longs for a more expansive life, where everything is splendid and impressive, and she writes from New York: "When I saw the large steamers at the New York landing, ready for their European voyage, I felt in my heart inclined to sigh that poverty was my portion. I often laugh and tell Mr. Lincoln that I am determined my next husband shall be rich."

BOOK THREE

FIGHTER

Keen was the disappointment, Mary's as well as Lincoln's. Had he been defeated in a great battle, had he been in the position of a leader who with renewed courage is preparing for a fresh struggle, it would have been easy for him to adapt himself once more to the narrows of his old environment, to look upon life in this little town and the still primitive West as merely a pause between fights. But his day seemed to be over; it had been a day of no particular note; to himself, perhaps, no less than to his fellow citizens, he might well appear to be nothing more than a private soldier who had been sent to guard an outpost for a time, and had now been withdrawn. He no longer had a seat in the local legislature; his practice as a lawyer had been injured by his absence; instead of receiving considerable allowances for his services as congressman, he had now to content himself with his modest fees; and, as far as his subjective state of mind was concerned, he had brought back with him from Washington, not so much a picture of a wider world, as the conviction that the capital was a swamp, and that political life was a marsh in which honest folk got hopelessly bogged.

It was natural then, that, with some remnants of ambition, he should try to secure a post which would provide a more expanded environment without burdening him with the cares of congressional life. Immediately after his return to Springfield, he made moves to get the appointment of Commissioner of the General Land Office at Washington, for this was to be given to a Whig, and probably to an Illinois man. It would be an interesting position, politically important; the salary was a good one; his previous experiences as farmer, land surveyor, and lawyer would be most useful in this office. To President Taylor, who was under obligations to him, he gave eleven reasons why he should have the job; and to his political friends he wrote numerous canvassing letters, for this, as he had learned in the capital, was the customary practice of representatives on such occasions. Here is one of these letters :

"Dear Sir, I am about to ask a favor of you, one which I hope will not cost you much. I understand the General Land Office is about to be given to Illinois, and that Mr. Ewing desires Justin Butterfield, of Chicago, to be the man. I give you my word, the appointment of Mr. Butterfield will be an egregious political blunder. . . . Now, if you can conscientiously do so, I wish you to write General Taylor at once, saying that either I or the man I recommend should in your opinion be appointed to that office, if any one from Illinois shall be. I restrict my request to Illinois because you may have a man from your own State, and I do not ask to interfere with that. Your friend as ever."

To another he writes :

"Butterfield will be Commissioner of the General Land Office, unless prevented by strong and speedy efforts. . . . If you agree with me that his appointment would dissatisfy rather than gratify the Whigs of this State, that it would slacken their energies in future contests, that his appointment in '41 is an old sore with them which they will not patiently have reopened, . . . write Crittenden to that effect. . . . Not a moment's time is to be lost. Let this be confidential."

These letters are written with the skill of a practised diplomatist. Precisely because, with good reason, he warns against the appointment of his rival, he refrains from advancing his own claim too strenuously ; gives the name of another suitable Whig and thus, though he is putting himself forward more than ever in his life, he shows a perplexing lukewarmness in the matter. His old friend Herndon explains : "Besides his lack of persistence, he had an unconscious feeling of superiority and pride that admitted of no such flexibility of opinion as the professional suitor for office must have, in order to succeed." The shortness and straightforwardness of these letters, in which there is never a touch of adulation, makes them much blunter in tone than many of those he wrote, both when he was representative and afterwards, to solicit, with success, lesser posts for others. A minor position, however, was not what he wanted for himself. He writes at this date:

"There is nothing about me to authorize me to think of a first-class office, and a second-class one would not compensate me for being sneered at by others who want it for themselves."

Here we have both pride and modesty, both diffidence and self-esteem, with a subtle and ironical outlook upon his fellows. The sentence effectively summarizes Lincoln's attitude toward the world; and if, in days to come, the premier position in the State should fall into his grasp, he would accept the gift modestly enough, but without any surprise.

Yet he is surprised when he finds that some of his friends are censorious because he has applied for this position in the Land Office. It appears that Edwards, an old comrade of the Vandalia days, had wanted the job for himself, and feels slighted.

Lincoln writes to an acquaintance:

"Mr. Edwards is unquestionably offended with me in connection with the matter of the General Land Office. He wrote a letter against me which was filed at the department. The better part of one's life consists of his friendships; and, of them, mine with Mr. Edwards was one of the most cherished. I have not been false to it. At a word I could have had the office any time before the department was committed to Mr. Butterfield — at least Mr. Ewing and the President say as much. That word I forbore to speak, partly for other reasons, but chiefly for Mr. Edwards' sake — losing the office (that he might gain it) I was always for; but to lose his friendship, by the effort for him, would oppress me very much, were I not sustained by the utmost consciousness of rectitude."

Lincoln goes on to give detailed evidence to show that Edwards' suspicion of treachery is unwarranted; but the proofs are superfluous, for Lincoln's whole nature is sufficient evidence of the truth. He is deeply wounded by the suspicion. He is a lonely man, with few friends, and he values these much more than appointment to any office. That is why he is so much hurt when Edwards finds fault with him, and when he hears that some one or other in

Washington, with the customary cynicism, has spoken of the tall Springfield lawyer as one of those place hunters who will sacrifice everything else in the pursuit of money and power.

Since neither he nor Edwards has secured the coveted position, Lincoln can write tranquilly: "I am not greatly dissatisfied. I wish the offer had been so bestowed as to encourage our friends in future contests, and I regret exceedingly Mr. Edwards' feelings towards me. These two things away, I should have no regrets — at least I think I would not." Thus quickly does he withdraw into his inner self when an objective aim has been frustrated. Shortly afterwards, when the President offers him in compensation the office of secretary of Oregon, after brief reflection, he refuses.

Mary's wishes played a part in promoting this refusal. Her view was that if they removed to those western wilds to accept a position there, however good, there might be no possibility of a return to Washington. Her disinclination to play the part of governor's lady in the Far West, her preference even in this hour of disappointment for the uncertainties of their future in the little town of Springfield, show that her conviction in the greatness of Lincoln's future had not been shaken. Events were to justify the wisdom of her decision, for herself, for him, and for the nation.

She had helped him too in another way — by contraries! Had their life together been harmonious, he would have been inclined to spend more of his time at home. Since it was disharmonious, he became more and more disposed to go on circuit as a lawyer, for a wandering life was more congenial to his gypsy temperament than a strained domesticity in stiffly furnished rooms, with regular meals, social duties, and careful dress. When a Chicago colleague offered him a partnership, he rejected the proposal on the ground that he was consumptive, and that a sedentary existence would be the death of him.

Life as a lawyer on circuit was less remunerative, but there were compensating advantages. Half the year, all the spring and autumn months, he was on the road. He was not forced to spend day after day sitting at his desk in the same house, in the same street. He was freed from the burden of having to keep fixed hours; and he was not pestered at meal times with chatter about children, cooks, relatives, and shopping. There was no occasion for him to tidy himself up in the evening, to brush his stovepipe hat, retie his necktie, and go to some party where he would have to talk to the ladies about the latest fashions in basket chaises in Europe, or even about slavery.

How much pleasanter it was to drive from one little town to another through the lovely flower-decked prairies of Illinois. Three or four would drive together in some old rattletrap of a carriage, or, better still, he would ride on horseback, in the company of the judges and of one or two other lawyers. Toward noon, court would open, and the farmers who had suits to bring would appear: there would be disputes about land; assault cases; a man would be charged with the theft of a hog. The lawyer's business was to wash the sinner as white as he could; to put up the best possible case for the debtor; or, perhaps, to help the creditor to his due. After a few hours of this, they would all adjourn to the inn, Lincoln carrying his old, green, straight-handled umbrella, tied up with a piece of string; in the other hand, his documents in a carpetbag. At supper, the litigants would talk about crops, farm stock, land values. He would hear at first hand from the farmers what the needs of the countryside were, whether railroads or waterways would be best, and what the effects of the protective tariff were in actual practice. Now Lincoln would clear up a dubious point by telling one of his anecdotes, and thereupon people from the other tables would crowd around to listen. He had been on circuit there before, this long, thin fellow, "Honest Abe." They knew how amusingly he could talk. The judges, prosecutors and defendants, witnesses, those who had been at odds all the afternoon, would throng around this extraordinary man whose fund of witty sayings seemed inexhaustible. Herndon writes:

"In the rôle of a story teller I am prone to regard Mr. Lincoln as without an equal. I have seen him surrounded by a crowd numbering as many as two and in some cases three hundred persons, all deeply interested in the outcome of a story. . . . His countenance and all his features seemed to take part in the performance. As he neared the pith or point of the joke or story, every vestige of seriousness disappeared from his face. His little gray eyes sparkled; a smile seemed to gather up, curtain-like, the corners of his mouth; his frame quivered with suppressed excitement; and when the point — or 'nub' of the story, as he called it — came, no one's laugh was heartier than his. These backwoods allegories are out of date now, and any lawyer ambitious to gain prominence would hardly dare thus to entertain a crowd, except at the risk of his reputation; but with Lincoln it gave him, in some mysterious way, a singularly firm hold on the people."

A number of the stories, Herndon goes on to say, "would not bear repetition; . . . but many of them had morals which, while exposing the weaknesses of mankind, stung like a whiplash. Some, no doubt, were a thousand years old, with just enough 'verbal varnish' and alterations of names and dates to make them new and crisp. . . . Every recital was followed by . . . laughter and . . . cheers. After this had all died down, some unfortunate creature, through whose thickened skull the point had just penetrated, would break out in a guffaw, starting another wave of laughter which, growing to the proportions of a billow, would come rolling in like a veritable breaker. . . . I have seen Judge Treat, who was the very impersonation of gravity, sit up till the last and laugh until, as he often expressed it, 'he almost shook his ribs loose.' The next day he would ascend the bench and listen to Lincoln in a murder trial."

Having grown up in such close touch with the common people, and bound by ties of blood to men like these, he shared intimately in their feelings, and was continually learning from them. In successive journeys of this kind, he became well known throughout the whole length and breadth of Illinois, laying the foundations of a popularity without which he would never have secured his great victory of ten years later. As to meal times, and what was served up to him, he was as indifferent as he had been twenty years earlier, when in some such little country town he would saw wood or peddle buttons. Just as, in those early days, he would lie down on the

counter of his shop in order to read, so now his partner (who sometimes accompanied him on circuit) describes him as lying in the bed
the two men shared, with his long legs projecting beyond the foot,
reading Euclid till two in the morning, to the accompaniment of
the snores of the occupants of the other beds in the room.   Or he
would sit up till midnight, playing chess with the judge.   Then,
seated on the edge of his bed in a yellow flannel nightshirt which
was always too short for him, he would engage in a protracted discussion on slavery. At length the other would fall asleep, to
awaken in the morning and see Lincoln sitting deep in thought,
just where he had been overnight, ready, as if there had been no
interval, to resume the argument with the words : "Let me tell you
that this nation cannot continue to exist half slave and half free."

There is always something to learn, on the road and elsewhere.
He comes across an itinerant with a magic lantern, and takes the
thing to pieces, to discover how it is made.   Another time, a small
traveling exhibition happens along, and over the inn fire that
evening Lincoln talks about the electrical machine he has seen.
He gets hold of a German grammar, dips into it, and, making little
progress in his studies, scribbles on it, in German : "Nix kommt
raus !"   Whenever there is a chance, he gives a helping hand to
folk, sawing wood or milking the cows, for he does not wish to get
quite out of practice, and these countryside clients have actually
more respect for this lawyer of theirs when they find that he can
milk the cow that is to figure in to-morrow's suit.

All his companions like him, especially Trumbull, Browning,
young Swett, Judge Davis (a fine figure of a man, like a Franz Hals
picture), his fellow travelers on these journeys for years. But
no more than Lincoln himself do they realize that they will in due
time be involved with him in a much more formidable movement,
and will then render him loyal service. For politically they are all
of much the same way of thinking, influence one another in interminable discussions, and finally come to form the nucleus of a
new party which will ultimately be constituted in this State of
Illinois. Only when Judge Douglas comes along are there likely
to be dissensions. It is just as well that he is now a senator and

would rather pass his time at the Capitol or the club in Washington, than have to rough it in the primitive inns or on the primitive roads of Illinois.

At present the careers of these sometime rivals seem to be diverging. Douglas is giving himself up more and more to politics, whereas Lincoln, between the ages of forty-one and forty-six, devotes himself mainly to law, although he does not abandon politics completely.

II

"Persuade your neighbors to compromise whenever you can. Point out to them how the nominal winner is often a real loser — in fees, expenses, and waste of time. As a peacemaker, the lawyer has a superior opportunity of being a good man. There will still be business enough.

"Never stir up litigation. A worse man can scarcely be found than one who does this. . . . As a general rule, never take your whole fee in advance, nor any more than a small retainer. When fully paid beforehand, you are more than a common mortal if you can feel the same interest in the case as if something was still in prospect for you, as well as for your client."

These extracts from the notes for a law lecture disclose a theoretical outlook which Lincoln incorporated still more vividly in his daily practice. Though he was never passionately devoted to the practice of the law, from very early days he was animated by a keen sense of justice, so that his adoption of a legal career was not a mere matter of chance. Only when we understand his thoughts, and still more when we understand his feelings, upon such matters, can we understand the thoughts and the feelings he manifested in political life; but when we understand the former, we understand the latter readily enough. His was one of those characters whose every trait secures practical expression. Nothing that he ever did was accidental, underhand, or furtive; he was inviolably true to his inner nature, was genuine through and through, was at every moment Lincoln, and so comparable only to himself. To defend a poor woman against the machinations of a usurer was no more

LINCOLN IN 1854

From a daguerreotype made in Chicago

and no less important, in his eyes, than to defend the traditions of the fathers of the country against the encroachments of party passion, or to defend millions of Negro slaves against the injustice of their masters.

Yet there was nothing of the prophet or the preacher about him. The hardships of his early life, his struggles for a livelihood, his wanderings, his service, the lack of any protectors, had strengthened him in the school of the world without blunting his sensibilities. In his practice as a lawyer, he would turn his knowledge of men to account, would mingle wit and sarcasm to undermine the credibility of a witness, of a prosecutor or a defendant.

"You are called J. Parker Green. What does 'J' mean?"

"'J.' means John."

"Is that so? But why don't you call yourself 'John P. Green' just like other folk?"

This sally makes the jury smile; and while Lincoln is playing pitch and toss with the witness's two Christian names, his victim's prestige is being undermined.

In another case, Logan, his former partner, is opposing counsel in a horse-stealing trial. It is hot weather; they are all in shirt sleeves, and Lincoln sees that Logan has put on his shirt wrong side before. Lincoln opens his speech for the defense by saying: "Mr. Logan has been talking for an hour about horses, in order to show these worthy farmers what he has learnt about the animals from a book on veterinary surgery. But how can we trust his knowledge of horses when he does not even know enough to put on his shirt properly." Logan is made ridiculous — and loses his case.

A rich man had assaulted another man, and had struck him with a stick. The injured party had sued for ten thousand dollars moral damages. Lincoln was defending counsel. The counsel for the prosecution had reduced the court to tears by depicting the honorable character of the victim, who was poor, and by talking about the arrogance of the wealthy aggressor. Now Lincoln rose slowly to reply, adjusted his coat, looked thoughtfully at a piece of paper lying on the table in front of him, took it up, scanned it yet more carefully, and burst out laughing. Those who were watching him grew curious, and wanted to share in the joke. He laid down the paper, took off his necktie, took up the paper once more, and laughed yet more heartily. By the contagion of example, the others were forced to join in. Then Lincoln repeated the panto-mime, having taken off his coat this time, while the court rocked with laughter. Then the advocate made his excuses, explaining to the court the reason for his mirth. This paper showed that the plaintiff had, to begin with, valued his wounded honor at one thousand dollars, and only after the discovery that the assailant was a rich man had he come to the conclusion it was worth nine thousand dollars more. Thereupon Lincoln offered the plaintiff a few hundred dollars, told one of his humorous anecdotes, and persuaded the court to leave it at that.

Often Lincoln gets to work with all a farmer's shrewdness. A lawyer owes a wealthy man two dollars and fifty cents, and, since he will not pay up, the angry creditor wants to sue for the amount. Lincoln dissuades him, saying; "It will cost you more than you will get out of it."

"That does not matter."

"Very well, then, you must pay me a fee of ten dollars right away."

Thereupon Lincoln calls on his colleague, tells him what has happened, shares the ten dollars with him, and makes him pay his debt of two dollars fifty..

Sometimes he wins a case by the talent that would have brought him a fortune on the stage. The anecdotalist, relating some humor-ous incident of everyday experience, pulls the lawyer out of a diffi-culty. Here is another assault case, and the settlement of the issue turns upon the question as to who began it.

"My client was in the position of a man who was walking along the road with a pitchfork on his shoulder when suddenly a savage dog ran out of a farmhouse he was passing and attacked him. To save himself, the man killed the dog with the pitchfork."

"Why did you kill my dog?" said the angry farmer.

"Why did the dog try to bite me?"

"Why didn't you fend him off with the blunt end?"

"Why didn't your dog go for me with his blunt end?"

Lincoln mimics what would have been the absurd movements of a dog running backwards to attack the jury, and convulses them with amusement. They give a verdict for his client.

If he has no detailed knowledge of the law books, that is all the better for his diction, inasmuch as what he has to say is free from the sophistries of legal terminology. He never splits hairs. His clear and pithy sentences, sharply and distinctly carved like his features, are those of a countryman, and appeal to the countrymen who make up the jury. According to current report, Lincoln, when he repeats the arguments of the opposing counsel, makes them much clearer than they were before — as a preliminary to demolishing them by his keen logic. In this manner, his instinct for comparisons and his fondness for drawing them are useful. With an impartiality rare among lawyers, he enumerates and balances the claims of both parties to a suit, thus winning the confidence of the court quicker than can one whose only object is to put forward the side of his own client.

In the simplest and most natural way in the world, there are fused in his character the lineaments of the poet with those of the righteous man, and those of the logician with those of the moralist. Lincoln would have been an ideal judge. In the end, he became judge for the nation. The result of his peculiarities was, as all his colleagues declare, that he made a very poor advocate when, during the course of the proceedings, he came to feel that his client was in the wrong. Should he be sure of this when first approached, he would refuse to undertake the case. A lady sent him a check for two hundred and fifty dollars, asking him to act for her. He returned it with the remark: "I have not a single nail on which to hang your claim."

When a man of whose criminality he was convinced sought his help, Lincoln handed the case over to a colleague, saying, "This man is guilty. I cannot defend him. You can." Another time he had a talk with the opposing counsel before the hearing of the case, made up his mind about the matter, and said, "As I see that my client is in the wrong, I shall advise him to withdraw the suit."

Yet, though his humor would sometimes lead him to great lengths, there was always a moral boundary which he would not overstep. It seemed as if, like a thoroughbred horse, he was shying against an unseen obstacle. In one case Herndon heard that there was a point about which the other side was very anxious and therefore threw out a plea, purely fictitious as a matter of fact, in which this secret doubt of the other side was taken full advantage of. Lincoln, who has been away, asks on his return whether the plea is founded on fact.

"Not? Hadn't we better withdraw that plea? You know it's a sham, and a sham is very often but another name for a lie. Don't let it go on record. The cursed thing may come staring us in the face long after this suit has been forgotten."

The practical caution of the experienced politician obviously played a part here, and one who did not know the speaker might readily imagine that caution influenced him more than morality. Nevertheless there are hundreds of purely altruistic decisions of the kind on record, and morality was certainly the dominant consideration in this instance. Before his partner, however, Lincoln wishes to avoid a pharisaical pose, and would (here, as in general) rather represent himself as shrewd than as fanatically truthful.

If, on the other hand, Lincoln believes that his client is being unjustly treated, he will hit back unmercifully. When a soldier's widow has been cheated out of half of her pension by an agent, Lincoln, as prosecuting counsel, tells Herndon to listen to his address to the jury, "for," says he, "I am going to skin Wright, and get that money back."

Another time, in a murder case, when he regarded the sentence as unjust, he sprang to his feet and, "alarming of aspect, he roared like a lion disturbed in its cave", and made a passionate speech lasting ten minutes.

For success in court, Lincoln needed, not only a conviction that the cause he was advocating was just, but also plenty of time. Just as he walked slowly, ate slowly, and digested slowly, so he was never quick at improvisation, and was deliberate in attack. Here was a man who had never fought in battle, but had made plentiful use of the woodman's ax. Since he never thought of trying to shine, since both as lawyer and as politician he thought a great deal about the cause in which he was engaged and never thought about himself, he was not able to produce the effects of the brilliant orator. Herndon tells us that he used to grow restless at Lincoln's slow movements and speeches in court, and once begged his partner to speak with more vim. Lincoln had an answer ready: "Give me your little penknife with its short blade, and hand me that old jackknife, lying on the table." Opening the blade of the penknife, he said, "You see, this blade at the point travels rapidly, but only through a small portion of space till it stops; now the long blade of the jackknife moves no faster but through a much greater space than the small one. Just so with the long, labored movements of my mind. I may not emit ideas as rapidly as others, because I am compelled by nature to speak slowly; but when I do throw off a thought it seems to me, though it comes with some effort, it has force enough to cut its own way and travel a greater distance."

III

How small the capital of Illinois seemed when one returned to it from the wide spaces of the open country! Was it not natural that to Lincoln, a man of nomadic temperament, Springfield should appear duller than ever when he came back to his house and his office after several months on circuit? He, indeed, avoided the place when his journey had brought him within range of it, and when his companions devoted week-ends and holidays to revisiting their homes and families. What was there to attract him back to Springfield? Not even its rapid growth.

Every one knew him there, of course, and when he went to and fro between house and office, all greeted him in the friendliest fashion. If he had forgotten some little girl's name, he would say, "Good morning, little sister," as he went by. People were familiar, too, with his strange manner of walking. He always put his whole foot down flat on the ground and lifted it up in the same way, and yet he did not look ungainly, for there was power in his stride. His little son, who often came with him on these rounds, could hardly keep up with the long-legged father on the frozen sidewalks nor could the boy get much out of Lincoln by pulling at the great, bony hand, for the father was full of his own thoughts. When people saw him as he went by, wearing around his neck an old gray shawl twisted into a rope, they spoke of him as "old Lincoln", though he was little over forty; for, even as a young man, he had not looked young. Those who turned to glance at him, did so sympathetically; indeed, his friends assure us that this general sympathy with the melancholy of his aspect was one of the causes of his success. Should any one speak to him, he would stop short in surprise, clasp the other's hand in both his, say "How d'ye do?" and then, unfailingly, detain the acquaintance to tell one of his famous anecdotes.

In the office, work was done haphazard, as of yore, although there was a good deal more to do than formerly. There was never anything meticulous about Abraham Lincoln, and we feel that there was a slightly contemptuous ring in the tone in which he sometimes said to his partner, "Well, Billy, let's hear what there is in the books."

What he likes better than anything else is to stretch himself on the old sofa and read. Shakespeare is continually in his hands, and he quotes out-of-the-way passages from this author. He has several editions of Byron's "Don Juan", and they are all freely underlined. He is extremely fond of Burns, and once he reads aloud to his partner one of the Scotsman's poems. The early poems of young Walt Whitman are also discussed in this office. They make a strong impression on Lincoln; he takes the book home with him, but promptly brings it back again next day, with the grim remark that it has narrowly escaped being "purified in fire", for "the women didn't like it." Of other new books, he will merely flutter the leaves, let them drop on the floor, close his eyes, and murmuringly repeat the substance of what he has just been reading. He does not store up books. On the parlor table at home there are no books to be seen beyond a number of Mary's gilded albums. He prefers to borrow what interests him from the Council House library. But one day Herndon, who is a great book buyer, brings to the office a volume of the *Annual of Science*. Lincoln promptly buys the whole series, for, he says, "I may, by this book, correct my errors and save time and expense. Men are greedy to publish the successes of their efforts, but reluctant to publish their failures. Men are ruined by this one-sided practice of concealment of blunders and failures."

He tries to win clear ideas concerning the new researches in botany and physics, to understand the working of machinery, and to grasp the import of the newly developing science of electricity. He recommends these novelties to the farmers, going out to meet advances in technique with the hopefulness of the social thinker who has had to perform arduous manual labor without loving it.

The lawyer of riper years can turn this same young man's experience to account. In a trial where the working of a waterwheel comes in question, he amazes the judge by his knowledge of technical details; and when, acting for a railroad, he has to defend the building of a bridge across the Mississippi whose construction is resisted by a shipping line, the sometime raftsman knows what arguments are best to use, while the politician can contribute more recent knowledge, for he is already interested in the linking of East and West.

Calculations have been made to show that he won many more law cases than he lost; and that he far more often was counsel for defendant than for plaintiff. His fees were extremely moderate. Since he never calculated them in accordance with the amount of money involved in the case, he once asked $3.50 from a man for whom he had won $600. He was almost forty years of age before he earned more than one hundred dollars in a single case; then his reputation grew, and he earned more than three thousand dollars a year. But when a new hotel paid him twenty-five dollars for preparing some necessary law papers, he wrote: "You must think I am a high-priced man. You are too liberal with your money. Fifteen dollars is enough for the job. I return to you a ten dollar bill."

But he would not let himself be imposed upon. After he had won a very important law case, on behalf of the Illinois Central Railroad, the counsel for the other side being his sometime partners, Stuart and Logan, he sent in a bill for two thousand dollars. The company expostulated, remarking, "Why, this is as much as a first-class lawyer would have charged!" and refused to pay more than two hundred dollars. Thereupon Lincoln sued for a fee of five thousand dollars, and won his case.

Such successes helped him to overcome his constitutional diffidence; but, as a self-taught man, when he was pleading before the court, no less than in ordinary everyday life, it was his way to rely on his reasoning powers rather than on what was written in the law books, and on his sense of justice even more than on his reasoning powers. After Clay's death, he said, in a memorial address, that Clay's scant opportunities for education were a useful lesson that in the United States no one was born so poor as to be unable to get sufficient education, if only the will were not lacking. To a young man who wanted to study law under his guidance he wrote:

"If you are resolutely determined to make a lawyer of yourself, the thing is more than half done already. It is but a small matter whether you read with anybody or not. I did not read with any one. Get the books, and read and study them till you understand them in their principal features; and that is the main thing. It is of no consequence to be in a large town while you are reading. I read at New Salem, which never had three hundred people living in it. . . . Always bear in mind that your own resolution to succeed is more important than any other one thing."

Seldom, indeed, was he himself animated by such a resolution! Dreams of an unattainable Elysium had induced a mood of general renunciation, which interfered with the growth of his ambition. There can be no doubt that by the time he was forty years of age, Lincoln had become fully aware of his own worth. But he failed to recognize, as yet, how great is the power of the voice of the people to overcome the machinations of the politicians; though he felt that nothing but the voice of the people could guide him and sustain him. At this period, perhaps, after his political experiences in Washington, he felt more at home in the young western State. For him, there, politics had now become a pastime, engaged in for its own sake, and not for any advantages it might bring. Still, for the party to which he belonged and for the cause which he had espoused, there was work to do, even in this out-of-the-way corner of his country. His life during these years exhibits numerous instances of such activities. For even now, Lincoln never lost touch with politics.

He took part in elections and by-elections; when important posts were vacant, he was more vigorous in canvassing on behalf of his party friends than he had been when he wanted such a job for himself; he drew up lists of voters; and he declared that the sending of personal letters to voters was much more effective than the circulation of printed documents. When a letter came from an elector, he scrutinized style and handwriting, believing that from this he could obtain valuable information as to the mood of the writer.

His skill as a negotiator (arising out of his fine perception of people's moods, and fortified by his ever lively sense of justice) increased with the passing of the years; his work as a lawyer and his experience as a politician interacted on one another helpfully in this respect. Of the two men who stood closest to him in political life, one declared him to be the finest diplomat in the world. The other said: "He is secretive, communicates no more of his own thoughts and purposes than he thinks will subserve the end he has in view; he has the faculty of gaining the confidence of others by apparently giving them his own. . . . He is one of the shrewdest men I have ever known; he is by no means the unsophisticated, artless man that many take him to be." Here is a similar judgment, from a professional colleague: "One who should believe Lincoln to be a simple, harmless fellow, would soon be undeceived — in the ditch." Those who had watched him playing chess, described him as cautious, on the defensive, always waiting for the moment when he could attack with confidence as to the result. Lincoln once said of himself, " My mind is like a piece of steel — very hard to scratch anything on it, and almost impossible after you get it there to rub it out."

What guided Lincoln's footsteps in the political world is shown by the answer he once gave when asked what special ability was most valuable for a winning politician. "To be able to raise a cause which shall produce an effect, and then fight the effect." A profound saying, deep as a well, in whose depths, far below the midday glare of everyday life, we see the stars of human wisdom shining. The lambent shafts of the speaker's irony are directed against the cunning of the leaders and the weaknesses of the led; but at the same time what he says is instinct with the ethical fervor of one who would fain see mankind better than it is.

For always, when Lincoln thinks politically, he is thinking of mankind in the concrete, of humanity at large. Springfield and Illinois may be his starting point, the matter of immediate concern may be some detail of the local party struggle; his gaze may be fixed on the consequences in Washington, where decisions affecting the whole country are taken; but his heart throbs responsively to a world far wider even than the great world of the United States. What he said of Henry Clay applies also to himself: "He loved his country warmly, because it was his home; but he loved it even more because it was a free country." In an after-dinner speech, he expressed this idea as follows: "Public opinion has always one central thought, from which all other thoughts radiate. From the first, and until recently, the equality of mankind was this central thought, and although public opinion has had to tolerate the inequality which seemed necessary, it steadily progresses towards a true equality of all human beings."

The man who, as a routine practice, unhesitatingly has four hundred copies made and distributed of a recommendation to some post which he thinks can be filled in a particular way to the advantage of the party, is animated by other motives, is spurred on by his general sense of justice and responsibility, when he suddenly and spontaneously makes up his mind to write the following letter to the Secretary of State in Washington:

"It is with some hesitation I presume to address this letter — and yet I wish not only you, but the whole cabinet, and the President too, would consider the subject matter of it. My being among the people while you and they are not, will excuse the apparent presumption. It is understood that the President at first adopted, as a general rule, to throw the responsibility of the appointments upon the respective departments; and that such rule is adhered to and practised upon. This course I at first thought proper; and, of course, I am not now complaining of it. Still I am disappointed with the effect of it on the public mind. It is fixing for the President the unjust and ruinous character of being a mere man of straw. This must be arrested, or it will damn us all inevitably. It is said Gen. Taylor and his officers held a council of war, at Palo Alto (I believe); and that he then fought the battle against unanimous opinion of those officers. This fact (no matter whether rightfully or wrongfully) gives him more popularity than ten thousand submissions, however really wide and magnanimous those submissions may be. The appointments need be no better than they have been, but the public must be brought to understand that they are the President's appointments. He must occasionally say, or seem to say, 'By the Eternal, I take the responsibility.' Those phrases were the 'Samson's Locks' of Gen. Jackson, and we dare not disregard the length of experience."

What motive induced a man devoid of political power to write such a letter? He would not write in that critical vein, if his purpose were merely to remind the central authorities at Washington of his existence. Is he trying to shake a reputation? No, he is trying to establish one more firmly. Does he desire to increase his prestige in his own town, by having the news that he has written this letter bruited abroad? No one knew anything about it until forty years after his death. The letter is written for the reason it bears on its own face. This half-forgotten man is moved to give unasked advice by concern for the public welfare; literally this, and nothing else.

His opposition to slavery is but an expression of his concern for the sufferings of all mankind. The melancholy look in his gray eyes is in eyes that are ever turned towards his brothers. He is eager to be just and tolerant to all and sundry. When there is an agitation against the Germans, who at this time are arriving in vast numbers as immigrants, he asks some of the agitators, "Who are the native Americans? Do they not wear the breechclout and carry the tomahawk? We pushed them from their homes, and now turn on others not fortunate enough to come over so early as we or our forefathers."

Such are the thoughts that course through a brain which is always ruled by the heart; such are the things that stir Lincoln to action — not ambition, nor money, nor family concerns. But he has consideration for individuals, as well as for causes. To a New York firm, writing to ask him about the financial standing of a Springfield man, he answers:

"First of all, he has a wife and a baby; together they ought to be worth $500,000, to any man. Secondly, he has an office in which there is a table worth $1.50, and three chairs, worth, say, $1. Last of all, there is in one corner a large rathole, which will bear looking into. Respectfully, A. Lincoln."

IV

"Within the last three weeks there has been a party almost every night, and some two or three grand fêtes are coming off this week. I may surprise you when I mention that I am recovering from the slight fatigue of a very large, and, I really believe, a very handsome and agreeable entertainment, at least our friends flatter us by saying so. About five hundred were invited; yet, owing to an unlucky rain, three hundred only favored us by their presence."

This is Mary, writing to her sister, and it gives a clue to the general tenor of her thoughts and cares, her wishes and triumphs. Driving in her own carriage — the carriage he has bought for her, though he never uses it himself — to pay a round of calls in the little town, she can tickle her fancy with the thought that, on however small a scale, she is keeping up a Parisian style. He is earning more money now and has paid off all his debts, so she has a second story built to their house. That renders the place more presentable. Besides, owing to the growth of Springfield, it is now in quite a central situation, which makes it all the more charming to her, and, we need not doubt, all the more uncongenial to him. She does not care for the only tree left near the house and has it cut down; but she loves her wonderful new chandeliers, and she delights in the musical box between the two cut-glass inkstands on her writing table. But of what avail are all these splendors when her husband still insists on cleaning his own boots; when he replaces a missing trousers button by a wooden peg, hitches it to his suspenders, and humorously calls the arrangement a "gallus?"

Certainly, she has a far from easy time with him. Often, when dinner is ready, he does not come. She has to send the two older boys to look for their father, and they find him in one of the shops, sitting on a nail keg, chatting with and listening to a crowd of the customers. At length he gets up to come home, but stops again in the street outside the shop, the center of a little group, the two boys hanging on to his coat tails, while he finishes his anecdote. Then, when he is on his way home, the youngsters begin to cry.

"What on earth is the matter?" asks a passer-by.

"What on earth is the matter?" rejoins Lincoln. "I have three walnuts, and each of them wants to have two."

Is it surprising that Mary is fretful at home? When one of the boys mispronounces the word "gentleman", which means so much to her and nothing to him, he is pleased, and tells all his friends about it. When he is asked why the Todds spell their name with two *d*'s, he answers, "For God one *d* is enough, but the Todds need two."

He is not the man to see to it that his boys are brought up properly, according to his wife's likes. On Sundays, he takes the two elder ones to his office while the mother is in church, sits plunged in thought or deep in his books, and never notices how they amuse themselves by messing up the pens, upsetting the inkpots, throwing legal documents on to the floor, and dropping pencils into the spittoon. It is left for his unhappy partner to discover on Monday that the young Lincolns have been up to mischief in the room.

At home, he usually shows a yielding disposition; does not ask how much Mary spends; leaves money lying about where she can take it whenever she pleases; is content with whatever arrangements

she may prefer in matters concerning the house and the garden —
and thus irritates her nervous susceptibilities and fosters her contradictoriness by his very passivity and indifference.

"He is of no account when he is at home," says Mary. "He
never does anything except to warm himself and read. He never
went to market in his life. I have to look after all that. He just
does nothing. He is the most useless, good-for-nothing man on
earth." Yet when her sister praises him, and says she would
be glad to have a husband with so much intelligence, Mary is
delighted, and agrees that his faults are only trifles. While she
wrangles with every one, with her sisters, with the servants, and of
course with him, he, on the other hand, records it as a principle:

"Quarrel not at all. No man resolved to make the most of himself can spare time for personal contention. Still less can he afford
to take all the consequences, including the vitiating of his temper
and the loss of self-control. Yield larger things to which you can
show no more than equal right: and yield lesser ones, though
clearly your own."

On these terms, they are able to rub along together; and the
death of one of their sons at the age of four years may have helped
to promote a closer union between them. When she is afraid Lincoln
is becoming consumptive she urges the doctor to conceal the fact from
him. In important matters, she never pushes Lincoln too far, and
she says of him after his death: "He was mild in his manner,
but a terribly firm man when he set his foot down. I could always
tell when, in deciding anything, he had reached his ultimatum. At
first he was very cheerful; then he lapsed into thoughtfulness,
bringing his lips together in a firm compression. When these
symptoms developed, I fashioned myself accordingly, and so did
all others have to do sooner or later."

But things did not always go as well as this. On one occasion he
had ordered a new newspaper to be sent to his house; Mary wrote
to the editor canceling the subscription, the letter was published,
and Lincoln could not openly repudiate what she had said, but the
matter made him quite ill. Here is another instance: Lincoln
is at home, talking business with a legal colleague, when Mary

bursts in at the door, asking whether he has done something he has promised to do. When he replies in the negative, she exclaims that he neglects her shamefully, and goes out, slamming the door after her. The visitor is amazed. Lincoln laughs the thing off, saying, "Why, if you knew how much good that little eruption did, what a relief it was to her, how she really enjoyed it, and if you knew her as well as I do, you would be glad she had had an opportunity to explode, to give vent to her feelings."

Sometimes, however, the atmosphere at home became unbearable. Then Herndon would find him in the office at seven o'clock in the morning, lying on the sofa, gazing moodily at the ceiling; or else sitting hunched up on a chair, his feet on the window sill, and only able to answer his partner's good morning with a grunt. If Herndon went out, Lincoln would bolt himself in. If Lincoln went out, it would be to the law court, or to some necessary business. At dinner time, though his house was so near, he would return to the office with some cheese and biscuits; would stay there till late in the evening, sitting on a box at the top of the stairway, talking to any one who came along. There he would remain till hours after closing time. Not until the night was well advanced would he slowly stroll homeward among the trees.

Lincoln was not one to complain of these home troubles. So far as we know, the only occasion on which he spoke of them was one on which he informed Herndon that he had been himself to blame. He had been sitting in gloomy silence all the morning, but at length told his partner what had happened. His wife, that morning, had "got out of the wrong side of her bed." Everything he did had been a cause of offense. He had not answered back to her scolding, but had himself grown more and more out of humor. He had left the dining room, and then had to go back in to it for some forgotten trifle. She greeted his reappearance with a fresh outburst. Losing patience, he seized her by the arm, pushed her through the door into the kitchen, thrust her across this room, and almost out through the open door into the street. This had been within sight of people coming down the street on their way to church. He was bitterly ashamed of his violence.

Can we be surprised, in view of the actual circumstances of his home life, that never in all these years did he venture to ask any one to dine at his house? We have testimony as to Mary's outbreaks of fury from no less than six witnesses, some of whom even tell us that they saw her drive her husband out through the door with a broomstick. We know that Lincoln's parents, who lived only eighty miles away, never came to pay him a visit; and that the only one of his relatives, one of the Hanks cousins, to enter the house was made a drudge of by Mary, so that Lincoln had to interfere. On the other hand, Mary always had a warm welcome for her fine friends from the South.

Have we not, then, good reason to agree with an intimate friend of Lincoln's who declared:

"The fact that Mary Todd, by her turbulent nature and unfortunate manner, prevented her husband from becoming a domestic man, operated largely in his favor; for he was thereby kept out in the world of business and politics. Instead of spending his evenings at home, reading the papers and warming his toes at his own fireside, he was constantly out with the common people, was mingling with the politicians, discussing public questions with the farmers who thronged the offices in the Court House and the State House, and exchanging views with the loungers who surrounded the stove on winter evenings in the village store. The result of this continuous contact with the world was, that he was more thoroughly known than any other man in his community. His wife, therefore, was one of the unintentional means of his promotion."

What might have seemed more likely than that Lincoln should have fallen in love with somebody on one or other of his long journeys? He was not a misogynist by nature, only shy. What he avoided and despised were the trivialities of ordinary society life. What he wanted was sympathy and understanding. Had he been fortunate enough to marry a woman of an affectionate and patient disposition, one easy to guide, he would himself have been amenable to her guidance in many matters, would have been able to rid himself of his all-pervading melancholy, would have become gentler and happier. He went so often to hear a certain woman singer that

people teased him about it, and even shook their heads at him
warningly.   His answer was, "Let me alone, she is the only woman
that has ever said nice things to me."   But at a later date, when
political feeling was running so high against Abraham Lincoln, not
one of his enemies was ever able to reproach him with an infringement of the strict moral standards of his time; and there is no
record that Mary, though she was so often left alone, and for such
long periods, though she was suspicious and irritable, was ever
jealous of her husband during their life in Springfield.

In some instances he appears in divorce cases.   Once when a
group of sturdy wives were prosecuted for entering a saloon, where
their husbands made it a daily habit to get drunk, and emptying
away all the whisky, Lincoln, with his oratorical gift, was able
to secure their acquittal.   He would even, on occasion, take a
woman's part in defiance of the law.   A cobbler who lived near
by, a wife-beater when in his cups, had been warned by him
several times.   Out of patience at length, and hearing the poor
woman's screams at a new beating, Lincoln got two or three friends
to help, seized the offender, dragged him out of his house, and tied
him to a post.   Giving the wife a whip, they told her to give her husband a sound lashing, which, after momentary hesitation, she
accordingly did.   Our worthy lawyer might well have been prosecuted and punished for the offense!   This man who, for the greater
part of his life, in defiance of the dictates of his own heart, resisted
the proposal to free the slaves by force, on the ground that such a
step would have been illegal — was induced in this little matter to
play the ringleader in an escapade which was not altogether seemly
in a man of his age and position.   Yet it was a natural outburst.

We see that he was at one and the same time a man drawn
towards women, and a man who held aloof from women.   When
he was asked why he seemed to take so little pleasure in women's
society, he answered with an anecdote: "When we lived in Indiana,
once in a while my mother used to . . . make some gingerbread.
. . . One day I smelled the gingerbread, and came into the house
to get my share while it was still hot.   My mother had baked me
three gingerbread men.   I took them out under a hickory tree to

eat them.   There was a family near us poorer than we were, and
their boy came along as I sat down. . . .   'Abe,' he said, 'gimme a
man !'   I gave him one.   He crammed it into his mouth in two
bites, and looked at me while I was biting the legs off my first one.
'Abe,' he said, 'gimme that other'n.'   I wanted it myself, but I
gave it to him, and it followed the first.   I said to him, 'You seem
to like gingerbread.'   'Abe,' he said, 'I don't s'pose anybody on
earth likes gingerbread better'n I do — and gets less'n I do.' "

Does the voice of premature age breathe through this little story?
Do we not, rather, see in it mingled sadness and roguishness,
renunciation joined with the conviction that renunciation is the
wiser course?   He is asked about his attitude toward women, from
whom he finds it harder to keep away than any one knows.   The
question makes him think of his mother's gingerbread cakes, of the
hickory tree, and the neighbor's little boy.   But he does not bring
up the incident in order to present himself in a sentimental light,
as a man who has always renounced the good things of life for others'
sakes.   He identifies himself with the poor youngster, who liked
gingerbread so much, and so seldom got any.   Beneath the shade
of that hickory tree in Indiana there revive in memory all the
bitter thoughts of a man who, first of all because he could not
boast of good looks and because of the death of his betrothed, then
by his nervous anxiety, and at length by his moral sentiments, had
been deprived of that companionship with women which would
have given a lighter touch to his essentially virile nature.

V

How far back, already, seem the days of youth!   Can it really
be twenty years since the burial of sweet Ann Rutledge?   Ah,
yes, it is twenty years since McNamar, who had once been betrothed
to her, had returned to seek her, and had had to content himself
with the story of his rival.   McNamar had liked this rival of his,
had thought him an honest, straightforward fellow, at that time
only a land surveyor.   He kept up the acquaintanceship later on,
when the surveyor had blossomed out as a lawyer in Springfield.

Lincoln looked after McNamar's local business interests, would write to the man whom he had then regarded as the spoiled child of fortune, whose courtship of Ann had then been a cause of so much distress to him, letters beginning:

"Honored Mr. McNamar, With regard to the taxes on the land you have purchased. . . ."

His father and his brother seemed quite as far away as McNamar. Old Thomas Lincoln, now well on in the sixties, lived a life of ups and downs, much as he had done in the days of his first marriage, troubled by debts and by dread of competitors. When things have taken an exceptionally bad turn with him, he applies for help to the son who has got on so well in the world.

"My dear Father . . . I very cheerfully send you the $20, which sum you say is necessary to save your land from sale. It is singular that you should have forgotten a judgment against you; and it is more singular that the plaintiff should have let you forget it so long, particularly as I suppose you always had property enough to satisfy a judgment of that amount. Before you pay it, it would be well to be sure you have not paid, or at least, that you cannot prove that you have paid it. Give my love to Mother and all connections. Affectionately your son, A. Lincoln."

His doubts as to the truth of his father's statement are very delicately concealed, and yet only half concealed. It is the letter of a son who is also a lawyer, and of a lawyer who is also a lover of the truth, and who even where strangers are concerned is disquieted by any transactions that bear a shady complexion. He wants to avoid betraying the discomfiture he feels that his own father should not be perfectly straight with him; and yet every line discloses his sorrow that men are what they are, and that his own family should be no better than the rest.

One day he opens his heart to Herndon about these private family concerns. The two men are driving together to see a client who wants to make his will. Some chance association recalls to Lincoln's mind the mystery of his mother's parentage, and he talks to his friend and partner about the matter. Should he himself, he adds, be more highly gifted than the other members of the family, it is unlikely that this talented strain comes either from the Lincolns or from the Hankses, none of whom have ever displayed conspicuous ability. It must derive from his unknown grandfather in the South. His theory is that illegitimate offspring are apt to be more highly gifted than legitimate. May we not suppose that such thoughts, which for decades in this lonely man's mind have been directed toward the unknown, must have tended to sever him all the more from those relatives with whom nothing now kept him in touch but their wish to get what they could out of him? If he is cold toward them, it is not because he has won a position, a reputation, and sufficient means, while they remain impoverished and obscure; for even when his name has become far more widely celebrated, we shall find that Lincoln, in his intercourse with the poorest of farmers, is as simple and homely as ever. What he misses is signs of affection from his old home; and with a melancholy that is untinged with pleasure, he withdraws into the stronghold of his reserve.

Two or three years later, his half brother writes to tell him that the father is breaking up. Will Abraham pay a visit home? "You already know," he rejoins, "I desire that neither Father nor Mother shall be in want of any comfort, either in health or sickness, while they live; and I feel sure you have not failed to use my name, if necessary, to procure a doctor, or anything else for father in his sickness. My business is such that I could hardly leave home now, if it was not as it is, that my own wife is sick abed. . . . I sincerely hope father may recover his health, but, at all events, tell him to remember to call upon and confide in our great and good and merciful Maker, who will not turn away from him in any extremity. He notes the fall of a sparrow, and numbers the hairs of our heads, and He will not forget the dying man who puts his trust in Him. Say to him that if we could meet now it is doubtful whether it would not be more painful than pleasant, but that if it be his lot to go now, he will soon have a joyous meeting with many loved ones gone before, and where the rest of us, through the help of God, hope ere long to join them. Write to me again when you receive this. Affectionately, A. Lincoln."

Every word, every phrase, is carefully adapted to the mentality of a dying farmer, who has certainly given far less thought to God than has the writer, but who no less certainly has a much stronger faith in God. The letter contains only the familiar consolations of an extreme unction, and Lincoln writes them because, his religious convictions and his nature being what they are, he could not utter them by word of mouth. How could it be painful to the father for the two to meet; how could it be anything but pleasant to the old man to see the son's tall form coming through the low door, and to look once more into Abraham's clear, gray eyes? But the son fears his father's deathbed just as he had feared his own wedding bed. His loneliness, his great loneliness, makes him dread such encounters and withdraw into himself.

From afar, he has for his stepbrothers and stepsisters been both helper and counselor. We do not know all that he did for them; what we do know is, that not one of them did anything for him. Just as in the early days he strode along beside the wagon in which the others were seated; just as, of old, he had vigorously plied ax and saw to build house and fence for them: so, now, though living apart, he is still for them the strong helper and protector. Only a few days before the date of the letter just quoted, he had written to his stepbrother, who lived close by Tom Lincoln, as follows:

"Dear Johnston, your request for eighty dollars I do not think it best to comply with now. At the various times when I have helped you a little, you have said to me, 'We can get along very well now'; but in a very short time I find you in the same difficulty again. Now, this can only happen by some defect in your conduct. What that defect is, I think I know. You are not lazy, and still you are an idler. I doubt whether, since I saw you, you have done a good whole day's work in any one day. You do not very much dislike to work, and still you do not work much merely because it does not seem to you that you could get much for it. This habit of uselessly wasting time is the whole difficulty; it is vastly important to you, and still more so to your children, that you should break the habit. It is more important to them, because they have longer to live, and can keep out of an idle habit before they are in it, easier than they can get out after they are in. You are now in need of some money; and what I propose is, that you shall go to work, 'tooth and nail,' for somebody who will give you money for it. Let father and your boys take charge of your things at home, prepare for a crop, and make the crop, and you go to work for the best money wages, or in discharge of any debt you owe, that you can get; and, to secure you a fair reward for your labour, I now promise you, that for every dollar you will, between this and the first of May, get for your own labor, either in money or as your own indebtedness, I will then give you one other dollar. By this, if you hire yourself at ten dollars a month, from me you will get ten more, making twenty dollars a month for your work. In this I do not mean that you shall go off to St. Louis, or the lead mines, or the gold mines in California, but I mean for you to go at it for the best wages you can get close to home in Coles County. Now, if you will do this, you will soon be out of debt, and, what is better, you will have a habit that will keep you from getting in debt again. But if I should now clear you out of debt, next year you would be just as deep in as ever. You say you would almost give your place in heaven for seventy or eighty dollars. Then you value your place in heaven very cheap, for I am sure you can, with the offer I make, get the seventy or eighty dollars for four or five months' work. You say if I will furnish you the money you will deed me the land, that if you don't pay the money back, you will deliver possession. Nonsense! If you can't now live with the land, how will you then live without it? You have always been kind to me, and I do not mean to be unkind to you. On the contrary, if you will but follow my advice, you will find it worth more than eighty times eighty dollars to you. Affectionately your brother, A. Lincoln."

In this simple letter, Lincoln reaches an altitude of tone which he will hardly transcend in the finest of his great political speeches. He says not a word which can affront the lazybones, who is a married man with a family; nor does he adopt a paternal note (like that in the previous letter), in order to deliver a homily on the blessing of labor. When these two brothers talk about places in heaven, they do it in the spirit of farmers, and not in the vein of the pious.

Johnston is shrewd. He knows that Abraham Lincoln has a kindly heart. It will be all right to mortgage the land to brother Abraham, who will never claim the pledge. But at bottom, Lincoln is the shrewder of the two. Kind-hearted though he be, he does not propose to go on throwing money into a yawning hole in the ground. Eighty dollars? Oh, yes, John Johnston shall have eighty dollars, but in the course of eight months, in which he must earn eighty for himself. Lincoln, wishing both to teach the other and to avoid promising too much, limits his offer as regards time, though not as regards amount. Herein we have Lincoln, the practical idealist, the philanthropist who wants to do his best for every one, but only on a realistic basis; the man in whose temperament heart and brain exercise a joint control.

Besides, Lincoln has good reason to be concerned, not so much about the fate of his money, as about the fate of his stepbrother and the latter's children, for John Johnston is really incorrigible. When Tom Lincoln dies, and Johnston wishes to overreach his mother, there is a new tone in Abraham Lincoln's letters, a harsh and bitter tone, for only by the menace of authority can he save his stepmother from the clutches of her own son.

"When I came into Charleston day before yesterday I learned that you are anxious to sell the land where you live, and move to Missouri. I have been thinking of this ever since, and cannot but think such a notion is utterly foolish. What can you do in Missouri better than here? Is the land richer? Can you there, any more than here, raise corn and wheat and oats without work? Will anybody there, any more than here, do your work for you? . . . You have raised no crop this year, and what you really want is to sell the land, get the money and spend it. . . . I feel it is my duty to have no hand in such a piece of foolery. I feel that it is so, even on your own account, and particularly on mother's account. The eastern forty acres I intend to keep for mother while she lives: if you will not cultivate it, it will rent for enough to support her; at least it will rent for something. Her dower in the other forties she can let you have. . . . To go to work is the only cure for your case."

Thus harsh is the voice of the man who, only a few months earlier, had still been trying to persuade and teach his stepbrother. So firm can Lincoln be when enmity rears its head against him, and his adversaries prove unteachable. His style recalls that of the Bible, in its combination of metallic and tender sounds, for both obey a moral law. Ensuing circumstances, indeed, make him withdraw his opposition to the sale of the land, when he finds that his mother's position is assured: but he writes to his brother, "Before I will make a deed, the money must be had, or secured beyond all doubt, at ten per cent." There is further shuffling on Johnston's part, and Lincoln writes a fortnight later:

"Your proposal about selling these forty acres of land is all that I could want or could claim for *myself;* but I am not satisfied with it on *mother's* account — I want her to have her living, and I feel that it is my duty, to some extent, to see that she is not wronged. She had a right of dower (that is, the use of one third for life) in the other two forties; but, it seems, she has already let you take that, hook and line." Johnston's proposal was to pay his mother eight per cent. on two hundred dollars, . . . "making her the *enormous* sum of sixteen dollars a year. Now, if you are satisfied with treating her in that way, I am not. I am confident that land can be made to produce for mother at least thirty dollars a year, and I can not, to oblige any living person, consent that she shall be put on an allowance of sixteen dollars a year. Yours, etc., A. Lincoln."

When Lincoln signs himself "Yours, etc.", it means that the weather is stormy. He goes on fighting on behalf of his stepmother against her own son; and he offers to take one of the nephews to educate. But, for reasons we can easily divine, he avoids asking his stepmother to come and stay with him. Instead, he advises her to accept the invitation to live for a while in the house of an old friend.

A couple of years later, after making a speech in the church of a little town, he takes aside a man whom he can trust, and says, "In your prison there is a youngster I want to see, but no one must know anything about it. Please arrange matters for me with the overseer." The youth, who has been charged with theft before, has this time stolen a watch, and probably a musket also. He is a son of John Johnston. "I will help him out of his difficulties, but for the last time. If he steals again, I will have nothing more to do with him." He goes to the grating in the wooden hut which serves as a prison, and talks to the lad inside. The latter, blubbering, holds forth a dirty Bible, and makes all manner of promises. The uncle has a private talk with the injured parties, who agree not to prosecute, and the authorities set young Johnston free. "Lincoln was profoundly unhappy," reports an eyewitness. "I have never seen him look more melancholy."

A sad moment, indeed. His heart is sore, for himself, for his relatives, for humanity at large, when he stands there at the grating of the prison, looking in at the idler's son who is suffering the results of a bad upbringing. He, who at this lad's age had already been known as "Honest Abraham", he who is now a man of standing, invited hither to give an address on public questions, has in secret to visit a little thief, to have furtive interviews with those whose goods have been stolen and whom he doubtless compensates out of his own purse, and can only make the best of a bad job by securing his nephew's release in defiance of the letter of the law. And all this because his father had married a widow whose children had turned out ill! Or did he do it for his stepmother's own sake, for the sake of the old woman to whom he ever remains thankful? Yet he often did quite as much for strangers. Perhaps the story of his own life may be summed up as the attempt of a lover of mankind to make law and compassion run in double harness.

VI

"His melancholy oozed from him as he walked." In this fine image, Herndon describes the fundamental tone of Lincoln's character. Had not his mother been of a like temperament? The gloomy trend was reinforced by his mother's premature death, by speculations upon the uncertainty of his descent on the maternal side, by his father's restless disposition with the consequent lack of a permanent home, by the numerous failures of his adolescence.

by his yearning towards women and his dread of them. Again and again he had dreamed of Elysium, only, on awakening, to find himself thrust out of this imagined paradise, and here was a sorrow which deepened the melancholy of eyes that seemed ever to be asking a great question of mankind. Perhaps the most salient indication of the man's true greatness is that his melancholy never made him bitter, never made him hate his fellows.

On circuit, once, Stuart drew a fellow lawyer's attention to Lincoln. Here is the latter's account:

"I turned a little, and saw Lincoln sitting alone in a corner of the bar, remote from any one, wrapped in abstraction and gloom. . . . I watched him for some time. He seemed to be pursuing in his mind some specific painful subject, regularly and systematically through various sinuosities, and his sad face would assume, at times, deeper phases of grief. No relief came till he was roused by the adjournment of court, when he emerged from his cave of gloom, like one awakened from sleep." Another who had been sharing Lincoln's bed in the inn, writes:

"I was awakened early, before daylight, by my companion sitting up in bed, his figure dimly visible by the ghostly firelight, and talking the wildest and most incoherent nonsense all to himself. A stranger to Lincoln would have supposed he had suddenly gone insane. Of course, I knew Lincoln and his idiosyncracies, and felt no alarm, so I listened and laughed. After he had gone on in this way for, say, five minutes, while I was awake, and I know not how long before I was awake, he sprang out of bed, hurriedly washed, and jumped into his clothes, put some wood on the fire and then sat in front of it, moodily, dejectedly, in a most sombre and gloomy spell, till the breakfast bell rang, when he started as if from sleep, and went with us to breakfast. Neither Davis nor I spoke to him. We knew this trait; it was not remarkable for Lincoln, although this time to which I refer was a radical manifestation of it."

When he heard sad songs sung, he would ask the singer to be good enough to write down the words for him. On a sheet of paper he notes:

"Poem — I like this."

" Tell me, ye winged winds
That round my pathway roar,
Do ye not know some spot
Where mortals weep no more?
Some lone and pleasant vale,
Some valley in the West,
Where, free from toil and pain,
The weary soul may rest?
The loud wind dwindled to a whisper low,
And sighed for pity as it answered, No.

" Tell me, thou mighty deep
Whose billows round me play,
Know'st thou some favoured spot,
Some island far away,
Where weary man may find
The bliss for which he sighs;
Where sorrow never lives,
And friendship never dies?
The loud waves rolling in perpetual flow
Stopped for awhile and sighed to answer, No."

On a starry night, Lincoln was one of a company sitting on the
terrace in front of a Chicago house, overlooking the great lake.   The
hostess says of him:

"He seemed enthralled by the beauty of the scene.   In the gentle
tones customary to him when his heart was moved, and which were
so well suited to the hour and the place, he began to speak of the
mystery which for thousands upon thousands of years had en-
wrapped those distant worlds and separated them from our own;
of the sense of loveliness and poesy which had so often filled the
seers of ancient days when Orion and Arcturus had become visible
on their nightly wanderings: of the discovery of the telescope, and
of the wonders of science, which was able to measure the vast dis-
tances separating us from the sun and the other planets.   He went

on to speculate about the knowledge yet to be revealed by the hidden powers of the lens.   When it had turned cold and we had gone indoors, he sat down on the sofa, stretching his long legs straight out in front of him across the carpet, folded his arms behind his back, and went on to speak of other discoveries."

Thus does his spirit rise to the stars, and then return to the clarities of earth, now visionary, now matter of fact; ranging between a yearning for the infinite and a search for immediate knowledge; yet invariably choosing in the end the middle path of truth.

But he is not always master of his nerves, and nothing but his sense of humor enables him to make headway against his melancholy.   Lincoln's irony must in great measure be regarded as in the nature of a life belt with which he is able to keep his head above water.   His unceasing flow of comic anecdotes is a sort of unconscious spiritual hygiene.   He actually carried about with him in his pocket a manuscript book filled with such sallies, as another might carry about a spirit flask or a bottle of smelling salts.   That was why he was so often absent-minded.   Sometimes he would brood for twenty minutes or more, and then end his musings by retailing some pointed witticism or lively tale — though it was plain enough to any one who had been watching him that his ponderings had been far from diverting.   Once he was among the audience at a reading of tedious poems.   The others were listening in a bored but well-bred silence, when there suddenly came from Lincoln an outburst of loud laughter, which embarrassed the offender quite as much as it did every one else.   In the same way, greatly to every one's alarm, he would at times suddenly begin to speak altogether out of season.

Occasionally his nerves would completely fail him at a critical moment.   He drove over once to New Salem to make a funeral speech at an old friend's burial.   For the first time after many years he saw the familiar faces of those who crowded around the coffin and were waiting for his words.   Suddenly he lost composure, was unable to utter a syllable, made a vague sign to the bearers to carry on the coffin, and stayed speechless where he was.   He had been unable to face the situation, just as he had been unable to face the situation on his wedding day.

His mental characteristics are rooted in his bodily peculiarities. From earliest youth he had been a man perpetually on the move, disinclined to a sedentary life; and, like many famous philosophers, he declared that he could always think best when he was walking. Just as everything about him was abnormally long and slow, just as his gaze was tranquil, his gait cautious, so did his long, bony head suggest a man of thought and observation rather than a man of action. The quadrangle formed by the blunt end of his long and prominent nose, the two projecting cheekbones, and the chin with its forward curve — traversed by the great, dry lips — might have belonged to a man with a taste for the material things of life. But below was the fine and vigorous neck, the virile sustainer of this head; above was the nobly domed forehead, with its craggy eyebrows, and beneath them the iron-gray eyes, which imposed silence on others because they were so obviously the eyes of a man with a vast fund of reserve.

Everything indicates that so far as constitution went, this man was predestined to live on into old age. For the very reason that he had in truth never been young and never ardent, because already in adolescence he was interested rather in the things that interest a philosopher than in the things that interest a youth, he needed a long, long time to develop the activities which would enable him to answer the great test. His moderation in all things was determined by his bodily nature, and this moderation itself became the determinant of his political ideas. "Am I a temperance man? No, but I am so moderate that I don't drink."

Once his only companion in a stagecoach was a jovial Kentuckian, who successively offered him tobacco to chew, a cigar to smoke, and a drink from a pocket brandy flask. All were politely declined. When they parted in the afternoon, the Kentuckian said, good-humoredly, "See here, stranger, you're a clever but queer companion. I may never see you again, and I don't wish to offend you, but I want to say this: my experience has taught me that a man who has no vices has damned few virtues. Good day." Lincoln was fond of telling this story against himself, and there may have been times of depression when he was more than half inclined to believe what his traveling companion had said.

If he was a man of strictly moral behavior, this was not from any Pharisaical love of display, but because he had an inborn sense of justice and right. He was no puritan to renounce money and its advantages on religious grounds; if he wore the same old overcoat year after year, and was content to drive hither and thither in rattle-trap carriages, it was because his thoughts were absorbed in other matters, and these trivialities did not interest him. If he was irregular in many of his ways, it was because he valued his independence more than most, and would not sacrifice it to be punctual at meals or appointments. He liked to eat when he was hungry, and to sleep when he was tired; what he ate and where he ate and slept, were indifferent to him; he detested fixed rules in these matters. Avoiding, as he did, all forms of ceremonial, making even his oratory as simple as it could possibly be, he could never play a set part — not even that of husband and father.

It is characteristic of such rare natures as Lincoln's that these men do not treat others, or even judge others, according to the friendship or the hostility they may display. Imaginatively, Lincoln puts himself in another's place; excuses what another does, because he understands why it has been done; acts on another's behalf as he knows that other would wish him to act. "I should very much like Logan to be elected judge of the Supreme Court; first of all, because he would be the best man in the post; secondly, because he would suffer more than any of the others if he should fail to get it."

Yet Lincoln is anything but an anchorite. Throughout life he remains the countryman, the farmer, the man who has a keen eye to his own advantage — but when Lincoln thinks of his own advantage, he thinks of what will give him more political influence. Certainly Lincoln was ambitious, for when, with the advance of years, he knew himself to be a man of exceptional gifts; when he aspired to free the oppressed, or at least to prevent the passing of laws which would oppress those who were already free, he had to aspire to posts which would put power in his hands. That is why, when he enters active political life for the second time, he will do so with an impetus for which, during these seemingly quiet years, he has been taking a long breath. "How hard it is to die," he says to Herndon, when they are driving together, "and leave one's country no better than if one had never lived for it! The world is dead to hope, deaf to its own death struggle. One made known by a universal cry, What is to be done. Is anything to be done? Who can do anything? And how is it to be done? Do you ever think of these things?"

These memorable words give us a deep insight into the mind of a man who longed to alter things. Not after the fashion of the artist, who alters the form; not after the fashion of the thinker, who deals with consequences; not after the fashion of the man of the world, who wants to change things so that they may redound to his personal advantage. The thoughts just quoted are the soliloquy of a lover of mankind, are the self-communings of an observer who has developed into an educator, and who is seriously asking himself whether he is called upon to build up order out of chaos. He thinks he knows what ought to be done. What puzzles him is how and by whom it is to be done. Then he cuts himself short, like a man of mark who has unbent for a moment to his secretary, and recloses the shutters of his inner self with a half question to which he does not expect an answer.

VII

Here lies poor Johnny Kongapod,
Have mercy on him, gracious God,
As he would do if he was God
and you were Johnny Kongapod.

This cheerful epitaph, composed by Lincoln for a Kickapoo Indian, embodies the brotherliness, mutuality, and comradeship that formed the essentials of his religious faith; it is instinct with the broad sympathy for his fellow men which was his leading char-

acteristic throughout life; and the rogue in him peeps through in
the irony which cannot be suppressed even on a tombstone.   Here,
too, it is compensation, justice, which he seeks; here, likewise,
there should be neither master nor slave, neither punishment nor
reward.   With one voice his friends declare that neither at twenty
nor yet at fifty, nor even later, despite the religious tenor of some of
his speeches, was Lincoln a Christian in the orthodox sense of the
term.

In New Salem, already, he was spoken of as an infidel, an atheist,
a fatalist, in spite of his fondness for quoting the Bible; and at a
later date he declared that his doubts became intensified when Ann
Rutledge died.   Writing of him when he was thirty years of age,
Herndon quotes an early friend of Lincoln as saying:

"Sometimes he bordered on atheism.   He went far that way,
and shocked me.   I was then a young man, and believed what my
good mother told me. . . .   He would come into the clerks' office,
where I and some young men were writing and staying, and would
bring the Bible with him; would read a chapter and argue against
it. . . .   Lincoln was enthusiastic in his infidelity.   As he grew
older, he grew more discreet; didn't talk much before strangers
about his religion."

Lincoln's first partner, Stuart, uses almost the same words:

"He . . . went further against Christian beliefs and doctrines
and principles than any man I ever heard. . . .   Lincoln always
denied that Jesus was . . . the Son of God as understood and maintained by the Christian Church."   Ten years later, according to
Judge Davis, Lincoln " had no faith in the Christian sense of the
term, had only faith in laws, principles, causes, and effects."

Another acquaintance writes: "Mr. Lincoln told me that he
was a kind of immortalist; that he never could bring himself to
believe in eternal punishment."

Here is still another report:

"He believed in a Creator of all things, who had neither beginning nor end, and, possessing all power and wisdom, established a
principle in obedience to which worlds move and are upheld, and
animal and vegetable life comes into existence.   A reason he gave

for his belief was that in view of the order and harmony of all nature which we behold, it would have been more miraculous to have come about by chance than to have been created and arranged by some great thinking power. . . . Evidence of Christ's divinity came to us in a somewhat doubtful shape; but . . . the system of Christianity was an ingenious one, at least, and perhaps was calculated to do good."

Others among those who knew Lincoln best are agreed in affirming that his religion was this ethical and undogmatic Christianity which he shared with all lovers of mankind before and since. "His expressed views on these and kindred topics were such as, in the estimation of most believers, would place him outside the Christian pale. Yet . . . his principles and practices and the spirit of his whole life were of the very kind we universally agree to call Christian." After his death, Mary said, "Mr. Lincoln had no faith and no hope in the usual acceptation of those words. He never joined a Church; but still, as I believe, he was a religious man by nature. . . . It was a kind of poetry in his nature, and he was never a technical Christian."

Herndon writes: "No man had stronger or firmer faith in Providence — God — than Mr. Lincoln, but the continued use by him late in life of the word 'God' must not be interpreted to mean that he believed in a personal God. In 1854 he asked me to erase the word 'God' from a speech which I had written and read to him for criticism, because my language indicated a personal God, whereas he insisted no such personality ever existed."

He was as frank, as straightforward with himself about religion and morality as he was in all his doings. He said that his code was like that of an old man he had once heard speak at a church meeting: "When I do good I feel good, and when I do bad I feel bad, and that's my religion." He could not have any other religion than this; and even though he read Kant and Locke, Fichte and Emerson, was acquainted with the writings of the Illinois freemasons, and also with certain monistic books from Scotland, they were of little interest even to his brain, and could certainly never touch his heart. When he was making an old woman's will, he could indeed, at her request, repeat for her a psalm out of his head; and when, after the death of their little boy Eddie, Mary joined the Presbyterians, he rented a pew in the church, and became friendly with the minister; but he would not himself become a church member. He said, "Probably it is to be my lot to go on in a twilight, feeling and reasoning my way through life, as questioning, doubting Thomas did."

Yet when his son was bitten by a mad dog, he took the boy to distant Indiana to touch a famous wonder-working stone there. He had grown up among simple-minded farmers and woodmen, and the knowledge and the doubts of riper years had not uprooted his primitive superstitions, but only refined them. Indeed, they actually became intensified as he reached the climax of his career.

This was natural enough. His loneliness, the growing recognition of his own eccentricity, inevitably inclined the skeptic to believe in signs and wonders; and such a belief was accordant with the essentials of his general outlook on life. "There are no accidents in my philosophy. Every effect must have its cause. The past is the cause of the present, and the present will be the cause of the future. All these are links in the endless chain stretching from the finite to the infinite." He smiled at the idea of the freedom of the will, said we were only entitled to speak of the freedom of the spirit, and was fond of quoting Hamlet's saying: "There's a divinity that shapes our ends, rough-hew them how we will."

So firm was his faith in predestination, that he said, "Brutus was forced to kill Caesar, by laws and conditions lying outside the power of his own will." Long after this, and after he had met his own fate at the hands of the Brutus who awaited him, this conviction of his was recorded by his wife, who said, "Lincoln's only philosophy was that what would happen, would happen, and that no prayer could avail to alter what was predestined." There is, then, a tragical ring in what Lincoln once said to Herndon: "Billy, I fear that I shall meet with some terrible end."

So firm a conviction that everything which happens is an inevitable concatenation of causes and effects leaves one who holds it no room for choice. The feeling that he is under the dominion of necessity inclines him, nevertheless, to pay heed to signs which may forewarn him of coming events. Warn him merely, not enable him to avert them. Lincoln's superstition was passive, and never led to active decisions. In the crises of his destiny he tried to interpret dreams and visions, but he did not act on their indications. All he hoped was that he would be able to get a glimpse through the veil hiding the future, to learn what was coming, though he would not be able to alter it. We never find that he changes his plans because this sign or that has disquieted him; but he not infrequently has forebodings. Even on the last day of his life we see him pensive in the shadow of such an anticipation.

All the same, just as in the little matters of everyday life, so likewise in the pursuit of wider aims, he guides his footsteps by reasoning, puts his trust in understanding. He must use his senses, must see and feel, must win experience, must have time. Is a man to refrain from action because everything is predetermined? How is it going to happen, and through whose instrumentality? Surely the hand and the brain of the individual are needed to carry into effect that which lies already in the nature of things? Why do we trouble to make all these analyses, if we are not going to turn them to account? Study men's motives, and try to change them! "There is no such thing as a disinterested action. The prompting to every action comes from the self." When Herndon tries to confute this, the elder man piles reason upon reason until the younger man concedes the point. No wonder that Herndon should be one of those radical abolitionists who want to make an end of slavery at a single blow, whereas Lincoln is among those who are glad if they can prevent any extension of the evil. Herndon is an idealist, Lincoln is a skeptic. The former believes that we can force on the coming of a better world; the latter knows that none of us can master destiny. That is why, though he has such broad sympathies and so kind a heart, he shows a crystal clarity in his actions, and has been called cold.

"Lincoln looked upon things as fixed, rather than as in motion. With a mind free from illusions, he ground the inexact, the pretentious, and the false, to powder; nothing was to remain hazy in out-

line, the lens with which he examined things was always accurately
focused. . . . All his great qualities were swayed by the despotism of his logic."

Only through this unceasing interaction between kindliness and
skepticism, only through such a balance between clarity and sympathy, could there gradually develop a statesman who, on the
devious paths of party politics, could stride slowly forward toward
one of the great goals of mankind.

VIII

For a while, the struggle had almost ceased to rage; but now, of
a sudden, it was clamorously resumed.

Eighty years before, when the Union had been founded, it had
been impossible to persuade the gentlemen of the South to send all
their Negro slaves back to Africa. They were under the spell of
traditional prejudices; they owed their wealth to their privileged
position; and if they accommodated themselves to the high-flown
and uncongenial principles of the North, they did so only because
and only in so far as it was to their interest to do so. Those of the
fathers of the country who had come from the South, being among
the few Southerners who had shaken off the traditions of their caste,
had to content themselves with reducing the numbers of their own
slaves, with improving the treatment of these, and with freeing
some of them.

In the new century, the oppositions between North and South
had become intensified. Beginning, as that century did, a new kind
of enslavement, the enslavement of human beings to machines, it
thereby cheapened commodities, generalized their use, and supplied
the poor with substitutes for some of the advantages enjoyed by
the rich. This machine development narrowed the gulf between
master class and servile class, and introduced an aspiring class
between the two. At the same time, it multiplied a hundredfold the
output of cotton goods, in which the new millions were clothed —
but these new millions had no inclination for the work of planting
and harvesting cotton in a sub-tropical climate. Thus it was that,

at the very time when the demand for universal equality was echoing around the world, and when the slaves were being urged to break their chains, the labor of the Southern Negroes became more indispensable than ever.

Why did not the masters themselves free the slaves? They were afraid to do so, and they believed that slavery served their interests best. Who would voluntarily pay for work, when he could get it done for nothing? Would a farmer hire a laborer to do a job which an ox could do just as well? The hundreds of Negroes a Southern planter owned, being fecund, spontaneously replaced those whom death claimed. But what would these hordes have done to their masters, if one day their chains had been struck off, if the overseer's whip and pistol had been laid aside, and if they had been told they were free in the name of humanity? Would the Christianity so laboriously implanted in them make them gentle, make them show loving kindness towards their sometime lords? Nay, they would devastate the cotton fields, break their working utensils, stave in the whisky vats, storm the arsenals, tear the overseers limb from limb, shoot the white men, and rape the white women. There was no help in abolition. Patience was the only help, prevention of the import of slaves, restriction of slavery to the States where it was already established and seemed to be needed. If the malady could be confined to outlying organs, there was no grave danger to life, as there would be if it invaded the central regions. Such was the compromise which circumstances forced on the grandsons of the men who had succeeded in establishing the Union, despite this internal contradiction. Had the South contented itself with its freedom to go on living in the old way, cotton might still be grown there by slave labor — just as elsewhere, to-day, there are mines in which Negroes, ostensibly "free" and paid a wage, are for practical purposes kept, under contract, in a slave status.

But the North went on growing. Men, money, the forces of production, new machinery and new thoughts combined within a few decades to produce a far-flung strength which threatened and ultimately overcame the dominance of the South. The sound of the

pioneers' axes cutting new roads toward the West wakened alarm
and then defiance in the minds of the Southern magnates; and they
began to realize that since they would soon be outnumbered by this
peripheral growth, they must at least do their utmost to maintain
a majority at the center of things in Washington. The opening
of innumerable fresh channels for labor; the perpetual influx of
Europeans who turned forests into fields, prairies into meadows,
thickets into towns; the awakening of the land from its millennial
sleep; the compulsion that was put upon it to disgorge gold and
silver, iron and lead — all the growth of the new West — were a
nightmare to the South, for these changes were wrought by white
hands. Every new cell built into the united honeycomb to enrich
the hive was a white cell, and therefore a menace to the supremacy
of the black ones. The Southern lords felt they must bestir themselves if they were to retain the upper hand in Washington; and
they knew that if they lost their dominant position there, the institution of slavery was doomed.

What was the best way of enforcing their will on the North? A
threat of secession! Cuba and Central America were close at
hand. Like the Southern States, but yet more tropical, and therefore even more athirst for Negro labor. Surely England would
protect those who should gainsay the rebellion of the eighteenth
century, thanks to which the American colonies had cut adrift from
the mother land? Would not England look favorably on those who
should weaken the Union by seceding? If the grandsons of the
rebels of 1776 were to break loose from their Northern cousins, might
they not expect to be rewarded? Of course no one would try to
deprive them of their freedom, but the weakened North would be
given pause in its victorious progress. Perhaps by intervention,
certainly by economic measures, it would be compelled to make to
Europe the concessions it was now unwilling to grant.

In this perplexing situation, the North was prepared to compromise. The first arrangement was that, after Missouri, no new slave
State was to be founded, north of the line 36° and 30′ extended westward from Missouri. Thereafter the South and the North strove
to preserve the balance between the sections by the admission of

States in pairs, and this policy continued until a new crisis was caused by the imminent exhaustion of Southern territory out of which to create new slave States. Subsequently, by yet another compromise for which the famous Whig statesman, Henry Clay, was responsible, an arrangement was made for solving the slavery issue in the territory acquired from Mexico, by allowing California to be admitted as a free State. Yet at the same time, by an additional concession to the South, the law for the capture and return of runaway slaves was strengthened. Thereby, the principle that a slave was a chattel and not a person was made valid even into the farthest limits of the North, with the result that those in whom the anti-slavery spirit was active were up in arms. It was monstrous, they said, that every citizen should be under the obligation of arresting a runaway Negro he might happen to meet in the high road, and should be tempted to become a slave hunter by the offer of a ten-dollar reward for every runaway.

Moderate men, of course, held a position somewhere between two extremes. Clay and Webster, the most sagacious leaders of the nation, raised warning voices in Congress; and Lincoln, reading the reports of their speeches, must have echoed their sentiments in his heart. Clay, now an old man, foreseeing the most terrible danger the twentieth century would hold for the United States, declared boldly that the Negroes must be sent back to Africa. The mixing of blood, the birth of innumerable mulattoes and other crosses between blacks and whites, was the peril. As some one then wrote: "The blood of our race flows in the veins of thousands who are bought and sold as beasts of burden." Yet at the same time Clay told the abolitionists that such impassioned propaganda as that of "Uncle Tom's Cabin" (now making a great noise in the world) could serve only to exasperate the South.

At this juncture was heard the voice of one saying, as against Douglas, "There is a higher law than the Constitution!" The speaker was Seward, who, a decade later, was to be so closely connected with Lincoln.

IX

Destiny was getting to work through two individual men. A senator wished to become President, and a slave wished to become free. The senator was named Douglas. Having calculated his chances, he secured the passage of a law which was to make him popular. In due course, however, it led to confusion, broke up his party, brought about the formation of a new one, and ultimately insured the victory of this latter. The slave was named Dred Scott. Suing for his freedom, on the ground that his master had taken him for a time into a free State, he won his case in the court of first instance; but, on an appeal, this decision was reversed by the Supreme Court in 1857, the whole country being convulsed about the matter. Both men failed to achieve their end. The senator did not become President, and the slave did not become free. The Union, however, after a decade of fierce internal struggles, including four years of civil war, emerged from the great crisis intact. By then, the senator was dead; the slave, if still living, had become free, together with millions of his black brethren.

Meantime, in 1854, with the presidential election due in two years, Douglas, the most influential and most popular of the Democrats, was steering towards his goal. This could only be reached with Southern aid, and he could only win the South by favoring the extension of slavery into the new territories. A year before, indeed, he had referred to the Missouri Compromise as sacrosanct. But now, when he practically held the position of Southern envoy to the North, and was at the same time representative of the thousands of Northern Democrats whose main desire was that the vexatious question of slavery should not be a cause of interference with business, the formation of two new States gave him an opportunity for a decisive change of policy.

Kansas and Nebraska were still in the condition of those early embryos whose sex is not yet determined. Situated northward of the dividing line fixed by the Missouri Compromise, and therefore by the terms of that compromise to be inaugurated as States in which slavery was prohibited, they were now besieged by both

parties with appeals to decide (as the case might be) in favor of or
against slavery — for North and South were equally interested
in securing the new senatorial votes. Douglas, as chairman of the
committee on the Kansas-Nebraska question, was on the lookout
for some way of settling the difficulty which would not raise him up
enemies either in the North or in the South. He declared that to
tie the hands of a new State was opposed to the spirit of the Constitution, whose basic principle was the sovereignty of the people.
In accordance with this principle, the citizens of each State had
a right to draft its constitution as they pleased, and to decide for
themselves whether they would or would not permit slaveholding
within their borders. A generation before, Calhoun had said that
one had just as little right to forbid a man to take his slave with him
into another State, as to forbid him taking his cattle, his furniture,
or his walking-stick. It was not the object of the Kansas-Nebraska
Bill, said Douglas, either to introduce slavery into any new State,
or to prohibit its introduction there. The inhabitants of the new
State were to be left perfectly free to arrange their own domestic
affairs as they pleased, subject to the general provisions of the
United States Constitution. Of late years the rights of citizens in
this respect had been restricted; now full rights were to be restored.

The Kansas-Nebraska Bill, very cleverly drafted by Douglas,
was ostensibly based on Clay's last compromise in the matter of
fugitive slaves, seeming merely to develop this a stage further.
It was an appeal to the Whigs, in so far as Douglas professed to be
following in the footsteps of the great Whig leader, recently deceased; to the Northerners, since it was believed that the majority
in Kansas was opposed to slavery; to the Southerners, who might
hope by promoting immigration from the South to turn the Kansas
vote the other way. By shrewd management, Douglas was able
to obtain the passage of the bill through both houses, but it had a
stormy time. Its first passage of the Senate, by a majority of
three to one in the small hours of the morning, was announced in
Washington by a salvo of artillery. In truth, these were the first
shots of the Civil War, though the actual fighting was not to begin
till seven years later.

For the nation answered with an outburst of indignation such as had not been known since the foundation of the Union. Thanks to the cleverness of an ambitious senator, people found themselves suddenly confronted with the fact that henceforward any new State could introduce slavery. Douglas, who had secured the passage of this law, played the martyr, exclaiming, "Fanatics will attack me and rail against me; many of those who used to have confidence in me, will come to hate me; I shall be hanged in effigy!"

The voting in Kansas reflected the general excitement. By climate and soil, that Territory, which the South hoped to organize as a slave, and the North as a free State, was suited for colonization by white men, rather than for cultivation by slave labor; yet when the enumeration of 1855 was taken, the settlers from the South had a majority of several hundred in a total of about eight thousand. The Emigrant Aid Company of Massachusetts, and other similar societies elsewhere in the North, expended considerable sums to promote the colonization of Kansas by anti-slavery families. The number of these emigrants were not many, but their influence was extensive. From the South, also, came bands of emigrants to maintain the pro-slavery majority. There was intense excitement in Kansas and in the adjacent State of Missouri when the Territorial Legislature was elected in March. Hundreds, perhaps thousands of swashbucklers crossed the border from western Missouri, and cast illegal ballots for the pro-slavery candidates. A spark at any moment might produce a conflagration, and ere long events occurred to set off the explosion which made "Bleeding Kansas" the leading topic of discussion throughout the nation. Wrong was done by both the Free State Party and the Law and Order Party, so called. The "border ruffians", as Horace Greeley named them, ravaged the country. Murders took place from time to time, and one or two outrageous atrocities. But a great tide of immigration set in from the North which soon overturned the numerical superiority of the Southern party.

This upshot was a blow to Douglas as well as to his party. His senatorial term had just expired, and it was essential he should go

to Illinois on a campaign to secure his reëlection as senator by the
local legislature. In this wide-flung State, extending from the
Great Lakes in the north to the Kentucky border in the south,
there were two traditions, a Northern and a Southern, and the net
result of Douglas' duplicity had been to offend them both. He had
never expected so violent a reaction. Many Northern newspapers
were raging against him, were ruthlessly exposing his secret motive,
his presidential ambitions. They railed against him as a mon-
strosity, a Northerner with a Southern heart. Still, he must make
the venture.

When he reached Chicago, he found that boat flags had been
half-masted; and in the evening, when he was to speak at a great
meeting, the church bells were tolling as if for a funeral. Eight
thousand excited people were packed to hear him in the great
square. He was fiercely heckled, lost patience, answered back
angrily, in a way that led to brawls between the furious multitude
and the small minority of his supporters. He stood there dumbfounded, face flushed, brows knitted, fists clenched. "You have
entered into a conspiracy with the South," shouted the crowd.
He could not make himself heard; he was howled down. After
facing the storm for two hours, at midnight he looked at his watch,
and yelled :

"It is now Sunday morning — I'll go to church, and you may go
to hell !"

In continuance of his oratorical campaign, Douglas made his
way to Springfield, and spoke there for three hours in the State
House, getting a far more patient hearing than at Chicago. Towards
the end of his speech, he said, "I hear that Mr. Lincoln of this town
wishes to answer me. I hope that he will do so."

Taking up the challenge, Lincoln next day made a four-hour
speech against the Kansas-Nebraska Bill, and against slavery.
The response was deep, rather than loud, but Lincoln had made his
first great speech. Among the auditors was Douglas, who said at
the close, "My friend Mr. Lincoln has asked me to listen to him
and to reply. I thank him for his courteous challenge."

This first duel remained indecisive.

X

Thirteen years earlier, Lincoln, on a Mississippi voyage, had written to Speed's sister:

"By the way, a fine example was presented on board the boat for contemplating the effect of condition upon human happiness. A gentleman had purchased twelve Negroes in different parts of Kentucky, and was taking them to a farm in the South. They were chained six and six together. A small iron clevis was around the left wrist of each, and this fastened to the main chain by a shorter one, at a convenient distance from the others, so that the Negroes were strung together precisely like so many fish upon a trot-line. In this condition, they were being separated forever from the scenes of their childhood, their friends, their fathers and mothers, and brothers and sisters, and many of them from their wives and children, and going into perpetual slavery, where the lash of the master is proverbially more ruthless and unrelenting than any other where; and yet, amid all these distressing circumstances, as we would think them, they were the most cheerful and apparently happy creatures on board. One, whose offense for which he had been sold was an over-fondness for his wife, played the fiddle almost continually, and the others danced, sang, cracked jokes, and played various games with cards from day to day. How true it is that 'God tempers the wind to the shorn lamb', or, in other words, that He renders the worst of human conditions tolerable, while He permits the best to be nothing better than tolerable."

Such is Lincoln's voice when he is letting his imagination run lightly over the great themes, and when, with the skepticism of wisdom, he is pondering the limitations of his aims, and the relativity of the human happiness for which he would gladly fight. His fondness for parable, and his faculty for entering into other people's minds, must make this experience memorable to him; but it does not upset the fixity of his purpose. True, many years before, he had been deeply moved at the sight of the nude mulatto girl, exposed to the covetous glances of the buyers and trembling before the threat of the slave-dealer's whip; but he is no longer a young man, and his own and others' experience has taught him that white folk, too, have grievous troubles, and that the heart can be sorely wounded, no matter what the tint of the skin beneath which it beats. What drives him onward is the sense of human dignity that was outraged as he watched those slaves making light of their troubles on board the steamer. When he described the incident at that time, his tone was lyrical; now it has become more forcible, more virile, when, at the age of forty-six, he makes the following answer to his old friend, Joshua Speed, who has been defending himself for being a slave owner.

"You know I dislike slavery, and you fully admit the abstract wrong of it. So far, there is no cause of difference. But you say that sooner than yield your legal rights to the slaves, especially at the bidding of those who are not themselves interested, you would see the Union dissolved. I am not aware that any one is bidding you yield that right; very certainly I am not. I confess I hate to see the poor creatures hunted down and caught and carried back to their stripes and unrequited toil; but I bite my lips and keep quiet. In 1841, you and I had together a tedious low-water trip on a steamboat from Louisville to St. Louis. You may remember, as well as I do, that from Louisville to the mouth of the Ohio there were on board ten or a dozen slaves shackled together with irons. That sight was a continued torment to me; and I see something like it every time I touch the Ohio or any other slave border. It is not fair for you to assume that I have no interest in a thing which has, and continually exercises, the power of making me miserable. . . . I do oppose the extension of slavery because my judgment and feelings so prompt me, and I am under no obligations to the contrary. If for this you and I must differ, differ we must. You say, if you were President, you would send an army and hang the leaders of the Missouri outrages upon the Kansas election; still, if Kansas fairly votes herself a slave State, she must be admitted or the Union must be dissolved. You say that if Kansas fairly votes herself a free State, as a Christian you will rejoice at it. All decent slaveholders talk that way, and I do not doubt their candor. But they never vote that way. . . . Our progress in degeneracy appears to me to be pretty rapid. As a nation we began by declaring that 'all men are created equal.' We now practically read in 'all men are created equal, except negroes.' When the Know-Nothings get control, it will read 'all men are created equal, except negroes and foreigners and Catholics.' When it comes to this, I shall prefer emigrating to some country where they make no pretence of loving liberty, — to Russia, for instance, where despotism can be taken pure, without the base alloy of hypocrisy."

Judgment and feeling prompt him, says Lincoln; but when, as here, he is trying to convince an old friend, as later he tries to convince the myriads, he restrains his feelings lest he should himself be carried away, and should affront instead of convince. Feeling, no doubt, prompts him to action; memories of his own harsh experiences as a poor white; memories of the many reverses he and his forefathers had to suffer; and (who can doubt it?) at times the imprint left on his imagination by the shadowy figure of that Southern gentleman who had been one of his grandfathers, and had left a poor girl to face her trouble alone. But when now, after long years, he again seems to hear the rattling of the chains which those slaves had worn on the Mississippi steamboat, he has forgotten the fiddle-playing and the singing; and the heart of the Northerner who lives far away from slave States is filled with anger rather than sympathy. The voice of mankind is calling to him.

Head and heart are joint factors of the craving for justice which is so powerful that at times we are tempted to think Lincoln was less concerned to liberate the black than he was to make the white humane. Indeed, he once said as much in plain terms, declaring that if he could be sure that no free man could any longer be a slave owner, this would mean more to him than that no slave could any longer be a slave. To that ideal of justice he is ready to sacrifice everything he wishes and every one he loves. Douglas' bill having become law, law it is, and Kansas can in due form of law declare itself a slave State. If Speed defends slavery, he and Lincoln must part company, though Speed is his oldest and best friend. There has begun in Lincoln's inner self that conflict which will lead him on to momentous decisions. Which does he love more, liberty or his country? He does not allow any phrases to obscure the clarity of mind which makes him a critic of his homeland, for at about the same date he writes:

"When we freed ourselves from political slavery to King George, we said the principle 'all men were created equal' was an immanent truth. Now, when we are full fed, and have no fear of being made slaves again ourselves, we have become so greedy to be masters that we declare the very reverse of this maxim to be an immanent truth. . . . The tsar of the Russias would be readier to take off his crown and declare all his subjects free, than our American gentlemen would be to set their slaves at liberty."

Within a few years, the Tsar of all the Russias was to free the serfs, thus doing what Lincoln thought so unlikely, for a new wind was blowing across Europe, and what the New World had learned from the Old as a theory and had first carried to practice, reacted on the Old World and revolutionized it.

That same new spirit breathes through Lincoln's speeches when he leaves the main topic of slavery to voice his class feelings where the whites are concerned. Large farms, he tells the farmers, are unpractical; just as a weapon or a tool can be too heavy. He goes on to show why, in the United States, no one need spend his whole life as a day laborer. He continues, "Labor is prior to and independent of capital. In fact, capital is the fruit of labor, and could never have existed unless labor had first existed. Labor can exist without capital, but capital could never have existed without labor. Hence, labor is the superior — greatly the superior — of capital."

He unmasks, also, the love of ostentation which makes the slave owners defend slavery. A man who owns many Negroes can parade his wealth far more easily than a man who simply owns much land. He did not forget what a Kentuckian had once said to him:

"You might have any amount of land, money in your pocket, or bank stock, and, while traveling around, nobody would be any wiser; but if you had a darky trudging at your heels, everybody would see him and know you owned a slave. It is the most glittering property in the world. If a young man goes courting, the only inquiry is how many negroes he or she owns. Slave ownership betokens not only the possession of wealth, but indicates the gentleman of leisure, who is above labor and scorns labor."

A man who feels thus keenly, wants to act; but Lincoln was averse to hurried action; he and his friends hesitated long before they would use force. He was not an abolitionist of Herndon's type, much as Herndon would have liked him to be. To a physical-force abolitionist, he said, "In a democracy, where the majority rule by the ballot through the forms of law, these physical rebellions and bloody resistances are radically wrong, unconstitutional, and are treason. . . . Revolutionize through the ballot box."

None the less, he acts. Whereas most of his colleagues refused to defend a Negro, he was counsel in a number of such trials, regardless of the sneers of "society people." One case was that of a young colored man, the son of a free colored woman in Springfield. He had gone to New Orleans as one of the crew of a Mississippi steamboat. Not having the requisite papers, he was arrested there, and was kept in prison until after his boat had left. He was liable to be sold into slavery to defray prison expenses. The mother appealed to Lincoln for help. Lincoln tried to induce, first the governor of Illinois, and then the governor of Louisiana, to intercede; but both refused to move. The times were critical, and they were disinclined to face trouble for the sake of a mulatto boy. Lincoln circulated a subscription list, and raised enough money to pay the prison charges and bring the lad back safely to the North.

XI

The Douglas affair had done even more than Mary's urgings to revive Lincoln's repressed ambition after the lapse of five years. He decided to run for the Senate. The restlessness inspired by the feeling that he could make a better job of it than his rival, the belief that Douglas was animated by self-seeking, the long-standing awareness of the conflict between their characters — these things, in conjunction with the politician's natural desire to take advantage

LINCOLN IN 1857

From an ambrotype made by Alschuler, Urbana, Illinois

of the weakness of Douglas' present position, induced him to come forward as a candidate. He described his opponent privately as "the most dangerous enemy of liberty, because the most insidious one"; and he said, "You can't overturn a pyramid, but you can undermine it; that's what I've been trying to do." He was full of hope and confidence, writing that he had a very good chance, and doing his best to enlist the support of influential people.

Mary was filled with enthusiasm. To become a senator's wife would repay her for all these dull years of waiting. She could already fancy herself in Washington, in a position much more important than that of a congressman's wife, so she naturally did her utmost to promote his election. What a pity Lincoln was not a Democrat! She could never quite get over her regret that he did not belong to what seemed to her the more gentlemanly party. Writing to her sister, she made excuses for him:

"You must not include him with so many of those who belong to that party, an Abolitionist. In principle he is far from it. All he desires is that slavery shall not be extended, let it remain where it is. My weak woman's heart was too Southern in feeling to sympathize with any but Fillmore. I have always been a great admirer of his. . . . If some of you Kentuckians had to deal with the wild Irish, as we housekeepers are sometimes called upon to do, the South would certainly elect Fillmore next time."

Mary's present utterance concerning servants is akin to her former utterances concerning slaves. Authoritative by temperament, she sighs at her troubles with the "wild Irish." Just as, in her own household, this woman would like to rule unchallenged over things and over men, just as the outlook of the master comes naturally to this lady from a slave State, so is it with her relatives and with the worthy Speed in Kentucky, who may be supposed to treat their slaves better than do the cotton-growing aristocrats of the South, but find them absolutely essential to their comfort.

Lincoln has now to devote considerable attention to party matters, and has become as clever as any professional politician in the minor manipulations of the trade. When the conservative *Journal* of Springfield wins too much influence, he determines to undermine this. He succeeds in "planting" on the simple-minded editor an apologia for slavery published by one of the Southern newspapers, and suggests its reprint in pamphlet form. This ruins the prestige of the *Journal*, which loses so many subscribers that it has to cease publication.

The Whigs really do not know how far their influence extends, for here in Illinois, as elsewhere, half of the Democrats are forming front against Douglas, and are voting against slavery, thus favoring Lincoln's chances of the senatorship. But, at the eleventh hour, the shrewd Democrats put forward another candidate, Trumbull, opposed to slavery, and one of Lincoln's close friends. This leads to Lincoln's defeat, greatly to the wrath of Mary, who is in the gallery of the legislature while the voting is taking place.

Lincoln speedily reacted from the depression of this reverse, writing to a friend next day: "I regret my defeat moderately, but am not nervous about it."

Matters ripened as the time for the presidential election drew near. While the Democrats, though to outward appearance they still formed a compact body, were inwardly disunited, the Whig party actually broke up, and it was decided to form a new party. The discontented Democrats who were known as the "Free Soilers" and the anti-slavery section of the Whigs joined forces, animated by the approval (expressed in both prose and in verse) of some of the best-known men in America. Calling themselves Republicans, in honor of Jefferson who had been Lincoln's exemplar for twenty years, they got together at Philadelphia, and chose as presidential candidate John C. Frémont, pathfinder and pioneer, who in age and appearance, in record and in views, was the best possible counterpart to old Buchanan, the Democrats' nominee.

In his own State of Illinois, Lincoln was naturally to the fore in the foundation of the new party. Indeed, there was some feeling that it was in large measure his creation, so that even at Philadelphia, where he was personally unknown, he secured a large number of votes for the vice-presidential nomination. His destiny was, indeed, working itself out. The abandonment of the Missouri Compromise and the passage of the Kansas-Nebraska Bill had been the outcome of Douglas' ambition; thence had arisen the crisis in the Democratic Party, leading to the formation of the Republican Party; and the burden of the new party was being to a considerable extent upborne by Lincoln's strong shoulders. It was natural, therefore, that he should wield considerable influence in its councils and secure widespread support, as had been shown in Decatur, where the constituent committee of the party recommended him as candidate for the governorship of Illinois.

Every one knew that this would be a step towards the presidency. He promptly declined the recommendation, saying, "If I were chosen, the Democrats would say we were only trying to put new life into the old body of the Whigs; I should be elected as a Whig, and our new ideas would come to nothing." He recommended, as alternative, a man whose nomination would bring over a great many Democrats to their side. The old diffidence, the old caution; but in the mixture of motives prudence now took the lead over modesty, for there are many indications that his self-confidence was growing throughout this year.

In the crucible of the new party very various ingredients were to be smelted together. It included outspokenly abolitionist elements, like Herndon, now mayor of Springfield. When Herndon called a meeting of those in Sangamon County who favored "the policy of Washington and Jefferson", to select delegates for a convention to be held at Bloomington, he included Lincoln's name among the summoners of the convention, without consulting his partner, who was absent on circuit. Some of Lincoln's old Whig friends disapproved, so Herndon wrote to Lincoln for an endorsement. Lincoln replied: "All right; go ahead. Will meet you — radicals and all." Thus did Lincoln declare himself a Republican.

In Bloomington, at this first Republican State Convention of Illinois, he delivered a unifying speech, a masterpiece of passion and shrewdness, diplomacy and conviction, designed to supply a common platform for those who had hitherto been representatives of three conflicting tendencies. For a remarkable reason, there is no detailed report of this speech. A few minutes after the orator had begun, the reporters dropped their pencils and devoted themselves to listening with breathless attention. Eyewitnesses say that Lincoln had the appearance of a man who is approaching a crisis in his life. He began hesitatingly, with suppressed emotion, but grew vigorous and impassioned as he went on. As he moved slowly toward the front of the platform, eyes flashing, he seemed to the audience to grow taller and taller; once, indeed, he increased his great height yet further by rising on tiptoe, and a member of the audience said afterwards: "At this moment he looked to me the handsomest man I had ever seen in my life."

The reason for this excitement was the rapid advance, in the South, of a movement tending towards secession from the Union. Lincoln was aware of the imminence of this danger; he dreaded the consequences; and he earnestly desired to prevent the disaster. Clay and Webster, whom he took as his models, had long since prophesied that civil war would be the upshot of an agitation for the freeing of the slaves. Here Lincoln spoke more of the Union than of slavery. He strove to warn rather than to convince. The phrasing of his speech was perfectly simple; but the battle-ground seemed to have been transferred from an economic and moral question to the very fundamentals of existence. The audience heard the rumble of the coming thunderstorm, and the pleasure of their applause was mingled with alarm. At the climax, apostrophizing invisible adversaries, Lincoln exclaimed, "We won't go out of the Union, and you sha'n't!"

The fame of this speech soon spread throughout Illinois. No detailed reports were available, but those who had heard it declared that the speaker was ripening for the presidential chair.

XII

Buchanan was elected President. Once more the Democrats had been victorious, but a third of their votes had been transferred to the new party. Some of the leading spirits of the nation had fought on the side of the Republicans. Emerson, Motley, and Longfellow had refrained from a proposed European tour in order to vote against slavery. The leaders of the Republicans in the new

Senate were Chase, author of an anti-slavery proclamation, a young
and resolute man, of a lively temperament, and Seward, ambitious
but thoroughly trustworthy, a lover of mankind, but too much of
an optimist to escape disappointments. In contrast with the old
leaders, these two men had always strongly advocated the continuance of the Missouri Compromise.

But the most notable of them all, a man of swiftly moving intelligence, was Sumner, likewise a senator, professor of law at Harvard,
who had as a young man studied for three years in Europe. He
was fearless, ardent, and, like Lincoln, endowed with a keen sense
of justice. In the Senate, during the debate on the Kansas affair
at the time when excitement about the election in that State was
at its height and a senator took the floor with a pair of cavalry
pistols buckled round his waist, Sumner denounced the Kansas-
Nebraska Bill as a swindle, and held Senator Butler, of South
Carolina, up to the scorn of the world. Two days later, Brooks,
a relative of Butler, attacked Sumner as he sat writing at his desk
in the Senate chamber, and beat him brutally over the head with a
cane, so that he fell unconscious to the floor. Sumner's health was
for years seriously impaired by this outrage.

The attack on Sumner was, in fact, the first blow struck in the
Civil War. By the champions of the South, Brooks was acclaimed
as a hero. A number of students clubbed together and presented
him with a gold-headed cane. The Northerners were scoffed at
as cowards, because no one issued a challenge against Brooks.
In reply, the men of the North spoke sarcastically about the honor
of Southern gentlemen, and mocked at their readiness to use pistols
as well as bludgeons. The whole country was convulsed with
excitement, and every one took sides with Sumner or with his
assailant.

A final decision of the Supreme Court, during these days, added
fuel to the flames. A Southern gentleman had migrated to one
of the northwestern States, taking his slaves with him. One of
these, more intelligent than his master knew, and aware that he
was north of the Missouri Compromise line, claimed freedom for
himself and his family, taking the case through one court after

another, up to the Supreme Court. Taney, the chief justice, was a learned and venerable man, one of the pillars of the nation. But the air of Washington, the prevailing opinion of the society in which he moved, the ruling-class mentality of the Southern slave owners, and to some extent, no doubt, party feeling, influenced Taney and other justices of the Supreme Court, men appointed for life, but pledged to guard the Constitution as if it had been a sacred flame. They decided that a Negro slave was not entitled to sue in the United States courts, and that neither Congress nor a local legislature could forbid any one to take back his slave from a free State to a slave State.

To understand the excitement that this decision aroused, it must be remembered how widespread was the feeling that Dred Scott, a solitary figure, was the representative of millions of slaves. It must also be remembered that, in a pamphlet issued not long before, Dred Scott's plea in the District Court of St. Louis had been voiced for him in the following terms:

"The judge said that, according to these laws, while I was in Illinois and Wisconsin, I was a free man — just as good as my master — and that I had as much right to make a slave of a white man, as a white man to make a slave of me.

"I was sorry nobody ever told me that while I was there. Yet I was glad to hear the judge talk so, for I thought he would set me free.

"But, after a little while, the judge said that as soon as my master got me back this side of the line of Missouri, my right to be free was gone; and that I and my wife and my children became nothing but so many pieces of property.

"I thought it hard that white men should draw a line of their own on the face of the earth, on one side of which a black man was to become no man at all, and never say a word to the black man about it until they had got him on that side of the line. So I appealed to the Supreme Court of the United States.

"My fellow-men, can any of you help me in my day of trial? Will nobody speak for me at Washington, even without hope of other reward than the blessings of a poor black man and his family?

I do not know. I can only pray that some good heart will be moved by pity to do that for me which I cannot do for myself; and that if the right is on my side, it may be so declared by the high court to which I have appealed."

Thus the voice of this lone Negro had echoed through the United States, touching the hearts of men. But the answer to the appeal was the decision of Taney and his colleagues, just quoted.

If the highest judges in the land protected slavery, the program of the new political party was unconstitutional. The North was furious; the South exulted, and expressed its firm intention to secede unless the Northerners bowed before the decision of the Supreme Court.

A fresh cause of turmoil came when the new constitution of Kansas reached Washington. This Lecompton Constitution was entirely the product of the advocates of slavery, for the Free State men had refrained from going to the polls to elect delegates to the constitutional convention. The debate filled many weeks in Congress. It was over one salient feature of this constitution that Douglas broke with President Buchanan. In the end, after a long deadlock between the Senate and the House, a compromise bill, which gave the people of Kansas a chance to vote on the new constitution in its entirety, but with the confident expectation that they would repudiate the instrument, mustered enough votes to pass both Houses.

Two lightning flashes had clarified the situation. With one exception, all the leaders knew exactly where they stood. The exception was Douglas, whose position had now become extremely complicated. He had been the great champion of State sovereignty. How was he going to reconcile that championship with the Dred Scott decision, and with the coercion that had been exercised upon Kansas? How could he at one and the same time, in the ensuing year, placate the Illinois voters upon whom he depended for his reëlection to the Senate, and satisfy the Southerners to whom he must look subsequently to send him to the presidential chair? After all, the matter of the Negro was not of such pressing importance; but the blow against Kansas could not be justified. Deciding that the Northern voters were more important to him for the moment, he voted against a slave State constitution for Kansas. Feeling that a defeat in the senatorial election would wreck his future, he hastened back to Illinois.

At this juncture came an unexpected offer, whose acceptance would have required more youth than was left to Douglas and more courage than he had ever possessed. Since the line he had taken upon the Kansas question had to some extent estranged him from the Democrats, it seemed to the Republicans that there might be a chance of attracting this man of outstanding talent and reputation to their service. Horace Greeley (editor of the *New York Tribune* and the most influential journalist of the North), Seward, and some of the New England leaders, wishing to conciliate as many sides as possible, hoped that under Douglas' leadership they could win. With Douglas at their head, too, it would be easier for them to keep in touch with the South, to accommodate matters in a way which seemed essential to the business affairs, the repose, nay, the very existence of the Union. Greeley, especially, considered the line that was being taken by the Republicans unduly sentimental. He wanted what he called a practical policy; and he advised his readers in Illinois to vote for Douglas, hoping thereby to win over Douglas to the Republicans.

Thereupon, for the first time, Lincoln took a strong line. As leader of the left wing of the Republicans in Illinois, he insisted that such machinations were a danger to the integrity of the newly formed party.

"Greeley does me an injustice. I am a true Republican, and have always stood in the forefront of the battle. Now he is negotiating with Douglas, the typical compromiser, at one time the tool of the South, and now opposed to the South. This is the man he is trying to put in our front line. . . . He thinks Douglas' superior position, reputation, experience, and ability, if you please, would more than compensate for his lack of pure Republican position, and therefore his reëlection to the general cause of Republicanism would do more good than would the election of any one of our better undistinguished pure Republicans. What does the *New York Tribune* mean by its constant eulogizing, and admiring, and

magnifying Douglas? Does it, in this, speak the sentiments of
the Republicans at Washington? Have they concluded that the
Republican cause, generally, can be best promoted by sacrificing
us here in Illinois? If so, we would like to know it soon; it will
save us a great deal of labor to surrender at once. As yet, I have
heard of no Republican here going over to Douglas; but if the
Tribune continues to din his praises into the ears of its five or
ten thousand Republican readers in Illinois, it is more than can be
hoped that all will stand firm. I am not complaining — I only
wish a fair understanding."

Here is a new Lincoln — a fighting Lincoln! He is indignant;
he feels that he is being unjustly sacrificed for the sake of a cunning
adversary. Doubtless these letters will go the round in Washington, and it will surprise a good many to learn of the temerity of this
tall lawyer in Springfield who ventures to measure swords with
Douglas. No one saw the anger that flamed up in the heart of the
man who had been waiting so long, when he found his old rival
represented as a sort of colleague, and one who was to be preferred
to himself. To have Douglas as an enemy was tolerable, and was
a spur to competition; to have Douglas ranking as a comrade and
a superior in the struggle against slavery roused Lincoln's ire.

Was the party in actual fact still young and inviolate? Was
it not already old enough to be rent with dissensions? The leaders
were quarreling one with another; were quarreling on personal
grounds rather than on grounds of principle. The new leader
had to send forth scouts, not to find out what the enemy was doing,
but simply in order to scrutinize the mood of his own adherents.
Herndon, his most trustworthy assistant and his most faithful
informant, now brought back disquieting news from the East.
Seward, it appeared, was jealous; Greeley was intriguing on his
behalf; two years after the presidential election, preparations
were already being made for the next. New York was suspicious
of Springfield; and Lincoln, who had just been nominated as candidate for the Senate, had to give proof that he was not intriguing
against Seward. "I have made no move as regards the nomination
for the next presidency, or as regards the governorship of Illinois,"

he writes. "Neither directly nor indirectly have I taken any steps in these matters. We must be careful to avoid having any unjust suspicions of one another."

XIII

His political career being thus uncertain, Lincoln was obliged to devote himself for the time being more assiduously to his law practice; and at this juncture, when his career as a lawyer was almost finished, he won several cases which greatly enhanced his fame, and thus reacted favorably on his position in the political struggle. His success in the suit of the Illinois Central Railroad had made his name known to thousands of the electors. Another famous case was a murder trial, in which socially prominent people of his town were involved. In a brawl, a young man had fatally stabbed another, and was tried for murder. The accused was the grandson of Peter Cartwright, who twenty years before had charged Lincoln with being no Christian. In the trial, Lincoln put the aged Cartwright in the witness box, and was able to elicit evidence which induced the jury to acquit the accused.

In the West of those days, deadly quarrels, as the outcome of drink and political animus, were still common. One day, Lincoln read in the newspaper an account of such a dispute during a drinking bout, as a sequel of which two young fellows were accused of murdering a third. One of these youths had been condemned to eight years' imprisonment; the other had still to be tried. The latter, said the newspaper report, was named Armstrong. Lincoln was startled. Could that be the son of Jack Armstrong, the friend of his youth?

In fancy, Lincoln sees himself as a young flatboatman, newly arrived at New Salem, wrestling with the village champion, Armstrong, and winning. He recalls how the vanquished wrestler had defended him against the angry villagers, how he and Armstrong had become fast friends, how Armstrong's house had sheltered him more than once in time of need; he pictures himself sitting beside the fire, rocking the baby's cradle. This was Duff Armstrong, now in danger of being hanged.

" Dear Mrs. Armstrong, I have just heard of your deep affliction, and the arrest of your son for murder. I can hardly believe that he can be capable of the crime alleged against him. It does not seem possible. I am anxious that he should be given a fair trial, at any rate; and gratitude for your long-continued kindness to me in adverse circumstances prompts me to offer my humble services gratuitously in his behalf. It will afford me an opportunity to requite, in a small degree, the favors I received at your hand, and that of your lamented husband, when your roof afforded me a grateful shelter, without money and without price."

A country lawyer is writing to a poor widow whom he has not seen for twenty years, recalling the hospitality of her simple home, and yet the words sound as if addressed to humanity at large, as if spoken in the voice of one who feels an eternal responsibility. There is no excess of sentiment. He deliberately minimizes the moral foundation of his offer; implies that if he gives his legal services gratuitously, it will only be repayment of the hospitality which had been so freely bestowed on him. Writing to a farmer's widow, he sets forth motives which she will readily understand; yet at the same time, he writes as her friend, and as a lover of mankind.

Nevertheless, as regards details, he showed great caution and knowledge of affairs in preparing his case. Since local feeling had been running high against Duff Armstrong, he asked for a change of venue and succeeded in getting the trial removed to Beardtown. Believing that young men would be more sympathetic than old towards a hot-blooded youth, he saw to it that, as far as possible, the members of the jury should be young. In his examination of the principal witness against the accused, Lincoln was able to show that this witness had an animus against Duff, whereas Duff had been no enemy of the man who was killed. This witness testified to having seen Armstrong strike his victim in the right eye with what appeared to be a slung-shot. This had been within the edge of a wood, at eleven o'clock at night. Lincoln asked the witness how he had been able to see so clearly.

"By the light of the moon."

Lincoln sent for an almanac, consulted it, and gave it back to the attendant. The proceedings continued. Examining a medical witness, Lincoln showed that both the injuries to the dead man's head might have been caused by the same blow; either by a fall, or by a blow struck by the other assailant. As to the slung-shot, which Armstrong was alleged to have used, another witness testified to having made this particular slung-shot, which had been in his possession on the day of the fight, and the day after had been thrown away by him at the place where it was found. Lincoln cut open the slung-shot, and showed that it had been made as the witness had sworn. When other evidence, less favorable to the accused, was being put in, his mother, who was in court, began to cry. Lincoln went up to her and said, "Be easy, Hannah. Duff will be freed before nightfall." She looked up at his long, stooping figure half incredulously, and yet hopefully.

He began his speech for the defense slowly and cautiously, dwelt on the conflicting character of the evidence, seemed to be feeling his way. But when he came to discuss the evidence of the chief witness who had testified to having seen the murderous attack by moonlight, he sent for the calendar once more, and showed that, at the hour named, the moon had not been high in the heavens but low in the western sky, within an hour of setting.

However, the main force of Lincoln's speech for the defence lay in his appeal to the sympathy of the jurors. He spoke of the youth of the accused, described what he had himself owed to the kindness and friendship of young Armstrong's parents, referred to the recently deceased father's determination to devote all his worldly goods to the defense of his son; referred to the hopeless plight of the widow if Duff should be taken from her. As he had promised Hannah Armstrong, the young man was acquitted before nightfall.

Naturally the tale of this case went the rounds at the time; and it was still contributing to his popularity long after his death. Strange, is it not, how the temptations and the opportunities, the puzzles and the tests, of fate come to the right person? A murder trial in which there was false witness, defended and won by any chance lawyer, might speedily have been forgotten; but that letter in which Lincoln announces his determination to intervene, the emotional impetus with which he takes up the matter even before the accused's innocence has become plain to him, in conjunction with the caution and versatility of the born orator, are as typical of the man as his general behavior on the slavery question. The way in which he saves an innocent man from the hangman's noose is closely akin to that in which, a few years later, he will liberate millions of human beings from slavery. He is guided by the practical idealism of one whose gaze is fixed on what is eternally right, but at the same time knows how to realize his aims in the hard world of reality. Such is Lincoln's way. He moves forward slowly, convincing his hearers by facts, and then suddenly exposing the weakness of his adversary; but he does not disclose the essential substratum of his feelings, regarding this as incommunicable and private; and in his public demonstration he almost always puts forward the brain as representative of the heart. Just as, before nightfall this day, he frees young Armstrong, so, in the end, before night closes in on his own life, he will free the slaves. In his wisdom and his sadness, in his justice and his growing power over his fellows, does he not remind us of the aging King Saul?

He seems to conceal the wonderful power that radiates from him, keeps in close touch with ordinary folk as of old, converses with all and sundry in the streets, sits chatting in the shops, asks questions and tells anecdotes; and yet he is, substantially, though secretly, a king. Notwithstanding, amid the multitude, he is lonely, very, very lonely, so he seeks and finds a young knight and companion. Ward Hill Lamon was nineteen years younger than Lincoln; a Southern dandy, with broad shoulders and finely modeled limbs; an aristocrat with black, carefully oiled hair and a small mustache; distinguished and frivolous; usually surrounded by wine bottles, horses, and women; and always enveloped in an atmosphere of music. A lawyer by profession, he had made Lincoln's acquaintance on circuit, and now became the elder man's representative in a small provincial town. The two had many talks together, though it is likely enough that these seldom turned on legal questions, and even less on politics, for the young man's leanings on the slavery problem were those of the class from which he sprang, that of the slaveholders of Virginia.

But Lamon was a great singer of sailor chanteys and coon songs; was a troubadour to match Lincoln the anecdotalist, a singer to match Lincoln the reflective. Separated though they might be in the world of politics, in that other world of song and story they were extraordinarily congenial, and would spend evening after evening together, until their colleagues wondered what Lincoln could find in common with a man whose store of learning was so scantily furnished, with one who ranked among those "gentlemen" who shared neither Lincoln's ideals nor his aims. But Saul knew well enough what he wanted of David. Deep called to deep; the poet in Lincoln to the poet in Lamon, whom Lincoln addressed by the familiar name of "Hill." When disheartened and overtired, when seized by one of those accesses of melancholy to which he was prone, Lincoln would ask the always cheerful Hill to take his banjo and sing some songs of the people and the prairie, merry or grave, tender or stirring. These melodious strains would gradually charm away the heaviness from Lincoln's heart, would make him forget for a while the great problem of his mission; and he, who drank no wine, never hunted women, neither gambled nor sang, would drift back in imagination into the domain of a rose-tinted youth — which, in reality, Lincoln had never known.

XIV

"A house divided against itself cannot stand!"

In the crowded hall at Springfield Lincoln thundered forth this Biblical aphorism, which sounded like a trumpet calling to war. It was part of a speech which, contrary to his usual custom, he had committed to writing beforehand, and had talked over with some of his friends. They had objected to this sentence in particular, as unwise. "But are you not on the side of the abolitionists?" Lincoln had asked them. For Douglas had come to Illinois, and his double-tongued utterances had roused Lincoln to the attack. He said what he had planned to say, and his hearers were startled. He went on, "I do not expect the house to fall; but I do expect it will cease to be divided. It will become all one thing, or all the other. . . . I believe this government cannot endure permanently half slave and half free." Then he challenged Douglas, who was absent, to say clearly, unambiguously, what he thought about Kansas and the Dred Scott decision; to say in plain terms whether he wanted to see slavery restricted or enlarged. None the less, he protested against the theories of those abolitionists who advocated forcible interference with any attempt to recapture runaway slaves; he insisted that the Dred Scott decision, though morally unjustified, was good in law, and could only be fought by legal methods.

At Chicago, two or three weeks later he spoke as follows: "I protest, now and for ever, against that counterfeit logic which presumes that because I did not want a negro woman for a slave, I do necessarily want her for a wife. My understanding is that I need not have her for either, but, as God made us separate, we can leave one another alone, and do one another much good thereby. There are white men enough to marry all the white women, and enough black men to marry all the black women; and in God's name let them be so married."

"The Divided House" speech inflamed the enthusiasm of his auditors, and the news of it spread like wildfire through the country. Lincoln understood the importance of this utterance. Rather pathetically he said, "If I had to draw a pen across my record, and erase my whole life from sight, and I had one poor gift or choice left as to what I should save from the wreck, I should choose that speech and leave it to the world unerased." The shadows of coming events were beginning to cast themselves into his mind, and by slow degrees he was growing aware of his position as a historical figure.

Nor did Douglas miss the historical significance of this address. He felt that a crisis was approaching, but, characteristically, he would fain have avoided an open duel. "I do not feel, between you and me, that I want to go into this debate. The whole country knows me, and has me measured. Lincoln, as regards myself, is comparatively unknown, and if he gets the best of this debate —

and I want to say he is the ablest man the Republicans have got —
I shall lose everything and Lincoln will gain everything. Should I
win, I shall gain but little. I do not want to go into a debate with
Lincoln."

In public, however, Douglas assumed another tone. Then he
represented Lincoln as one of the most conspicuous among the abolitionists. Lincoln's "Divided House" speech, said Douglas, was
manifestly designed to promote friction and separation, in defiance
of the will of half of those who dwelt in the house. Lincoln rejoined
that Douglas was twisting his utterances. "I expect to die, but I
am not eager to." Douglas answered patronizingly, "Mr. Lincoln
is a kind, amiable, intelligent gentleman"; and he went on mis-
quoting Lincoln's speeches.

Now Lincoln determined to do a thing that had never before been
done in American history : he challenged his opponent Douglas to an
oratorical duel : "Will it be agreeable to you to make an arrangement
for you and myself to divide time, and address the same audiences
in the present canvass? Mr. Judd, who will hand you this, is
authorized to receive your answer; and, if agreeable to you, to
enter into the terms of such arrangement." This was both bold
and shrewd, for in this way Lincoln would be able to get the ear of
Douglas' audiences. That prospect was far from agreeable to
Douglas, who would gladly have evaded the issue if he could. He
said that he had already made all the arrangements for his campaign speeches, and he was surprised that Lincoln had not come
forward with the proposal earlier. Still, he then proposed several
towns. Lincoln protested against the implication of unfairness,
and agreed to speak at the seven places named. "As to the
other details, I wish perfect reciprocity and no more. I wish as
much time as you, and that conclusion shall alternate. That
is all."

And now they begin in Ottawa, on a platform, in the open, their
first duel for a seat in the Senate : Douglas one hour, Lincoln one
hour and a half, then Douglas half an hour. Huge audiences flock
to hear these redoubtable champions; all Illinois is talking and
writing about the contest; the telegraph gets to work, and after

LINCOLN IN 1858

*From a second ambrotype similar to that said to have been made by
T. P. Pearson in Macomb, Illinois*

the third debate all the country knows about it and asks: Who are
the two fighters on the platform?

Look at them; they are irreconcilable. The one, called the Little
Giant, is only just over five feet high, but strongly built, with powerful neck and shoulders, deep chest, and massive head, vigorous and
tenacious, but all the same lively, even elegant. His clothes are
well cut, and his linen is spotless. As he speaks, he often shakes his
long gray-sprinkled hair back with a quick movement of the head;
his features are mobile; there is the deep furrow of a strong will
between his eyes — those fine, blue eyes which exercise a seductive
force; not until he stops speaking, not until his face is in repose,
does one notice the dull and unwholesome tint of his skin, due to
drink and town life. His shapely hands, too, are those of a man
unused to the rough and tumble of open-air life.

But if this man is unduly short and thickset, the other is
unduly tall and lean; Lincoln is bony, whereas Douglas is muscu-
lar. Lincoln's nose is bold; his gaze is questing rather than piercing;
his wrinkled visage has no brilliancy of expression. His ill-fitting
clothes hang awry on his ungainly form. They are creased and much
too short. His great feet are those of a man who walks slowly and
cautiously; his huge, sinewy hands are those of one who has been
accustomed to carry loads. It takes a poet to decide at first sight
for Lincoln.

What were the two men's records? The one, born forty-five
years ago as the son of a physician, had passed his early youth in
poor circumstances, had earned his school money as a land laborer,
as a carpenter in the college of his father, and, saving a little money
for his studies, became a teacher at twenty, at twenty-one a lawyer.
By enormous diligence and ambition, climbing step by step, he
became a member of the State legislature, then Secretary of State in
Illinois, and later a judge of the Supreme Court of Illinois. He
entered Congress very young and was soon known for his amiability.
Spoiled by Washington society, he soon learned to mingle business
with politics, speedily acquiring wealth by judicious land speculations.
Before he was forty he had become a senator. He had already been
a formidable candidate for the presidency. Douglas had married a

daughter of a Southern slaveholder, and upon her death he visited Europe. In Russia he was received by the Tsar. When he remarried, a few years later, it was once more to a lady from the South, a famous beauty, who became the leader of Washington society. Thus Douglas was one of the chiefs of his party, and one of the most outstanding men in the Union; wealthy, powerful, and dreaded; and more, a man of charm, chivalry, and suggestive force.

Lincoln was not drawn by ambition or money, nor by the wish to shine in the world or to win power; nothing but the growing conviction of his own talents had drawn him, by slow degrees, out of the narrow circle of provincial life. While his rival unrestingly, purposively, had heaped stone on stone of the steep turret of his success, to gain the wide outlook of the leader, Lincoln had strolled quietly along through the land of his companions, watching and questioning, aimless as a rule, and yet with his eyes fixed on a distant goal, on the towering and unattainable peak of a mighty ideal. If, once or twice, in response to his wife's urging, he left the plains to climb one of the foothills, he soon shrank from the difficulties of the ascent, and, instead of fighting his way upward, he quizzically inquired what was the use of it all. Would power and influence make him any happier? Would success be worth the sacrifice of inner freedom? One man finds it easy to build himself a light raft on which he can steer through the rapids of party life into a safe and comfortable haven; where he gets wind of the plans for a new railway, buys up land, is able to influence the course of the line, sells his land at enormous profit, and becomes rich between night and morning. Another buys up a bankrupt store, lies on the counter reading instead of trying to push his business, heaps up debts instead of money, debts which cumber him for a dozen years to follow; he will not push himself forward in opposition to his friends, and thus he loses his chance of an important and lucrative official position; he shuns the social life of the capital, and even the social life of his town; he prefers to drive to and fro on bad roads, to lodge in poor village hotels, to tell innumerable anecdotes illustrative of human weaknesses.

Thus it comes to pass that the swift, short man has outrun the slow, tall man in all things except the story of the heart; that the little man is able to talk of the splendors of emperors and queens, and to tell how court chamberlains have bowed before him, whereas the tall man can tell only of queens of fable and has no word to say of any one's bowing before him — and has himself, in truth, never bowed to any other. Thus it comes to pass that the purposive will reaches a culminating point whose altitude above the level of society can easily be calculated, while depising or forgetting the unattainable peak on the horizon; whereas an aimless longing rises above life plunged in dreams of Elysium that cannot attain reality. Thus it comes to pass that he who never bowed once in his life borrowed one hundred dollars from the other who so often bowed, and returned them without feeling indebted. Once only, so far, has the tall man got the better of the short — in the wooing of Mary Todd; but here the struggle was fought out in the recesses of Mary's mind, and the victory was a Pyrrhic one.

There is no doubt about it; Douglas has won. Look at him; is he not, virtually, the king of Illinois? He travels by special train, or at least in a private car; and attached to the train is a truck with a field gun on board, a gun which is fired to announce Douglas' arrival at a town. It is answered by a salute of thirty-two rounds, symbolizing the number of the still united States. The finest carriage in the town, drawn by six horses, is waiting for him and his wife. Round it are grouped two-and-thirty men and women on horseback, who conduct him in triumph to the Town Hall or to the inn. Douglas stands bareheaded in the carriage, bowing right and left, pluming himself on the thought that the whole country lies in the palm of his hand.

There is no special car for Lincoln, who has to travel, like other common folk, in crowded day coaches. Douglas sweeps by Lincoln, who is sidetracked in an accommodation or freight train, while Douglas' flag-bedecked special has thundered by, and ejaculates the ironically superior words: "The gentleman in that car evidently smelt no royalty in our carriage." No salute from thirty-two guns heralds Lincoln's arrival; his friends come to fetch him in a hay wain, drawn by horses taken from the plough; and if there be music, it is that of a brass band whose noise disturbs the hero.

When the Little Giant receives visitors shortly before the debate, his courteous smile remains on his lips for an hour. He shakes every one cordially by the hand, not with the dignified pose of a senator, but as a man of the people, who recognizes them all, and asks after their troubles individually, who chews and spits freely, and offers drinks with hospitable lavishness; but his wife must warn him under her breath to be careful in his own consumption, lest the drink for which he has a fondness should run away with his wits. Yet even in these matters, what a contrast!

The long lawyer, surrounded by curiosity, shadowed by the shyness of sensibility, is not so good in winning people's graces. The questioning eyes make him uneasy, so that he cannot chat comfortably to the bystanders. If the moment comes when he ought to speak flatteringly to a local leader, he stands there as stiff as an ancient Roman, as unyielding as Coriolanus.

The two men mount the platform. Now let us listen! Douglas is the opener this time, and is hailed with salvos of applause, which he acknowledges with a gracious gesture, as he stands there, the center of approving glances. He speaks in a vigorous but mellow baritone; his pronunciation is clear; he can suit the action to the word, and what he has to say comes trippingly from the tongue; he fetters his audience by the skill of his sophistical fencing, charms them for the very reason that he has not a popular style, but speaks somewhat above their heads. He is artful and aggressive, blunt and straightforward, bold and self-possessed, by turns, thus holding their attention like a corruscating firework — which is forgotten a minute after it has burned itself out.

After so sparkling an exit, Lincoln makes a bad entrance. Ungainly of aspect, he stands on this platform, everything hanging loose about him: clothes, arms, and head. His feet are planted rectangularly, one next to the other; he stands free, no leaning against walls, and when he folds his hands, perhaps twiddling his thumbs, you might think him a schoolmaster with a bad digestion, beginning, with harsh aloofness, to cross-examine his pupils. Very soon, however, he warms to his subject, his tones are more convincing, he lets himself go, he swings his left arm backward, props his right arm akimbo, makes gestures with his head rather than with his hands, but sometimes expresses his emphasis by pointing his theories into his hearer's heads with a long, bony forefinger. When, at some great moment, he flings both hands upward, to show joy, or when he clenches his fists in silent condemnation against slavery, the audience feels the power of these rare gestures. Ungainly though the orator may be, and in spite of his narrow chest, in such a moment he stands on the platform an imposing figure, and every one feels his emotion to be genuine.

He begins by making far-reaching concessions to his adversaries. His righteous feeling, his Socratic logic, here on the political platform no less than in the law courts, find the strong points in his rival's case, and with manly consideration he does his best to expound them. This frankness inspires confidence. But he goes on, by degrees, to expose the fallacies of the opposing arguments, cutting these arguments open as if he were in the post-mortem room, pitilessly laying bare all the weak spots. Then, with crystalline clarity, he proceeds to the offensive. Drawing his instances out of happenings in the daily lives of the farmers who form the majority of his audience, men among whom he has lived and worked, he proceeds from inference to inference in a lucid and simple style. Now, as always, his aim is a heartfelt one, a moral aim; but the path thither is logical.

In debate, Lincoln is transfigured. When he has finished, Douglas, the wily gladiator, proceeds to falsify Lincoln's arguments, since he cannot disprove them; the applause of his friends encourages him to be personally abusive, and whereas Lincoln has poked genial fun at Douglas, Douglas tries to make Lincoln seem ridiculous. The diplomat proves a less successful debater than the lawyer; the man used to platform oratory is troubled by the local acoustics, but the lawyer masters them, getting his words home. The short man influences the crowd, the long one influences isolated individuals; the former's influence is strong but evanescent, the latter's is slower and lasting. "So that is what the big chiefs in Washington are like," think people when they hear Douglas. But when they see Lincoln, they say to themselves, "If only we could have a man like this in Washington!"

Douglas is successful now, and for a brief space; Lincoln is successful later, and in the long run.

XV

Destiny stood behind Lincoln, driving him on into the slavery fight. Looking back on the pre-war period with a knowledge of the disastrous events that followed, we cannot but ask ourselves whether so fierce a controversy was essential; whether there was no possibility of such a compromise as the moderates of both parties desired. The Illinois debates did not actually cause the war, but they had exceptionally wide reverberations; they went further than the discussions of Congress; they gave birth to catchwords full of significance, which arrested the attention of millions; they certainly helped to intensify the conflict.

"I do not claim, gentlemen, to be unselfish," Lincoln said in a debate. "I do not pretend that I would not like to go to the United States Senate; I make no such hypocritical pretense; but I do say to you that in this mighty issue, it is nothing to you, nothing to the mass of the people of the nation, whether or not Judge Douglas or myself shall ever be heard of after this night. It may be a trifle to either of us, but in connection with this mighty question upon which hang the destinies of the nation perhaps, it is absolutely nothing."

The immanent moral law which guides Lincoln's whole life, and which will in the end lead him to the cross, drives him forward in such a fashion that the nearer he comes to personal power, the more is he impelled to think only of the cause.

Douglas, too, feels that the forces of destiny are at work. He sends a message to his opponent: "Tell Lincoln I have crossed the river and have burned my boats." An emotional note, very different from his usually elegant manner, and he probably believes what he says, for he declares more than once, "I do not care whether the vote goes for or against slavery. That is only a question of dollars and cents. The Almighty himself has drawn across this continent a line on one side of which the earth must for ever be tilled by slave labor, whereas on the other side of that line labor is free."

Lincoln's voice rings out clear against Douglas: "This is a world of compensation; and he who would not be slave, must consent to have no slave. Those who deny freedom to others deserve it not for themselves." Yet he remains the practical politician, quoting the Declaration: "I believe the declaration that 'all men are created equal' is the great fundamental principle upon which our free institutions rest. That negro slavery is violative of that principle; but that, by our frame of government, that principle has not been made one of legal obligation; that, by our frame of government, States which have slavery are to retain it, or surrender it, at their own pleasure. . . . I believe our government was thus framed because of the necessity springing from the actual presence of slavery, when it was framed. I believe that such necessity does not exist in the Territories where slavery is not present."

Commenting on the Dred Scott decision, he ends: "In those days, as I understand, masters could, at their own pleasure, emancipate their slaves; but since then such legal restraints have been made upon emancipation as to amount almost to prohibition."

He shows that Douglas' doctrine of popular sovereignty would necessarily make slavery a national affair, would inevitably lead to the reopening of the African slave trade.

"No one can forbid me to take my slave to Nebraska, just as I can take my horse thither. Why did our fathers make it a capital offence to import slaves from Africa? Why did they not make the catching of wild pigs a capital offence? Why is the slave dealer in the South a person regarded with such contempt that no one will shake hands with him; a person whose children are not allowed to play with the children of the Southern gentry, although the children of the slaves may play freely enough with the children of the slave owners? Why have so many slaves been set free, unless from the promptings of conscience? If we once abandon the principle of our fathers, that all men are born free and equal, and if we declare that negroes are not the equals of whites, the next step will be to declare that not all the whites are equal. . . . What will then become of the fundamental idea of our Constitution, that no one is entitled to issue orders to another, unless that other be a consenting party? . . . Those who like to play the master will always tell you that really they have no taste for mastership, but are only thinking of the interests of people who are better off when ruled. This argument of kings becomes none the more forcible because it is employed by the members of a higher race against the members of a lower."

The general concept of social equality always underlay these utterances. When Douglas railed against the Northern bootmakers who were on strike for better wages, Lincoln rejoined, "God be thanked that we have a labor system in which people can go on strike!"

Rarely, in these debates, does he give his passion free rein. What especially moves his bile is, not the curse imposed on those with black skins, but the curse from which those with white skins suffer because of the indolence of their hearts. That is why, in his inner self, he dislikes the ostensibly neutral Douglas more than he dislikes the slave owners of the South, who have a moral code of their own.

"I loathe such indifference!" he explains in one of his speeches. "It weakens the sense of justice in our State; it gives the enemies of a peaceful constitution the semblance of a right to regard us as hypocrites; and, at the same time, it gives the true friends of liberty a good reason to doubt our sincerity."

And another time he says:

"Accustomed to trample on the rights of those around you, you have lost the genius of your own independence, and become the fit subjects of the first cunning tyrant who rises among you. And let me tell you that these things are prepared for you with the logic of history, if the elections shall promise that the next Dred Scott decision and all future decisions shall be acquiesced in by the people. . . . You can fool all the people some of the time, and some of the people all the time, but you cannot fool all the people all the time."

From such sentiments, he speedily returns to irony and to popular imagery, which is ever ready, like a scherzo, to follow the dignified largo of his nature. When he wants to show how Buchanan, Douglas, Taney (the chief justice of the Supreme Court), and a former President have long since put their heads together, he says, using the Christian names of these men, which are familiar to his audience:

" When we see a lot of framed timbers different portions of which we know have been gotten out at different times and places and by different workmen — Stephen, Roger, Franklin, and James, for instance, and when we see these timbers joined together, and see they exactly make the frame of a house or a mill . . . we find it impossible to not believe that . . . all understood one another from the beginning and all worked upon a common plan."

Again, wishing to exemplify the various attitudes which might be taken by the old States and the new Territories toward slavery, he says:

"If I saw a venomous snake crawling in the road, any man would say I might seize the nearest stick and kill him; but if I found that snake in bed with my children, that would be another question. I might hurt the children more than the snake, and it might bite me. Much more if I found it in bed with my neighbor's children, and I had bound myself by a solemn compact not to meddle with his children under any circumstances. . . . But if there were a bed newly made up, to which the children were to be taken, and it was proposed to take a batch of young snakes and put them there with them, I take it no man would say there was any question how I ought to decide!"

Such vigorous metaphors are interspersed with witticisms and mischievous sallies, with slogans and apt rejoinders, Douglas being good at these, but Lincoln much better. Douglas, in one of his early speeches, stigmatizing Lincoln as an abolitionist, produces in evidence an old radical program bearing Lincoln's signature. In actual fact, the document is a forgery; and when, later, Douglas makes reference to other documents, Lincoln tells him to his face that the evidence he adduces can no longer be regarded as trustworthy.

Another time, when Douglas alters his opinion and denies his former one, Lincoln says: "I say that you took your hat off your head, and you prove me a liar by putting it on your head. That is the whole force of your argument."

Sometimes Lincoln succeeds in making Douglas appear ridiculous by expanding one of the latter's utterances into a formula.

Douglas: "When the struggle is between the white man and the negro, I am for the white man; when it is between the negro and the crocodile, I am for the negro."

Lincoln: "We gather from this that as a white man is to a negro, so is a negro to a crocodile; and as the negro may rightfully treat the crocodile, so may the white man rightfully treat the negro."

Again: "The sovereignty of the people means the right of the people to govern themselves. Did Judge Douglas invent this? Not quite. The idea of popular sovereignty was floating about several ages before the author of the Nebraska Bill was born — indeed before Columbus set foot on this continent. . . . If Judge Douglas did not invent this kind of popular sovereignty, let us pursue the inquiry and find out what kind he did invent. Was it the right of immigrants to Kansas and Nebraska to govern themselves, and a lot of 'niggers', too, if they wanted them? Clearly this was no invention of his, because General Cass put forth the same doctrine . . . six years before Douglas thought of such a thing. Then what was it that the 'Little Giant' invented? It never occurred to General Cass to call his discovery by the odd name of popular sovereignty. He had not the face to say that the right of the people to govern 'niggers' was the right of the people to govern themselves. . . . And here I submit to you was Judge Douglas' discovery, and the whole of it. He discovered that the right to breed and flog negroes in Nebraska was popular sovereignty."

Thus drastic can Lincoln be when it is a question of nailing false coin to the counter. When Douglas asks him why he had voted against the war credits at the time of the Mexican War, instead of replying in set terms that Douglas is misinformed, Lincoln summons to the platform from amid the audience one of Douglas' intimate friends, who ten years earlier had been one of Lincoln's fellow congressmen.

"I ask you, Sir," said Lincoln, "did Mr. Douglas speak the truth about my vote on that occasion?" And amid general laughter Douglas' friend must deny his statement.

Lincoln raises a laugh by describing Douglas as a cuttlefish, darkening the waters to evade pursuit. He lets all his wits play to ridicule his rival:

"Senator Douglas is of world-wide renown. All the anxious politicians of his party, or who have been of his party for years past, have been looking upon him as certainly, at no distant day, to be the President of the United States. They have seen in his round, jolly, fruitful face, post-offices, land-offices, marshalships, and cabinet appointments, chargeships and foreign missions, bursting and sprouting out in wonderful exuberance, ready to be laid hold of by their greedy hands. And as they have been gazing upon this attractive picture so long, they can not, in the little distraction that has taken place in the party, bring themselves to give up the charming hope; but with greedier anxiety they rush about him, sustain him, and give him marches, triumphal entries, and receptions beyond what even in the days of his highest prosperity they could have brought about in his favor. On the contrary, nobody has ever expected me to be President. In my poor, lean, lank face, nobody has ever seen that any cabbages were sprouting out. These are disadvantages, all taken together, that the Republicans labor under. We have to fight this battle upon principle, and upon principle alone."

Once Lincoln sets a snare for Douglas. The question he puts contains the magic antithesis between the two rivals:

"Can the people of a United States territory, in any lawful way, against the wish of any citizen of the United States, exclude slavery from its limits prior to the formation of a State Constitution?"

The questioner knew that Douglas' own measure of popular sovereignty, which declared that the people of a territory should be left to regulate their domestic concerns in their own way, subject only to the Constitution, was incompatible with the decision of the Supreme Court in the Dred Scott case, to the effect that slaves, being property, could not under the Constitution be excluded from a territory. Lincoln knew that if Douglas answered the question in the negative, his reëlection as senator for Illinois would become impossible. If Douglas said "Yes", he would estrange the Southern voters and could never become President. For the moment, Douglas wriggled out of the dilemma adroitly enough:

"It matters not what way the Supreme Court may hereafter decide as to the abstract question whether slavery may or may not go into a territory under the Constitution; the people have the lawful means to introduce it or exclude it as they please, for the reason that slavery cannot exist a day or an hour anywhere unless it is supported by local police regulations."

There were thousands of farmers and shopkeepers listening to these subtleties, recognizing only that a shrewd question had been shrewdly answered. They began to shout from both sides, and the rival bands began to play simultaneously, each trying to drown the other. Amid the clamor, no one seemed to know the importance of that question, not even Lincoln's closest political friends. And yet Lincoln's clever trick became a matter of destiny when the lawyer developed into a statesman.

Two years later, matters were to turn out as he had foreseen. From the first, when Douglas' answer became known, the South turned against him, for it was the general demand of the slave owners that the Union should everywhere enforce the protection of slavery. To win reëlection as senator, Douglas forfeited his chances of the presidency. What was Lincoln's motive? Did he only wish to annihilate a man he considered mischievous? Had he no personal interest in the struggle of two years hence? However this may be, he had long since summed up Douglas, and in private letters described him as a humbug, and had said that Douglas' endeavors to convey the impression of a triumphal march through Illinois were "as bombastic and hollow as Napoleon's bulletins sent back from his campaign in Russia." And he also said, "He is a man with tens of thousands of blind followers. It is my business to make some of those blind followers see." Would he take up the fight with Douglas in the future?

One of Lincoln's party friends describes meeting him in a Springfield hotel.

"The day was warm, and at the first chance he broke away and came out of the hotel for a little fresh air, wiping the sweat from his face. As he passed the door he saw me, and, taking my hand, inquired for the health and views of his 'friends over in Vermilion County.' He was assured that they were wide awake, and further told that they looked forward to the debate between him and Senator Douglas with deep concern. From the shadow that went quickly over his face, the pained look that came to give quickly way to a blaze of eyes and quiver of lips, I felt that Mr. Lincoln had gone beneath my mere words and had caught my inner and current fears as to the result. And then, in a forgiving, jocular way peculiar to him, he said, 'Sit down; I have a moment to spare, and will tell you a story.' Having been on his feet for some time, he sat on the end of the stone steps leading into the hotel door, while I stood closely fronting him.

"'You have,' he continued, 'seen two men about to fight?'

"'Yes, many times.'

"'Well, one of them brags about what he means to do. He jumps high in the air, knocking his heels together, smites his fists, and wastes his breath trying to scare somebody. You see the other fellow, he says not a word' — here Mr. Lincoln's voice and manner changed to great earnestness, and repeating — 'you see the other man says not a word. His arms are at his side, his fists are closely doubled up, his head is drawn to the shoulder, and his feet are set firm together. He is saving his wind for the fight, and as sure as it comes off he will win it, or die a-trying.'"

Lincoln lost the first round, won the second, but he died a-trying.

XVI

Douglas had won the first round. He had inflicted a signal defeat on Lincoln, and had returned as senator to the capital, whereas the other went back to his lawsuits in the small town; it seemed to be a case of "as you were." Lincoln had encountered some terrible moments: in Petersburg, when he had been hooted for half an hour; in Ottawa, when some stalwart young fellows had carried him about triumphantly on their shoulders, with his long legs hanging down, and his trousers rucked up to the knees; in yet another town, when he was decorated with garlands. He had to put up with these things, but he hated them. A lady had teased him by dangling a nigger doll in front of him, but he had turned the laugh against her by tranquilly inquiring, "Ma'am, is that your baby?" But when, at an open-air meeting, a gentleman on horseback rode close up to the platform, and shouted, "Would you like to sleep in the same bed with a nigger?" Lincoln did not deign to answer, but looked so contemptuously at the questioner that the latter turned about and rode off, followed by the booing of the auditors.

And, in truth, it was not a case of "as you were." A notable thing had happened. All America had got to know the name of Abraham Lincoln. While the Democrats took the chairmanship of the Committee on Territories from Douglas because of his ambiguous rôle, all the North spoke of "Abe the Giant Killer"; and a couplet was going the round:

"Westward the star of empire takes its way;
    The girls link on to Lincoln, their mothers were for Clay."

There was a new town in Illinois that took his name — against his will.

A stranger wrote to him: "You are like Byron, who awoke one day to find himself famous. People wish to know about you. You have sprung at once from the position of a capital fellow and a leading lawyer in Illinois to a national reputation." The upshot of it all was that his Illinois supporters began to think, not only that he could be useful to the party, but also that he must really be a great man.

What was Lincoln's own view?

On a summer's eve during the debates, Lincoln was waiting with Henry Villard at a station. A thunderstorm came up and the two fled into a freight car and squatted down in the dark. In these primitive surroundings, without light, without chairs, Lincoln's thoughts roamed back for twenty years and more, that compared to-day and yesterday. Soliloquizing, he said that when he had been a country store clerk at New Salem, his highest ambition had been to get into the State legislature. "Since then," he went on, laughing, "of course, I have grown some. But as to running for senator, my friends got me into it. . . . Now, to be sure, I am convinced that I am good enough for it; but in spite of it all, I am saying to myself every day: 'It is too big a thing for you; you will never get it.' Mary insists, however, that I am going to be senator and President of the United States too!" As he squatted there on the floor, hugging his knees, he shook with laughter at the thought of his wife's ambition for him to be President, and said: "Just think of such a sucker as me being President."

One of the most vivid scenes in Lincoln's life is here realistically described by a shrewd observer. There is the man after a day filled with speechifying, brass-band playing, and the waving of flags — the hero of the day, with a journalist, sitting on the hard floor of the dark and stuffy baggage car — just as he had sat many a night in the cabin in Indiana. The discomforts do not depress him; instead, the reminders of old days cheer him up and loosen his tongue. The darkness, too, makes it easier for this reserved being to converse. His lambent ironies about human endeavor and his own person vibrate through the empty car like goblin music. There he sits and reveals the hidden motives of his activities; and, even in disclosing Mary's ambition, the man's imaginative nature peeps through, the nature of one who sees in pictures and parables, though outwardly he may appear to be only fighting for such dry things as laws. Fundamentally modest, his glimpses behind the scenes of political life have taught him that political power comes often enough and easily enough to persons who have neither genius nor character. For weeks, now, he has been living in close touch with the most famous tactician of America — with the inevitable result that his respect sank and his self-respect rose.

If, though somewhat later than most American politicians, he has in his leisurely fashion at length begun to think of himself as a possible President, it is no longer a doubt in his own capacity that makes him question whether he is likely to fulfill his wife's supreme wish, but he sees himself faithfully reflected in the mirror of his own heart.

It never occurs to him that, as his opponents would declare, he is not well bred enough for such a position. His fine perceptions have long since enabled him to acquire a sufficiency of the culti- vated manners of which the gentlefolk of the Washington drawing- rooms are so proud. Nor does he forget that Benjamin Franklin had been a working printer, and Andrew Jackson a saddler's appren- tice. But his own bony frame makes him laugh because it counter- acts all diplomatic elegance.

After this failure, when he finds that none the less the circum- stances attending on that defeat have made his name known far and wide through the land, his self-confidence goes on growing, and he turns to consider new possibilities. When he was asked how he was bearing up under his defeat, he answered in words which admirably summed up this *entr'acte* mood: "I feel like a lad who has knocked his shins, in too much pain to laugh about it, but too grown up to cry." Writing to his old friend and physician Doctor Henry, he said:

"I am glad I made the late race. It gave me a hearing on the great and durable question of the age, which I would have had in no other way; and though I now sink out of view, and shall be for- gotten, I believe I have made some marks which will tell for the cause of civil liberty long after I am gone."

The man's proud spirit of self-renunciation is conveyed by these words; we learn from them that the cause of freedom is more to him than the prospect of a presidency. Is he not the same young enthu- siast who, twenty years earlier, in the Springfield debating society, had spoken of two great men, Caesar and Napoleon, to whom a presidential chair would have seemed no very great thing? The man who was to bestow the gift of human dignity upon thousands of slaves was not so undignified as to strive after power with the eagerness for it which characterized his wife.

But what of the reality of power? What if only by getting this into his hands, can he realize his ideal of freedom? The chain of

LINCOLN ABOUT 1858

From a photograph by Alexander Hesler, Chicago

thoughts and the chain of feelings, ambition and idealism, person and cause, intersect in this, as in every great life, and are forever inseparable.

That autumn, in Bloomington, he meets an acquaintance who says to him, "Everywhere I hear you talked about. Very frequently I have been asked, 'Who is this man Lincoln?' I have usually answered that we had in Illinois two giants instead of one; that Douglas was the little one, as they all knew, but that you were the big one, which they didn't all know. . . . I have a decided impression . . . you can be made a formidable, if not a successful candidate for the presidency."

Lincoln rejoins that he is scarcely known outside Illinois, and that Seward or Chase is much more likely to be put forward by the Republicans for the presidency.

The other demurs, and says that the Republicans in general do not want a New Yorker. He would like some autobiographical details, which can be circulated with a view to putting Lincoln forward for the presidency.

Lincoln: "I admit the force of much that you say, and I admit that I am ambitious and would like to be President. I am not insensible to the compliment you pay me, and the interest you manifest in the matter; but there is no such good luck in store for me as the presidency of the United States; besides, there is nothing in my early history that would interest you or anybody else; and, as Judge Davis says, 'It won't pay'."

Thereon, wrapping a thick gray-and-brown wool shawl round his bony shoulders, and saying good night, Lincoln departed.

On a reiterated demand, he did give his data, as follows:

"I was born February 12, 1809, in Hardin County, Kentucky. My parents were both born in Virginia, of undistinguished families — second families, perhaps I should say. . . . My paternal grandfather, Abraham Lincoln, emigrated from Rockingham County, Virginia, to Kentucky about 1781 or 1782, where a year or two later he was killed by the Indians, not in battle, but by stealth, when he was laboring to open a farm in the forest. His ancestors, who were Quakers, went to Virginia from Berks County, Pennsylvania. . . .

"My father, at the death of his father, was but six years of age, and he grew up literally without education. He removed from Kentucky to what is now Spencer County, Indiana, in my eighth year. We reached our new home about the time that State came into the Union. It was a wild region, with many bears and other wild animals still in the woods. There I grew up. There were some schools, so called, but no qualification was ever required of a teacher beyond 'readin', writin', and cipherin'' to the rule of three. If a straggler supposed to understand Latin happened to sojourn in the neighborhood, he was looked upon as a wizard. There was absolutely nothing to excite ambition for education.

" Of course, when I came of age I did not know much. Still, some-how, I could read, write, and cipher to the rule of three, but that was all. I have not been to school since. The little advance I now have upon this store of education, I have picked up from time to time under the pressure of necessity.

"I was raised to farm work, which I continued till I was twenty-two. At twenty-one I came to Illinois, Macon County. Then I got to New Salem, at that time in Sangamon, now in Menard County, where I remained a year as a sort of clerk in a store. Then came the Black Hawk war; and I was elected a captain of volunteers, a suc-cess which gave me more pleasure than any I have had since. I went to the campaign, was nominated, ran for the legislature the same year (1832), and was beaten — the only time I ever have been beaten by the people. The next and three succeeding biennial elections I was elected to the legislature. I was not a candidate afterwards. During this legislative period I had studied law, and removed to Springfield to practice it. In 1846, I was once elected to the lower house of Congress. Was not a candidate for reëlec-tion. From 1849 to 1854, both inclusive, practised law more assidu-ously than ever before. Always a Whig in politics; and generally on the Whig electoral tickets, making active canvasses. I was losing interest in politics when the repeal of the Missouri Compro-mise aroused me again. What I have done since then is pretty well known.

"If any personal description of me is thought desirable, it may be said I am, in height, six feet, four inches, nearly; lean in flesh, weighing on an average one hundred and eighty pounds; dark complexion, with coarse black hair and gray eyes. No other marks or brands recollected."

Was ever tone so dry? Not a word about things that vanity might like to make known, but a good deal that might speak against it. The wealth of metaphor that adorns his style, the finesse of his letters, the impetuous rhythm of his speeches — all these are lacking in this arid document, and only an expert would recognize an eminent stylist. We feel much as we should feel if a celebrated chef were to prepare large quantities of a tasteless soup in order to feed those who had heard much of his culinary skill, and wanted to know his secret.

And yet, this fragment is a masterpiece in what it says and in what it conceals. People may like to know of the grandfather who fell as a pioneer, leaving his son to be educated by the wild bears. They will be amused, too, by the joke about the "wizard." But Lincoln is too proud to talk about his strenuous efforts to gain access to the wells of knowledge. Enough for him to say that he has picked up education here and there, from time to time, under the pressure of necessity. Not a word does he say about his work in the local legislature, about the matters he fought for in Congress. But he does not mind revealing the real acquisition of popularity with comrades and townsmen, true to him in war and campaign. Personal details? Is he to tell people the name of his favorite poet; that he does not care for drink, and is fond of telling anecdotes; that he would rather chop wood in his shirt sleeves than go to parties in a frock coat? Six feet, four inches high ("nearly", to keep within the strict letter of the truth); a hundred and eighty pounds, coarse hair, and no birthmarks. With this splendid formula à la Don Quixote, he ends his epistle.

XVII

The results of the debates, for Lincoln, were that he returned home about twenty pounds heavier and several thousand dollars poorer. His income from the law business had fallen off with only his partner Herndon to look after it, while his expenses had been heavy; and although he might now expect that he would be able to restore the balance, for the moment he was short of money for current expenses. When Judd, Chairman of the Republican State Central Committee, wrote asking for his financial help, he replied:

"As to the pecuniary matter, I am willing to pay according to my ability, but I am the poorest hand living to get others to pay. I have been on expenses so long without earning anything, that I am absolutely without money now for even household purposes. Still, if you can put in $250 for me, towards discharging the debt of the committee, I will allow it when you and I settle the private matter between us. This, with what I have already paid, and with an outstanding note of mine, will exceed my subscription of $500. This, too, exclusive of my ordinary expenses during the campaign, all of which, being added to my loss of time and business, bears pretty heavily upon one no better off in this world's goods than I. But as I had the post of honor, it is not for me to be over nice."

It was usual enough in the United States of those days for a political party to expect liberal contributions from its standard bearers. The unusual thing was that Lincoln, in his actual position, should have agreed to contribute, for he had not secured the senatorial post with its emoluments, and had rendered more services to his party than others. Still, he was somewhat embarrassed. The land granted him in Iowa for his military services in the old days was not remunerative. That and some other pieces of land, the home in Springfield, together with various moneys owed him, may have represented a nominal value of nearly twenty thousand dollars. His law practice brought him in his best years more than three thousand dollars.

Mary's demands were considerable. She thought this a suitable occasion to buy a new carriage, and Lincoln paid the bill without a word. She knew how to live up to his growing reputation, how to keep house, how to smile at the right moment, how to make the prevailing crinoline fashion advantageous to her stoutness; but she sometimes aroused comment and made enemies by her overbearing

manners, as when, at a ball, she criticized the playing of the band
in such loud tones that the musicians heard what she said. She
always disliked Herndon, and would gladly have seen his partnership with Lincoln dissolved, for it did not seem fair to her that the
junior partner should net half the income from the law practice
when the senior conducted all the big trials. She looked down on
Herndon for his lowly origin — for having grown up in a tavern, for
being a radical and an anti-clerical, for occasionally getting drunk;
and his outspoken abolitionist views reacted, so she thought,
unfavorably on his partner's position. She wanted Lincoln to
enter into partnership with a relative of hers, a gentleman from
Kentucky, but for Lincoln this was no recommendation and,
besides, he was a man who was faithful to his friends, Herndon
above all.

Also he had been too profoundly moved by the public experiences
of recent years, by the storms of national passion, and by the imminence of a great crisis, to settle down comfortably any longer as a
provincial lawyer. However, when asked to speak in the country,
he declined, writing: "It is bad to be poor. I shall go to the wall
for bread and meat if I neglect my business this year as well as
last." But an inner urge drove him forward. He had been careful to file the newspaper reports of the debates with Douglas, and
determined to have them printed. Not being able to find a pub-
lisher who would venture the whole risk, he contributed fifty dollars
toward the cost of issuing his first and last book. He took the
reports of Douglas' speeches from the Democratic press, determined to be absolutely fair to his opponent; and he protested
against having the speeches touched up, refusing to tone down his
own animated utterances. He issued this book as a historian, not
as a campaigner, believing that in historical retrospect he would be
regarded as the victor. In common with the whole nation, he felt
that the struggle was not yet over. Not even the speech-making
contest. For soon the rivals were on the stump again in the West;
and everywhere it was the defeated Lincoln who (to his great
annoyance!) was welcomed by the braying of bands. In his
speeches, now, he tore Douglas' theories to tatters:

"What, at bottom, is this popular sovereignty? . . . It is, as a principle, no other than that if one man chooses to make a slave of another man, neither that other man nor anybody else has a right to object. . . . Another's enslavement seems a little matter to Senator Douglas. He is so put up by nature that a lash upon his back would hurt him, but a lash upon anybody else's back does not hurt him at all. . . . This policy of popular sovereignty is what chiefly stands in the way of a permanent settlement of the question. I believe there is no danger of it becoming the permanent policy of the country, for it is based on a public indifference. There is nobody that 'don't care.' All the people do care one way or the other! . . . Senator Douglas is the only man in the nation who has never said whether he regards slavery as just or unjust."

In the course of this campaign, Lincoln speaks in far more resounding tones than have hitherto been customary with him.

At Cincinnati, on the Kentucky border, apostrophizing the Kentuckians in particular, he says:

"We Republicans mean to remember that you are as good as we; that there is no difference between us other than the difference of circumstances. We mean to recognize and bear in mind always that you have as good hearts in your bosoms as other people, or as we claim to have, and treat you accordingly. We mean to marry your girls when we have a chance — the white ones, I mean — and I have the honor to inform you that I once did have a chance in that way."

That is a superior tone, the tone of a practised orator who does not have any difficulty in gathering audiences, the tone of one whose thoughts have already moved farther on, of a man who is impatient. He even continues ironically:

"Will you make war upon us, and kill us all? Why, gentlemen, I think you are as gallant and as brave men as live; that you can fight as bravely in a good cause, man for man, as any other people living; that you have shown yourselves capable of this upon various occasions; but, man for man, you are not better than we are, and there are not so many of you as there are of us. You will never make much of a hand at whipping us. If we were fewer in number than you, I think that you could whip us; if we were equal, it would likely be a drawn battle; but, being inferior in numbers, you will make nothing by attempting to master us."

What is going on within him, that now from time to time he speaks in this Shakespearian vein as a leader of the people? Is this a reaction to a tension unduly prolonged? Does he feel like an actor who has grown weary of the part he has been playing? Or has there been slowly gathering within him the sense of a great responsibility? Is he still shrinking in alarm from the acceptance of a mission which, in secret, he has long known to be his?

A man who was in danger of being jailed for helping a runaway slave complained to Lincoln: this is "not only unconstitutional, but inhuman."

Lincoln, animated but mournful, brandished his right arm. "Oh, it is ungodly! It is ungodly! No doubt it is ungodly! But it is the law of the land, and we must obey it as we find it."

"Mr. Lincoln, how often have you sworn to support the Constitution? We propose to elect you President. How would you look taking an oath to support what you declare is an ungodly Constitution, and asking God to help you?"

Lincoln's head drooped, he ran his fingers through his hair, looked desperately puzzled, but a moment later placed his hand gently on the other's and said quizzically, "It's no use to be always looking up these hard spots."

Thus he was full of doubt as to where events were going and as to what he should do. He was anxious, disquieted. And something happened now which could not fail to increase his discomfiture. John Brown was a farmer of sorts, a fanatical abolitionist, an idealist and a militant. Three years before, he had played a conspicuous part in the border troubles of Kansas. The Southerners had killed his son and on his own head they had set a price. He was a lean, handsome old fellow, with the aquiline nose of an aristocrat and the beard and flowing locks of a frontiersman; a passionate lover of freedom; and inspired with a religious maniac's conviction in God's approval and God's help. With a guerilla force of only eighteen men, five of whom were Negroes, he had captured a United States arsenal, intending to make this the base for starting a slave revolt in the South. This naïve raid failed, he was captured, tried, sentenced, and hanged. Within a few weeks he became the martyr of the Northern Abolitionists; legends and poems gathered round his name; and while Douglas was able to make much of the disastrous consequences of this agitation, Lincoln was not slow to grasp how much damage Brown had done.

Ere long he had a chance of saying this in public. The year of the presidential election had come round once more; it was February, 1860, and the nominations were to take place in May. Not for decades had there been such universal excitement, for every one knew that the integrity of the Union was involved in the election. Only in the South, indeed, was there talk of secession. But the North was uncertain as to its own wishes. Business men there, as a rule, would vote Republican, but would do so with uneasy hearts. Among Northern intellectuals, however, the old Puritan spirit was still alive, or had been reborn; the spirit of those who held that fundamental principles were at stake in this contest. Northern susceptibilities, too, had been outraged by the increasing arrogance of the Southerners, who were continually threatening to break away from the Union, as if this decision rested upon their wills alone. The Northerners naturally resented this, knowing that more than half of the industry and wealth of the present power and the future possibilities of the United States were vested in them.

Issues and moods being thus uncertain, people in the Eastern States wished to see this eccentric Westerner, Lincoln, for themselves, and to see and hear him with their own eyes and ears. His intention to speak in Brooklyn had aroused so much interest that, at the last moment, he was asked to deliver his speech at the famous Cooper Institute in New York. From the start Lincoln was somewhat embarrassed at having to face these shrewd and superior persons, whose moral cloak (he felt) was padded with cotton. Such unsympathetic feelings were, to begin with, reciprocal. The audience noted with disapproval the old-fashioned cut of the speaker's clothes; while he, for his part, found his thoughts continually wandering from his topic to dwell upon the contrast between the elegant attire of his auditors and his own ill-fitting coat — a new one, indeed, but rumpled by bad packing.

Extracts from the reports of two eyewitnesses:

"His head was propped on a long, lean stalk, and not until he opened his hands in a gesture did I realize how huge they were. He began in a deep voice, like one accustomed to open-air speaking and afraid of talking too loud; said 'Mr. Cheerman', and used other antiquated expressions. I said to myself: 'Old fellow, you won't do; it's all very well for the Wild West, but this will never go down in New York.' . . . In all respects he looked like one of those simple folk with whom he was glad to be numbered. There was nothing imposing about his appearance; his clothes hung loosely on his giant frame; his features were dusky, pale, colorless, roughly chiselled, bearing the signs of privation; and his deep set eyes were full of care . . . But as he developed his theme, his face was lit up by inner fires. . . . His voice rang out. His oratory was terse; he had, in great measure, the extreme simplicity of the Bible. . . . There was such profound silence while he was speaking, that in the pauses one could hear the hissing of the gas-jets. But at the climaxes there were terrifying thunders of applause. When he wound up, I leapt to my feet and yelled like a mad Indian. So did the others. An amazing fellow!"

The speech had been as carefully prepared as a sermon, and, like a sermon, it was framed to a text from Douglas: "Our fathers, when they framed the government under which we live, understood this question just as well, and even better, than we do now." Setting out from plain constitutional and historical considerations known to every child, he went on to the methodical and logical development of the inferences therefrom. Then came a part of the speech that was directly addressed to the Southerners, as if they had been sitting there in the hall.

"You will not abide the election of a Republican President! In that supposed event, you say, you will destroy the Union; and then you say, the great crime of having destroyed it will be upon us! That is cool. A highwayman holds a pistol to my ear, and mutters through his teeth, 'Stand and deliver, or I shall kill you, and then you will be a murderer!'"

Yet he expressly repudiated any connection between the Republicans and John Brown — a dangerous, or, at any rate, an unpopular thing to do in the North at this particular moment.

"John Brown's effort was peculiar. It was not a slave insurrection. It was an attempt by white men to get up a revolt among slaves, in which the slaves refused to participate. In fact, it was so absurd that the slaves, with all their ignorance, saw plainly enough it could not succeed. That affair, in its philosophy, corresponds with the many attempts related in history of the assassination of kings and emperors. An enthusiast broods over the oppression of a people, till he fancies himself commissioned by heaven to liberate them. He ventures the attempt, which ends in little else than his own execution. . . . We cannot object to old John Brown's execution for treason against a State. We cannot object, even though he agreed with us in thinking slavery wrong. That cannot excuse violence, bloodshed, and treason."

This one evening suffices to win for Lincoln in the East the reputation of a great orator. Other States invite him to speak. A professor delivers a lecture on his Cooper Institute speech. The widening of his fame reacts, not only on Illinois, but also on himself. For the first time he has directly contemplated what is known as the "great world"; has appraised himself by its standard, has come to recognize the power of its external, the weakness of its internal qualities, and yet in the end the preponderant strength of the profounder elements of this noisy world of business affairs. On his way home, he finds his own name in the papers as among the possible Republican candidates for the presidency. Only a few weeks before, in a list of thirty-four political notables, there had been no mention of Abraham Lincoln. Six months earlier, in a letter expressing a doubt as to whether Chase was the most suitable candidate for the presidency, he added: "I must say I do not think myself fit for the presidency."

But these six months had taught him much. In April he wrote to Trumbull:

"As you request, I will be entirely frank. The taste *is* in my mouth a little; and this, no doubt, disqualifies me, to some extent to form correct opinions. You may confidently rely, however, that by no advice or consent of mine, shall my pretensions be pressed to the point of endangering our common cause."

This remark, in a private letter, is absolutely true. Lincoln analyzes himself and his own position just as conscientiously as if the case were that of another. Being able to look God in the face, he is not afraid to look at his own, and is ready to acknowledge that he entertains wishes which he would not condemn in another. But he is on his guard: "Remembering that when a not very great man begins to be mentioned for a very great position, his head is very likely to be a little turned, I concluded I am not the fittest person to answer the questions you ask."

His critical faculties are fully alert during this period of hope and waiting.

We should be mistaken, therefore, to think of Lincoln at this period as passive, as waiting upon events; on the contrary, he was more active than ever, writing numerous letters to his party associates, giving them advice where to fight and how, for, as one of his friends said, "his tactic was to put himself in the right position so that events might find him there." The press, too, he knew how to manage, as an extract from a letter written a few years before will show:

"Friend Harding, I have been reading your paper three or four years, and have paid you nothing for it. Herewith is a receipt of Sylvanus Sandford for two claims amounting to ten dollars. If he has collected the money, get it from him, and put it into your pocket, saying nothing further about it. And now, if you please, I should be glad for you to put in your paper of this week the name of Stephen T. Logan as a candidate for judge of the Supreme Court; and of Stephen A. Corneau, for clerk of the Supreme Court."

Recently, for the sum of four hundred dollars, he had bought the *Illinois Staats-Anzeiger*, one of the two German newspapers published in the State, doing it so privately that not even Herndon knew of the matter. This periodical was being discreetly used as a means of propaganda on his behalf; and he took other measures to secure immigrant support.

Abraham Lincoln could be cunning enough on occasions. But there was no justification for calling him a fox, as some of his adversaries did at this time, for, as far as he was concerned, the use of such measures was exceptional, not typical. In the struggle of politics, however, he had suffered too much from the artifices of the other side not to feel inclined, at times, to pay back in the same coin. For decades he had fought for others and was too little of a Pharisee, too much of a farmer, not to use his wits on behalf of a great cause which was his country's as well as his own.

XVIII

Now Lincoln suddenly recognized more enemies within his party than without. The power of the Republicans was growing so rapidly, their program was so well designed to catch the popular imagination, that one who secured the Republican nomination was likely to become President, and for that very reason many were against his nomination. His rivals were stronger and more influential men than himself, and Herndon writes:

"He had no money with which to maintain a political bureau, and he lacked any kind of personal organization whatever. Seward had all these things, and, behind them all, a brilliant record in the United States Senate with which to dazzle his followers."

It seemed natural to expect that Chase, Governor of Ohio, or Seward, ex-Governor of New York, would be preferred to Abraham Lincoln. Their record in the anti-slavery campaign was longer than and as honorable as his, and Chase had been even more radical; both were senators, famous lawyers, and men with wide political experience in Washington and elsewhere. Seward, in especial, by his record and by the breadth of his culture, had many advantages over the poor provincial who had only once, a dozen years before, been in Congress without attracting any attention. Had he not been in the bad books of Greeley, the influential newspaper man of the East, Seward's chances would have been better.

As chance would have it, the Republican State Convention of Illinois was held at Decatur, the town into which Lincoln had driven so many years before with an ox-wagon.

There they wanted to come to an agreement before the Republican National Convention. At the tavern table, wire pullers and place hunters calculate and compromise, and the faces of the candidates are studied as to their usefulness, as Lincoln once had analyzed the face of Douglas. But there! What is that for a procession, with music and a strange flag tied to two old fence rails? People go outside to see them; Lincoln too. Is that a ghost, in the full light of noon, carrying ghostly weapons?

No ghost, but his cousin John Hanks, who thirty years before had helped him build a house for his father. John is eager to tell them all about it: that had been one of the first houses in the district, the house that he and honest Abe had built, in days when a road was only just being made through the wilderness. For Abe's father had been one of the pioneers, and had fought here for his country in the days when there were still wolves in the forest. Then the tall lad Abraham had worked for wages, had swung an ax, felled trees, and split three thousand rails. Here were two of them!

The crowd is fascinated by these two old rails; every one's mind is stirred by the image of the pioneers; and the man who had split three thousand rails becomes more to them than had been the man who had won an oratorical victory over Douglas. Lincoln stands there with mixed feelings. His father, who had never been much good, is now being described as a famous pioneer; and he himself, who had only swung an ax for the sake of the half dollar a day he earned by it, is now to be far more richly repaid for his labors after the lapse of a generation! Does he smile or chuckle to himself? Does he understand how important the old fence rails will be to-morrow? "I suppose I must say something about them. That was a long time ago. It is possible I may have split these rails, but I cannot identify them. . . . I can only say that I have split a great many better-looking ones!"

There is further cheering, and a shrewd onlooker declares "Seward's chance is gone." A new symbol had been found, a new name: Lincoln, the Rail Splitter. That was even better than "Honest Abe." Within a few weeks, every child in the country was talking of him as the Rail Splitter. Lincoln owed this turn of fortune to cousin John Hanks, the only relative that ever helped him after he had grown up.

When in May the National Republican Convention opened in Chicago in a newly built frame hall, which had been christened the Wigwam, forty thousand strangers had flocked to the youthful city for the great occasion. Brass bands and supporters had turned out in exceptional force. The general belief was that, at this first Republican Convention in the grand style, Seward would be nominated. Two thousand of his supporters had come from New York, some of them rather shady customers. Of course Lincoln's friends were busy too: Herndon and Logan; Davis and Swett, and other judges and lawyers who had been old-time associates on circuit; the *Chicago Tribune* had espoused his cause. He was also favored by the circumstance that the supporters of other possible nominees were prepared to concentrate on the new man rather than on Seward. They also managed to prevent Lincoln from being nominated for Vice President, which he had at once refused. At the eleventh hour, he imperiled his prospects by his honesty, by sending a wire that no binding engagements were to be made on his behalf, and thus preventing his intimates from buying support by the customary promises of office.

While this went on Lincoln remained at home in Springfield, as excited as Carmen outside the bull ring, being kept in touch with the progress of events by telegrams from his friends which he went to fetch from the telegraph office. He tried to compose his nerves by reading Burns; tried to pitch horseshoes, hoped and doubted, threw himself on a friend's old office sofa, saying, "Well, Conkling, I believe I will go back to my office and practice law." In the end, he was taken by surprise when a messenger boy handed him a telegram, with the exclamation, "Mr. Lincoln, you have been nominated!" Shouts from the bystanders! Lincoln stood silent for some minutes and then said, "I reckon there's a little short woman down at our house that would like to hear the news."

Probably the moment of this return home was the happiest in all their married life.

Next day the pair received the little delegation that had come to announce the nomination officially. Lincoln responded in a few grave words, without excitement or embarrassment. Mary behaved tactfully. As for Lincoln, he won golden opinions. "Why, Sir, they told me he was a rough diamond," said one member of the delegation, "but nothing could have been in better taste than that speech."

Another delegate said, "We might have done a more daring thing, but we certainly could not have done a better thing." That evening, when a crowd assembled in front of his house and clamored for a speech, he refused to make one, saying, "Fellow citizens, there are moments in every politician's life when the best thing he can do is to keep his lips closed. I think such a moment has now come for me."

But when he had to write the formal letter of acceptance, he was troubled in his mind, wondered whether he could write it properly — he who, in twenty-two years of his legal practice, had penned thousands of documents. What does he do to-day? He goes with the letter to the superintendent of education and says, "Mr. Schoolmaster, here is my letter of acceptance. I am not very strong on grammar, and I wish you to see if it is all right. I wouldn't like to have any mistakes in it." The other glanced through the document, and said, "There is only one change I should suggest, Mr. Lincoln. You have written: 'It shall be my care to not violate or disregard it in any part'; you should have written 'not to violate.' Never split an infinitive, is the rule." Lincoln took the manuscript, regarding it for a moment with a puzzled air. "So you think I better put those two little fellows end to end, do you?" he said, as he made the suggested change.

Has ever a king or a president adopted a more charming attitude? Lincoln has not been, like a king in a fairy tale, taken from the plow to rule the people. He is a man over fifty, grown gray-headed in the practice of the law, in business affairs, and in political life. After having made many great speeches to the nation, after years of campaigning, he has been selected to run for the highest office in the land. He knows too that he is fit for the job. But there are little matters that men born to be kings, the Douglases, know all about — the well-ironed coats of the New Yorkers, the well-fitting trousers of the Washington gentlemen. These "little fellows" in grammar that have to "sit" properly like a necktie, have to be "well brushed" like a stovepipe hat. It would be fatal to make a slip here! Mary, of course, understands about shoes and collars; she can even talk French, but when the question is one of how to word a letter properly, it is better to go to the schoolmaster. Besides, he will know how to keep a still tongue, and even should he gossip, there will be nothing to Lincoln's discredit.

And so the President of to-morrow goes over to an old teacher to ask advice on matters he had not learned in Indiana, for there he had to split rails.

XIX

A poet was the first to understand what was happening here; Bryant wrote, "A poor flatboat-man — such are the true leaders of the Nation!" He found himself alone in this opinion for, in general, the Republican leaders were far from happy. One of them writes:

"I remember that when I first read the news on a bulletin board as I came down street in Philadelphia that I experienced a moment of intense physical pain, it was as though some one had dealt me a heavy blow over the head; then my strength failed me. I believed our cause was doomed."

In the eastern States it was said that Seward had been sacrificed; he was the real chief of the young party, he was even advised to ignore the decision of the Chicago Convention, and to have himself nominated. But Seward, being a gentleman, was prompt to congratulate his rival and when the New Yorkers found no one to write an article on Lincoln he wrote the first, though rather a cold, estimate.

The tone of the Democratic papers about Lincoln was savagely derisive. He was "a third-rate country lawyer." He was "a

LINCOLN IN 1860

From a photograph by Hesler, Springfield, Illinois

nullity." He was "in the habit of making coarse and clumsy jokes."
He "could not speak good grammar." He was not a gentleman:
was accustomed to sit in his shirt sleeves; tilted his chair. He
could split rails: that was all he was fit for. As for his looks, he
resembled a gorilla.

The results of the nomination were ominous. For months the
Southerners had been vociferating that the Union would break up
if a Black Republican were elected President. Now, when there
had been a nomination far more offensive to the South than that of
Seward would have been, the question of slavery passed suddenly
into the background, and the whole nation was inquiring whether
Lincoln's election would not involve the break-up of the Union.
The change was such as occurs when a man who, in the course of his
career, has often had to decide whether to turn to the right or to
the left, is suddenly overtaken by grave illness, so that the only
question with him now is, "Shall I be alive next week?"

Never, since the foundation of the United States, had the hatred
of the South for the North flamed so fiercely. Only the South
hated, and that was because the Northern condemnation of the
"peculiar institution" of the South was a moral one. Those who
feel that others regard them with moral contempt react with passion rather than with argument.

"Free society?" wrote a Southern newspaper. "We sicken of the
name. What is it but a conglomeration of greasy mechanics, filthy
operatives, small-fisted farmers, and moon-struck theorists! All
the Northern and especially the New England States are devoid of
society fitted for well-bred gentlemen. The prevailing class one
meets with is that of mechanics struggling to be genteel, and small
farmers who do their own drudgery, and yet who are hardly fit for
association with a Southern gentleman's body-servant."

While this fresh campaign is in progress, certain officers in border
forts announce if Lincoln is elected they will throw up their commissions and withdraw to the South. Northern business men take
alarm, trade is bad, Southern debtors will not pay their Northern
creditors, the stock market becomes jumpy, money is tight, the
financial situation "borders on panic." Everywhere there are

meetings in favor of maintaining the Union and urging compromise. In Boston, an anti-slavery gathering is broken up by an angry mob. Ere long, however, the Northerners begin to realize that the prospect of Lincoln's election as President is, for the South, a mere pretext. Many of the Southerners do not want compromise; they no longer desire union with the North; they wish to set up a separate confederation of the Southern States.

No one is more watchful than Lincoln.

In his provincial nest he receives the first secret information about war preparations from an army major. He meditates: Has he more authority, in these moments, than any other American, he who to-morrow may be outvoted and forgotten? He cannot demand further information though it would be most useful. He begs the major to continue, if it would not be unprofessional or dishonorable — "of which you are to be judge."

What must he think of the corruptibility and the stupidity of his fellow men when he learns that at the Chicago Convention, as soon as the current seemed to be setting in favor of his nomination, a number of the delegates who had been voting for some other nominee showed themselves overready to welcome the rising sun, and to register their votes in favor of the man who would in a little while have places to dispose of? What must he think when the interviewers flock to Springfield that they may describe his home, his family, and his habits — in order to prove that the Republican nominee does not live "in low Hoosier style." Must not his sardonic humor be tickled when the reporters declare with great satisfaction that his daily wear is a broadcloth suit "almost elegant"; that his wife speaks French fluently; and that he has a son at Harvard College?

But among the farmers he finds that the story of his having been a rail splitter is a stimulus to enthusiasm. Great play is made with this, rails are figured on campaign medals and on tobacco pipes, songs are sung about Lincoln the riverman, the tree feller, the patriarch. People are already quarreling about the genuineness of the rails; two are put on show at the party headquarters in New York and a political club announces that it possesses the ax originally used by Lincoln.

Meanwhile there is a split among the Democrats, as Lincoln with the eye of the statesman had foreseen, two years before. If Lincoln is the "rail splitter", Douglas might just as well be called the "party splitter." He wobbles between North and South and ruins his chances; the South repudiates him, and pays no heed to the flattering tones in which he addresses it. Soon there are three candidates in the field in opposition to Lincoln, but they are more concerned to fight one another than to fight him. This split had been prepared by Douglas and forced into existence by him, so he can be said to have personally calculated and decided this election.

During his electoral campaign, Lincoln had to change his habits a little, and yet he remained the same man as ever. In the morning, when he was seen leaving the post office, laden with the heavy mail (for he never thought of sending for it), everybody could walk up to him and accompany him to the Capitol, where there was no porter, and where the door of his room was open all the morning, although threats of assassination had already been uttered. He had, however, now taken a secretary, Nicolay, of German origin, serious-minded, diligent, taciturn; a student learning under him, and who later was himself assisted by Hay, a law student with a poetical disposition, humorous and musically inclined. These two men were qualified later on to write the first great source of detailed information concerning their chief.

All who now flocked to Springfield in search of information or advice, or hoping for the promise of a place, were received with equal friendliness — and with equal reserve, and he tried personally to answer as many of the thousands of letters as he could. "I see that you have not read my speeches; here is a copy of them," he would often say. Hundred of copies of this reprint of the debates with Douglas were given away and in many more instances a question was answered with an anecdote. In cases of public misunderstanding or misrepresentation, he preferred to reply in private, to avoid giving his adversaries fresh cause for controversy, being of opinion that this was a time when it was "best for him to keep his lips closed." At length, when letters asking his political views were multiplied beyond bounds, he found it necessary to have a standardized form of reply :

"Your letter to Mr. Lincoln of" — such and such a date — "by which you seek to obtain his opinion on certain political points, has been received by him. He has received others of a similar character, but he also has a greater number of the exactly opposite character. The latter class beseech him to write nothing whatever upon any point of political doctrine. They say his positions were well known when he was nominated, and that he must not now embarrass the canvass by undertaking to shift or modify them. He regrets that he cannot oblige all, but you perceive it is impossible for him to do so."

Thus the inquirer was made to feel that Lincoln's refusal to answer was not dictated by personal reluctance, but was the expression of a general sentiment as to what ought to be done. In this way the aim of discretion could be achieved without giving offense. But once :

"While talking to two or three gentlemen and standing up, a very hard-looking customer rolled in and tumbled into the only vacant chair and the one lately occupied by Mr. Lincoln. Mr. Lincoln's keen eye took in the fact, but gave no evidence of the notice. Turning round at last, he spoke to the odd specimen, holding out his hand at such a distance that our friend had to vacate the chair if he accepted the proffered shake. Mr. Lincoln quietly resumed his chair."

This is the behavior of a man who has sprung from the common people, has outdistanced but not forgotten them. Towards this man who is rude, he shows no irritation, nor yet a forced geniality, nor does he ignore the affront; but he adopts the device of an experienced wrestler, who lures his opponent out of a favorable position ; and he does it in a way which any diplomat might envy.

Throughout, however, Lincoln remained perfectly easy in his ways, and when Carl Schurz was to speak for him in Springfield, he himself walked with Schurz to the place of the open-air meeting. It was a hot day in August, and Lincoln had left coat and waistcoat at home, wearing instead a long dust coat, much weather-worn, and on his head was "a somewhat battered stove-pipe hat." In this guise, side by side with Schurz, he strolled through the streets of the town, accompanied by the braying of the band, and greeting acquaintances as he went: "Good evening, Ben!" — "How are you, Joe?" — "Glad to see you, Dick!" And so he travels while the crowd laughs and applauds, shouting, "Three cheers for old Abe!"

One of the strangest of the letters he received came from a little girl, who seems to have made an inquiry about Lincoln's family, and to have told him that he ought to grow a beard. Here is the reply:

"Springfield, Illinois, October 15, 1860. My dear little Miss, your very agreeable letter of the 15th is received. I regret the necessity of saying I have no daughter. I have three sons — one seventeen, one nine, and one seven. They, with their mother, constitute my whole family. As to the whiskers, having never worn any, do you not think people would call it a piece of silly affectation if I were to begin wearing them now? I am your true friend and sincere well-wisher, A. Lincoln."

In actual fact, however, almost immediately after this, he did begin to grow a beard. This may have been an old topic of discussion between himself and his wife, for we can hardly suppose that, at so late a date, he would have undergone this unfavorable change without her consent. However this may be, during the next weeks the good citizens of Springfield were able to watch black bristles sprouting on the familiar countenance — familiar and unforgetable in its wrinkled and bony nakedness, whereas the beard and whiskers gave his visage a softer and more yielding aspect, deprived the broad mouth of some of its defiance, hid the pointed chin and the scraggy neck and the prominent Adam's apple.

At length, in November, came election day. According to all the indications, his election was practically certain, so that at Springfield and throughout Illinois interest mainly turned on the question how big the majority was going to be. Just as had happened twenty-five years before in New Salem, so now in Springfield even the Democrats cheered loudly in favor of their beloved townsman, although they could not vote for him. That was what Lincoln wanted, what he had underlined in his autobiographical sketch. Nothing could have been more gratifying to him, whose fundamental honesty and straightforwardness made him rejoice in the affectionate approval of those among whom he lived; just as nothing was more painful to him at this time than the unanimous hostility of the clergy of Springfield.

In the election, Lincoln received nearly 1,900,000 votes, and Douglas 1,400,000. The other two candidates secured, between them, another million and a half votes, so that in actual fact Lincoln was elected by a Northern minority. Out of three hundred three electoral votes, Lincoln received one hundred eighty. In fifteen States of the Union, he got no electoral votes; and in ten States, not a single popular vote. But for the first time in the history of the Union, the North had used its preponderant numerical strength to vote down the South. This was menacing, but it was also symbolical, for it showed what would be the outcome of a civil war, should war come.

Would it come? That was the question which this serious man was now turning over in his mind day and night; suffocating the humor which helped him to live, tormenting him when jubilant crowds were filing in procession past his house. There were thousands upon thousands coming to pay homage to him! Had he, then, won a great battle? Had he saved the country, or unified it? Whither was destiny, in which he believed, now leading him? What struggles were awaiting him in the uncongenial Washington, where people loved the South? He knew his own strength, and he knew his own limitations, for he could contemplate himself dispassionately. Was he strong enough to withstand that Douglas atmosphere which could out-weary the strongest? Would the North support him, when so many Northerners were in favor of compromise? Or would they want him to resign? Could he effectively represent a cause which had, indeed, been espoused by the majority of the nation, when the minority was so hopelessly refractory that the Union made by their fathers was about to be broken?

Thus must he have pondered moodily, as from his wooden balcony he watched the interminable procession, listened to the bands, and to the triumphant choruses of the campaign songs, while Mary stood beside him, laughing unweariedly, and graciously acknowledging the acclamations of the crowd. She, at any rate, was happy and so were the children pressing to her side; she shared unhesitatingly in the general delight. Abraham Lincoln alone had a heavy heart, thinking that he who, as a boy in a log cabin long ago, had with a glowing heart read by the firelight, from a tattered book, the story of George Washington — was now to be his fifteenth successor.

XX

Not yet, indeed! Four months had still to pass before he could take up the reins of office, and the interval was perhaps the most trying period of his life. In peaceful times, a man who had been nominated for the presidency could devote the many months that had to elapse before he could begin to wield power to the study of personalities and conditions, to the marking out of a line of action. It was like the epoch of a betrothal, during which he could revolve in an orbit around the presidency as a pledged lover circles at a distance around his fiancée.

For Lincoln, however, there was vouchsafed no such forecast of perfect happiness. He was listening, in imagination, not to the strains of the Wedding March, but to the threatening pulses of martial music. Evil tidings came to trouble his peace of mind. There was firing on all sides of the President elect. On the day after the poll, the *Charleston Mercury* published the information of Lincoln's election under the caption "Foreign News", the governor of South Carolina officially advocated the purchase of arms and munitions, and in private entered into arrangements with the governors of the other Southern States, which for the last four years had been resolved to break away from the Union should a Republican be elected President.

Four days after the election the United States senators from South Carolina resigned; a week later the South Carolina journals issued extras, announcing in gigantic headlines the dissolution of the Union. This, which raised a hubbub in the streets, was premature; but only five weeks afterwards the South Carolina legislature passed an ordinance of secession, and began to organize an independent government.

The North, meanwhile, was clamoring for compromise. Some of the points in the Republican program must be withdrawn; the trouble, said these weak-kneed Northerners, was not due to the recalcitrancy of the Southern States, but to the excesses of the radicals. Above all, Lincoln was to blame! He received sacks full of scurrilous letters, in which he was abused as a Negro, mulatto, buffoon; in which he was threatened with caning, burning, shooting, and hanging. For his part, he was looking neither to the North nor to the South, but towards Washington.

Everything there depended on the conduct of the retiring President. If he remained true to his oath to safeguard and maintain the Union, if he counteracted every attempt at treason, if he strongly upheld the rights of the Union and was prepared to use all the force at his disposal against any State that should try to disintegrate the Union, could he have prevented secession?

Buchanan was a venerable-looking old man, with white hair, but somewhat shifty eyes. He always wore a white necktie, which gave him a clerical aspect. In truth, he was cold and obstinate, cautious, and, none the less, unstable. Those who extolled him as eminently practical did him too much honor, for his cleverness lacked grip, and he was timid in his shrewdness. Apart from his character and his record, it was natural enough that an old man, approaching the end of his term of power, should be loath to imperil his reputation, his peace of mind, and perhaps his life. Let the tall lawyer from Illinois deal with these thorny matters when the time came! Buchanan, elected by the South, had, by his election, become chief of the whole Union. Typically enough, therefore, he adopted a middle course; and his main desire was that the crisis should be held in suspense for another twelve weeks, until he could retire to his Pennsylvania home, and there play the part of dispassionate spectator. Therefore, in a message to Congress, he

declared that, while a State had no legal right to secede, the Federal
Government had no power forcibly to prevent secession. It need
hardly be said that this message was an encouragement to the South
to secede and that its effect in Europe was to promote a conviction
that there was no possibility of maintaining the Union.

He was really led by his cabinet, in which there was a majority
for the Union, although its most influential personalities favored the
South. Two members who remained perfectly straightforward
were General Cass, the man whom Lincoln had once made fun of
in Congress, and who resigned at this juncture; and Stanton, who
went frankly to Buchanan, saying, "It is my duty, as your legal
adviser, to inform you that you have no right to hand over the
property of the State, no right to let your enemies take its soldiers
and its ships. The line now being taken by the secretary of the
interior is treasonable, and will involve you and all who collaborate
in treason!" Thereupon he handed in his resignation.

The President had virtually abdicated in the final months of
1860, only in the two months of 1861, which completed his term,
to take a somewhat firmer line under the influence of the strongly
Union members of his cabinet, especially Black and Stanton.
The cabinet, however, contained several members sympathetic
with the South, who allowed the transfer of property and munitions from Federal forts and arsenals, and the depletion of the
funds in the Federal Treasury before relinquishing their offices.
Cabinet members came and went with bewildering rapidity between those months of the election of Lincoln and his induction
into office. One cabinet member, Thompson, while still in charge
of the Interior Department, encouraged the State of North
Carolina to secede and allowed the impression to prevail that the
President endorsed his mission.

To one of the senators from North Carolina, Thompson said:

"I am appointed negotiator to bring about the secession of your
State."

"I did not know," answered the senator, "that you had resigned."

"I have not resigned, and do not intend to. Buchanan wants us
all to remain in office until March 4th."

"But does Buchanan know what you are planning in North Carolina?"

"Of course."

"Never before," said the amazed senator afterwards, "did I hear of any instance of a ruler sending a member of his own cabinet to organize a revolution against his own government."

While conspiracy was thus tolerated in the cabinet, the Southern senators, continuing to draw their salaries, were sitting on commissions appointed to effect a compromise; were listening to Seward's proposals for a compromise; were laughing at Corwin, the veteran, whose failing voice issued a last warning to the country; were rejoicing in the applause of the gallery; were planning to make Washington the capital of the new confederation; and of an evening, in the new club, were vying one with another in witticisms concerning the badly dressed backwoodsman who fancied that he was about to become President of the United States.

All the while Lincoln was living quietly in his little house in Springfield, far from the great happenings; listening, pondering, ceaselessly questioning his brain and his conscience. When he read the newspapers in the morning, or at eventide went to one of the newspaper offices to glance at the latest telegrams — what news? He learned day by day that another stone had crumbled away from the strong tower which the fathers of the country had upbuilded; day followed day on which the post brought warnings from the North and threats from the South — threats which often took the form of pictured daggers; every day came urgent requests for a word of consolation, or at least of guidance to the country. He held his peace, however, for, though elected to carry out a policy whose details he had expounded, he was not as yet in a position to put any of his plans into operation. Every intriguing secretary in the capital had more power to-day than the man who had been chosen to be President on the morrow.

Meanwhile he was besieged by visitors. When advised to deny himself to most of them, he replied, "They ask very little, and get still less. I must see them." There speaks the man of the people, who needs this perpetual contact with his fellows to strengthen his inner convictions.   One writer tells us:

"When receiving such visitors, his shrewdness of insight speedily enabled him to grasp the newcomer's character and peculiarities. He adapted himself to these, was willing to answer any suitable question, and always answered suitably.   Since he invariably had some original argument at his command, if there was any difference of opinion, he usually kept the upper hand."

But when Horace Greeley came to Springfield, and did not seek out Lincoln, the latter, President elect of the United States, called at Greeley's hotel.   They conversed for an hour without coming to an understanding, and Lincoln took his leave discouraged, without having told a single anecdote.

Should he resign?   He was publicly advised to do so.   Would anything be gained thereby?   Only with a surrender.   Ought he to surrender?   Never!   In this matter the new President is unyielding from the first, and will remain unyielding to the last.

"We are told in advance the government shall be broken up unless we surrender to those we have beaten, before we take the offices. In this they are either attempting to play upon us or they are in dead earnest.   Either way, if we surrender, it is the end of us, and of the government.   They will repeat the experiment upon us *ad libitum*.   A year will not pass till we shall have to take Cuba as a condition upon which they will stay in the Union."

A few weeks after the election he writes:

"Prevent, as far as possible, any of our friends from demoralizing themselves and our cause by entertaining propositions for compromise of any sort on slavery extension.   There is no possible compromise upon it but which puts us under again, and leaves all our work to do over again.   Whether it be a Missouri line or Eli Thayer's popular sovereignty, it is all the same.   Let either be done, and immediately filibustering and extending slavery recommence.   On that point hold firm as with a chain of steel.

At about the same date, through Seward's instrumentality, a new compromise in the matter of latitude is proposed to him privately, with the same result.

The Southerners' attitude towards every proposal made by the
North frees him from any qualms of conscience; from any conflict
between will to power and love of country. Lincoln finds wonderful parables:

"Go to the river bank with a coarse sieve and fill it with gravel.
After a vigorous shaking you will observe that the small pebbles
and sand have sunk from view and fallen to the ground. The next
larger in size, unable to slip between the wires, will still be found
within the sieve. By thorough and repeated shakings you will find
that, of the pebbles still left in the sieve, the largest ones will have
risen to the top. Now, if war is inevitable and will shake the
country from center to circumference, you will find that the little
men will fall out of view in the shaking. The masses will rest on
some solid foundation, and the big men will have climbed to the
top. Of these latter, one greater than all the rest will leap forth
equipped — the people's leader in the conflict."

Or he tells the tale of a township which wanted to build a bridge.
It was looking round for an engineer, and a man noted for his piety
recommended some one as highly efficient, technically speaking,
though not a church member.

"I'm ready to build a bridge to the infernal regions, if necessary,"
said the engineer, to the horror of the worthy townsfolk, who looked
questioningly at the man who had given the recommendation.

The latter said, "I know Jones. . . . If he says he can build a
bridge to Hades, why, I believe it; but I have my doubts about
the abutments on the infernal side."

Such is Lincoln when his native shrewdness makes him ready
to defy the onslaughts of fate. But that is a rare mood. Now,
week by week, he grows more anxious. His appetite fails, he becomes thinner than ever, his friends declare that the melancholy of
his visage is a danger; he responds by making jokes, and thus
estranges a good many people. When really irritated, he will retort
with unusual warmth. A visitor comes from New England, a business man, to speak of the danger to the manufacturing interests of
that region, and bringing letters of the same tenor. Lincoln divines
the mercenary nature of the appeal, and says he will make no truck

with his principles. The delegate shows him an additional letter, bearing a number of signatures, and asks him if he does not recognize names that are a power. Glancing at them, Lincoln rejoins sharply, "Yes, I recognize them as a set of liars and knaves who signed that statement about Seward last year." Then, cooling off a little, he adds with a laugh, "It annoyed me to hear that gang of men called respectable."

Artists came to take Lincoln's likeness. One of them, a sculptor, wanted a cast of his hands, and said he must have something firm to grip. Lincoln went out to the woodshed and came back to the dining room with an old broom handle, which he proceeded to whittle carefully. The sculptor said he need not be so particular as all that. "Oh, well," said Lincoln, "I thought I would like to have it nice." Here is a man who now has scarcely a moment to spare, little interest in the work of portraiture, and no real need to whittle the broomhandle so carefully; but he cannot help himself; he has whittled plenty of sticks carefully before, and from childhood upwards has been wont to take more pains about such things than about the writing of documents.

When a fashionable portrait painter was sent to him by a snob, Lincoln at first declined to give another sitting, but at length agreed to do so. Next morning, at the appointed time, he threw himself into the chair which had been arranged for him, and sat there as if petrified, impenetrable in his abstraction, preoccupied with gloomy thoughts. The artist could see nothing but the rough features of a working man; he had had his mind filled with reports of Lincoln's coarse manners and low stories; and believing he must speak to him in the vulgar tone to which Lincoln is accustomed, makes a flippant remark. Now Lincoln lifts his eye and looks at him with a wonderful expression — "a mingling of instant shrewd apprehension of the whole attitude of mind at back of my remark, pained disappointment at my misunderstanding of him, and patient tolerance. In a flash, I saw I had made a mistake."

As in a tragic scene, motives and effects of two different characters are developed here. The elegant painter who most likely left for Springfield with a joke on his lips to paint the curious fellow for

the money of a rich man, cannot intrude into the mysteries of the
frozen features, sees only his lowly origin, the only thing in which the
great man may be his inferior. He concludes most superficially as
to the character of his model and wants to seize his attention by some
vulgar obscenity. The other at once perceives the thoughts of the
artist; but instead of getting rid of him with a single movement,
that human feeling of partnership arises in him, the old disappointment about the abyss of misunderstanding, and he shoots a look at
the stranger that humiliates the man but elevates the artist.

Gillespie, one of his oldest friends, comes to sit by the fire in the
evening, and tries to distract Lincoln from his troubles by talking
over old times: "Yes, yes, I remember," Lincoln would rejoin,
listlessly. Gillespie says:

"The oldtime zest was not only lacking, but in its place was a
gloom and despondency entirely foreign to Lincoln's character as I
had learned to know it. . . .   He sat with his head lying upon his
arms, which were folded over the back of his chair, as I had often
seen him sit on our travels after an exciting day in court. Suddenly
he roused himself. 'Gillespie,' said he, 'I would willingly take out
of my life a period in years equal to the two months that intervene
between now and my inauguration to take the oath of office now.'
'Why?' I asked. 'Because every hour adds to the difficulties I am
called upon to meet, and the present administration does nothing
to check the tendency towards dissolution. I, who have been
called to meet this awful responsibility, am compelled to remain
here, doing nothing to avert it or lessen its force when it comes to
me.' A little later, 'It is not of myself I complain,' he said, with
more bitterness than I ever heard him speak, before or after, 'but
every day adds to the difficulty of the situation, and makes the
outlook more gloomy. Secession is being fostered rather than
repressed, and if the doctrine meets with a general acceptance in the
border States, it will be a great blow to the government. . . .   I
have read, upon my knees, the story of Gethsemane, where the Son
of God prayed in vain that the cup of bitterness might pass from
him. I am in the garden of Gethsemane now, and my cup of
bitterness is full and overflowing.' . . .   When I retired, it was the

master of the house and chosen ruler of the country who saw me to
my room. 'Joe,' he said, as he was about to leave me, 'I suppose you
will never forget that trial down in Montgomery County, where the
lawyer associated with you gave away the whole case in his opening
speech. I saw you signaling to him, but you couldn't stop him.
Now, that's just the way with me and Buchanan. He is giving
away the case, and I have nothing to say, and can't stop him.
Good-night.'"

Here we see Lincoln at close quarters; manly, in spite of his
despondency, restrained in his emotions, careful, even in this hour
of crisis, to avoid exaggeration. He does not say that he would
give his life to skip this interval; he said two years — a high price,
but not an absurd one. If he compares his position with that of
Jesus in the Garden of Gethsemane, he does so briefly and in out-
line; next moment he is back in the world of facts, reminds his friend
of a trial and says epigrammatically, Buchanan is giving away my
case. Next morning he is in better spirits. "I only wish I could
have got to Washington to lock the door before the horse was
stolen," he says. "But when I get to the spot, I can only find the
tracks."

He is on the watch for signs and portents. Between the field
of the country lad and the field of the philosopher stands the huge
and ancient tree of superstition, casting its shade on either side.
Here is a happening recorded by a friend in Lincoln's own words:

"Once, after a tumultuous and tiring day, I threw myself down
on an old sofa at home.

"Opposite where I lay was a bureau with a swinging glass upon it,
and looking in that glass, I saw myself reflected nearly at full length;
but my face, I noticed, had *two* separate and distinct images, the tip
of the nose of one being about three inches from the tip of the other.
I was a little bothered, perhaps startled, and got up and looked in
the glass, but the illusion vanished. On lying down again, I saw
it a second time, plainer, if possible, than before; and then I noticed that one of the faces was a little paler — say, five shades —
than the other. I got up, and the thing melted away, and I went
off, and in the excitement of the hour forgot all about it — nearly,

but not quite, for the thing would once in a while come up, and give
me a little pang, as if something uncomfortable had happened.
When I went home again that night, I told my wife about it, and a
few days afterward I made the experiment again, when, sure enough,
the thing came again; but I never succeeded in bringing the ghost
back after that, though I once tried very industriously to show it
to my wife, who was somewhat worried about it. She thought it
was a 'sign' that I was to be elected to a second term of office, and
that the paleness of one of the faces was an omen that I should not
see life through the last term."

Must this not alarm him? How often, during these weeks, he
must have asked himself whether he ought not, for the sake of peace,
to retire, to leave the way open for a fresh election, to assuage the
intensity of popular passion under new conditions, to prevent the
outbreak of civil war by the withdrawal of his personality? If he
did not give way to such promptings, his decision to persist must
(his character being what it was) have been dictated by positive
considerations. But now he is startled by a sign. Though, as his
manner is, he tries to explain what happens, though he speaks with
the utmost precision of "three inches" and "five shades", though he
forgets "nearly but not quite", though he looks for the manifestation again, finds it, and then fails to find it — there remains, in the
end, a disquietude which he cannot banish from his heart.

But Mary faces up sturdily to the uncanny phenomenon. Her
vitality is such that she refuses to accept it as a warning of anything
that would cost her the goal of her ambition; and yet her infallible
instinct, which long before had made her anticipate Lincoln's
career, now discloses to her Lincoln's end.

XXI

In December, there was one Southern fortress left to the Union: in
Charleston Harbor. It was held by Major Anderson, in an extremely difficult situation. From Washington he had received
orders and counter orders to deliver up guns, and when he was in
need of reinforcements and had become convinced that the authorities were playing double, he at last retired on his own responsibility

LINCOLN IN 1860

From an ambrotype made in Springfield, Illinois

to the strongest position, Fort Sumter. There was an uproar alike in the North and in the South; and early in January the President yielded to popular clamor, sending a vessel, the *Star of the West*, to Anderson with supplies. The ship was fired on by the South Carolinians as she entered the harbor, and had to withdraw. This was, in reality, the opening of the war. In Charleston there were exultant demonstrations, in which people trampled on the banner of the Union. During this same month of January, five additional States seceded: Florida, Alabama, Georgia, Louisiana, and Mississippi. Like South Carolina, they all proceeded to make ready for war.

Black had been transferred from his place in the cabinet as Attorney General to the premier place of Secretary of State in succession to Cass, who had resigned. Cobb, now that he had emptied the Treasury, had also resigned, saying openly that it would be his business henceforward to work for the Confederate government. President Buchanan, nerving himself at length for a deed, hoping to check the progress of national disaster, ordered a general Fast Day! When, at Washington on this occasion, General Scott wanted to hold a review of the troops, Buchanan forbade it at first, and then allowed it. By turns, the President commissioned officers to the forts, and issued counter orders when they arrived. It was common talk in the White House that documents were being stolen from the archives.

Panic was widespread in the North; there was a general desire for peace. Should business be ruined, should well-being be undermined, for the sake of a few thousand slaves? For an idea? Leading Northerners wrote to the South, proposing a compromise: and similar attempts were made in Congress.

The deep-seated reason for the Southern secession was not yet fully understood in the North. The North did not realize how fierce an anger animated the South; above all, although North and South had formed one community for more than eighty years, the Northerners did not even now understand in how all-pervading a sense the Southern States were aristocratic; that they had remained a country of the old kind, of masters and servants, of command and obedience, a place where those who thought and led were few in number. Passion in this crisis was mainly on the side of the South, where alone there were reasons for it.

The Southerners wanted to be independent of the North; to be free from incessant criticism of their way of life. In their view, if secession involved them in a fight, it would be a fight for freedom; they looked upon themselves as enslaved by their union with the North.

"It has been proposed," writes a Southerner, "to reopen the African slave trade, but Congress will never agree to this. We ought to annex Mexico and Central America, to secure a neutral road for the import of slaves. If we cannot do this peacefully, we must do it by force of arms. God created negroes for no other purpose than to be hewers of wood and drawers of water for the whites. We Southerners, who constitute one of the most virtuous, enlightened, and powerful among the peoples that now exist, have too long been lacking in self-esteem. The North will never be able to rule the South. If love of country does not stand in the way, then the love of cotton and tobacco will do so. The enslavement of negroes is justified by the Bible, by humanitarian considerations, and by a sound philosophy."

Lincoln was still waiting in Springfield, powerless. Writing from Washington, Seward urged him to come thither earlier. Had he been, like Seward, a senator, or, like Douglas, a man well known personally to all the chiefs in the political world, he might have followed this advice; but, as a stranger, exposed to criticism and without any backing, he could not venture on any such step. Nor could he possibly follow the counsel of others, who wanted him to put himself at the head of a hundred thousand Wide Awakes, who could be found, enter the capital and take over the government, a few weeks before the date prescribed by the Constitution. Lincoln as triumphal warrior; the friend of peace as the armed conqueror of his own capital!

For news of his own country he was dependent on smuggled letters and secret messages: he was an imprisoned king. When a captain in the Charleston fort wrote secretly to a brother in New

York, the President elect in Springfield was glad to get a glimpse of the letter; and it was good luck that old General Scott, considering himself snubbed by the President, applied indirectly to the incoming one and received the indirect answer: "I shall be obliged to him to be as well prepared as he can to either *hold* or *retake* the forts, as the case may require, at and after the inauguration." Thus cautiously had the elected of the nation to negotiate with a defender of the Union, as if both of them had been spies. Trumbull in Washington was nearer to him, and many letters were exchanged between them. On Christmas Eve, Lincoln wrote:

"Dispatches have come here two days in succession, that the fort in South Carolina will be surrendered by the order, or consent at least, of the President. I can scarcely believe this; but if it prove true, I will, if our friends at Washington concur, announce publicly at once that they are to be retaken after the inauguration. This will give the Union Men a rallying cry, and preparation will proceed somewhat on their side, as well as on the other."

To that side Lincoln knew of only one bridge and he made the best use he could of it for the very reason that he could not yet feel himself to be the head of the nation. The "Lincoln" of the South, the moderate man of the South, at this juncture was Alexander Stephens of Georgia. Twelve years before, he and Lincoln had been Congressmen together, not neighbors, indeed, for Stephens was a Democrat; but they had been together in mind, for both of them were practical idealists. It was the same Stephens who had made Lincoln, a solitary unknown Congressman, shed tears over his speech on the Mexican War, when Stephens had expressed a wonder "whether the free people of this country have so soon forgotten the principles of their ancestors as to be so easily awed by the arrogance of power." Stephens and Lincoln had joined forces in founding the Taylor Club, to promote the election of Taylor as President. They must have made a strange-looking pair as they went about together, the lean giant, and the little, slim, pale, consumptive-looking man from the South; but their faces were alike in this, that both of them had dry and wrinkled skins. Stephens, however, had delicate features and fine eyes, which made him more attractive at first sight than Lincoln — though Stephens was diffident as to his own aspect, writing once in his diary: "I believe I shall never be worth anything, and the thought is death to my soul. I am too boyish, unmanful, trifling, simple in my manners and address."

Since then, the two men had remained in touch, even after the conflict had grown fiercer, and when they respectively had ripened to leaders of hostile parties. A few months before nomination, Lincoln had written to Stephens "the longest letter I ever dictated or wrote", a criticism of Stephens, but couched in tones of friendship growing chilly. Now, in December, Lincoln read two great admonitory speeches of Stephens. Lincoln's election, said the latter, had been perfectly constitutional. Rebellion was an uncertain method; a war would be very likely to end with the abolition of slavery, whether under martial law or by civil proclamation. This, the last warning from the South before the Southern States gave way to passion, made a profound impression throughout the country, and not least on Lincoln, who wrote to Stephens, begging for a revised copy of the speech. Stephens replied courteously, saying that the speech had not been revised, but that the newspaper report was sufficiently accurate for practical purposes: "The country is certainly in great peril, and no man ever had heavier or greater responsibilities resting upon him than you have in the present momentous crisis." Lincoln answered promptly:

"Do the people of the South really entertain fears that a Republican administration would, directly or indirectly, interfere with the slaves, or with them about the slaves? If they do, I wish to assure you, as once a friend, and still, I hope, not an enemy, that there is no cause for such fears. The South would be in no more danger in this respect than it was in the days of Washington. I suppose, however, this does not meet the case. You think slavery is right and ought to be extended, while we think it is wrong and ought to be restricted. That, I suppose, is the rub. It certainly is the only substantial difference between us."

How manly is this letter in its terseness, in its utilization of the last opportunity to assure one of the leaders over there of the

Southern independence. But, at the same time a simple moral word as if, while the old friend was still within earshot, to remind him how they two had, in long conversations, always been able to come to an understanding about humanity. Stephens' answer is also concise and grave. Lincoln was putting the institutions of nearly half the States under the ban of public opinion and national condemnation. For a while, none the less, Stephens continued to do his utmost to restrain Georgia from secession. Ere long, however, came the time when the nearer home seemed more important to him than the farther one; when Georgia, with its familiar streams and forests, Georgia and its sister States of the South, were more to him than the artificial Union; when, swept away by the current of Southern opinion, he came to the front as vice president of the rebel Southern confederacy.

In the beginning of February, the representatives of seven Southern States assembled at Montgomery, Alabama, and founded the Confederate States, with a constitution very similar to that of the Union. Jefferson Davis, United States Senator for Mississippi, became president. Stephens, speaking at Savannah a few weeks after his inauguration as vice president, explained matters as follows:

"The new constitution makes an end, once for all, of the disturbing problems that have arisen out of our institution, slavery. This was the immediate cause of the rupture and of the revolution. The prevailing ideas entertained by Jefferson and most of the leading statesmen at the time of the formation of the old Constitution, were that the enslavement of the Africans was in violation of the law of nature; that it was wrong in *principle*, socially, morally, and politically. . . . Our new government is founded upon exactly the opposite idea. Its foundations are laid, its corner-stone rests upon the great truth, that the negro is not equal to the white man; that slavery — subordination to the superior race — is his natural and normal condition. This, our new government, is the first, in the history of the world, to be based upon this great physical, philosophical, and moral truth. Secession became necessary when the North refused to recognize the great moral, political, and religious truth that there can be no other solid foundation than the slavery of the negro. . . . It is, indeed, in conformity with the ordinance of the Creator. . . . The great objects of humanity are best attained when there is conformity to His laws and decrees, in the formation of governments as well as in all things else."

The voice is the very same that once had reduced the unsentimental Lincoln to tears. So quickly does a catchword win power over the brain of a man when his heart is more strongly attached to his country than to the cause of all mankind. Lincoln was never faced with the dilemma which Stephens had to face at this juncture, but everything we know of Lincoln leads us to suppose that he would have answered differently to such a test.

XXII

"You are President elect. I congratulate you and thank God. The great object of my wishes and labors for nineteen years is accomplished in the overthrow of the slave power. The space is now clear for the establishment of the policy of freedom on safe and firm grounds. The lead is yours. The responsibility is great. May God strengthen you for your great duties."

This was among the first congratulations received by Lincoln after his election; it came from his rival Chase. When Lincoln formed his cabinet, his main desire was to include Chase and Seward, though both were accounted extremists. By patient persistence in the face of their own hesitancy, and the opposition of some of his advisers, the President elect induced Seward to become Secretary of State and Chase, Secretary of the Treasury. There was a chaffering about the other cabinet offices which Lincoln found extremely distasteful. He told a friend: "If I could choose a cabinet from among the lawyers I traveled with on the Eighth Circuit, I would be able to prevent a war."

"But those lawyers are all Democrats."

"I would rather have Democrats I know than Republicans I don't know."

The little hotel in Springfield became a kind of public exchange, where places were sought and allotted, for Republicans flocked hither to secure posts for themselves or their friends. Disputes raged around the appointment of Cameron, a man whose probity in public affairs was challenged, but on whose behalf pledges had been given in Lincoln's name at Chicago; the question whether Cameron should or should not get an appointment cost Lincoln much anxious thought; but when his old friend Judge Davis was importunate in demands for office, Lincoln was sore at heart; "I know it is an awful thing for me to say, but I already wish some one else was here in my place." With Hamlin, on the other hand, the vice president elect, he soon came to an understanding, and entered into a friendship which lasted till the end.

Many of his old friends, however, proved of sterling metal. He met Speed and his wife, and they talked over old times.

"Speed, are you pretty well off these days?"

"Mr. President, I fancy I know what you are going on to say. I'm fairly well off, thank you. I don't think I want any place you would be likely to offer."

Lincoln's heart warmed. Here, at length, was a friend of long standing who was not a place hunter.

Acquaintances who had not troubled about him for decades emerged suddenly from the void. Even one of the Grigsbys, who had treated his sister so badly once, turning up before the election in the rôle of old friend, wishing to bask in the rays of the rising sun, received the friendly answer:

"Of our three families who removed from Indiana together, my father, Squire Hall, and John D. Johnston are dead, and all the rest of us are yet living, of course the younger ones are grown up, marriages contracted, and new ones born. I have three boys now, the oldest of which is seventeen years of age. There is now a Republican electoral ticket in Missouri, so that you can vote for me if your neighbors will let you. I would advise you not to get into any trouble about it. Give my kindest regards to your brother Charlie."

Before removing to the turmoil of Washington, Lincoln is drawn to the quiet places of his early youth. He rides about in that old country, meets the surviving members of the Hanks and Johnston families, orders the neglected grave of his father to be cared for.

They laugh when they see him, recalling his funny stories; the graybeards remember the stalwart young fellow who drove oxen. Only his good stepmother is silent and at parting seems to have warned him of his enemies. Also old Hannah Armstrong. He reassured her with a jest, "Hannah, if they do kill me I shall never die again."

But the wine has been poured out, and the time has come to drink it. There is not much to arrange at home. He stores his furniture, lets his house, gives a bundle of papers to a niece with the instruction that if he somehow should never return she can do what she likes with them. He burns stacks of letters, although he had, a short time ago, carefully put away his verses.

Before leaving, he prepares his inaugural address, using only, as aids, Clay's, Jackson's, and Webster's speeches, and the United States Constitution. He shuts himself up alone in order to write it. Herndon, referring to the composition of this speech and of previous speeches, tells us that Lincoln was exclusively responsible for it.

"I never wrote a line for him, nor did he ever ask me to do so. I never exercised any influence on him in these matters. He would occasionally consult me upon a point of style, . . . would ask me about the proper use of a word or a phrase. But if I wanted him to change any word which seemed to him to express his feelings well, he was unbending."

This testimony throws a good light on Herndon's character and gives the lie to some suspicions that have been uttered regarding him. What would have been easier than for Herndon, who had for so many years been the great man's partner, to have made much of the part he had played in molding the President's style, or in advising him in choosing his cabinet? The speech was actually written by Lincoln with his own hands, and was very little corrected. Then it was privately printed.

Mary was full of cheerful anticipations, spoke continually of "our promotion", and enjoyed the present of a new tall hat for her husband. She had made a shopping expedition to New York, traveling by special train, accompanied by her sister, and bubbling over with delight.   She gave a great reception, "dressed plainly, but richly, wearing a beautiful full trail, white moiré-antique, with a small French lace collar.   Her neck was ornamented with a string of pearls.   Her headdress was a simple one, a delicate vine arranged with good taste. . . .   She is a lady of fine figure and attractive manner, and is well calculated to grace and do honor at the White House."

In the afternoon before the departure, Lincoln came down to his law office to examine some papers.   Then he threw himself on the sofa, and there was silence for a time.

"Billy, how long have we been together?"

"Over sixteen years."

"We've never had a cross word during all that time, have we?"

"No, indeed we have not."

Lincoln then recalled some incidents of his early practice, gathered up a bundle of books and papers, and started to leave, but paused at the signboard which swung on its rusty hinges at the foot of the stairway.

"Billy, let it hang there undisturbed.   Give our clients to understand that the election of a president makes no change in the firm of Lincoln and Herndon.   If I live, I'm coming back some time, and then we'll go right on practising law as if nothing had ever happened."

As the two men went home together, he said: "I am sick of office holding already, and I shudder when I think of the tasks that are still ahead."   That evening, at the hotel office, Lincoln himself wrote the labels for his trunks: "A. Lincoln, White House, Washington, D. C."   Then he roped the trunks with his own hands.

And why not?   Why should he strike a new attitude because he is about to take over the leadership of the State?   His own native dignity, which is so perfect a counterpoise to his general sense of the dignity of mankind, will unquestionably sustain him at the White House; but is there any reason why he should give up the practice of doing his own chores because he has become President of the United States, and because a hotel porter and one or two other quidnuncs are scrutinizing his actions?   Is there any reason for taking down the old signboard at the law office because some one may think it improper that the President's name should hang at the street corner to attract clients? Who feels this way cannot offend him and those whose opinions he respects will understand his motives. He is only giving an example and is not even the first to do so. Here is still a native expression of the American spirit. We might call it the American idea, that the President should rope his own trunks the night before his departure.

It is a cold morning in the middle of February. At the little station there are a thousand people to bid him farewell. In the car are his old friends Judd and Davis, the new secretaries Nicolay and Hay, two governors, some army officers, and Wallace. One of the travelers is a man with a cheerful countenance, and fine teeth: This is "Hill", whom Lincoln has summoned to come to him, the David who is to cheer up the melancholy Saul.

Mary is on the platform. She will join him later and show tact and courage. But to-day he is alone, when he leaves this Springfield that he long ago entered and where he shall never return. There he stands with his curious stovepipe hat, and, while the rain is falling, he steps on to the platform of his car and says a few words:

"My friends, no one not in my situation, can appreciate my feeling of sadness at this parting. To this place, and the kindness of these people, I owe everything. Here I have lived a quarter of a century, and have passed from a youth to an old man. Here my children have been born and one is buried. I now leave, not knowing when or whether I may ever return, with a task before me greater than that which rested upon Washington. Without the assistance of that Divine Being who ever attended him, I cannot succeed. With that assistance, I cannot fail. Trusting in Him who can go with me, and remain with you, and be everywhere for good, let us confidently hope that all may yet be well. To His care commending you, as I hope in your prayers you will commend me, I bid you an affectionate farewell."

The drizzling rain falls slowly on the bared heads and also on his. The sadness of his word about the grave and the timid "yet" of hope, have deeply moved the auditors. No one feels hopeful as the train vanishes in the morning mist.

He spends ten days on this journey through the Northern States, for everywhere people wish to see him and to listen to him. A good many are disappointed, for his prevailing mood is one of depression, but sometimes he amazes adversaries whom curiosity has brought to his meetings. On the whole, he is pale and sad throughout this journey, and only cheers up when Hill plays the banjo and sings coon songs to him. He feels, as a great many others doubtless feel, that torchlight processions and serenades are out of keeping with the conditions of the time. He has, moreover, to be extremely careful in what he says; and sometimes, after preparing a speech, he has to modify it at the last moment because of telegraphic news from Alabama, where the Southerners are holding a congress at this very moment. That is why the speeches made during this journey are so unequal. Nevertheless, they are one and all adorned by the way in which they are addressed to the heart of the people, and by their conciliatory tone.

"Fellow citizens of Kentucky — friends and brethren, may I call you in my new position?"

In New York City: "And now, my friends, have I said enough? [No, no!] There appears to be a difference of opinion between you and me, and I really feel called upon to decide the question myself."

At Indianapolis: "I wish you to remember, now and for ever, that it is your business, and not mine; that if the union of these States and the liberties of this people shall be lost, it is but little to any one man of fifty-two years of age, but a great deal to the thirty millions of people who inhabit these United States, and to their posterity in all coming times. . . . Constantly bear in mind that not with politicians, not with Presidents, not with office-seekers, but with you, is the question: Shall the Union and shall the liberties of this country be preserved to the latest generation?"

Addressing the Senate of New Jersey, he speaks of the struggle at Trenton nearly a hundred years before, speaks of reading about the matter in early youth:

"I recollect thinking then, boy even though I was, that there must have been something more than common that these men struggled for. I am exceedingly anxious that that thing — that something even more than National Independence; that something that held out a great promise to all the people of the world for all time to come — I am exceedingly anxious that this Union, the Constitution, and the liberties of the people, shall be perpetuated in accordance with the original idea for which that struggle was made."

In Philadelphia, finally, speaking in the Hall of Independence, and overpowered by memories of the fathers of the country, he breaks his resolution, and, for the one and only time on this journey, refers to what should be done and left undone:

"I have often inquired of myself what great principle or idea it was that kept the Confederacy so long together. It was not the mere matter of separation of the colonies from the motherland, but that sentiment in the Declaration of Independence which gave liberty, not alone to the people of this country, but hope to all the world for all future time. It was that which gave promise that in due time the weight would be lifted from the shoulders of all men, and that all should have an equal chance. This is the sentiment embodied in the Declaration of Independence. Now, my friends, can this country be saved on that basis? If it can, I will consider myself one of the happiest men in the world if I can help to save it. . . . But if this country cannot be saved without giving up that principle, . . . I would rather be assassinated on this spot than surrender it. Now, in my view of the present aspect of affairs, there is no need of bloodshed and war. There is no necessity for it. I am not in favor of such a course; and I may say in advance that there will be no bloodshed unless it be forced upon the Government. The Government will not use force unless force is used against it. My friends, this is wholly an unprepared speech. I did not expect to be called on to say a word when I came here. I supposed it was merely to do something towards raising a flag. I may, therefore, have said something indiscreet. But I have said nothing but what I am willing to live by, and, if it be the pleasure of Almighty God die by."

Every one in that great hall must have felt the truth of those closing words, and we feel their truth to-day after the lapse of seventy years. For Lincoln says he is willing to die for his convictions, and this is not idle talk. . . . Soon reality will confirm it. Before reaching Baltimore he is warned by a detective that there is a plot to assassinate him there. He will not believe it at first and wants to continue his route, but when soon after this, Seward's son brings a warning from his father, he compares the two informations, and finding them identical and independent makes up his mind to a change of plan. Some of his friends considered that it would make a bad impression. Lincoln, however, was too shrewd, was too much the countryman, to risk his life needlessly for the sake of a public reception, the hundredth during these weeks. Had there been a battle imminent in Baltimore, had it been that the coming of the President was essential for the encouragement of the troops in such a battle! But he would not, simply to make a parade of courage, put himself in the power of a group of cowardly conspirators. Leaving the last reception at Harrisburg by a side door, in a soft hat, and ignoring the special train that was waiting to take him to Baltimore, he drove to the station and boarded the ordinary train, which had been detained to receive "an important parcel for Washington."

With Lincoln on this journey were "Hill" Lamon and Allan Pinkerton, the detective. His wife, his sons, and all the other members of the party continued on the special train. Only one of those who started with him from Springfield stayed with him during this last adventurous part of his journey: Hill, from whom he was inseparable.

In February it is still dark at six o'clock in the morning. The streets are lost in dusk, for the lights are out. Only two persons know who is arriving: Seward and Washburne, who come to meet him. Now the four drive to a hotel. The town lies still asleep, though some of the conspirators may have been in Washington, eagerly awaiting news of a successful coup in Baltimore. None of them knew that the man of whom they had hoped to rid themselves was already driving through the lonely streets. Had any of the Southern cavaliers passed the carriage on their way home from a late party, they may have supposed the travelers to be business men, come to Washington on the chance of a munitions contract — or, perhaps spies?

Unrecognized, a stranger, Abraham Lincoln, drove in the dark through his capital, to become the successor of Washington.

XXIII

If, in the gray of morning, he compared his present position with that he had held when he quitted Washington twelve years before, how high had he climbed! But neither the moment nor his nature were inclined to such reflections; he might rather have thought how much this chilly hotel room was like the one of those days, how uncertain even to-day his future was and how he was alone. For his wife was not with him, and would not join him until the special train arrived next day.

What does he first catch sight of, when he looks out of the window? Slaves! For the first time since the crisis began, he is in a slave district. What sounds come first to his ears? The strains of "Dixie", and other defiant Southern songs. On what sort of faces do his eyes light in the streets? Anxious faces, questioning faces; for every one is afraid of every one else, and the air is full of talk about spies and attempts at assassination. He knows nobody and nobody knows him, for everybody is bent on some business except himself. He can guess, easily enough, what people will have been saying in their drawing-rooms yesterday. "Perhaps something or other will happen to the fellow! Soon he will be sent home again, alive or dead. Then Jefferson Davis will come here as a real President, and the whole nightmare will be over!" It is only a few days from the time fixed for the inauguration, and here in Washington, in "good society", people are still laying odds that he will never be inaugurated.

How taciturn Seward is; how cold and discontented his mien! When Lincoln consults him about anything, there is nothing cordial about his aspect, and his tone is frosty. Is there no friendly face here? Were Hill not here, he would feel utterly forlorn. What news from the forts? What from Alabama? As discouraging as ever! But here is an interesting item from Europe, and all at once a warm breeze blows through the cold. "The Tsar of all the Russias has emancipated all the serfs of Russia." That stirs the heart of the man who wants to do the same thing here, and who in the New World is being hindered from doing that which Old Europe, that which despised Russia, has already done! It seems as if the sun were rising at midnight from out of the sea.

Soon, however, things begin to move about the lonely man. As soon as his arrival is known, people flock round him as at Spring-field, eager to see him, some moved by simple curiosity, some by hostility, some by friendliness. The passages are thronged, all the doors are open, no precautions are taken, so that the would-be assassins of yesterday have free access. There comes Douglas among the other visitors, and these two men, the short man and the tall one, who on the platform said such kind things about one an-other, and who in the recent campaign had had little occasion to resume friendly relations, now shake hands, smile at one another, and declare themselves charmed to meet once more — while Douglas is probably thinking, "I'm glad I don't stand in Lincoln's shoes to-day!"

Four days after his arrival in Washington, replying to a cold address of welcome, Lincoln says:

"I think very much of the ill-feeling that has existed and still exists between the people in the section from which I came and the people here, is dependent upon a misunderstanding of one another. I therefore avail myself of this opportunity to assure you, and all the gentlemen present, that I have not now, and never have had, any other than as kindly feelings toward you as to the people of my own section. I have not now, and never have had, any disposition to treat you in any respect otherwise than as my own neighbors . . . in a word, that when we shall become better acquainted — and I say it with great confidence — we shall like each other better. I thank you for the kindness of this reception."

A masterpiece: regal, affable, ceremonious, and yet ending with the unvarnished truth, clearly implied if not actually stated, that at present we do not like one another!

The fight for places in the cabinet rages more furiously than ever in these days. Strong objections are made to every one whom the President proposes to appoint. Senators and Congressmen try to get posts for themselves or their friends, and to keep enemies out of office. The trafficking of Springfield is resumed; and the first acquaintance Lincoln makes with many of the notable personalities of the capital is as place hunters.

Seward seems bitter, and is taciturn. Must he not feel piqued when his new chief, occupying the post he had wanted for himself, does not ask him to compose the inaugural address — as much more experienced Presidents had done? How is he to remain responsible if this will be the order of the day. When, at length, the address is submitted to him for approval, he is alarmed by its outspokenness, and writes:

"You must allow me to speak frankly and candidly. In this spirit, I declare to you my conviction, that the second and third paragraphs, even if modified as I propose in my amendment, will give such advantages to the Disunionists that Virginia and Maryland will secede, and we shall within ninety, perhaps within sixty, days be obliged to fight the South for this capital, with a divided North for our reliance, and we shall not have one loyal magistrate or ministerial officer south of the Potomac. . . . I therefore most respectfully counsel the omission of those paragraphs. . . . The argument is strong and conclusive, and ought not to be in any way abridged or modified. But something besides or in addition to argument is needful — to meet and remove prejudice and passion in the South, and despondency and fear in the East. Some words of affection — some of calm and cheerful confidence." Seward's aim was to strike people's imaginations, and make them forget the diplomatic caution of the main body of the document, whereas Lincoln wanted to win his hearers by a clarity conformable to his own clear logic.

Therefore Seward recommended the concluding phrases:

"I close. We are not, we must not be, aliens or enemies, but

THE LINCOLN LIFE-MASK

Made by Volk in 1860

fellow countrymen and brethren. Although passion has strained our bonds of affection too hardly, they must not, I am sure they will not, be broken. The mystic chords which, proceeding from so many battlefields and so many patriot graves, pass through all the hearts and all hearths in this broad continent of ours, will yet again harmonize in their ancient music when breathed upon by the guardian angel of the nation." Lincoln modified it as follows:

"I am loth to close. We are not enemies, but friends. We must not be enemies. Though passion may have strained, it must not break our bonds of affection. The mystic chords of memory, stretching from every battlefield, and patriot grave, to every living heart and hearthstone, all over this broad land, will yet swell the chorus of the Union, when again touched, as surely they will be, by the better angels of our nature."

Thus does the statesman suggest to the poet a fine poetical conclusion, which the latter knows how to develop to its full beauty. But Lincoln did not accept all of Seward's suggestions, confident of his judgment of their effect on the masses. Partially, perhaps on account of chagrin, but mainly because of jealousy of Chase, Seward surprises the President elect. For on the day before the inauguration, Lincoln gets a letter from Seward withdrawing his previous acceptance of his office. A serious blow, this, at so critical a moment! What is to be done? Lincoln puts aside the letter until the morrow.

The fourth of March dawns. Even yesterday, in the capital, people were still betting against Lincoln's chances. But now, at noon old Buchanan drives up to Lincoln's hotel in an open carriage! Clerical of aspect, as usual, with his white necktie, a face much wrinkled, his head twisting to the left, for he has a wry neck, wearing a broad-brimmed, low-crowned hat, and an old-fashioned swallow-tailed coat. They drive off together. For the first time, the streets leading to the Capitol are occupied by troops. Now the stately procession emerges from the entrance of the Senate. The terraces are not as full as they might have been, for a good many people have been kept away by dread of bullets, but there is none the less a brilliant assembly. All eyes are centered on the tallest man in the advancing company, who, carrying hat and stick, walks slowly through the corridor to the platform in front of the east portico in full view of the multitude of spectators. His old friend Senator Baker introduces Lincoln, amid the cheers of the assembly.

When he glances around, to take in the scene, his eyes light first on the notables. To his left sit the diplomats, who are strangers to him; to the right, the senators, and quite close to him, hard by the steps leading to the orator's pulpit, he sees Douglas; just below him are his wife and his three sons. What do the audience see? They look up at the speaker, but his friends are little pleased by his aspect.

"His newly grown beard was short and stubbly like a shoe brush: grizzled, stiff, and hideous; disfiguring a face that without it expressed power and deep feeling. He wore a brand-new suit, with a swallow-tail instead of the customary frock coat; he had a very shiny stovepipe hat, evidently just taken out of the bandbox, and a huge ebony stick, with a gold head as large as an egg. In this unusual rig-out, he looked so uncomfortable that it was quite pathetic. Matters were even worse when he reached the platform, for he did not know what on earth to do with his hat and his stick. There he stood, a target for thousands of eyes, holding these two encumbrances, the image of hopeless perplexity. After a little hesitation, he leaned his stick against the rail, but could not find any place except the floor for his hat, and, as I saw, he did not wish to put it down there. Douglas, who noted his embarrassment, came to the help of his old rival, relieved him of the hat, and held it until the owner wanted it again."

There he stands burdened with things which his fashionable wife must have forced upon him, too elegantly attired, lest he should look like a backwoodsman — a man used to wearing his clothes just anyhow, decked out with a useless walking cane, transformed into a comedy figure and all the more a mark of silent sarcasm. There he stands for the first time he is to speak to the nation as a whole, but he is embarrassed by this fine new stick with a gold knob and the terribly shiny top hat. What is he to do? Dreadful moments, but fate has sent him his longtime enemy, who, as if in irony, is watching his plight at close hand. Douglas it is who comes to his rescue; Douglas as a valet, Douglas who stretches out his short arm to take the hat and hold it for half an hour, like a footman, till all is over, and the new President can take it back from the senator with a friendly nod.

Douglas sits listening to the address, but at times his thoughts may have wandered to the hat he was holding, an exceptionally large one. And to the question if his head would not be too small for it, and how strange Lincoln would look in his hat. Perhaps he peeps inside, to see whether there are any odd papers stuck under the leather band, for, like every one else, he is familiar with Lincoln's trick of using a hat as a portfolio. Then, perchance, his thoughts turn to the head of the wearer, comparing Lincoln's intelligence with his own, naturally to his own favor; and, with the resignation of conscious superiority, he will listen once more to his adversary's words.

Lincoln has begun by saying that his party has never made any attempt to interfere with the institution of slavery in States where it exists. "I take the official oath to-day with no mental reservations and with no purpose to construe the Constitution or laws by any hypercritical rule." During the seventy-two years that had elapsed since the first inauguration of a President under the national Constitution, fifteen different citizens had, in succession, governed, and generally with success.

"Yet, with all this scope of precedent, I now enter upon the same task . . . under great and peculiar difficulty. A disruption of the Federal Union, heretofore only menaced, is now formidably attempted. . . . The power confided to me will be used to hold, occupy, and possess the property and places belonging to the Government, and to collect the duties and imposts; but beyond what may be necessary for these objects, there will be no invasion, no using of force against or among the people anywhere. . . . That there are persons in one section or another who seek to destroy the Union at all events, and are glad of any pretext to do it, I will neither affirm nor deny; but if there be such, I need address no word to them." He goes on to ask how, physically speaking, can the North and the South separate? Is force to be used? If so, what will happen then?

"Can aliens make treaties easier than friends can make laws? Can treaties be more faithfully enforced between aliens, than laws can among friends? Suppose you go to war, you cannot fight always: and when, after much loss on both sides, and no gain on either, you cease fighting, the identical old questions as to terms of intercourse are again upon you. . . .

"Why should there not be a patient confidence in the ultimate justice of the people? Is there any better or equal hope in the world? In our present differences, is either party without faith of being in the right? If the Almighty Ruler of Nations, with His eternal truth and justice, be on your side of the North, or on yours of the South, that truth and that justice will surely prevail by the judgment of this great tribunal of the American people."

There had been applause here and there at notable passages. Buchanan had listened attentively; so had Douglas, who, the instant the speaker had finished, jumped up, shook hands with him, and expressed cordial approval. But here comes the clerk with the Bible. All rise to their feet, and Buchanan, the retiring President, with his crooked head, takes his stand beside Lincoln. A very aged man presides over the ceremony, pushing his mummy-like shape, in his black robe, to the front: Taney, the chief justice who had been responsible for the famous Dred Scott decision. No less patriotic a man than Lincoln, his features betray the emotion he feels when administering the oath. Lincoln, after glancing respectfully at Taney, lays his huge hand on the Bible, and slowly pronounces the oath:

"I, Abraham Lincoln, do solemnly swear that I will faithfully execute the office of President of the United States, and will, to the best of my ability, preserve, protect, and defend the Constitution of the United States."

Now the company disperses, the outgoing President and the newly inaugurated one walking away through the corridor arm in arm. One man remains to the last, a man who, in a conspicuous position, has watched the affair throughout with challenging attitude, standing on the top of the pyramid of onlookers. This was a well-known senator for Texas, who, with crossed arms, has been leaning against the top entrance listening with contempt — the last of the Southern senators to remain in Washington; envoy and symbol of the South; the future enemy personified.

Now the carriage drives off to the White House. Mary is radiant. This posse of servants, male and female, these silent liveries, cannot fail to remind her of the slave State of her youth. It had been a long journey — eight days and, before that, twenty years, but now at last they have arrived. She is both tired and excited; the goal is reached, the dream has become reality. How quickly she takes in the suites of rooms and halls, the handsome vases, the soft carpets; how the gilded chairs and the glittering chandeliers flatter her eyes like those of the children who follow her. It seems to her that there is a good deal to be improved, but there will be plenty of time. She has four years, anyhow; nothing but death can expel her from this house before those four years have passed.

But Lincoln is heavy-hearted as he stalks through these same apartments, wondering within himself whether there may not be other forces than death to drive him, and the Union, out of this house. And while Mary is admiring the damask hangings of the walls he is asking himself what they may have heard within the last three months; and knows that whatever it may have been, nimble tongues have swiftly carried the tidings South. All that awaits him is a writing table, more heavily laden with work than was his old office table in Springfield, even in the busiest days; and, as he begins to dictate, perhaps his eyes rove among the cold splendors in search of a familiar leather-covered sofa.

The very first letter he writes on the same evening, and bearing the superscription "Executive Mansion" is to William H. Seward, and runs as follows:

"My dear Sir, Your note of the 2d instant, asking to withdraw your acceptance of my invitation to take charge of the State Department, was duly received. It is the subject of the most painful solicitude with me, and I feel constrained to beg that you

will countermand the withdrawal. The public interest, I think,
demands that you should; and my personal feelings are deeply
enlisted in the same direction. Please consider, and answer by
9 o'clock A.M. to-morrow.

"Your obedient servant."

The same regal dignity, the same skillful reserve; an expression
of personal esteem, but an ultimatum for the very next morning;
a formal, though polite signature.

The rats are deserting the ship, thinks the captain; deserting it
at the very moment he is taking command. And as he looks out
through the window into the night, what does he see and fancy?
Those dark shadows, are they spies, assassins, or slaves? Is the
town really full of rebels? Surely it must also contain well-wishers,
kind citizens, who are looking up to the lighted windows, considering
the strength of the new man? Over there is the Treasury; it is
empty. That other house over there, the War Office, may contain
stacks of documents, but the forces inscribed in the lists are all but
useless; firearms and ammunition have been sent to the South;
and there is scarcely a ship left to the North.

In the distance, broad as a sea, flows the Potomac; he can make
it out from the window. Beyond it stands the enemy under arms,
with forts, money, and men — and hearts fired with passion. To-
morrow they will strike; or, if not to-morrow, within a few weeks.
Is he, then, master of the White House, or only its prisoner?

All depends on one thing: to be strong enough for destiny.

BOOK FOUR

LIBERATOR

I

If we describe as "tragical" a conflict which is a life-and-death struggle between two contending powers, both of them animated with a conviction of being in the right and both of them determined to make the right prevail; if we term "tragical" the war of ideas which goes on in a purer light behind the clouds of interests, ambition, and money, and is as rarely visible to the eyes of human fighters as were the figures of the gods who did battle on behalf of one side or the other in the great contest described by Homer — then we shall certainly compare the American Civil War to a Greek tragedy. It arouses sympathy and inspires dread, and ends by evoking a feeling akin to that which arises in us when the landscape brightens after the atmosphere has been cleared by a storm.

When one of a later generation acclaims the victory of freedom over slavery, he must not be misled into condemning those who were defeated in the struggle — however sure he may feel that as its contemporary he would have espoused the cause which proved victorious. If he despises the lords of the South for the mere reason that their power was based upon the shameful oppression of innocent human beings, he will be unable to explain to himself and others the confusion that prevailed in the leading minds of both parties of that day; he will not even understand the subsequent decision by the rude arbitrament of force, in an issue which could only be settled once for all by the power of ideas. He will be equally unable to do justice to the deeds of the minority, who for four years resisted as valiantly as the Trojan heroes, and to the splendid patience and moderation of the Northern leader who, during the fifteen hundred days of his presidency, during as many days and nights of changing fortunes on the battlefield and fluctuations of popular favor, lost neither his nerve nor his faith, neither his sense of humor nor his wisdom, but amid incessant difficulties was able to preserve his virtues, to strengthen his faculties, to make his very weaknesses productive in order to realize one thought — or rather two thoughts which in his mind became gradually fused into a unity tinged with deep feeling. No one who fails to admire the enthusiasm, the conviction of rectitude, and the tenacity of the South, can appraise Lincoln at his true worth.

Besides, is it so hard to do justice to the South? Invariably the effect of a long tenure of power has been to arouse in the grand-children of those who achieved it by conquest the conviction that it was held by right. Everywhere the aristocrat, in the ancient struggle between masters and slaves, has looked upon himself as morally justified by an uninterrupted chain of heritage, by un-troubled centuries of inviolable tenure, has seen his claim to author-ity sanctioned by a time so immemorial that the bronze and the iron of force have become encrusted by the patina of antiquity. Did ever knight and baron unresistingly hand over their abundance in response to the demands of a new time, peacefully surrender their strong fortresses in obedience to the claims of a loftier insight, merely because the champions of a more enlightened morality came knocking at the gates?

And those who knocked, were they sincere apostles, one and all? Cold-hearted men of business, the Southerners thought them; the offspring of Anglo-Saxon peasants, intent on profits, who had made money enough now to indulge in the luxury of a little virtuous indignation; determined, it would seem, to grasp the leadership of the Union, though as unfit to rule as they were lacking in culture. But the Southerners knew themselves to be the descendants of the Norman nobility; they had the manners and customs of English peers; their representatives had occupied the presidential chair time and again, this making them responsible for the guidance of the destinies of the Union; they supplied twice or thrice as many of the cabinet members and leading judges as the North. Were they, men born to rule, men of honor, the true leaders of the nation both in peace and war — were they to take it lying down when they were stigmatized as immoral?

This had been going on for a generation, but during the last

decade it had become intolerable — and why? Because thousands
upon thousands of immigrants had streamed into the North, men
of broken lives, the scum of old Europe, lured by Californian gold,
set upon earning money quickly and anyhow, even if it were by
degrading tastes fit only for a Negro. Of course, where there is
paid work for every one it is easy to talk of liberty and democracy,
since there money means freedom. Where steam engines do the
rough work instead of men, there is no need for Negroes to put their
backs into it. Where great towns, the centers of plebeian industry,
are numerous, there is not much danger in talking about an equality
which is in truth contrary to the laws of God. If during the last
ten years the population of the North has increased to nineteen
millions, while in the South there are only eight million whites, it
is natural enough that the North should have a third more Congressmen than the South, and should command a majority in the Senate.

Swayed by such thoughts, the Southern leaders (a small but
powerful group) were naturally impelled in the direction of increasing self-assertion, until at length the elections of 1860 fanned into
open flame the fires which for a decade had been smoldering beneath
the surface. The men of the countryside were marshaled against
the men of the towns, sportsmen and cavaliers against accountants
and factory owners, army officers against commercial clerks,
venerable tradition against impatient innovation, class against
class, one race against the defenders of another, the passions and
the customs and the pride and honor of those born to rule against
the leveling force of the conception of social equality; indeed, in
this matter, the new continent was once again marshaled against
Europe, so that the South could count upon European sympathy.

The Southern sense of superiority seemed to be sanctioned alike
by legal and by economic considerations. Could not Calhoun's
authority be quoted in favor of the dictum that the Union was
nothing more than a contractual league from which any member
could withdraw if it felt that the terms of the contract were being
infringed? As regards the natural riches with which God had
gifted the Southern soil, one of the senators from South Carolina
expressed most Southerners' honest conviction when he said, "No

one can defy the slaveholding South. There may be temporary disorders, but cotton, tobacco, and rice rule the world. Without us, the North will remain a motherless calf, which can do nothing but low, and will soon die of hunger."

Nevertheless, in the passionate South every one, even the women, seemed to favor a defensive attitude; whereas the North, cooler and more critical though it was, was forced into an offensive which harmonized ill with the temperament and the dissensions of the Northerners, and was out of keeping with their motives. If the secession of six Southern States occurred at this juncture, there were two good reasons for the step: either the Southerners' bluff would be successful, and the alarmed North would again yield ground, as so often in previous years; or else there would be war — and then this would be the last moment for the South to resist the threat of the steadily growing population of the North. Otherwise the South (from which only the most radical were proposing to take away anything, and, least of all, the slaves) would after so long a struggle have been willing to outface another four short years in the hope that, when the time of the elections came around once more, it would be able to enforce its will as it had frequently done before. After all, the "black" President did not command a majority in either House, nor really among the people.

"On both sides they stand like bulldogs spoiling for a fight," wrote Thomas Corwin at this time. Can we be surprised, seeing that for months, all over the South, trees of liberty had been set up; that everywhere Southerners were defiantly singing the "Marseillaise" and thereby reducing to absurdity their slaveholding policy by voicing the sentiments of this most entrancing of all the songs of freedom; that thousands of wealthy young idlers, the sons of the Southern gentry, were exercising their fine horses and practising with their pistols in the hope that ere long they would be able to use them before a greater public than a handful of intimidated whites and blacks; that the blaring of the bugles, the rustle of the banners, the call of honor had intoxicated an almost unanimous master class, subject to no check from a common people able to murmur or to warn; that, at last, secession had come, dissolving the ties of the State, so that there was not even left intact an authority to disobey?

How could the South fail to regard itself as unquestionably superior in military matters? True, they were in a minority, as far as the counting of heads was concerned; but before the first shot was fired the South had twice as many men under arms as were contained in the whole effective force of the North, and the right to call up thrice that number. Unless the war should prove a lengthy affair, the South could reckon on every advantage: on obedience, which had been inculcated on the poor whites, had been strengthened in them by a sense of danger, and had not been seriously undermined by democracy; on officers who had gained renown in former campaigns, and whose mode of life and caste prejudices fitted them for the part they would have to play in war; on practical immunity from the spirit of faction; and, when it should come to actual fighting, on holding an inner line, along which troops could be concentrated with all convenient speed. Contrast with this the situation of the North. There every volunteer had ideas of his own, was a man of independent character, one inclined to cavil whenever an order was issued; the officers were fresh from business; the rank and file were townsmen wearied by forced marches of long duration trying to encircle the enemy, and having to do this in hostile territory amid legions of irregular sharpshooters and spies; party disputes were rife, and could not fail to hamper the conduct of the war. Add to this that the Northerners were not yet animated by a feeling of common peril, nor were they yet fused by a common passion, but the motive for their great offensive was hardly more than an idea which had the force of conviction for only a part of the North.

The one thing, therefore, the South had to fear was a long war, in which the North would be able to call upon its inexhaustible reserves of men and supplies, to train officers and privates, and to starve the South by the weapon of blockade. But the political dissensions in the North, and the lack of fighting impetus in that part of the world, made a prolonged contest unlikely. If the

North were to show the military zeal which the risks of the situation made a matter of course in the South, it could only be due to a leader holding sway over the generals, a man at the head of affairs who should be at once strong and popular — and there seemed little reason to suppose that such a leader would be forthcoming in the person of the new President.

II

When Lincoln awakened for the first time at the White House, the day after being sworn in as President, there was a letter from Fort Sumter on his table. It came from the commandant, who now addressed himself to the new President, the old one having given him no help for months past. The writer said that, unless reinforcements were sent, he would not be able to hold the fort for more than a few weeks longer. And Lincoln had sworn to maintain the possessions of the Union, and the fort in question was one of these. "If Anderson evacuates Fort Sumter, I shall have to evacuate the White House," he said.

Since January this fort on an island in Charleston Harbor, garrisoned by no more than a hundred men but well supplied with artillery, had been the object of a sort of implicit truce. The unexpressed compact between the hostile brethren was that no attack would be made by the Southerners so long as no attempt was made by the North to reinforce it.

Seward, however, now advised surrender; and even old Scott declared the stronghold to be untenable. Here was the first instance of discouragement, and time and again during the next few years we shall find that the hesitating President will be forced to stimulate the hesitating military arm. The question was not merely one of courage; it was one of diplomacy as well. Evacuation would set an example which would encourage the South all along the line. On the other hand, to send troops and munitions would be an open challenge to the enemy, would start the war, would from the first put Europe out of humor with the North, and would provide all the local adversaries with catchwords for use in their criticisms.

Are not these criticisms already acrimonious enough? Through-out the country the radical press is declaring that the President is blind, incapable, or cowardly, and that he has been infected with Seward's pacifism. What has he done? The one positive action with which he can be credited is his refusal to receive a deputation from the rebels. On the other hand, the Democrats are clamoring for the evacuation of the forts, and for peace at any price. They want no truck with the "black" Republicans. At the same time the wildest rumors are current, one of them being to the effect that more and more officers of the regular army are deserting to the South. Lincoln listens to it all, reads the papers; hears what visitors, experts, and ordinary folk have to say; and throughout March is pondering a solution.

At length he finds one. March is drawing to a close, Anderson's difficulties are increasing, and probably the garrison is already on short rations. Now comes the first grand reception at the White House. Lincoln appears in a new swallow-tailed coat beside his elegantly attired wife, and hundreds of people are watching mali-ciously for some breach of decorum. He is the same man as usual, easy-going, cheerful, and sociable; and next day the *Times* correspondent is able to report that the President regaled the company with numerous anecdotes concerning horses, drunken drivers, and other incidents of Western life. In view of this, the guests must have thought, as they came away, that there could be no imminent danger — the very impression Lincoln had wished to produce. But to his cabinet members he spoke otherwise. Requesting them to stay after the reception, he told them how Scott was urging him to evacuate Fort Sumter on the instant. They left the White House, greatly excited, to return in a few hours for an early morning session, and to learn the President's decision. Lincoln was going to send a ship laden with provisions to the fort, and would officially inform the governor that the aim was merely to save the garrison from starvation. If the governor did not take the step amiss, the prestige of the United States Government would have been restored and the garrison's most urgent necessity would have been relieved. If, on the other hand, the governor should prove as bellicose as he had given himself out to be for weeks past, he would regard the action as provocative, and would retaliate by firing the first shot, thus relieving the tension, making the South responsible for the commencement of hostilities, and arousing in the North the indignation without which a victory could never be won.

The notion was that of a farmer and a diplomatist, and all happened as he had foreseen. After driving back the relieving ships, the Southern forces bombarded the fort, shot down the flag, and continued firing until Anderson capitulated and withdrew the garrison. All the world took note of this date, April 14, on which the Civil War actually began; but no one foresaw with whose blood the same date was to be rebaptized four years later.

The effect is terrible, but it is uplifting. A cry rises everywhere from the North: "The star-spangled banner has been shot down by Southern troops!" A clamor for revenge unifies for the instant all the millions of the North; party disputes are stilled, opponents become reconciled or cease to quarrel; every one feels that a dreadful thing has happened, something unparalleled since, eighty years before, the Stars and Stripes had first waved above Washington's head. At this moment, and only now, Lincoln has the country in his hands. An appeal for seventy-five thousand volunteers is answered within a few days by ninety-two thousand; in June there will be three hundred thousand. But they are enrolled for three months only, the longest period allowed by the law.

For the nonce, however, not a soldier is to be seen. The total force available numbers only three thousand. Where are the volunteers? How can they be assembled, armed, and trained in the twinkling of an eye? Where will be the seat of war? No plan of campaign has been drawn up for this struggle, since it is a civil war. What will the border States do? Above all, what will be the decision of Virginia, at the very gates of the capital? People come and ask him laconically what is his attitude towards the Confederate States. He makes an ambiguous reference to his inaugural address, saying that his line is laid down in that: "I recommend a careful study of this speech, which contains the best statement of my intentions."

Immediately afterwards, Virginia announces its withdrawal

from the Union, and thus the Potomac becomes the frontier. The enemy is only just across the water, within sight of the White House. Things have turned out as the new President had feared they might when he assumed office five weeks before.

The news of Virginia's secession has a paralyzing effect in Washington. Where are the troops? The capital has suddenly become an island amid hostile waters; it can even be threatened from the rear, where a deep valley is in the hands of the enemy. Alarming rumors are rife in the town. To-morrow the place may be besieged. It must be provisioned forthwith. Barricade the Capitol with tubs of cement, and with sheet iron as well! Clear out the women and the children! Who is in command? Scott, an old man of seventy-five, the new Secretary of War, who up to now has been a financier, and Lincoln, whose military glory has been the rescue of one Indian.

No reinforcements, not a solitary new soldier within sight! Lincoln, pacing his room, is asking himself, "Why don't they come?" The report runs that they have been taken prisoners in Virginia. A few days later the President confided to Schurz that at this moment he had felt utterly forsaken and helpless. A small detachment of Southerners might easily cross the long bridge over the Potomac, to capture him and the whole cabinet. Suddenly he hears cannon fire. There they are! He expects news from instant to instant. Nothing. He goes down and asks the officials. Nothing. On into the street, farther and farther, till he reaches the arsenal, which is practically unprotected, so that any one might rifle its stores. He asks the few men on duty there whether they have not heard distant gunfire. Not a sound. Then he recognizes that he must have been a prey to autosuggestion. So sensitive are his nerves in moments of stress, to-day as on his wedding day long ago. He is surely the most unwarlike commander in chief known to history! Will he grow to meet the necessities of war?

At length comes the whistle of the long-expected locomotive. The whole population of the town flocks to the station; the New York regiment has arrived. People draw deep breaths of relief, but only for a moment. Where are the others?

"I am beginning to think that there is no North," says Lincoln to the troops. "The 7th regiment is a myth. Rhode Island is another. You are the only reality!"

The words (unquestionably injudicious, likely to arouse the disfavor of the newcomers, or likely to be misunderstood by them) give a clue to the oppression which is weighing him down. He is a stranger; he has never held executive office before, and now he has been suddenly thrust into the highest position in the Union; he has to cope with a situation unprecedented in the history of the country; alone, unaided, without Congress, and with an unwilling cabinet, he has to make the gravest decision ever made by a President of the Union.

A kingdom for a military commander! The best would be Lee. He is over in Virginia, has always been loyal to the Union, and has opposed secession. Lincoln offers him the commandership in chief. Lee refuses the post, saying that he cannot be a party to an invasion of the Southern States. At the same time he sends in his resignation to General Scott, his superior officer and a fellow-Virginian, thus withdrawing from the United States army.

"This is a more serious loss than would be the going over of 20,000 men," says the veteran Scott, and he is right.

At the same time Baltimore demands of the President a pledge that he will cease conveying troops through that town.

All right, they can make a detour round it. "No," says Baltimore, "we are neutral, and the troops must not march round us either."

"We must have troops," rejoins Lincoln. "As they can neither crawl under Maryland, nor fly over it, they must come across it." Thereupon the Marylanders break down the bridges, so that on three sides now, Washington is cut off from reinforcements, while on the fourth side it lies open to the enemy. Then comes the first brush with the Southerners, and wounded are borne back on stretchers through the streets on their way to the Capitol.

It is the blood of his brothers that Lincoln for the first time sees oozing through the hastily improvised bandages; the blood of innocent youngsters, who have no interest in politics, and are neither for slavery nor against it; men who have only rallied to the colors in response to the cry: "The Union has been broken." This first blood, made visible at the Capitol to the great lover of mankind, gives him proof of the soundness of his inward conviction that, as far as the popular imagination is concerned, the Civil War is not being waged on behalf of an abstract ideal. People are giving their blood, not for the freedom of African blacks, but for the sake of their American fatherland.

III

While two families can readily, and with much tumult, break with one another betwixt night and morning, a quarrel between two brothers in the same house is no such easy matter to carry into practical effect. After the first stormy days, this Civil War began with a three months' truce, which was devoted on both sides to preparation, but also to overcoming a certain amount of perplexity; it was a pause for equipment, but also one of decency.

Lincoln's moral and historical conception of the struggle was expounded by him in a magnificent speech, a message to Congress on July 4. It was a discourse such as in Europe never, and in America hardly before, could have been delivered in justification of a war. The President began by demanding four hundred thousand men and four hundred million dollars. "The sum is less than a twenty-third part of the money value owned by the men who seem ready to devote the whole." He went on to compare the present crisis, in which the Union had to be preserved, with the crisis in which the Union had been founded; pointed out how much richer the country was than in those earlier days, and said, "Surely each man has as strong a motive now to preserve our liberties as each had then to establish them." Turning to the problem of "State rights", he showed that a monetary question was involved, that the nation had "purchased with money the countries out of which several of these (Southern) States were formed. Is it just that they shall go off without leave and without refunding?"

Ere long he sounded a deeper note, insisting that the new constitution of the Confederate States justified conclusions regarding juridical and philosophical differences between North and South. "Our adversaries have adopted some declarations of independence in which, unlike the good old one, penned by Jefferson, they omit the words 'all men are created equal.' Why? They have adopted a temporary national constitution, in the preamble of which, unlike our good old one, signed by Washington, they omit 'We, the People', and substitute 'We, the deputies of the sovereign and independent States.' "

He went on to deduce the intrinsic nature of what was "essentially a people's contest. On the side of the Union it is a struggle for maintaining in the world that form and substance of government whose leading object is to elevate the condition of men — to lift artificial weights from all shoulders; to clear the paths of laudable pursuit for all; to afford all an unfettered start, and a fair chance in the race of life. . . . Our popular government has often been called an experiment. . . . One [point] still remains — its successful maintenance against a formidable internal attempt to overthrow it. It is now for them [our people] to demonstrate to the world that those who can fairly carry an election can also suppress a rebellion; that ballots are the rightful and peaceful successors of bullets; and that when ballots have fairly and constitutionally decided, there can be no successful appeal back to bullets; . . . Such will be a great lesson of peace: teaching men that what they cannot take by an election, neither can they take by a war; teaching all the folly of being the beginners of a war."

With what mastery does he speak here, first in figures and then in ideas, first to the electors and then to the world in general. If he speaks of the popular government of the United States as an experiment conducted before the eyes of all mankind, we have here, within the wrappings of demagogic statistics, at the core the substance of Lincoln's religion, the basic idea he expounded in youth, and often since; we have Jefferson's and Clay's conviction that more is at stake for the human race in this country than its mere existence as an independent State. We see that now, as ever, Lincoln's gaze is steadily fixed upon humanity at large; that he deems the Union more important than the slavery question, but less important than the principle of freedom; and that when he insists upon the need for giving a great moral demonstration to the world, he is speaking from his very heart.

All the more because here (as ever) he is more deeply concerned about the social than about the political aspect of the question. A few months later, in another message to Congress, he declares that the main object of the struggle is to save the principle of democracy, for in the South monarchy itself has been sometimes hinted at as a possible refuge from the power of the people.

"But there is one point, not so hackneyed as most others, to which I ask a brief attention. It is the effort to place capital on an equal footing with, if not above, labor in the structure of government. It is assumed that labor is available only in connection with capital; that nobody labors unless somebody else, owning capital, somehow by the use of it induces him to labor. This assumed, it is next considered whether it is best that capital shall hire laborers, and thus induce them to work by their own consent, or buy them and drive them to it without their consent. Having proceeded so far, it is naturally concluded that all laborers are either hired laborers or what we call slaves. And, further, it is assumed that whoever is once a hired laborer is fixed in that condition for life.

"Now, there is no such relation between capital and labor as assumed, nor is there any such thing as a free man being fixed for life in the condition of a hired laborer. Both these assumptions are false, and all inferences from them are groundless.

"Labor is prior to and independent of, capital. Capital is only the fruit of labor, and could never have existed if labor had not first existed. Labor is the superior of capital, and deserves much the higher consideration. Capital has its rights, which are as worthy of protection as any other rights. Nor is it denied that there is, and probably always will be, a relation between labor and capital producing mutual benefits. The error is in assuming that the whole labor of the community exists within that relation.

"A few men own capital, and that few avoid labor themselves, and with their capital hire or buy another few to labor for them. A large majority belong to neither class — neither work for others

nor have others work for them. In most of the Southern States
a majority of the whole people, of all colors, are neither slaves nor
masters. . . . Men, with their families . . . work for themselves
on their farms, in their houses, and in their shops; taking the
whole product to themselves, and asking no favors of capital on
the one hand nor of hired laborers or slaves on the other. . . . The
prudent, penniless beginner in the world labors for wages awhile,
saves a surplus with which to buy tools or land for himself, then
labors on his own account another while, and at length hires another
new beginner to help him. This is the just and generous and
prosperous system which opens the way to all, gives hope to all,
and consequent energy and progress and improvement of condition
to all. No men living are more worthy to be trusted than those
who toil up from poverty; none less inclined to take or touch aught
which they have not honestly earned. Let them beware of surrendering a political power which they already possess, and which,
if surrendered, will surely be used to close the door of advancement
against such as they and to fix new disabilities and burdens upon
them till all of liberty shall be lost."

Were these propositions inscribed in a textbook or announced
from a professorial chair, they would be little more than truisms;
written by the President, at this particular epoch, they are indeed
aimed at the farmers and the employees who will soon be reading
them throughout the country, and also at the poor whites of the
South, who may thereby be rendered skeptical as to the cause for
which they are fighting; but their force and their historical significance depend upon the personality of their author. As a
tactician and stylist (for by now he is both of these), he would never
tack a theoretical disquisition of this kind on to the brilliant close
of a long message on the war, were it not that his eyes are always
fixed on general issues, were he not disposed to speak to those who
in the 'sixties were willing to give ear to new social doctrines. He is
the sometime woodman and wage earner, who in this free country
need not, as in Europe, make a secret of his lowly origin, but can
point to it with pride; and, obviously speaking against his enemies,
against "good society" in Washington, he can tell them which

members of the community he regards as most worthy of trust —
he who has himself been a hired laborer, and has only made his way
upward thanks to his talents and his industry.

IV

Six o'clock in the morning, and the streets are almost empty,
though the spring sun had been shining brightly for a good while
now. Some one passing the White House sees a very tall man, in
blue socks and big slippers, standing in the doorway. This man,
whom he knows well enough by sight, calls to him in a friendly way,
"Good morning, good morning. I am looking for a newsboy.
When you get to the corner, I wish you would send one up this
way." Lincoln is still the same as when he was a lawyer in Springfield, where his plain farmer ways used to strike people as odd.
Even if he does not stand like this at the house door every morning,
the anecdote shows that restless curiosity is apt from time to time
to revive old habits.

Of course, if he wants anything, he need only tug at the fine,
long bell pull that hangs close to the great writing table. But as
he sits in his armchair now, a ring, while it will doubtless bring a
servant, will certainly not bring his secretary Nicolay at that hour,
for the President is the earliest worker in the United States — a
remarkable thing in a man not accustomed to regular hours, either
by disposition or training. His natural tendency is to be guided
by caprice as to what he does and leaves undone, and nothing but
a sense of responsibility has constrained him to adapt himself to
the rhythm of public affairs. To reach his office on the south side
of the White House, he had to pass through the hall. Thus, when
he does this at a later hour in the day, he has to run the gauntlet
of numerous persons waiting there on the chance of seeing him. Not
until three years later does he have a special doorway cut and
a side entrance made, enabling him to get to his office without
exposing himself to these importunities.

The office is roomy, since there must be space in the middle for
the oaken table at which the sittings of the cabinet are held. There

are two sofas, both of horsehair; but the fact that there are two, and that he (who loves to stretch out his long legs and to lie reading at full length) is thus enabled to change from one to the other, is perhaps the only gain in the way of personal comfort accruing to Abraham Lincoln in compensation for the manifold burdens imposed on him by the presidency. Of the pictures on the walls, the old one of Jackson was probably there when Lincoln took over, and he is not likely to look at it often; but the photograph of John Bright, the English free trader, is an addition of his own, and serves to show the President's esteem for the British radicals. There are also maps hanging on the walls, military maps which remind every visitor: "we are at war."

There is nothing, however, to remind one of the war in the aspect of the men who begin to arrive towards nine o'clock; and the cabinet by whose appointment Lincoln has startled the country would have been pretty much the same in time of peace. As he takes his seat at the head of the gathering, partly to read out his own report on current affairs, and partly to hear what the cabinet members have to tell him, he shows a tranquil self-confidence, and no one would ever dream that up to now, when he is fifty-three years of age, he has never taken the chair at any such meeting. Yet those who sit around the table and regard him more or less mistrustfully are all of them men with a wealth of practical experience, and therefore naturally inclined to believe in themselves rather than in him. Why did not this newcomer surround himself with personal friends? Instead, he sits among a phalanx of strangers, half of whom are members of an alien party, while the other half (though they belong to his own party) are personal adversaries. When asked why he has appointed four Democrats and only three Republicans, he replies, "I am a Republican myself, and that makes things equal." Surely it is a sign of unusual tolerance and political wisdom that he should make a special effort to enlist the services, above all, of the politicians who regard themselves as his rivals.

Is he merely out of humor and hypercritical, this man sitting beside Lincoln and scrutinizing him through half-closed lids?

Even if Seward were less vain than he is, it would be natural enough
that he, whose training and services, reputation and talents, would
seem to have destined him for the highest office in the land, should
now be disgruntled at having to serve another. A man of distinguished appearance, but the fine nose and mouth are marred
by a sour expression, and the shrewd eyes are clouded by ambition
and jealousy. When, during these early weeks, some one tells him
that the passing over of a certain man for a particular post will
arouse widespread disappointment, Seward bursts out :
"You talk to me of disappointment! To me, who had every
reason to expect that I should be chosen as candidate for the
presidency, and had to stand aside for a petty lawyer from Illinois!
You talk to *me* of disappointment!"

He has not been reconciled to his successful rival, but he has been
glad to accept office as Secretary of State and likes to be called
Premier (thus arousing cynical comment), and he likes to plume
himself on secret information of things he keeps to himself.

His vis-à-vis is likewise fuming with jealousy. He does not say
anything against Lincoln, but his silence is eloquent — for he, too,
was Lincoln's rival, and he considers that he has been cheated by
the party. But Chase has a well-knit frame and an open countenance; his beardless face is fuller and younger; he would seem
to be hoping for better luck next time, and is readier to forget his
personal mortification and to devote his energies to the common
cause. An unyielding opponent of slavery, of a more ardent
temperament than Seward and even than Lincoln, Chase, as Secretary of the Treasury, remains at once master and servant in the
sober realm of figures, and though he is at times somewhat pompous,
his self-conceit does not undermine his willingness to serve the man
who has in the end become the chosen representative of the people;
nor is he lacking in penetration as regards either personal questions or matters of business, and his abilities and his character
render control superfluous, so the President gives him a free hand.

The next man, no less honest and well-informed, is equally uncomfortable. This is Gideon Welles, whose general appearance
instantly arouses thoughts of the sea; he has keen eyes, though

the skin beneath them is baggy; a white spade beard shaved around the mouth to leave the lips free, and long, gray hair. He will hold his office for four years, and will prove the most successful of Lincoln's secretaries. We may imagine Fox, the young assistant secretary, an Anglophobe, sitting beside his chief; his is a bold spirit, constantly tending to outrun his cautious senior.

They go well together and work hand in hand, Fox and his brother-in-law, that fellow with a youthful, hard-bitten face, a pointed nose, piercing eyes, and a firmly compressed mouth, a man who might be taken for a mathematician; Blair, Postmaster General, member of an influential family with far-reaching connections, as passionately opposed to the rebels as Fox, and no less practical. Bates, the Attorney General, looks to be a man of cooler type; he is from Missouri, and is therefore likely to understand the South. As for Smith, the Secretary of the Interior, who hails from Indiana, he is a reputable citizen, who will probably have a better understanding of things close at hand than of those distant perspectives that shade off into the unknown.

When Lincoln lets his discerning eyes roam around the table, he cannot fail to be impressed by the uniqueness of the head of the seventh and last of these secretaries of his — though all six of them are extremely individual types. Number seven is beardless, has grayish-white hair, a well-shaped forehead, a big nose, penetrating eyes, and extremely pinched lips, the mouth of a man with a bent for silence and reserve; he looks like one little inclined to be accommodating, one who enjoys feeling contempt for his fellows, assumes a defiant attitude towards the world, and makes it his business to overreach others: this is Cameron, forced upon Lincoln by his party, and from whom the President will not be able to free himself immediately; to-day, as Secretary of War, the principal figure in the cabinet, in so far as Lincoln gives him as free a hand as his colleague, the Secretary of the Navy. But since neither Lincoln nor Cameron is an expert in matters military, the one being a man of affairs and the other the ruling father of his country, Cameron will not control the War Department unaided or for long.

It was a good while since a cabinet so amorphous had been assembled around this council table. The President's first and most difficult task was to unite these men of conflicting aims and temperaments, to convince them of his own capacity, and thus to subject them in the spirit to a leadership which as yet he held only in the letter. That was the crucial test applied to him as one able to know men and competent to manage them; that he stood this test was perhaps the greatest of Lincoln's victories, and beyond question the condition of victory in war. For here, where the elements of disunion were provided with a specious sanction by the falling away of half the nation; when thousands of heads and hearts, conjoined but yesterday, were fiercely antagonistic; when the conflict now raging had been the outcome, not of mere differences of internal interests, but of racial and national divergencies, and of a hopeless variance of outlooks among compatriots — it was inevitable that the spirit of discord should intrude into every discussion, into every public office, and ultimately into a cabinet whose members had been chosen, not in accordance with their general attitude towards the fundamental problem, but in accordance with partisan and political considerations, and who were now faced one and all by unfamiliar tasks of a kind with which only an expert as a rule can deal intelligently.

At the same time it was inevitable that the animus should be concentrated against a chief who had never been a chief before, against one who had not even been chairman of a Congressional committee. Instead of studying the new formalities and striving to observe them, Lincoln, as though he had been years in the saddle, rode with a loose rein, conducted the discussions as if they had been ordinary conversations, rarely asked a direct question, but listened to what every one had to say, distinguished clearly between what he understood and what he did not understand, brought to the front in the end only such matters as he thought expedient while tacitly ignoring those which seemed to him unessential, safeguarded himself against a usurpation of power on the part of his subordinates by daily visits to the departments and especially to the War Office — and did all these things, as his secretary assures us, in the politest fashion conceivable. "With a delicacy which has rarely been equalled, he respected, not merely their official authority, but also their sentiments, their judgments, their manhood."

Thus it was that, within the first few weeks, he was able, by a virile gesture, to maintain his leadership. Seward, who in the beginning of March, just before the inauguration, had wanted to retire, sent the President the following sermonizing memorandum when the war was on the point of breaking out:

"*First.* We are at the end of a month's administration, and yet without a policy, either domestic or foreign.

"*Second.* This, however, is not culpable, and it has even been unavoidable. The presence of the Senate, with the need to meet applications for patronage, have prevented attention to other and more grave matters.

"*Third.* But further delay to adopt and prosecute our policies for both domestic and foreign affairs would not only bring scandal on the Administration, but danger upon the country.

"*Fourth.* To do this we must dismiss the applicants for office. . .

"*Fifth.* The policy at home. I am aware that my views are singular, and perhaps not sufficiently explained. My system is build upon this *idea* as a ruling one, namely that we must,

" CHANGE THE QUESTION BEFORE THE PUBLIC FROM ONE UPON SLAVERY, OR ABOUT SLAVERY, for a question upon UNION OR DIS-UNION.

"In other words, from what would be regarded as a party question, to one of *Patriotism or Union.*" (He then recommends the evacuation of Fort Sumter.)

FOR FOREIGN NATIONS

"I would demand explanations from Spain and France, categorically, at once.

"I would seek explanations from Great Britain and Russia, and send agents into Canada, Mexico, and Central America, to rouse a vigorous . . . spirit of independence on this continent against European intervention.

"And, if satisfactory explanations are not received from Spair and France,

"Would convene Congress and declare war against them.

"But whatever policy we adopt, there must be an energetic prosecution of it.

"For this purpose it must be somebody's business to pursue and direct it incessantly.

"Either the President must do it himself, and be all the while active in it, or,

"Devolve it on some member of his Cabinet. Once adopted, debates on it must end, and all agree and abide.

"It is not in my especial province.

"But I neither seek to evade nor assume responsibility."

This was Seward's ultimatum. Once, in response to Lincoln's request, he had remained in office. Now he put a pistol to his chief's head, declaring, in the dry tone of a secretary who believed himself indispensable, that either he would manage foreign affairs as he pleased or not at all. The modicum of courtesy with which he conceded the possibility of the President's being master in his own household was revoked by the almost minatory ring of the concluding sentence. Lincoln, when reading this memorandum, might well feel much as he felt about the question of the evacuation of Fort Sumter, which came to a head at this time, and concerning which Seward once more took the erroneous line of advocating surrender. Just as the President rejected the idea of evacuation, considering that a step backwards in this matter would call forth a hundred fresh demands from the South, so did he refuse to make the other step backward demanded of him by Seward in the memorandum. In both cases alike, subordinate authorities were asking the chief of the country to yield something fundamental; a group of States in one instance, and a secretary in the other. If Anderson evacuated Fort Sumter, Lincoln had said, he himself would have to evacuate the White House. He felt the same as regards the proposal that he should surrender the control of foreign affairs. He answered Seward as follows, on the selfsame day:

"My dear Sir: Since parting with you I have been considering your paper dated this day, . . . In the inaugural, I said, 'The power confided to me will be used to hold, occupy, and possess the property and places belonging to the Government, and to collect the duties and imposts.' This had your distinct approval at the time; and, taken in connection with the order I immediately gave General Scott, directing him to employ every means in his power to strengthen and hold the forts, comprises the exact domestic policy you now urge, with the single exception that it does not propose to abandon Fort Sumter. . . .

"The news received yesterday in regard to St. Domingo certainly brings a new item within the range of our foreign policy; but up to that time we have been preparing circulars and instructions to ministers and the like, all in perfect harmony, without even a suggestion that we had no foreign policy. Upon your closing proposition, . . . I remark that if this must be done, I must do it. When a general line of policy is adopted, I apprehend there is no danger of its being changed without good reason, or continuing to be a subject of unnecessary debate; still, upon points arising in its progress I wish, and suppose I am entitled to have, the advice of all the cabinet.   "Your ob't servant, A. Lincoln."

This seems the tone of a man accustomed for years to command. In so far as the secretary has been a party to the issue, he is reminded of his previous approval; and in so far as his approval is not wanted, he is not made a party to the issue. The idea of war with two European powers is not even discussed, Lincoln being content to say afterwards in private: "One war at a time is quite enough." The control of foreign affairs is stabilized, the attempted invasion of the President's rights being met by a counterthrust — by a statement that if he should ever want advice, he would seek that of all the cabinet. — Your obedient servant.

What will happen now? Will Seward resign? Despite his ambition, the Secretary of State is man enough to acknowledge the other's superiority as soon as he recognizes it. In May he allows Lincoln to correct a critical dispatch to England; and in the beginning of June he writes to his wife: "Executive force and vigor are rare qualities. The President is the best of us."

V

As the store clerk with his customers, the lawyer with his clients, had conducted business informally, defying set rules, and deciding on the spur of the moment in accordance with the demands of the particular case, so does the President conduct his relations with his subordinates in defiance of all the rules of the White House. The state of war justifies and masks this informality, sometimes necessitates it. One might say that the unusual condition of the country, and therefore of the administration, harmonized better with the exceptional character of this President than would have a tranquil time; for in any case the peculiarities, chances, and needs of war blunt the points of conventional forms, and open the door to originality.

"The Secretary of the Treasury and the Commissioner of Internal Revenue will please see Mr. ——, one of the best men there is, and, if any difference, one they would like better than they do me."

Such is the tenor of one of Lincoln's letters of introduction. In conferring an appointment he writes:

"I now have a very special request to make of you, that you will make no war upon Mr. ——, who is also my friend, and of longer standing than yourself. I will even be obliged if you can do something for him if occasion presents."

Here is another letter:

"My dear Sir, God help me. It is said that I have offended you. I hope you will tell me how. Yours very truly."

The addressee answers that he is unaware of Lincoln's having offended him in any way. This letter the President returns with the endorsement, "Very glad to know that I haven't."

Again, he wants a trustworthy messenger to carry a document to the governor of Texas. "This is a confidential and secret message. No one besides my cabinet and myself knows anything about it, and we are all sworn to secrecy. I am going to swear you in as one of my cabinet. Hold up your right hand. Now, consider yourself a member of my cabinet."

"Hadn't you better send it by a government official?"

"No. Those Texans would hang any official caught with that paper."

"Me, too, if they caught me with it."

"I do not wish to have you hanged; and if you think there is so much danger, I will not ask you to take it. But as you live in Texas and are about to return, I was in hopes you would take it."

In this way he wins over the messenger. But when a governor excuses himself for slowness in sending troops, on the ground that the disbursing officer and the paymaster are delaying matters, Lincoln sends the following answer:

"Please say to these gentlemen that if they do not work quickly I will make quick work with them. In the name of all that is reasonable, how long does it take to pay a couple of regiments? We were never more in need of the arrival of regiments than now — even to-day."

When a certain senator was trying to talk him into a line of action he was disinclined to follow, and remarked, "You say you are the people's attorney. Now, you will admit that this course would be most popular," Lincoln replied, "But I am not going to let my client manage my case against my judgment. . . . They will have a chance to put me out by and by, if my management is not satisfactory."

He cannot respect such a senator, cannot even imagine feeling respect for a man of this stamp; but he, the sometime woodman, is impressed by corporal qualities, and wants to impress others by his own. Like most very tall men, he is rather annoyed when he encounters some one taller than himself. "So you are Mr. Sherman? Well, let's see if you are as tall as I." Such is his greeting to a senator, who is considerably disconcerted thereby. On a warship, seeing an ax in the chopping block, he is not easy till he has got hold of it, and has stood for some minutes stretching it out at arm's length, gripping the end of the handle with thumb and forefinger only. This feat surprises all beholders, and he is pleased to find that even the strongest bluejackets on board cannot do the like.

Such intercourse with the common people is an essential need for him; no dignities, no anxieties, are allowed to stand in the way.

As the years passed, he indulged in it more rather than less, and
it was another matter in which the wartime mood suited his peculiarities.   Twice a week, every one who wished to come was admitted
without formality — a sign of true democracy, and to-day still
characteristic of the White House, though up to his day nothing
of the kind was known at any royal palace or presidential residence
in Europe.   On these occasions the President, apt to be neglectful
of his dress, was carefully attired, and sat in his armchair listening
quietly to all and sundry.   "His 'yes'," we are told, "was amiable
and gave great pleasure; his 'no' was voiced in such a tone as to
deprive it of its sting.   For my part, when I left him I felt uplifted and encouraged."   At such audiences, he listened to his
visitors more attentively than they were aware, and often learned
more about the state of popular feeling than they learned about
their own destiny.   But his patience, as concerned individuals,
was inexhaustible.   For instance, when three poorly dressed girls
had found their way into the White House, and were shyly travers-
ing the reception room, he stopped them and shook hands with
each of them in turn.   If he heard the doorkeeper barring the way
to any one, he would promptly intervene; but he would make no
bones about keeping a senator waiting; and when a card had been
sent in to him, he would often come out to the door with it in his
hand, that he might himself bring the caller in.

He knows that he is humbugged sometimes, and yet when women
are pleading for the lives of sons who have deserted he will not
prove obdurate, even if they have falsely described themselves as
widows, or have brought along a borrowed child as their own.
Convinced that mercy is better than punishment, he would rather
err on the side of compassion.   Has not the war brought misery
enough into the land?

Continually he finds new illustrations, or tells some fresh
anecdote, to convince interlocutors, people who have come to
offer advice or to voice a grievance.   To one group of such he
says:

"Gentlemen, suppose all the property you were worth was in
gold and you had put it in the hands of Blondin, to carry across

the Niagara River on a rope. Would you shake the cable or keep shouting at him, 'Blondin, stand up a little straighter — Blondin, stoop a little more — go a little faster — lean a little more to the north — lean a little more to the south?' No, you would hold your breath as well as your tongue and keep your hands off till he was safe over. The government is carrying an enormous weight. Untold treasures are in their hands; they are doing the very best they can. Don't badger them. Keep silence, and we will get you safe across."

Another time, when, apropos of a visit he had paid to a military academy, false reports have been circulated regarding the dismissal of generals, he remarks in a brief speech:

"When birds and animals are looked at through a fog, they are seen to disadvantage, and so it might be with you if I were to attempt to tell you why I went to see General Scott. I can only say that my visit . . . concerned matters that you understand quite as well as if I were to tell you all about them. . . . The Secretary of War, you know, holds a pretty tight rein on the press, so that they shall not tell more than they ought to; and I'm afraid that if I blab too much, he might draw a tight rein on me."

This is a tone which is within the grasp of all his hearers, and every one of them believes what he says.

The one thing that rouses his ire is pretentiousness. He ignores the arrogance of self-styled experts and of diplomatists; pretends to be unaware of what they think and say about his ludicrous ways, his dress, and the questionable taste of his anecdotes. But when a young count with a letter of introduction from the Prussian embassy is brought to him by Schurz, and, in support of a request for a commission in the army, explains that his family is many centuries old, Lincoln interrupts (though in quite a friendly tone) by saying, "Never mind that. You will not find that to be an obstacle to your advancement."

Lincoln was a match for any one whom he could meet with the shafts of his humor. But place hunters were really more than he could face. During the early weeks of his presidency they were an even heavier burden to him than the fate of the nation, for this he expected to cope with, whereas the place hunters were too much for him :

"It was bad enough before I left Springfield, but there it was child's play when compared with the barbarism of the present situation. They hardly give me time to eat and sleep. Every one of the hungry pack looks on me as his lawful quarry."

To begin with, the staircase and the passages were filled with persons who were as busy calculating their chances as if they had been in the stock exchange; their friends patrolled the front of the house, and the new President was assailed by them even in the street. For the Republican Party was a new one, and had entered into power for the first time; and, since he aimed always at choosing the most efficient, since he wanted to allay the evils of the party system by appointing as many Democrats as possible, and since he set his face against nepotism, he found this cynical appeal to him as the dispenser of offices doubly distasteful in this hour of his country's need. He summed up his feelings in a brilliant epigram : "While the house is on fire, I must toil and moil on behalf of people who want me to find them quarters in the blazing mansion !"

Yet he rarely lost patience, and then only when the applicants' impudence passed all bounds. On one occasion a man wanted Lincoln's name in support of some money-making scheme, and would not take no for an answer. Thereupon the sleeping fires burst forth, "Do you look upon the President of the United States as a commission broker? You have come to the wrong place; and for you and every one who comes for such purposes, there is the door !"

Again, when a man short of a limb asked for a situation, and could produce no documentary evidence in support of his assertion that he was a war cripple, the President exclaimed, "What ! No papers, no credentials, nothing to show how you lost your leg ! How am I to know that you did not lose it by a trap after getting into somebody's orchard?"

We see here the farmer's son, who is familiar with such tricks, and will not allow himself to be overreached; but in the end he gives the applicant a recommendation.

Only his sense of humor lifts him to the height of reflective detachment. His ability to make fun of such people, to outwit them by his superior brains, without giving them offense, provides him with moments of refreshment; he is back again in the good old days of the circuit courts, and seems to look upon the office seekers as the opposing parties in a suit, and therefore as persons whose case has pros and cons as well as his own. Above all, it is the postmasters who approach him as a sometime colleague. Once when a Westerner happens along, and begins to talk of all kinds of irrelevant matters, the President (who is now always on the look-out for place hunters) lays a hand familiarly on the man's shoulder, saying, "You haven't such a thing as a postmaster in your pocket, have you?" The visitor is perplexed. "You see, it seems to me kind of unnatural. . . . Everybody I've seen for days past has had foreign ministers, and collectors, and all kinds, and I thought you couldn't have got in here without having at least a postmaster get into your pocket!"

Once he calls in his doctor to help him rid himself of a pertinacious bore. "Doctor, what are these blotches?" says Lincoln, holding out his hands. "That's varioloid, or mild smallpox," quoth the man of medicine. "They're all over me. It's contagious, I believe?" —

"Very contagious, indeed!" answered the skilled adviser.

The visitor departs with all convenient speed.

VI

His cabinet, and the political world generally, had least faith in him as regards the management of foreign affairs. How could this country bumpkin, this provincial lawyer, know anything about the fine art of diplomacy, which Douglas had been studying for decades in the lobbies and drawing-rooms of Washington? Seward could write notes; Sumner, who had now become chairman of the Senate Committee on Foreign Relations, was acquainted with the European style; Cameron knew how to force or wriggle his way through all the twists and narrows of political life; but the new

President was a man of the people and an anecdotalist? He must be carefully excluded from these fields.

This prejudice of the professional politicians and the long-lasting error of posterity (which failed to recognize Lincoln's shrewdness and oratorical ability, his skillful and worldly-wise arabesques, side by side with the broad lines of his character) are given their quietus by the resource, the finesse, and the patience he displayed in the management of neutrals — qualities not to be acquired by any process of ripening with the years, and among his fundamental attributes from the first.

His dealings with a hostile press are enough to prove him a diplomat. He admits the powerful Greeley — a man whose support was almost indispensable, and a man who had not been won over during a personal interview in Springfield — to a knowledge of all the plans of the government, on the understanding that Greeley shall open his newspaper to the advocacy of the governmental policy.

"He will be, in effect, my mouthpiece, but I must not be known to be the speaker. I need not tell you that I have the highest confidence in Mr. Greeley. He is a great power. Having him firmly behind me will be as helpful to me as an army of one hundred thousand men."

Greeley is to be told that if he ever objects to Lincoln's policy, "I shall be glad to have him state to me his views frankly and fully. I shall adopt his if I can. If I cannot, I will at least tell him why. He and I should stand together, and let no minor differences come between us; for we both seek one end, which is the saving of our country. Now, Governor, this is a longer letter than I have written in a month — longer than I would have written for any other man than Horace Greeley."

This epistle, very carefully worded in such a way that the recipient would be able to show it confidentially to the great journalist, was an attempt at mental bribery and corruption. If it was not more than half successful, this redounded to the credit of both parties.

More difficult was the management of the border States, those important neutrals, upon whose decision the upshot of the war might depend. Since a cleavage of opinion ran athwart them all, the essential point was everywhere to strengthen the feeling in favor of the Union. In Tennessee and Arkansas, the friends of the North, being few in number, were unable to prevent secession; but Delaware sent troops to support the Federal Government, although the Governor refrained from political action. Everything turned on insuring the loyalty of Maryland, Kentucky, and Missouri. This was possible, since they were not declared Southern States, though a good many slave owners lived in them; and from a moral and political standpoint it was of the utmost importance. In Missouri, the governor wanted to prevent the levying of troops for the North, but none the less the Germans (who here, as elsewhere, had whole-heartedly espoused the Northern cause) lent themselves to a recruiting campaign; on the other hand, the South hoped to maintain a footing in parts even of Illinois and Pennsylvania. Thus there were several vacillating States, whose attitude would be determined in the first instance by adroit handling, and later by occupation.

In these circumstances Lincoln, as diplomat, was careful to avoid legal pressure and emotional phraseology. When, for instance, the governor of Kentucky wanted the Union forces to be removed from the limits of that State, the President replied, "I most cordially sympathize with Your Excellency in the wish to preserve the peace of my own native State, Kentucky. It is with regret I search, and cannot find, in your not very short letter, any declaration or intimation that you entertain any desire for the preservation of the Federal Union. Your obedient servant."

The way in which the whole problem is here summarized in a single sentence packed with smooth civility and masked contempt, the way in which the sentimental notion of Kentucky as his birthplace is insinuated into a cold logical deduction, and in which, without breach of courtesy, the governor is invited to contemplate his own image in a pitiless mirror — do not these remind us of the skill with which, twenty-five years earlier, the half-engaged man had found it possible to escape from the net that had been cast round him by his corpulent lady friend?

To envoys from foreign parts (whom he will ere long handle in a way that will prove decisive for the issue of the war), he presents himself as a sovereign ruler who has occupied that position for years, finds the apt tone for every eventuality, and knows which of them he can suitably address in a popular vein.

One evening there come to him four Canadians, persons of standing, to find in his company a professor explaining to him by figures how industry is being damaged by the war.   Lincoln is not dressed for the part.   When he crosses his legs, his slippers dangle, and there is a liberal display of thick, blue woollen socks protruding from beneath his trousers; and now he tells a funny story about Negro life.   Yet these callers, different types though they are, are all agreed in describing the visit (each in his own way) as a delightful surprise;   the professor being charmed with the accuracy of the President's information;   and the Canadians with his classical dignity.   Another time, when a Swede and a Norwegian, army officers both, turn up, he quotes to them the English rendering of a Swedish poem which incorporates an ancient saga and describes a Scandinavian landscape.

When the King of Siam sends him various tokens of esteem, he writes a letter thanking His Majesty for "the royal gift . . . a sword of costly materials and exquisite workmanship, a photographic likeness of Your Majesty and of Your Majesty's beloved daughter, and also two elephants' tusks of length and magnitude such as indicate that they could have belonged only to an animal which was a native of Siam.   Your Majesty's letters show an understanding that our laws forbid the President from receiving these rich presents as personal treasures. . . .   Congress being now in session at this capital, . . . under their direction the gifts will be placed among the archives of the government."

Then the writer thanks the king for the tender of elephants, and continues:

"The government would not hesitate to avail itself of so generous an offer, if the object were one which could be made practically useful in the present condition of the United States.   Our political jurisdiction, however, does not reach a latitude so low as to favor the multiplication of the elephant, and steam on land as well as on water has been our best and most efficient agent of transportation in internal commerce. I shall have occasion at no distant day. . . .

"Your good friend, Abraham Lincoln."

Do we not see the twinkle in his eye, as he dictates this missive. There is no head of department to conduct relations with Siam, and Seward has neither the imagination nor the stylistic finesse that would enable him to achieve the subtle irony of the foregoing lines. A lawyer from the backwoods, who has seen nothing of the great world and knows it only through the medium of print, but one gifted with the art common to the statesman and the poet — the art of putting himself in another's place — is able, amid the threatening pressure of urgent public affairs, to fancy himself in Siam, and to return thanks for an ornamental sword (which can only seem absurd to him), and for the offer of a couple of elephants, of which he could only make effective use as the subject matter of his anecdotes.

This assured touch in all emergencies, or almost all, has certainly become more confident during the last ten years; it is in any case very remarkable in a man who by nature is essentially reserved, not to say shy, but now, encircled by mistrust, criticism, and mockery, almost a beginner, nevertheless substitutes the use of the spirit for the use of power, endeavoring in a hundred crises of the war to persuade rather than to command, and who is enabled in this very way to dominate conflicts. For the Civil War in this young democracy had to be carried on amid the fiercest dissensions in the States that remained true to the Union, and only one who was a master in the art of choosing, managing, and reconciling leaders could have conducted it to a successful conclusion.

Indeed, the evil germs of political corruption, partisan feeling, and place hunting flourished at this time most abundantly in the army.

VII

No European State was at that time so ill-prepared for a war as the American Union, and especially the North. There were men enough in the Northern States, and after the fall of Fort Sumter

there was enthusiasm as well; there was energy and there was
money; but no generals; still less, a commander. The President,
who was commander in chief of the army and the navy, knew no
more about war than most of his predecessors and rivals; and
even had he been an accomplished general, he would not have been
able to choose the leaders in the field solely on the strength of their
professional qualifications, for over the commander in chief there
was set a yet more supreme commander, mightier by far than in
England, to say nothing of the rest of Europe — public opinion.
With the aid of the press, the political clubs and associations, the
committees of Congress, and the banks, each party and each State
endeavored to have its own nominees appointed to leading positions,
and were able to exercise strong pressure in this direction, working
often by means of threats.

Who could compel the State governors to levy troops, unless
they were given cogent reasons for it by the occupation of strong
positions? Even later, when universal compulsory service had
been introduced, the supreme authority had to consider the susceptibilities of these men of might and of powerful groups in all parts
of the country, and must try to steer a safe course between contending influences. The members of the army headquarters, on
the other hand, were up in arms against this sort of thing, for
they had a perfectly reasonable objection to being bossed by either
officers or civilians whose only title to authority was the possession
of a political pull; while the lower-grade commanders were continually wrangling, after the manner of amateurs to whom one
another's deficiencies are obvious. Above all, the President's
moral sense was outraged by it, for, especially in the early days of
the war, he had to endure terrible internal conflicts over the choice
between intrinsic knowledge and extrinsic shrewdness, between
vital needs and political considerations. "You must make a job
of it, and provide a place for the bearer of this. . . . Make a job
of it with the collector and have it done. You *can* do it for me, and
you *must*."

This is but one letter among hundreds sent posthaste to General
Scott, on behalf of some man personally indifferent to Lincoln,

whom he has probably seen for the first time, and who is pretty certain to be incompetent. He sighs as he pens it, he is dispirited and weary, he feels all the bitterness of a fundamentally honest man who has never tried to win any advantage for himself and very seldom for a friend, but is now constrained to use his authority to promote the interests of strangers, not for the sake of the country or the army, but merely under stress of party considerations; in these circumstances he has to espouse the cause of the man whom he recommends to the generalissimo with the request to do it "for me."

At the same time he is perpetually tormented by the feeling that he lacks expert knowledge — a lack which the self-taught, more than all others, find unpardonable. The man who is not merely able to control lawyers and judges, but can take a saw into his own hands and show an incompetent carpenter how to use it to better advantage; the man who knows whether a frame house is well built or ill, and is no less efficient as referee at a wrestling match; the man who can manage horses and oxen, rafts and boats, and will during the war find encouraging opportunities for the use of these particular kinds of knowledge — this man can only with great internal disquietude force himself to give the final decision upon crucial matters relating to the war, concerning which for the time being he feels dependent upon the advice of his minister. These thoughts are obscured by the knowledge that the enemy has secured the ablest officers — for Lee is only one of many who have gone over to the South, and the North has none to whom the nation could suitably entrust supreme control in military matters.

There he stands now at the big window of his room, looking across the broad river. Through a telescope he can make out plainly enough the blue flag of the secessionists, which is fluttering as bravely in God's wind as the Union emblem on this side, and is held in no less honor. At night, when another sorrowful day has drawn to a close with nothing achieved, there arrives a confidential agent, a Canadian, bringing letters from English correspondents intercepted on their way to the South. The visitor hears the President sigh as he says, "I have slept with one eye open ever since I came to Washington; I never close both, except when an office-seeker is looking for me." Now, while Lincoln scans the impounded mail, he is astonished at the well-known names of some of the addressees, sorts the letters; the Canadian notes in him "traces of having passed through months of painful anxiety and trouble. There was a sad and serious look in his eyes that spoke louder than words of the disappointments, trials, and discouragements he had encountered since the war began. The wrinkles about the eyes and forehead were deeper; the lips were firmer, but indicative of kindness and forbearance."

Meanwhile the press is urging a forward move to Richmond, for there is dread of European intervention, and a general belief that the enemy, being equally ill-prepared, can more readily be forced back by a prompt onslaught. Is it only arrogance which has made the Confederates establish their new capital so close to the old capital of the Union? Why did not they choose New Orleans, far away to the South, instead of fixing upon a place only a hundred miles from Washington? Virginia is a powerful State, and one of the first importance, one from which pressure can most readily be exercised on the border States. Besides, the world shall see: "It is only a step to Washington and we shall soon be back!" Thus it was that the eastern theater of war was narrow, whereas the western was of almost boundless extent.

While the new regiments are streaming in, stronger than expected or demanded, but untrained and almost unled; while the Union capital, so close to the frontier, becomes an armed camp, and tens of thousands of soldiers must be quartered in the environs; while the President consecrates banners, visits hospitals, holds reviews, and sees the national will straining towards an advance — he cannot order this advance because he is short of generals. "I have more holes than pegs to put in them," he says in a powerful metaphor; and when he appoints Buell to the command of the Army of the Ohio, McDowell to that of the Army of the East, neither he nor the country knows anything to speak of about either man, and only Frémont, who takes charge of the Army of the West, has a name likely to inspire confidence.

Thus Lincoln and Scott are driven onward by the vague hope of the country. Lincoln, indeed, warns against a general attack, points out the inadequacy of railway communication, and advises that the initiative shall take the form of a feint attack which will lead to a dispersal of the enemy's forces and will obviate the possibility of a defeat; but Scott will hear nothing of this, orders a general onslaught by the Army of the East one Sunday in July, and sustains the first severe defeat at Bull Run, a tributary of the Potomac. There is a retreat upon the capital, the panic being intensified by senators and other sightseers who have driven out towards the scene of action in the hope of enjoying the spectacle of a victory. Rumor seeks to outdo rumor, and there is certainly good reason to expect the Southerners to follow up their victory by an advance. Amid the widespread confusion, while senators and Congressmen are losing their heads, the President is notable for his composure, ordering the necessary measures in the capital and wiring to the defeated general, "Save Washington and save the army." But to an old acquaintance, who calls on him that night, he explains that the Secretary of War has forbidden his imparting information to persons not in the military service. "These war fellows are very strict with me. . . . I must obey them, I suppose, till I get the hang of things."

Thus does Lincoln, immediately after the first reverse, make up his mind to get the hang of things for himself.

It is, however, too early for this; the immediate need is obviously to find a new military chief. The country wants a youthful hero, and Scott is seventy-five. Since no man of ripe experience is forthcoming, the President asks himself who is most loved by the soldiers and best known to the people. Who has a name that can exercise the suggestive force indispensable at such a moment? Who will be able to extract some positive achievement out of the first three months of the war? McClellan has quickly and successfully organized the new State of West Virginia (the part of the old Virginia that has remained loyal to the Union), expelling the last Southern elements from the region, and thus securing public approval. Not much of a qualification for an army commander, but it is more than

any of the others have done. Is he an officer on the active list?
He has been. Now he is a railroad executive, but in the Mexican
War he did good service as an engineer officer, and had served as
an army observer in the Crimean War. Is he a Republican? No,
a Democrat. All the better! The country will realize that he has
only been appointed because he is a man of genius. But is he?
Who knows? Anyhow, people say that he is a second Napoleon.

Certainly McClellan, now in the middle thirties, is a man whose
appearance makes people fall in love with him. He is a fine gentleman, with a good seat on horseback, has Southern manners, a big
nose, an overhanging mustache, deep-set eyes, pale cheeks, looks
through people rather than at them, and is of small stature — "a
little fellow, like Napoleon." He gets to work with the Corsican's
emotional touch, rechristening the Army of the East as the Army
of the Potomac, and, when he rides forth, is always attended by a
brilliant suite. He himself is splendidly mounted, and looks brood-
ingly ahead as he rides, a secret sounding from his lips: "I shall
carry the thing *en grande*, and crush the rebels in one campaign."
Another time, he writes to his wife as if he were Jefferson: "The
people call upon me to save the country. I must save it, and
cannot respect anything that is in the way." Listen to the cadence!
Every word literature!

The new commander begins by considering it necessary to devote
three months to the training of his quarter of a million soldiers.
Lincoln is extremely uneasy. Eastern Tennessee, threatened by
the South, is sending reiterated appeals for help, and he wants at
any cost to retain this Northern outpost thrust forward into the
enemy land. But he is thrall to the plans, nay the whims, of his
generals; he is a prisoner: public opinion swears by, the cabinet
believes in, the second Napoleon. When, at this juncture, an old
friend tells him that McClellan cherishes designs on the presidency,
Lincoln replies carelessly, "I am perfectly willing, if he will only
put an end to this war." Meanwhile, there is nothing to be done
but to leave the new commander busied beside the Potomac, drill-
ing his troops. What is going on in the West? There, perhaps,
we can discern more encouraging prospects of victory.

VIII

Here in St. Louis, likewise, there is a handsome general mounted on a fine horse and attended by a brilliant retinue; but Frémont, at any rate, has a great past, or the legend of one. He is the Western pioneer, the pathfinder. the romantic figure, the man whom the newly formed Republican Party had nominated as its first presidential candidate, and for whom Lincoln had fought. Did all that happen only five years ago? Too recently for Frémont to have forgotten it himself; too long ago for the public to remember without fresh laurels. For the time being, however, he is prized by Lincoln and the cabinet. Glitter, the power of silence, and the lack of experience as a commander in the field are qualities he shares with his colleague beside the Potomac; but he has worked out a specialty, creating a bodyguard, within which he ensconces himself, secludes himself undiscoverably, and under whose protection he is tardy in answering letters and telegrams from the government — or will not answer them at all. In their contempt for Washington and the government, the Eastern general and the Western make common cause; only in this, however, for in other matters they seem determined to work against one another.

But in contradiction to the Eastern organizer, the Western war lord is inactive in respect of the peaceful doings of the army as well, while his vanity makes him an easy prey to fraudulent army contractors (who perhaps are not unknown to the Secretary of War as well), and his main industry is to appoint brigadiers on his own initiative and without consulting the President. Within a few weeks, despite the iron wall of silence with which he has surrounded himself, materials for grave accusations against Frémont make their way to Washington. The man who was formerly an unsuccessful candidate for the presidency is said to aim at founding a Northwestern Union. The rumors lack foundation, and Lincoln does not credit them, but the fact that they are current serves to show what people regard as possible.

One morning in August, the President reads in a newspaper that General Frémont has issued a proclamation to the effect that

the property of all Missourians who shall take up arms against the
Union or shall in any other way help the South, will be confiscated
forthwith, and their slaves, if they have any, will be declared free.
What does Lincoln think and feel as he reads this? With the self-
restraint of a statesman, with the sense of responsibility proper to a
reigning sovereign, in defiance of his natural sentiments and wishes,
he has, since the beginning of the war, refrained from opening the
slavery question, being convinced that his first business is not to free
the slaves, but to save the Union. Only if the preservation of the
Union remains his war cry, can he count upon a Democratic majority
in the loyal States, and upon the neutrality of the border States.
If by any war measures on behalf of the slaves he shows that this
is a war for abolition and not a war for the maintenance of the Union,
he will lose ground, and therewith lose the war; and even in the
confiscation ordinances customary in war time he has been careful
to avoid mentioning slaves. Now comes one of his generals thrust-
ing clumsy fingers into this political web, completely ignoring the
subordination of the military arm to the political! Next day the
dormant controversy has been reawakened all over the country.
The radical press of the North applauds the bold soldier who has
outdistanced the hesitating President. The border States, on the
other hand, and Kentucky first of all, are infuriated at what
is now, they say, openly disclosed as the purpose of the war, and
once more they threaten to secede. Will not the general be
cashiered?

Not a bit of it. Lincoln writes him a friendly letter:

"I think there is great danger that the closing paragraph [of the
proclamation] . . . will alarm our Southern Union friends and
turn them against us; perhaps ruin our rather fair prospect for
Kentucky. Allow me, therefore, to ask that you will, as of your
own motion, modify that paragraph so as to conform to the first
and fourth sections of the act of Congress. . . . This letter is
written in a spirit of caution, and not of censure. I send it by special
messenger, in order that it may certainly and speedily reach you."

Amazing! In this matter Lincoln is too easy-going. His
endeavor to avoid harsh measures against men whom he con-

siders possessed of a wider national reputation than his own, his wish to repudiate the formal exercise of authority, lead him to be more complaisant than the risks of the situation justify. What is the upshot? First the general cannot be found; then he writes, asking the President himself to modify the relevant clause in the proclamation; and he sends this letter by Mrs. Frémont, an able and ambitious woman who has been described as the real chief of staff.

No, this is not a burlesque; things really happened that way!

The general's lady, fearing lest her husband may be removed, determines to take the offensive. Arriving at midnight, she insists on seeing the President then and there, berates him, threatens him with the possibility of Frémont's setting up an independent government. Will Lincoln pay her back in her own coin? He is said to be half a farmer, mannerless and boorish. "I had to exercise all the rude tact that I possess to avoid quarreling with her," he says afterwards. He does not want to use the iron hand; neither he nor the country is strong enough for that yet, and it is never his main purpose to seek popularity. He therefore proves accommodating in a way that is most injurious to himself — agrees to modify the clause under his own name as Frémont has requested, and incurs the anger of hundreds of thousands of Northerners, who regard him as cowardly and the general as a hero. Some of the newspapers declare that it would be well if Frémont were to take Lincoln's place, and one writer asks: "How many times are we to save Kentucky and lose our self-respect?"

In this matter, too, for Lincoln, policy outweighs ambition, and philosophy policy. Quite unconcerned, he ponders after his own fashion the underlying factors at work in this interlude:

"I have great respect for General Frémont and his abilities, but the fact is that the pioneer in any movement is not generally the best man to carry that movement to a successful issue. It was so in old times; Moses began the emancipation of the Jews, but didn't take Israel to the Promised Land after all. He had to make way for Joshua to complete the work. It looks as if the first reformer of a thing has to meet such a hard opposition and gets so battered and bespattered, that afterwards when people find they have to accept his reform they will accept it more easily from another man."

Thereupon he writes asking General Hunter to go to Missouri:

"He [Frémont] needs to have at his side a man of large experience. Will you not, for me, take that place? Your rank is one grade too high to be ordered to it, but will you not serve the country and oblige me by taking it voluntarily?"

Hunter, however, achieves very little, and writes letters no less arrogant than Frémont's. Thereupon he is reproved by his chief in this mild way:

"I am constrained to say it is difficult to answer so ugly a letter in good temper. I am as you intimate, losing much of the great confidence I placed in you, not from any act or omission of yours touching the public service . . . but from the flood of grumbling despatches and letters I have seen from you. . . . I have been and am sincerely your friend, and if, as such, I dare to make a suggestion, I would say that you are adopting the best possible way to ruin yourself. 'Act well your part, there all the honor lies.'"

And when, in the end, he finds it necessary to recall Frémont, his messengers cannot at first get access to the general at all, upon whom the letter has to be forced by a stratagem.

Thus delicately and grotesquely must the President of the Union handle his army commanders.

And McClellan? What is our handsome friend doing, meanwhile, beside the Potomac? During the last three months he has been training and grouping one hundred and seventy thousand men. Will he not attack now? Will the President order an advance, or discuss the matter with the general? McClellan does not want advice from any one, and least of all from Lincoln. He complains in private that the President's frequent visits to the camp are a nuisance. He writes:

"I am becoming daily more disgusted with this administration — perfectly sick of it. . . . I was obliged to attend a meeting of the cabinet, and was bored and annoyed. There are some of the greatest geese in the cabinet I have ever seen."

This is the way in which the man of the sword is apt to gird at the philosopher — but then why the devil does he not use his sword? Is the enemy too strong? Only one to three! McClellan does not believe this. His Napoleonic reputation has been acquired without his ever having fought a battle, and he fears to fritter it away in defeats. He perpetually demands troops, troops, troops; remains entrenched facing the enemy week after week, so that the morale of his inactive forces cannot but suffer; and when the Southerners, fearing a surprise attack, withdraw, evacuating Manassas, he is content to follow them only a little way, and then digs himself in once more, reporting daily, "All quiet upon the Potomac." The mood of the nation passes from uneasiness to anger, from anger to derision, from derision to mistrust. Does this Democrat cherish political ambitions; would he fain make his way to the highest office upon the field of inaction, rather than with renown on the battlefield?

Impossible, for the President promotes him. When the veteran Scott is now dismissed into honorable retirement, young McClellan is appointed commander in chief. Why? Lincoln has no one else for the job! He even puts up with discourteous treatment from the general, allows himself to be kept waiting in the anteroom, so that the matter gets into the papers, and arouses angry comment. Is the President himself put out of humor? Not in the least! He does not trouble about personal dignity, for his sole concern is to win the war. "I will hold McClellan's stirrup for him, if he will only win us victories." At length, one day, the general, on return-ing to his quarters, finds that Lincoln and Seward are waiting for him; he goes up to his room and sends down a message, saying he is sorry but is too tired to see them to-day. The Secretary of State is in a great rage, but the President remains unmoved. He pays no more visits to the general, however, and thenceforward his orders are curter.

The two men's relations assume a sinister tone, have a hollow ring, as if the foundations were being mined. "The Waleck River grows worse, the longer one looks at it," writes the general, who for six months now has been magnetized by the Potomac and its tributaries. Lincoln, when more troops are continually demanded, only to be swallowed up in the void, says it is "like shifting fleas across a barn floor with a shovel — not half of them ever get there." Again, he remarks, "Unless something is done soon, the bottom will drop out of the whole affair; and if General McClellan does not want to use the army, I should like to borrow it, if I could only see how it could be made to do something." Nevertheless he defends McClellan against the supervision committee of Congress.

In the West, at the same time, everything is at a standstill. The President, upon whom incessant demands for reinforcements, munitions, horses, etc., pour in, does not know what to make of the matter, feels that he is being humbugged in some way or other, but cannot see how to intervene. Here is a man in supreme command who knows nothing of the art of war, and a couple of generals who won't fight.

In this deadlock of depression, the scandal at the War Office had a certain ventilating effect. Cameron had unquestionably been too credulous in his dealings with army contractors, and many went so far as to say he was taking a share in the spoils. Socks that could be torn to pieces with a moderate pull, blankets that were too thin, knapsacks put together with glue instead of being stitched; all were laid to the Secretary of War's charge. A committee of inquiry was appointed, but Lincoln stood up for Cameron, declaring that he himself and the cabinet were jointly responsible for anything that was amiss. Even in the case of this man of dubious character, this man who had been forced on him, he preferred, without any need for it, to stake his own already much vilified name, and to bear his share of the blame for questionable machinations, rather than sacrifice a colleague when the battle was raging.

And this though he had a personal grievance against Cameron. The latter had, on his own initiative, come forward as an abolitionist, preparing in secret, almost simultaneously with the ripening of the army-contracts scandal, a report in which he declared:

"Those who make war against the Government justly forfeit all rights of property, privilege, or security derived from the Constitution and laws against which they are in armed rebellion, and as the labor and service of their slaves constitute the chief property of the rebels, such property should share in the common fate of war.'

For the second time Lincoln contemplated the fulfillment of his wishes, and again he had to take an adverse line. At this New Year of 1862 it seemed to him that the time was not yet ripe; nor was it. He had the pamphlet copies of the report recalled from the post offices by telegraph, and the controversial passage was deleted.

This is typical of Lincoln, who screens his secretary in personal difficulties, but disavows the same man in a matter where State policy is involved, although upon the latter question he is really in sympathy with Cameron, whereas in the former respect he is out of tune; and although the very reverse behavior in both instances would have been more favorable to his own reputation. How much importance he attaches to a cause and how little to personal concerns; how readily he can overlook a slight when he thinks an adversary can be useful to the imperiled nation, is strikingly proved at this juncture by his appointment of Stanton as Secretary of War.

Twice only had Lincoln seen this man, at one time a lawyer, and then Attorney General under Buchanan: for a moment only, nearly a year before, when he had himself assumed the presidential office; and once again, seven years ago. That had been in Cincinnati, on a day when Lincoln's self-esteem had been more gravely affronted than on any other occasion during the last twenty years. In an important trial, two noted Eastern lawyers had been briefed on the side which, for political reasons, a Westerner, Lincoln, was also summoned to support. The latter was really the best informed of the three regarding the topic of dispute; it was the first time he had traveled so far afield in a law case; and he had for several days been only a silent participator. When, at length, the time had come for him to speak, Stanton took the words out of his mouth, put himself forward as the chief counsel, and said to his friends that nothing would induce him to associate with "such a damned, gawky, long-armed ape as that." The two were staying at the same hotel, and for the whole week Stanton's manner toward his Western colleague was challenging and insolent.

Stanton had been disgusted by Lincoln's election as President — and not solely because he himself was a Democrat. During the subsequent months in Washington, he had continually abused Lincoln, who was an "original gorilla." Why, he asked McClellan, should any one go all the way to Africa in search of what could so easily be found at Springfield, Illinois? It is unlikely that the actual wording of these invectives reached the President's ears, but he was certainly acquainted with Stanton's general attitude towards himself.

Yet now he summons Stanton to one of the most important posts in the administration, and one which will involve constant contact between the two men. He does it because Stanton is inviolably faithful to the Union, and combines instinctive energy with knowledge, zeal with diligence, method with technical skill. Powerfully built, he has a broad head and a grizzled beard, a fine forehead, an emphatic nose; and one sees in him a person of practical bent, all-in-all a man. How well suited he is to Lincoln! Both of them are incorruptible, competent, and serious-minded; but whereas Lincoln is unduly cautious, Stanton is too forthright; and whereas the latter is inclined to put his head down and charge an obstacle, the former hesitates long before coming to a decision. They seem made to compensate one another's deficiencies, whilst in their merits they are akin and therefore reinforce one another.

Ere long they become fast friends.

IX

Abraham Lincoln was learning strategy. During these winter months, when nothing happened, when each general in turn had something fresh to ask for and found a new excuse for not marching against the enemy, when the war was dragging on and the differences between the commanders were growing, he realized that it had become necessary for him to gain a personal understanding of the main business of his post. If it was his duty as President to study

European diplomacy, he did so, to discover speedily that it was only a knowledge of men transferred from ordinary civilian life to the domain of political affairs. If, by the terms of the Constitution he was in supreme command both by land and by sea, and if there was not at his disposal any military leader in whose genius and character he could have full confidence, the practical needs of the situation, in conjunction with this lack of confidence and with his keen sense of responsibility, could not but impel him to the decision that he must learn that for which he was responsible.

Surely there could be no mystery about the art of war? With very little aid, he had learned to write; with none at all, he had learned history and the sciences. Had not a woodman with great, gnarled hands, transferred to a new nest as store clerk, been able, stretched out at full length on the counter, to apply himself to the study of the law, and to master the art of spelling? Had not Euclid opened stores of classical knowledge to him when, on circuit, he had lain in bed in the country inns, reading far into the night? And when he had entered the electoral field against Douglas, and had at first been inclined to doubt his own capacity, had he not quickly come to realize that these distinguished persons, no less than ordinary men, must use water to boil things in, and that in the last resort a senator needs only common sense and a good knowledge of men? Had it been necessary for him (like a dictator in ancient Rome) to place himself personally at the head of the army and to invite comparison with Jefferson Davis, his bodily energies would indeed have been equal to the test of battle, though his temperament would have unfitted him for leadership in the field. But what destiny now called on him to do was accordant with his nature and well within his competence. Lincoln, therefore, answered the call.

Day and night that winter, and especially in December and January, the President, so we learn from his secretary, was deep in the study of strategical works, maps, and other documents relating to the leadership of armies, their provisioning, their march. Predisposed to draw comparisons, gifted with imagination (the fundamental requisite of the great military commander), and at the same time a realist and a calculator (as the efficient farmer must be) — he had all the qualifications for success. Combining his memories of the little campaign against the Indians with the experiences of the last year, he could achieve a clear pictorial understanding of the extant military situation, and, his eyes on the map, could elaborate plans for encircling the enemy. He taught himself the fundamentals of war-making, as he had taught himself all that he had learned; and even if we do not know the precise course of his studies, the results, at any rate, show the extent of his acquirements.

For now he begins to take a new tone with his generals, no longer exhibiting toward them the demeanor of a perplexed layman. He writes rather tentatively to General Buell in January:

"For my own views, I have not offered, and do not now offer, them as orders; and while I am glad to have them respectfully considered, I would blame you to follow them contrary to your own clear judgment, unless I should put them in the form of orders. . . . With this preliminary, I state my general idea of this war to be, that we have the greater numbers and the enemy has the greater facility of concentrating forces upon points of collision; that we must fail unless we can find some way of making our advantage an overmatch for his; and that this can only be done by menacing him with superior forces at different points at the same time, so that we can safely attack one or both if he makes no change; and if he weakens one to strengthen the other, forbear to attack the strengthened one, but seize and hold the weakened one, gaining so much."

When illness now gives McClellan a new pretext for postponing the advance, and when a series of questions sent him by the President is returned with nothing more than fugitive penciled comments, Lincoln begins to address inquiries to the general's senior officers, and in this way learns a good deal more than is agreeable to that commander. The new Secretary of War, who has up to now been on friendly terms with McClellan, has an unpleasant way of going straight to the goal. He growls his discontent, and writes: "This army has got to fight or run away; and while men are fighting nobly in the West, the champagne and oysters on the Potomac must be stopped."

Lincoln goes more cautiously to work, invites the commander and his general to a cabinet meeting, lets the angry members put direct questions to the commander, and when McClellan refuses to answer unless the President expressly orders him to do so, the latter is content to inquire whether the former has any date fixed in his mind for an attack.

"Certainly I have," says the commander, curtly and mysteriously.

"In that case I close the meeting," says Lincoln, glad to avoid an outburst. But Stanton is furious, saying of the matter afterwards, "We had ten generals there, every one of them afraid to fight. . . . If McClellan had a million men, he would swear the enemy had two millions, and then he would sit down in the mud and yell for three."

Lincoln does not voice any complaints, but goes on learning, and since he is now becoming well-informed regarding questions of munitions and commissariat, he is often able to refute his generals' contentions that this or that is impossible. On the neighboring wharf he has everything explained to him as it arises, passing from practical instance to practical instance, this being the way in which the mind of the self-taught man works. Here is a brief note to the Secretary of the Navy: "I think I saw three vessels go up to the Navy Yard just now. Will you please send down and learn what they are?"

When an inventor brings a new gun, Lincoln, who has been unwilling to shoot even a dumb beast, will himself try its performance; he goes out with a clerk to the lawn south of the White House, fixes up a target cut from a sheet of Congressional notepaper, and shoots fairly well with it. Then he says, "I believe I can make this gun shoot better." Whittling a wooden sight from a pine stick, he adjusts it to the carbine, and does actually get a better result. Or, in his own room, with an admiral to help him, he will test a new gunpowder in the fireplace, carefully examining the residue, and making suggestions for further work on the powder.

He has a difference of opinion with the dilatory McClellan regarding the plans for the movement of the Army of the Potomac, the general wanting to march by way of the peninsula, while Lincoln favors a direct advance against Richmond. In order to hasten action by a general with whom he was losing patience the President then issued his much debated General War Order, Number 1:

"Ordered, that the 22d day of February, 1862, be the day for a general movement of all the land and naval forces of the United States against the insurgent forces. That especially the army at and about Fortress Monroe; the Army of the Potomac, the Army of Western Virginia; the army near Munfordville, Kentucky; the army and flotilla at Cairo, and a naval force in the Gulf of Mexico, be ready to move on that day."

The difference over the correct strategy required by the situation still persisted, however, and Lincoln at length addressed to McClellan one of his terse and precise letters:

"If you will give me satisfactory answers to the following questions, I shall gladly yield my plan to yours.

"*First.* Does not your plan involve a greatly larger expenditure of time and money than mine?

"*Second.* Wherein is a victory more certain by your plan than mine?

"*Third.* Wherein is a victory more valuable by your plan than mine?

"*Fourth.* In fact, would it not be less valuable in this, that it would break no great line of the enemy's communications, while mine would?

"*Fifth.* In case of disaster, would not a retreat be more difficult by your plan than mine?"

McClellan's reply lacks precision. At a council of war called shortly after, a majority of the soldiers present advocated the McClellan plan. The President was not convinced and he had able support in his views, but he adopted the counsel of prudence and allowed McClellan to have his way. Critics have not yet reached any general agreement as to which was right, the civilian in the White House or the general in the field.

In this gloomy period of the war, when he was exposed to political onslaughts from both sides, an object of derision for society people, despised by his generals, uncertain how and when the whole terrible business would end, groping his way forward toward light and knowledge amid a crowd of warring counselors — his two younger sons, infected at a hospital they had visited, fell sick, and Willie, the twelve-year-old boy to whom he was devotedly attached, succumbed within a few days. Lincoln watches with the nurse at the ailing children's bedside. He questions this nurse, a sincere Christian, as to her own situation; she tells him she is a widow, her husband and two children are in heaven, she is reconciled to her afflictions, and has learned to love God even more ardently than in happier days. How has that been brought about? By trusting in Him, and believing that all He ordained was for the best.

"Did you submit fully under the first loss?"

"Only by degrees. As blow followed blow, I learned better how to submit."

"I am glad to hear you say that. Your experience will help me to bear my afflictions. . . . This is the hardest trial of my life. Why is it? Why is it?"

When he is told that many Christians are praying for him, he says, "I am glad to hear that. . . . I need their prayers. . . . I wish I had that childlike faith you speak of, and I trust God will give it to me." He goes on to speak of his mother, buried so many years before in the wilds of Indiana. "I remember her prayers, and they have always followed me."

Nocturnal conversations, in the half light of a sickroom lamp, while the lean and careworn man stretches his legs towards the wall, and, as part of his personality escapes from its habitual restraints, his skepticism passes for a time into abeyance. His wife, being hysterically inclined, prowls restlessly up and down, on the verge of madness. But Lincoln sits quiet, thinking about his mother's prayers; asks the stranger whether it takes long before one can submit to affliction; and as soon as he goes out of the room it is to find Seward waiting for him with a menacing telegram from

Europe, or Stanton with bad news from the front, or an unhappy woman who wants to save her son from the clutches of martial law, and at the same moment his own son's life is being cut short prematurely in consequence of the war.

Is it not natural that he should run counter to the opinion of the Secretary of War, should make a practice of clemency in cases where severity might be expected to act as a more effectual deterrent? A young soldier has been sentenced to be shot for sleeping while on sentinel duty. "I could not think of going into eternity with the blood of that poor young man on my hands. It is not to be wondered at that a boy raised on a farm, probably in the habit of going to bed at dark, should, when required to watch, fall asleep."

A young officer attached to the service of the White House, and very dear to Lincoln, fell in the earlier days of the war.

"In the untimely loss of your noble son," he writes to the parents, "our affliction here is scarcely less than your own. So much of promised usefulness to one's country, and of bright hopes for oneself and friends, have rarely been so suddenly dashed as in his fall. In size, in years, and in youthful appearance, a boy only, his power to command men was surpassingly great. . . . And yet he was singularly modest and deferential in social intercourse. My acquaintance with him began less than two years ago; yet, through the latter half of the intervening period, it was as intimate as the disparity of our ages and my engrossing engagements would permit. To me he appeared to have no indulgences or pastimes, and I never heard him utter a profane or an intemperate word. . . . In the hope that it may be no intrusion upon the sacredness of your sorrow, I have ventured to address you this tribute to the memory of my young friend and your brave and early fallen child."

When before or since has the chief of a State penned such letters in the midst of a bloody war? Not a word about "a hero's death" to mar the 'cello tone of these lines, nor is there any flavor of the self-satisfaction of one in an exalted position from which the voice of human kindliness can only trickle down to those of inferior station. It is the letter of a poet. In like manner we see him pale, breast heaving with emotion, tears streaming down his face, both hands pressed upon his heart, as he leaves the quarters of General McClellan and walks down the street, not returning the salute of the sentinel before the door — when he has heard the news of the fall of Colonel Baker, an old friend and comrade of the Vandalia days. Can it really be no more than a year since he was sitting with another friend before the fire in Springfield, and talking of Gethsemane?

But there comes a clatter to his ears, and he knows that people are awaiting his decisions.

X

Where are all his old friends? At this critical time, surely, they will flock to his support? Most of them make a poor showing, as compared with his rivals. In the opening weeks of the war, Douglas hastens to Lincoln, to report the receipt of telegrams summoning him to Illinois that he may help to strengthen people's convictions there. Shall he go or stay? Let Lincoln decide. Thus does the little Douglas once more confront the tall Lincoln, speaking to him neither with cutting acerbity nor yet with fierce condescension; he does not this time hold the President's hat in his hand, but comes to ask his President what he had better do. Lincoln, who formerly would have given a good deal to keep his adversary out of Illinois, now sends him thither in support of the Northern cause. Douglas goes — to die there a few weeks later from apoplexy. Lincoln has the flag over the White House half-masted, and mourns for his opponent in this mansion for whose occupancy Douglas has vainly wrestled during all the active years of his life.

How glad he is to see the old faces sometimes. "Hill" has become an officer, and receives many favors from the President, but gets out of sympathy with him, and later writes against him. Others are recommended in letters as "the son of my very dear friend", or "my particular friend." Herndon gets a most affectionate note, though it is a short one: "Dear William, Yours of January 30th just received. Do just as you say about the money matter. As you well know, I have not time to write a letter of respectable length. God bless you, says your friend, A. Lincoln." When

Herndon comes, he is very welcome, but he is never intrusive, and asks nothing for himself.

A comrade of earlier days turns up and the sad visage of the President grows more cheerful. He will have other callers told that he is busy and cannot see them, while in the old friend's company he is "playful and sportive as a child, told me all sorts of anecdotes, . . . and inquired after several old characters whom we both knew in Illinois." Lincoln shows his visitor the war maps, demonstrating with bony fingers the actual situation, and explaining his own plans and those of the commanders in the field. Then comes an interruption, a general has called. "Well, as he is one of the fellows who make cannon, I suppose I must see him." The general's subsequent account of the matter was that he had left the President "closeted with an old Hoosier from Illinois, telling dirty yarns, while the country was quietly going to hell."

Another time he is sitting on the balcony of the White House when the band is playing, and a crowd of people is filing past. Among them he recognizes some one, jumps up, leans over the iron railing to beckon with his long arms, and calls, "Hubbard! Hubbard! Come here!" Since the key to the veranda gate cannot be found at the moment, he makes his friend climb over the railing to join him.

But while these familiar faces are friendly, hundreds of his sometime friends look at him askance. Many find it impossible to forgive him for canceling Frémont's abolitionist proclamation. When letters blaming him on this score come to hand, he does not ignore them, but answers them with his own pen.

"Yours of the 17th is just received; and coming from you, I confess it astonishes me. That you should object to my adhering to a law, which you had assisted in making and presenting to me less than a month before is odd enough. . . . The essential thing is to hold Kentucky, for the retention of Missouri and Maryland, and therefore the issue of the war, depend upon it. . . . If you will give up your restlessness for new positions, and back me manfully on the grounds upon which you and other kind friends gave me the election, and have approved in my public documents, we shall go through triumphantly. . . .

"Your friend as ever."

Sometimes bitterness and impatience are more plainly voiced. He answers by return of post the reproaches of an old acquaintance:

"You are ready to say I apply to friends what is due only to enemies. I distrust the wisdom if not the sincerity of friends who would hold my hands while my enemies stab me. The appeal of professed friends has paralyzed me more in this struggle than any other thing. . . . I am a patient man — always willing to forgive. . . . Still, I must save this government, if possible. What I cannot do, of course, I will not do; but it may as well be understood, once for all, that I shall not surrender this game leaving any available card unplayed. Yours truly."

Again, in the midst of intrigues, "I shall not do more than I can, and I shall do all I can, to save the Government. . . . I shall do nothing in malice. What I deal with is too vast for malicious dealing."

While he is thus disappointing erstwhile supporters, to whom he seems overcautious, he is winning new friends from among his adversaries, who revise their opinion of him now that they know him better. Especially does this happen with Seward and Stanton, though likewise with all the other members of the cabinet. That body is joined by Sumner, the senator who years before had been savagely assaulted by a political opponent, and had now become chairman of the Committee on Foreign Relations. Lincoln was impressed by Sumner for the simple reason that the latter was nearly as tall as himself; he could not fail to be doubly impressed because Sumner had the charm of manner and grace of movement which he himself lacked. This distinguished gentleman with the open countenance, high forehead, and straight nose, a man adorned with all the advantages of that European culture which was his by right of education, resembled the leading figures of the South, and seemed in aspect and nature to give the lie to the contention that a lordly character could only develop in a slaveholding community.

For many, many years, indeed, he had been an open and passionate opponent of slavery, and in so dogmatic a fashion that when he was reminded there were arguments on the other side he was wont to reply angrily, "There is no other side!" Being of this narrow and uncompromising type, he found it hard to understand Lincoln; whereas Lincoln, who was able to look at all sides of a question, could warmly admire such a character as Sumner's. The senator was poorly prepared by environment and experience to appreciate a man of Lincoln's type; and when Lincoln had come to take charge at the White House, Sumner had made horrified comments on the new President's aspect and manners. A New Englander, trained in the humanities at Harvard, handsome and proud, one for whom even a United States senator was invested with a quasi-Roman dignity, Sumner could not fail to be outraged and pained at the sight of this Western child of nature in the presidential chair. He did not, like Stanton, give uncontrolled expression to these feelings, but was filled with pity, partly for the country and partly for the man. Whereas Lincoln could delight in the brilliant conversation of this man of high breeding, the latter was repelled by the former's mentality, by his slow way of thinking, and above all by his humor. This last was often extremely perplexing to Sumner, who would occasionally ask to have the point of one of Lincoln's anecdotes explained.

Yet in a short while they had gained confidence in one another, and Sumner had become a trusted political adviser of the President. They were at one in the fight against slavery, and also in their pacifist trend, for fifteen years earlier, in a great speech, Sumner had said, "In our age, there can be no peace which is not honorable, and no war which is not dishonorable." Now they were called to the leadership of one of the factions in a civil war, and, though they were agreed in holding that the first essential was to save the Union, Sumner was more inclined than Lincoln to use the war as a means for combating slavery.

As yet, few besides Sumner understood Lincoln. Amid the chorus of invective, calumny, and mockery, the approving voices of isolated imaginative writers and statesmen were scarcely audible. Walt

Whitman, indeed, could not sufficiently extol the simplicity of the man who looked more modest than ever when surrounded by a guard of thirty cavalrymen with drawn sabers, himself "dressed in plain black, somewhat rusty or dusty; wearing a black, stiff hat, and looking about as ordinary in attire as the commonest man." This simplicity sets him apart, in Whitman's eyes, from the glittering generals who love to clank through the streets attended by a clanking suite.

Emerson, who knew him personally, wrote the fine sentence: "Lincoln was permitted to do more for America than any other American man." Carl Schurz, whose affection for the President seems to have been reluctant, wrote the following splendid characterization:

"He had great respect for other men's superior knowledge and higher culture, but these qualities did not make him afraid. In fact, he was afraid of no one and of nothing . . . to an extent that would lead him to surrender the independence of his judgment and his will. He would meet the greatest of men without a trace of embarrassment, as if he had been in the habit of meeting such persons all his life. . . . He was always able to recognize others' merits without being afraid that thereby his own would be eclipsed. No problem, however important, could perplex him, for he judged all that came his way in accordance with the principles of ordinary logic and the rules of common sense. . . . Yet there could be no one more receptive of honest advice, or more tolerant of criticism. . . . If he was attacked or misunderstood, he would invite the objector to a friendly exchange of views, instead of breaking off relations."

While Lincoln was still alive, Schurz expressed the following opinion in a letter:

"Free from the aspirations of genius, he will never be a danger to a free community. . . . He is the people personified. . . . His government is the most representative known to history. I will venture a prophecy that may sound strange. Within fifty years, and perhaps sooner, Lincoln's name will be inscribed in the honorable annals of the American Republic beside that of Wash-

MARY TODD LINCOLN

From a photograph taken during the early part of Lincoln's administration

ington. . . . The children of those who now persecute him will bless him."

Motley, then in the foreign diplomatic service, possessed of a profound knowledge of the human heart, and able as the intimate friend of Bismarck to compare Lincoln with another great statesman of the time, wrote:

"I went and had an hour's talk with Mr. Lincoln. I am very glad of it, for had I not done so I should have left Washington with a very inaccurate impression of the President. I am now satisfied that he is a man of very considerable native sagacity; and that he has an ingenuous, unsophisticated, frank, and noble character. I believe him to be as true as steel, and as courageous as true. At the same time there is doubtless an ignorance about State matters, and particularly about foreign affairs, which he does not attempt to conceal, but which we must of necessity regret in a man placed in such a position at such a crisis. Nevertheless his very modesty in this respect disarms criticism. . . . I feel that, so far as perfect integrity and directness of purpose go, the country will be safe in his hands."

Later: "He is the true, honest type of American democracy. There is nothing of the shabby-genteel, the would-be-but-couldn't-be fine gentleman; he is the great American Demos, honest, shrewd, homely, wise, humorous, cheerful, brave, blundering occasionally, but through blunders struggling onwards towards what he believes the right."

XI

Great, indeed, was Mary's disappointment! She had dreamed of a goal, had striven towards it, had attained it in defiance of all reasonable expectation — and, having done so, at length mistress of the White House, really the first lady in the land, it was to find, — what? War, which forbade her entertaining on a large scale. Once, when she gave a dance, there was acrimonious criticism in the newspapers; and anything of a public kind she attempted entailed embarrassing comment. She had overlooked one thing in all these years of anticipation; that it is hard to pass in one leap from Springfield to Washington, from the social life of a Western provincial town to that of a great capital; that the promotion (as she regarded it) would find her just as unprepared as her husband, the only difference between them being that her ambition was mortified, whereas he was unruffled. Towards her, born in the South, the Washington ladies of Southern extraction, whom marriage or political considerations had fettered to the side of the North, displayed a contempt which she had done nothing to warrant. It seemed as if they wished to wreak vengeance on the wife of the President for the vicissitudes of their own destiny; and they would even go so far, when she drove by in her carriage, as to run from the open window to the piano and strum the Southern song of defiance. He remained indifferent to criticism, whether printed or whispered, but she could not endure it, for she had come here to play a part; she had come to be something and to do something.

The most urgent and serious problem was that of dress. Between the election and the inauguration, she had been ordering clothes in New York; now she passed in review the dressmakers of all her Washington acquaintances. In the end she decided upon a Negress who was accounted the leading modiste in the capital. The fact that the woman had made gowns for Mrs. Jefferson Davis (a rival she simultaneously despised and admired) may well have weighed with Mary. The only person of color with whom the wife of the liberator of the blacks was on friendly terms was this dressmaker, who had for thirty years been a slave; indeed, she became by degrees intimate with Mrs. Lincoln, and remained a close friend in the days of misfortune. Now she made eighteen dresses for the President's wife.

The first, about which there were tears and a scene, because it arrived almost too late for the occasion, was a bright rose-colored moiré antique with an immense train, cut very low at the neck, as women who are ambitious rather than sensual love to have their dresses. It was suited to Mary's ample proportions; and, if one disregarded her unduly plump arms, she looked well in it. Her husband, at first sight of it, walked all round her with long strides, emitted a low whistle, and exclaimed, "Whew, what a long tail our cat has!" When she was inclined to take umbrage, he said, "No, no, it's very fine indeed; but it would look just as well if the head and tail were a little closer together." He spoke of such a costume as his wife's "full war-paint." When she found that the custom was for the President to go in first to dinner with the leading lady on his arm, and for the President's wife to bring up the rear on the arm of the leading gentleman, she declared that during her reign no other woman should take precedence of her, and she insisted on going first, arm in arm with her husband.

She knew, all the same, that they looked quaint side by side; but Lincoln took the edge off the absurdity in his broadly humorous way by introducing the pair of them at a small party with the words, "Ladies and gentlemen, here are the long and short of the presidency." Owing to the discrepancy in their appearance, she would never be photographed with him; but she consented to the publication of a "faked" group, a separate photograph of Lincoln having been adroitly combined with one of herself in which her head was brought up to the level of her husband's shoulder and her bust measure perceptibly reduced. She also ordered the destruction of the negatives of all photographs of which she did not approve.

Sumner seems to have been the only person who got on equally well with both husband and wife, Lincoln approving his mentality and Mary his manners. Otherwise, she associated with some rather dubious characters. Villard, who often saw her in the beginning, writes:

"His wife contributed not a little to Lincoln's troubles. She interfered, not only in the distribution of minor posts, but even in the appointment of cabinet members. She was also accessible to men and women who knew how to take advantage of her susceptibility to the grossest flattery, and were thus able to acquire great influence over her." Noteworthy among these was the Chevalier Wykoff, an adventurer, about whom there was a good deal of talk at the time, and who was really a spy in the White House for one of the New York papers. A man of the world, he had agreeable manners, self-assurance, and affability. "I heard him spread the butter so thick in his compliments to Mrs. Lincoln on her looks and her dress, that I should have expected her to blush, and to dismiss him as impudent beyond bearing. Instead, she took him into favor as a sort of master of the ceremonies, as authority upon questions of etiquette, as adviser in domestic and personal matters (toilet included), and as an ever welcome companion in the drawing-room and the carriage."

When the President's lady went to visit regiments, she preferred those which flattered her most and made most fuss over her. She was not invariably shrewd enough to see through the wiles of the Southern ladies who dressed themselves up as maidservants and sought employment at the White House, with the sole object of spying out the land. By her own family connections, moreover, she was linked to the South, a brother, three half brothers, and the husbands of three of her half sisters being in the Southern army. A cousin, who at the outset lived with her in Washington, tells of a farewell visit paid by a Southern politician at the outbreak of the war; on this occasion, a relative had said, "Dear Lizzie, I hope you won't be disappointed in your stay here. Better remain on as guest till we've taken Washington."

Instead of stressing the fateful character of this severance, she may have had a secret sympathy with the dashing officers who, down there in the South, were so chivalrously defending the ideals of the white lords. As to this, proof is lacking; but her pride, her early training, and her ties of kinship would make it perfectly comprehensible, for, especially at the beginning of the war, there was plenty of friction in the White House. When Lincoln wished to appoint his wife's brother-in-law to a much-prized post in the Northern army, the offer was refused, for the young man preferred to take service in the South, though he was a Kentuckian like Lincoln, and though his father remained true to the North.

It was natural enough that Mary should pull strings in favor of her sister in Illinois, and should secure a position for the family; but she was piqued because the beneficiaries ascribed the favors received to Lincoln, and not to her own good offices. In truth, everything depended on Lincoln, who was always loath to favor his own intimates, and in this matter had to write letters which went very much against the grain. To Mrs. Lincoln's brother-in-law Edwards:

"My dear Sir, It pains me to hear you speak of being ruined in your pecuniary affairs. I still hope you are injured only, and not ruined. . . . The thing you proposed, it seemed to me, I ought to understand myself before it was set on foot by my direction or permission, and I really had no time to make myself acquainted with it — nor have I yet. And yet I am unwilling, of course, that you should be deprived of a chance to make something, if it can be done without injustice to the government, or to any individual. If you choose to come here and point out to me how this can be done, I shall not only not object, but shall be gratified to be able to oblige you."

In the like vein to another:

"Dear Stuart, Cousin Lizzie shows me your letter of the 27th. The question of giving her the Springfield Post-office troubles me. You see, I have already appointed William Jayne, a territorial governor, and Judge Trumbull's brother to a land-office. — Will it do for me to go on and justify the declaration that Trumbull and I have divided out all the offices among our relatives. . . . I see by the papers a vote is to be taken as to the Post-office. Could you not set up Lizzie and beat them all? She, being here, need know nothing of it, so therefore there would be no indelicacy on her part."

What must be the feelings of this sorely tried man at the head of his nation, when he, who is contending with the parties about the highest military appointments, and who is being scrutinized by the hostile eyes of those who are eager to detect a weak spot in his armor of probity, is now asked to find posts for his wife's brother-in-law and other relatives. When he writes Edwards' address, must he not recall that New Year's Day when he had broken tryst at Edwards' house; and can he fail to ask himself, sometimes, whether the second wedding day had not been far more disastrous than the first. What had he gained by his marriage? One good thing, at any rate, is that Mary is not a coward. When the city is in danger, she refuses to betake herself and the children to some safe harborage and stays with him.

But her jealousy is so preposterous that she makes a black mark against any woman to whom he talks for more than five minutes at a time. Before a reception, she admonishes him not to act like a beardless schoolboy and conduct flirtations with silly women. And yet innocent flirtation would be the only suitable way in which he could get from women that indefinable stimulus for which he has been in search all his life. Will he not lose his temper, and show himself to be master in his own house as well as master of the country? Not a bit of it! He is content to tease her by making out a long list of the names of women she cannot abide, and with whom, he says, he intends to have amusing conversations.

For the rest, she was the mother of his children, and his love for these children grew with the passing of years and the increasing gravity of the situation. Of the four, only two survived. The eldest, a student, was almost always away. But Tad, now eight years old, a bright, gentle, and lively boy, was the darling of the White House, came into his father's room whenever he pleased, accompanied Lincoln everywhere, so that on visits to the camps one saw beside the lean tall-hatted giant on the big horse, a little figure in a gray cape, mounted on a pony — a lad whose rosy, cheerful face could not fail to put the soldiers in a good humor. Evening visitors would sometimes find Tad stretched on the carpet reading, beside the writing table where his father was hard at work; or the two would be busy over the same book, the little man learning and the big man relaxing his mind.

Close to the writing table was an escritoire with pigeonholes for filing letters, but there was no copying book. Lincoln preferred to make holograph copies of important documents, saying that these copies were less easy to steal than a copying book. In the same receptacle were always to be found the latest caricatures, and when Lincoln would read aloud to a visitor something humorous he had just come across — for instance, something grotesque and witty about the way in which the Negroes would flock to the North — the visitor, if a strait-laced New Englander, would assume a forbidding reserve, and would subsequently tell his friends he was amazed to think that the President could find time for such non-

sense. But no sourness of visage could wholly silence the Bohemian in Lincoln, and when he read poems aloud or asked for music
(Scottish songs and ballads), his favorites were still those which
dealt with the flight of time and memories of earlier days. For now,
when he was at the climax of his life, this melancholy man inclined
to the romantic but fallacious belief that things had gone much
better with him in his youth.

XII

The political aim of the Civil War was slowly shifting; to begin
with, it had been the rescue of the Union, by degrees it became the
abolition of slavery. Inasmuch as the former problem was still
far from being solved, and as the latter could only be solved by solving the former, there appeared very curious ironies and contradic-
tions; but everything that happened, and, yet more, everything
that could not happen for the moment, depended upon the person
of the President, was rooted in his heart and brain. Lincoln bore
the brunt; to Lincoln accrued the merit.

When the war began as a fight against rebels, the North had come
together as one man; but when the affair was protracted, there was
a revival of party dissensions, Democrat contending with Republican, and the moderate Republicans quarreling fiercely with the
radicals.

A new outlook, which had been decades in course of formation
and was now of a sudden being emphasized, could not be codified
all in a moment — perhaps could not be codified at all in war time.
The vagueness of the transitional state in which slavery was here
and there beginning to abolish itself without any legal warrant for
abolition, could not but arouse unrest and dissatisfaction in all
parties. Why, asked the Northern abolitionists, did the President
not at least incorporate into the army all slaves that escaped from
the South, or were captured by the Union forces, seeing that under
martial law his powers as commander in chief would enable him to
take far more drastic steps than this? Why, complained the negrophiles in the border States, did the troops treat the slaves that ran
away to them, and the slaves that fell into their hands, so badly?

Why, exclaimed the slave owners in these same border States, were the slaves between the lines protected in a way that infringed on the legal rights of the masters? Had not the South acted more wisely when, in its new constitution, it had prohibited the reopening of the African slave trade, and had also forbidden the import of slaves from the North? Thereby the neutral States were saved from the dread that the price of slaves would fall, but were at the same time inspired with alarm lest they should not be able to get any more slaves from the South!

Amid these discordant voices, what was Lincoln to do? In any case he silenced the voice of his own heart, and was content to weigh pros and cons as a politician. As far as the North was concerned, it was perhaps unnecessary for him to decide the issue, for there, whence his soldiers came, were as many negrophobe Democrats as negrophile Republicans. The abolitionist decree of Frémont in the West, even the proposal to arm fugitive slaves put forward by Secretary of War Cameron, both acting on their own initiative, would alienate the border States, and thus very likely turn the scale against the North. Thirty years before, Henry Clay (a negrophile like Lincoln, and in many respects his prototype) had said in warning: "The evils of slavery are nothing when compared with the greater evil that would arise out of its sudden, general, and indiscriminate abolition."

Conversely, there were other neutral States which were no less dangerous. These were in Europe, looking on, intent; and the majority of them — England in especial — were hostile to the North. Owing to the blockade enforced on the South, England was deprived of most of her supplies of raw cotton, and could not be won as long as the war-aim was the maintenance of a Union which had originally been formed against her and was still inconvenient to her; but if he were to inscribe abolition on his banner, the British puritans could hardly espouse the cause of the slave owners.

And yet, amid all his calculations, the pitiable condition of the blacks was a matter he had taken so long and so deeply to heart that he was little inclined to discuss it with the cabinet, or even with Seward. It was easier to write about it to Speed, with whom he had of old argued the problem of slavery, and who was now his trusted agent in Kentucky. But he seems to have talked things over again and again with Sumner, developing the idea that the border States should propose the purchase of slaves by the Union, whereupon other things would follow in due course. He was trying to find some transitional scheme.

Hoping to begin in Delaware by gradual abolition with compensation of the masters, he wrote private letters to senators who were opposed to the idea, endeavoring to convince them and the press that the purchase of all the slaves in four of the border States would cost the Union as much as eighty-seven days of the war. He told the impatient Sumner that they must wait until such a declaration would no longer disintegrate the North. When Sumner, who complained of Lincoln for his hesitation in this respect, just as Lincoln complained of the generals for delaying the advance, advised him to make abolition a New Year's present to Congress and the nation at the beginning of 1862, and sought to tempt him by referring to the fame he might thus win, Lincoln broke in with : "Don't say a word about that; I know very well that the name which is connected with this act will never be forgotten."

This is the voice of the man who at twenty-eight had declared that one ought not to die without having stamped one's name on the contemporary world, and when only twenty-five had been an enthusiastic admirer of the heroes of history. In the hidden depths of his soul there glows an ambition so intense that it had led him in youth, thirty years before, to declare that a mere seat in the presidential chair would not content him, and which is now battling with one of the crucial problems of mankind. Look at him as he lifts his long, bony fingers in the face of the elegant Sumner, drawing a veil over the passion that stirs his heart as he says "I know very well ——" Can we not feel the profound significance of these moments, succeeding one another for a year and more, in which the good will of the lover of mankind, memories of the earliest shadows that had been cast over his heart, and the enthusiastic aspirations of the idealist combine to dispel political skepticism. Stronger than ever before in Lincoln's life the internal struggle goes on between the realist and the dreamer, the lawyer and the philosopher; and nothing in his whole career bears more convincing testimony to the greatness of his character than that he should have refrained in this instance from following the call.

Suddenly, two weeks after his son's death, and in the darkest period of inaction, he sends to Sumner, asking him to come at once. "I want to read you my message to Congress. I want to know how you like it. I am going to send it in to-day." Thus does he overcome his own hesitation, and spur himself on towards the goal, being afraid lest some fresh considerations may shake the decision he has at length reached. Indeed, he would seem to wish to commit himself to the plan he has conceived, for when Schurz returns from Europe and gives him first-hand information regarding the state of feeling there, gets to work molding opinion in New York, undertakes the organization of an Emancipation Society, and submits to Lincoln the draft of a speech he intends to make in the beginning of March, the President says: "That's the right thing to say. And, remember, you may hear from me on the same day." The message to Congress, wired to New York, is delivered there to Schurz after he has made his speech. Amid general enthusiasm, he reads it aloud at midnight to the audience in the Cooper Union, the very place where, a few years before, Lincoln had first made an impression in the great city.

The message, which did not aim at more than a slow restriction of slavery, cautiously recommended Congress to adopt a resolution to the effect "that the United States ought to coöperate with any State which may adopt gradual abolishment of slavery, giving to such State pecuniary aid, to be used by such State in its discretion, to compensate for the inconveniences, public and private, produced by such change of system." This gradual and partial liberation of the slaves was only advocated by Lincoln as a means to peace:

"In my judgment, gradual, and not sudden, emancipation is better for all. . . . Such a proposition on the part of the general government sets up no claim of a right by Federal authority to interfere with slavery within State limits, referring, as it does, the absolute control of the subject in each case to the State and its people immediately interested."

This resolution was promptly adopted by Congress, and the sum of three hundred dollars was promised for every slave manumitted, but the resolution was ignored by the border States — was received with an icy silence. After four days of tense uneasiness, Lincoln invited the representatives of the five States to an interview, and spoke to them in urgent terms, but achieved nothing.

Yet, after all, something had been achieved. As before a *coup d'état*, the supreme authority had shown a benevolent determination to proceed slowly, by constitutional methods, and with payment of compensation — but with the implication: "If you don't like this, we have other means at our disposal!" Now the radicals and the moderates joined forces, things began to move, fresh ordinances forbade the army and the navy to aid in the return of runaway slaves, the Negro republics of Haiti and Liberia were recognized as independent, and one of the newspapers declared: "The guns which fired on Fort Sumter destroyed three-fourths of our boundary lines; this message has made an end of the remaining fourth!"

For the first time since the early weeks of the war, the President once more felt himself sustained by the wishes of the nation; he became more radical, and was at length able to secure something which he had proposed fourteen years earlier when he had been an inconspicuous Congressman, without then being able even to get the matter discussed. The District of Columbia, in which the capital of the United States is situated, was declared immune from slavery, a million dollars was paid as compensation to loyal slave owners, and schools and other institutions were established for the education of Negro children.

A few weeks later, another general again distinguishes himself by foolish and overbearing activities. He reads in the paper that General Hunter has issued an order declaring, "Slavery and martial law in a free country are altogether incompatible; the persons in . . . Georgia, Florida, and South Carolina heretofore held as slaves, are therefore declared for ever free."

The third instance of the kind! It is followed by a third repudia-
tion: "I, Abraham Lincoln, . . . declare that the government of
the United States had no knowledge, information, or belief of an
intention on the part of General Hunter to issue such a proclamation; nor has it yet any authentic information that the document is
genuine. And, further, that neither General Hunter nor any other
commander or person has been authorized . . . to make a proclamation declaring the slaves of any State free; and that the supposed proclamation now in question, whether genuine or false, is
altogether void so far as respects such a declaration. I further
make it known that whether it be competent for me, as Commander-in-Chief of the Army and Navy, to declare the slaves
of any State or States free, and whether, at any time, in any
case, it shall have become a necessity indispensable to the maintenance of the Government to exercise such supposed power, are
questions which, under my responsibility, I reserve to myself, and
which I cannot feel justified in leaving to the decision of commanders in the field."

This is Lincoln's resolute tone, the tone he is impelled to use when
an important means, and one he is actually looking forward to using,
is bunglingly applied at the wrong moment, and when he is constrained, in flat contradiction of his own general, his own party
comrade, and in opposition for the most part to public opinion and
the press, to disavow a procedure he is himself eager to initiate.
But when, in repeated circulars, he admonishes the governors of the
border States, who have exercised so stoical a self-restraint in the
application of the proposed method of partial liberation, he finds
a warmer, almost flattering tone:

"I do not argue; I beseech you to make the arguments for yourselves. You cannot, if you would, be blind to the signs of the times.
I beg of you a calm and enlarged consideration of them, ranging, if
it may be, far above personal and partisan politics. This proposal
. . . acts not the Pharisee. The change it contemplates would
come gently as the dews of heaven — not rending or wrecking anything. Will you not embrace it? So much good has not been done
by one effort in all past time, as, in the providence of God, it is now

your high privilege to do.   May the vast future not have to lament
that you have neglected it."

In his alternation between harsh revocation and gentle persuasion,
he pleases no one, and is once more besieged by the radical senators,
who want him to enroll the freed Negroes in the army.   The war,
they say, really came about for the Negroes' sake, and it is only fair
that the Negroes should lend a helping hand.

Lincoln replies: "Gentlemen, I have put thousands of muskets
into the hands of loyal citizens of Tennessee, Kentucky, and Western North Carolina.   They have said they could defend themselves
if they had guns.   I have given them the guns.   Now, these men
do not believe in mustering the negro.   If I do it, these thousands
of muskets will be turned against us.   We should lose more than we
should gain. . . .   I can't see it as you do.   You may be right, and
I may be wrong; but I'll tell you what I can do; I can resign in
favor of Mr. Hamlin.   Perhaps Mr. Hamlin could do it."

"The President must have been almost desperate," remarked
some one who at that time was well acquainted with him and his
situation.   Can we be surprised?   He himself is invested like a
fortress, and the fortress he is investing, the South, is as stubbornly
resistant as he is himself.

XIII

By the first anniversary of the opening of the war, only a little
had been achieved in the West, and nothing at all against Richmond.
McClellan was still postponing the advance.   He insisted that the
whole army must be shipped to the peninsula between the York and
the James rivers.   Why does he hesitate to act?   Had the thought
that this was a civil war aroused in him a sort of false chivalry?   Or
was he afraid to fight the master under whom he had studied the
art of war; the general the glamour of whose authority still overwhelmed him?   Had he, who was a Democrat, an idea that by
showing himself ready to treat rather than to make war, he would
weary both sides into a compromise, and then, as President, become
master of the situation?

Lincoln grew suspicious (how suspicious, we do not know), kept a

sharper eye on McClellan, made himself acquainted with details
that were not always known even to the Secretary of War.   His
letters to the inscrutable general, whom, in the face of public opinion, it was still expedient to support, were masterpieces:

"And once more let me tell you it is indispensable to you that you
strike a blow.   I am powerless to help this.   I always insisted that
going down the bay in search of a field, instead of fighting at or near
Manassas, was only shifting, not surmounting the difficulty. . . .
The country will not fail to note — and it is now noting — that the
present hesitation to move upon an intrenched enemy is but the
story of Manassas repeated.   I beg to assure you that I have never
written to you or spoken to you in greater kindness, nor with a
fuller purpose to sustain you, so far as in my most anxious judgment I consistently can.   *But you must act.*   Yours very truly."

This general, who is as sensitive as a girl, though by no means as
innocent, must be handled gently; and although he does nothing,
the President must unceasingly try to keep him in a good humor,
hoping that he will do something.   Thus Lincoln excuses himself
for having sent elsewhere a certain division that McClellan has
wanted, adding, "If you could know the full pressure of the case, I
am confident that you could justify it, even beyond a mere acknowl-
edgment that the commander-in-chief may order what he pleases."
As in the previous letter, there is a veiled menace.   One feels the
iron hand in the velvet glove, just as one does in the following:

"And here let me say, not as applicable to you personally, that
senators and representatives speak of *me* in their places as they
please without question, and that officers of the army must cease
addressing insulting letters to them for taking no greater liberty
with *them*."

In the end the President has to act more drastically, for it has
become essential to solve the problems of personality which are
spreading confusion in the conduct of the war.   Matters are just
as bad in the West as in the East, since Frémont will not budge to
capture Governor Jackson, who is really within his grasp.

At the same time the Northerners' command of the sea, their
most outstanding advantage, is being imperiled by bold deeds on

the part of the Southerners. They had the first armored cruiser, the *Merrimac*, which rammed and sank a number of Northern ships in Hampton Roads. The effect of this news was manifested in what Lincoln's secretary termed "perhaps the most excited and impressive cabinet meeting of the whole war." Would not the entire fleet soon be destroyed and the blockade lifted, if this vessel were to continue on the rampage? But Lincoln, we are told, displayed his wonted calm on this occasion, comparing the telegrams, and cross-questioning the officers. Next day the *Monitor*, a famous new model for war craft, but lately constructed in New York, fought off the *Merrimac* and saved the rest of the Union fleet. About eight weeks later Lincoln made a trip down the Chesapeake to observe the situation and took Chase and Stanton with him. The President and Chase opportunely discovered favorable places for the landing of troops to move upon Norfolk, and once a landing had been effected, the *Merrimac* found herself in an untenable position and was blown up, lest the vessel should fall into Union hands. Chase declared outright that if Lincoln "had not come down Norfolk would still have been in possession of the enemy and the *Merrimac* as grim and defiant . . . as ever." This he called the President's "brilliant week's campaign."

Meantime the brilliant exploit of Farragut in running the batteries on the Mississippi below New Orleans and the entrance into the city a few days afterward by Union troops, gave the North possession of the largest city of the South, a triumph which disturbed the confidence of Europe in the Confederacy.

But what about Richmond? Everything turns on Richmond! It is late in June, the incomprehensible procrastinator has at length begun the advance, has got within five miles of the enemy capital — to stop short once more. He leaves the adversary time to concentrate, and is then defeated in the course of what becomes known as the Seven Days' Battles. According to later critics, McClellan might have won an Austerlitz on this occasion. What says the new Napoleon?

"With ten thousand more men, I could gain a victory to-morrow," he wires in mingled rage and despair. "The Government must not and cannot hold me responsible. . . . The Government has not sustained this army. . . . If I save this army now, I tell you plainly that I owe no thanks to you or to any person in Washington. You have done your best to sacrifice this army."

Altogether in the tone of one who has been long accustomed to captivate people, and now disappoints others more than himself.

Lincoln thinks the man must have taken leave of his senses, and that since he cannot yet be replaced, he must be humored like a lunatic. Writing of McClellan's dispatches, the President says: "The later one of 6.15 P.M. . . . pains me very much. I give you all I can, and act on the presumption that you will do the best you can with what you have, while you continue, ungenerously I think, to assume that I could give you more if I would."

Next day: "Save your army, at all events. Will send reënforcements as fast as we can. Of course they cannot reach you to-day, to-morrow, or next day. I have not said you were ungenerous for saying you needed reënforcements. I thought you were ungenerous in assuming that I did not send them as fast as I could. I feel any misfortune to you and your army quite as keenly as you feel it yourself. If you have had a drawn battle, or a repulse, it is the price we pay for the enemy not being in Washington. . . . Had we stripped Washington" (such had been McClellan's wish) "he would have been upon us before the troops could have gotten to you."

Has ever a President had to carry on a dialogue like this with one of his defeated generals? A professional soldier holding such a position as Lincoln's would use a tone of simple command, a civilian would leave matters to the War Department. But in this instance the peculiar nature of the war modifies the character and the allotment of responsibility, and in addition the nature of the President modifies the moral equipoise. He is himself one of the weights in the scales, for he is not concerned merely to administer an office, but is swayed by his innermost feeling as to the duty of a ruler in the hour of his country's supreme need. And the country itself feels the hour to be one of supreme need. There is a sharp fall in the prices on the New York stock exchange; depression is widespread; and

LINCOLN IN 1863

From a photograph by Alexander Gardner, Washington

when three hundred thousand more men are levied for a term of three years, there is a general lack of enthusiasm in the response, and in popular parlance the recruits are said to be going into McClellan's trap.

Now is the moment for Lincoln to take all the strings into his own hands. It is he who writes soft words to the governors, inducing them to call up the requisite troops, and persuading them to send a moderate number promptly, rather than more in the vague future. It is he who smooths things over between governors and generals; and it is he who makes a point of seeing that there shall be rabbis with the armies to care for the spiritual comfort of Jewish soldiers. It is he who hastens to the front, to the battlefields first, and then to the war council on the Potomac, and interviews the subordinate leaders, since he no longer has confidence in the chiefs of this army.

"What amount of force have you now?"

"About eighty thousand; can't vary much; certainly seventy-five thousand."

"What is likely to be your condition as to health in this camp? Where is the enemy now?"

Each officer gives a different answer.

Immediately afterwards, he writes to McClellan about desertion:

"I am told that over 160,000 men have gone into your army on the Peninsula. When I was with you the other day we made out 86,500 remaining, leaving 73,500 to be accounted for. I believe 23,500 will cover all the killed, wounded, and missing in all your battles and skirmishes, leaving 50,000 who have left otherwise. No more than 5,000 of these have died, leaving 45,000 of your army still alive and not with it. I believe half or two-thirds of them are fit for duty to-day. Have you any more perfect knowledge of this than I have? If I am right, and you had these men with you, you could go into Richmond in the next three days. How can they be got to you, and how can they be prevented from getting away in such numbers for the future?"

The President, a civilian, does not merely write these things; he reckons them up, and he takes the initiative. Has he not really

become a general, Abraham Lincoln, the enemy of war and chase,
who never shot an animal, and only rescued an Indian? But while
the President is propounding military conundrums to the general,
the general is writing him political letters. In a private missive,
the latter says: "I am tired of serving fools. . . . Marcy and I
have just been discussing people in Washington, and conclude they
are a 'mighty trifling set.' . . . I begin to believe they wish this
army to be destroyed."

Lincoln is satisfied to take his revenge in the form of a postscript,
cutting in its irony: "If at any time you feel able to take the offensive, you are not restrained from doing so."

Then he turns to Seward, discusses every detail with the Secretary of State, and, at the close of a written order, sums up his
resolves in the splendid sentence: "I expect to continue this contest until successful, or till I die, or am conquered, or my term
expires, or Congress or the country forsakes me." That is Lincoln's lucid thought-world, animated with logic and with feelings
as resolute, virile, firm, as the great, bony hand with which, before
the eyes of the astonished bluejackets, he had vigorously and quietly,
for many minutes, held out the ax at arm's length — like the destiny of his country.

XIV

Unceasingly the war pressed for a decision of the slavery question; the worse things were for the North in the field, the better the
chance for the slaves. They were needed to replace the men leaving for the front, to quiet the Northern radicals, to influence Europe.
Letters and newspaper articles, threats and exhortations, multiplied. Garrison was urging the abolitionist case; a Swiss statesman had called attention to the danger that Napoleon III might
intervene in favor of the confederacy; Quakers and ministers of
religion were coming to Lincoln about the matter. Even though
emissaries from Kentucky turned up occasionally, to warn him
against interference with slavery, the suggestive force of their ad-
monitions was becoming less powerful.

"I intend no reproach or complaint," wrote Lincoln once more to the representatives of the border States, "when I assure you that, in my opinion, if you had all voted for the resolution in the gradual-emancipation message of last March, the war would now be substantially ended. And the plan therein proposed is yet one of the most potent and swift means of ending it. Let the States which are in rebellion see definitely and certainly that in no event will the States you represent ever join their proposed confederacy, and they cannot much longer maintain the contest. But you cannot divest them of their hope to ultimately have you with them so long as you show a determination to perpetuate the institution within your own States. . . . If the war continues long, . . . the institution in your States will be extinguished by mere friction and abrasion. . . . How much better to save the money which else we sink forever in war! How much better to do it while we can, lest the war ere long render us pecuniarily unable to do it! How much better for you as seller, and the nation as buyer, to sell out and buy out that without which the war could never have been, than to sink both the thing to be sold and the price of it in cutting one another's throats!"

Side by side with these sly considerations, addressed to the calculating minds of farmers and men of business, he shows all the ardor of the idealist when he exclaims to two noted abolitionists: "If only the border States would accept my plan! Then you and I would not have lived in vain!"

But when the border States are still recalcitrant, his own will is hardened by their stubbornness. On the very day when he has heard of the renewed rejection of his scheme, he is driving with Welles, Seward, and the latter's daughter-in-law. They are on their way to a funeral, for Stanton has lost a child, and Lincoln, whom the sorrow of his daily counselor cannot but remind of his own recent affliction, may well have had an unusual inclination to confidential utterance. His custom was to keep the great problem to himself, and in March he had taken his decisive step without consulting the cabinet. Now he speaks openly to his friends of this affair for the first time:

"I must save this government if possible. What I cannot do,

of course, I will not do; but it may as well be understood, once for all, that I shall not surrender this game leaving any available card unplayed. . . . I have come to the conclusion that it is a military necessity, absolutely essential to the salvation of the nation, that we must free the slaves or be ourselves subdued."

Free the slaves or be ourselves subdued; thus had the ideal been transmuted! What had at first been the purpose of the conflict, has become a means for conducting it; and what was to provide the moral justification of the Civil War when the case should come to be argued before the tribunal of history, has become an expedient for bringing it to a close. Painful, indeed, must have been Lincoln's reflections during these days and weeks, now that he had fully realized the paradox of such a development.

Even if destiny had singled him out to carry one of humanity's sublime ideas into effect, none the less it was his fate to make use of petty means and to direct his efforts for the moment towards transient aims; and only by a detour that was tragical in its irony could he advance towards the ideal of his youth.

He had to calculate, instead of dream. In the South the slaves were tilling the land, so that all the able-bodied whites could go to the front. If they were declared free, many of them would run away; the enemy's ranks would be thinned, and ours would be better manned; and the North would gain the labor power that was being taken away from the South. Legislative methods, even of the most suave kind, had failed to induce the border States to accept this plan, so military authority must here supersede that of Congress. Had not Adams prophesied a generation ago that if ever the South were to become the theater of a civil war or a war for the emancipation of the slaves, the commander in chief, in virtue of his supreme position, would be enabled to take independent action? If Lincoln were now to take this decisive step, he would make forever impossible the swearing of a sluggards' peace which would again obscure the whole problem after so heavy fighting; a new moral platform would have been established, and thenceforward every victory in the field would be a victory over slavery.

To-day, when the war had dragged on for fifteen months, it

seemed to him possible to take a step which, at the outset, would have rent the North in twain; for, since the North included four slave States, and the Democrats did not think the question worth so much bloodshed, he would not, at the outset, have felt himself backed up by his half of the nation. After the victory, the war measure might be made constitutional, and would then become law in the North as well; meanwhile there would be an inevitable contradiction, inasmuch as the North would free the Southern slaves and not its own; and the abolitionists, the champions of morality and human kindliness, would have to foster or endure the evil in their own household after they had made an end of it in the slaveholding South.

The working of Lincoln's mind before he finally came to this determination is disclosed in a letter written more than a year later to a Kentuckian whom he greatly esteemed:

"I am naturally antislavery. If slavery is not wrong, nothing is wrong. I cannot remember when I did not so think and feel, and yet I have never understood that the Presidency conferred upon me an unrestricted right to act officially upon this judgment and feeling. It was in the oath I took that I would, to the best of my ability, preserve, protect, and defend the Constitution of the United States. I could not take the office without taking the oath. Nor was it my view that I might take an oath to get power, and break the oath in using the power. I understood, too, that in ordinary civil administration this oath even forbade me to practically indulge my primary abstract judgment on the moral question of slavery. . . . Was it possible to lose the nation and yet preserve the Constitution?

"By general law, life and limb must be protected; yet often a limb must be amputated to save a life; but a life is never wisely given to save a limb. I felt that measures otherwise unconstitutional might become lawful by becoming indispensable to the preservation of the Constitution, through the preservation of the nation. Right or wrong, I assumed this ground, and now avow it. . . . When in March and May and July, 1862, I made earnest and successive appeals to the border States to favor compensated emancipation, I believed the indispensable necessity for military emancipation and arming the blacks would come unless averted by that measure. They declined the proposition, and I was, in my best judgment, driven to the alternative of either surrendering the Union, and with it the Constitution, or of laying strong hand upon the colored element. I chose the latter. In choosing it, I hoped for greater gain than loss."

Lincoln had deeply pondered the obligations entailed by the oath of office; he had repeatedly disavowed the abolitionist activities of his collaborators; he had so often and so urgently recommended the middle course — and it was, therefore, only by way of many moral perturbations that he could come to his great resolve. But on this occasion, as when he had been married, it was ostensibly a sudden determination. He wired for his old friend and fellow lawyer Swett, for at this juncture the frank advice of a familiar and trusted associate of early days would be worth more to him than the opinions of a dozen experts.

Swett arrives early in the morning, goes to the White House before breakfast, has to answer questions about some mutual friends, is shown a letter from Garrison in which the latter passionately urges abolition. Then, without asking Swett's opinion, Lincoln opens up the main theme, questioning himself and answering about the possible consequences from both sides, in a monologue which lasts more than an hour. The President, according to his auditor's description, "was simply framing his thought in words, under the eye of his friend, that he might clear up his own mind." When he had finished, he asked for no comment, made no inquiry, but expressed a hope that the visitor would get home safely, and sent messages to old acquaintances. That was the end of the visit.

Almost immediately afterwards, in the same impromptu fashion, and without having discussed the matter, he suddenly summoned his cabinet. He had resolved on his course, he told his ministers, and had not called them together to ask their advice, but to lay the subject matter of his proclamation before them. Suggestions as to it would be in order after they had heard it read. He showed once more a self-confidence which might have led strangers who knew nothing of him but this to regard him as dictatorial.   There he sits, at the green, oval table, surrounded by the silent faces, and reads aloud the original draft of the Emancipation Proclamation.   The document in its final form, as subsequently issued, much modified, but without any alteration of its intent, reads :

"I, Abraham Lincoln, President of the United States of America and Commander-in-Chief of the Army and Navy thereof, do hereby proclaim and declare that hereafter, as heretofore, the war will be prosecuted for the object of practically restoring the constitutional relation between the United States and each of the States and the people thereof, in which States that relation is or may be suspended or disturbed.   That it is my purpose, upon the next meeting of Congress, to again recommend the adoption of a practical measure tendering pecuniary aid to the free acceptance or rejection of all the slave States, so-called, the people whereof may not then be in rebellion against the United States, and which States may then have voluntarily adopted, or thereafter may voluntarily adopt, imme-diate or gradual abolishment of slavery within their respective limits; and that the effort to colonize persons of African descent, with their consent, upon this continent or elsewhere, with the pre-viously obtained consent of the governments existing there, will be continued.

"That on the first day of January, in the year of our Lord, one thousand eight hundred and sixty-three, all persons held as slaves within any State or designated part of a State, the people whereof shall then be in rebellion against the United States, shall be then, thenceforward, and forever free. . . .   The executive will, on the first day of January aforesaid, by proclamation, designate the States, and parts of States, if any, in which the people thereof, re-spectively, shall then be in rebellion against the United States."

In its final form the proclamation also called attention to the fact that officers have already been forbidden to use the forces under their command for the purpose of returning fugitive slaves to their sometime owners; and to a previously passed law enacting that "slaves found on or being within any place occupied by rebel forces

and afterwards occupied by the forces of the United States, shall
be deemed captives of war and shall be for ever free of their servi-
tude and not again held as slaves."

Here was a people which had been wearing out its energies in
struggles between slave owners and negrophiles. The quarrel had
at length eventuated in civil war, and the white inhabitants were
shooting one another down by thousands because of the blacks.
And when, at long last, the moment had come for the freeing of the
slaves by the fiat of the slave party, whom did the utterance of the
great word primarily advantage? Not the slaves of those who
called themselves the slaves' friends, but the slaves of those on the
other side of the fighting line, the slaves over whom the Northerners in truth could exercise no control. Thus an insoluble problem
had brought the clearest and noblest thinker of his nation to utter
contradiction because, while he had to use the sword in the attempt
to solve it, he could not simply hew his way through to victory.
The logic of facts had led Lincoln into a situation where he was
compelled to leave the slaves of his friends in the chains that he was
removing from the slaves of his foes.

The cabinet was astonished. "This measure," said Stanton,
"goes beyond anything I have recommended." What he and the
others had to object, the President had already calculated. Seward,
however, had a suggestion to make: "I approve of the proclamation, but I question the expediency of its issue at this juncture.
The depression of the public mind, consequent upon our repeated
reverses, is so great that I fear the effect of so important a step. It
may be viewed as the last measure of an exhausted Government, a
cry for help. . . . I therefore suggest that you postpone its issue
until you can give it to the country supported by military success,
instead of issuing it, as would be the case now, immediately after
the greatest disasters of the war."

Lincoln was quick to see the force of this consideration. He
locked the document in his desk and waited for a victory.

XV

The man who was leading the South had in youth been almost as famous for good looks as Lincoln had been for homeliness, and had, one might say, been dowered by fortune with nearly everything his great rival lacked — while, indeed, he lacked almost everything which Lincoln possessed.

Whereas Lincoln had grown to manhood in an atmosphere of poverty and deprivation; had depended for everything upon his strong arms and his sense of destiny; had made his own living as raftsman, handicraftsman, wage laborer, store clerk; and had meanwhile satisfied his craving for knowledge by the reading of whatever books chance threw in his way — Jefferson Davis, the son of a well-to-do landed proprietor, had, at the same age, from fourteen to twenty-four, been carefully grounded in the sciences and afterwards trained at the military academy of West Point as a cadet and an officer.   While Lincoln, at New Salem, was still lying on the counter conning a grammar, when he had lost the girl he loved and was at a loose end, Lieutenant Davis was already married to a colonel's daughter, and soon afterwards (what time Lincoln, burdened with debt and without any assured prospects, was about to try his luck as a lawyer) Davis' wealthy brother bought him an estate and a sufficiency of slaves to cultivate it, so that with his young wife he might settle down as a country gentleman instead of waiting about in the army for promotion.   After turning thirty, both Davis and Lincoln began to take a keen interest in politics; but Davis found his way into Congress after only two years' probation, and remained a member as senator, while Lincoln was to spend a whole decade without office or seat, and therefore without power; and when Lincoln at the age of forty-seven had vainly aspired to a place in the Senate, Davis was already Secretary of War and possessed of extensive influence at the seat of government.

The finely molded, resolute lineaments of his somewhat angular countenance indicate the determination of a man driven forward by ambition and self-confidence; of one who considers no opinions but his own valid or respectable, who looks upon tolerance as weakness, and who always feels himself to be on an assured footing and excellent terms with his caste and his family and his God. There is nothing problematical in him; and the spiritual composure of a man whose intelligence is essentially restricted despite its outstanding ability, fits him for the position of a second in command. He is one who will never mix with people who are of a lower class than his own, but will incline rather to seek out his superiors that he may pull himself up to their level; he is companionable, and likes a laugh, but you will not hear him tell amusing anecdotes; when he has accepted an official position, he will discharge its obligations punctually, just as he will order his whole life with precision, and his subordinates will dread him for his exactness and indefatigableness. As a farmer, he will pile up money and accumulate slaves; as Secretary of War, he will assemble soldiers; as an orator, he will be firm and extreme, but will only produce conviction in those who are already convinced.

His gait is springy and his speech is elastic; he abides by the Constitution, as he interprets it; and when he scrutinizes himself, he will always be satisfied with the result. Why should he ever suffer from depression, or question his own heart? There is no unguarded chink in his nature through which skepticism can enter. What can the people mean to him, who has never lived among them? Of course he is sorry for the poor, of course he must help them when he can, and, if their skins are black, he must give them medicine when they are sick and must see that they are provided with the consolations of Holy Writ; but the wealthy and the whites must never lay aside the power they have inherited, and he who unreasonably demands that they should is false to the spirit of independence. He has a serious personal trouble to contend with. This man who is in other respects healthy, a man of steel, a splendid horseman, and, if not as strong as Lincoln, is more adroit — has nevertheless been afflicted since youth by a grave affection of the eyes, which continually returns whenever he suffers from malarial fever, and occasionally blinds him for a time. Thus he lacks what Lincoln enjoys, robust health; but he has what Lincoln lacks, a devoted wife who shares undismayed all the dangers of a tempestuous career.

Yet this wife of his — his second wife, twenty years younger than the husband — had early recognized his weaknesses, for when she was only seventeen, before she was engaged, she wrote to her mother :

"He wounds me by his certainty that his own opinion is the only right one. Still, he is very agreeable, has a fine voice, and a pleasing way of expressing himself. I think he would be the sort of man to risk his life in order to rescue one from a mad dog, and would then meet the consequences with stoical indifference."

Such a man, especially since he soon became rich and made headway in the world, would naturally tend to be uncompromising wherever the life and honor of the South were concerned, and so, twelve years before the war, he could be heard exclaiming from the rostrum :

"We representatives of the southern States are not here to put up with affronts on account of our hereditary institutions. . . . If the civil war is to start from this side, let it come. For my part, I am ready to oppose every incendiary who betrays his country by applying the torch."

When the crisis came, as a leading orator he was extremely rhetorical, but his sentiment was in every word the precise opposite of Lincoln's. In the course of his great farewell speech as senator, just before leaving to take charge of the Southern government, he exclaimed theatrically :

"I feel sure that, however acrimonious the discussion may have been, there is not one among you to whom I cannot still say, in the sight of God, that I wish him well. . . . Mr. President and Gentlemen Senators, after having made to you the communication which the situation seemed to demand of me, the only thing that remains for me is to address you a last farewell!"

Subsequently in Richmond, when he took over the Southern presidency, at the close of his speech he raised eyes and hands to heaven, saying, "Full of humble thanks and with reverence I declare that the Constitution has manifestly protected the Confederacy during its brief but eventful existence. Trustingly, O God, I put myself in thy hand, and implore thy blessing on my country and my cause." When Lincoln became President for the second time, he said what was tantamount to the reverse of this.

Two worlds were in arms against each other, and the contrast between the belligerents only becomes accentuated to the pitch of symbolism in the leaders. Lincoln had said, "If slavery is not wrong, nothing is wrong." Long before this public utterance, Davis, at a congress apostrophizing his adversaries in the North, had exclaimed, "If slavery be a wrong, you have no part in it!"

An abyss lies between these two epigrams. A man who sets out from his own firm standing ground, from his friends' and his own legal rights to possession — transmitted by inheritance, and therefore inviolable — answers reproaches with the taunt that he and those who think with him will shoulder all the responsibility. Another man, setting out from moral sentiments, accuses no one, ignores the question of responsibility, and sees nothing but this: a wrong is being done. Although Lincoln is a party politician, and although Davis is as good a Christian (and in point of form a better one than Lincoln) — nevertheless the Southerner here contrasts with the Northerner as politician to philosopher, as realist to idealist. It is not a chance matter that these two men of conflicting temperaments should lead their respective parties, whose true exponents they in fact are. They have fundamentally divergent standpoints, from which they have started for the great struggle in which they are engaged.

A very different man from both of them was Lee, one of the finest personalities in American history, and, in the opinion of experts, one of the greatest military commanders. In early youth, already, he was lighted up by the torch of knowledge and by the flame of spiritual endeavor. His father, who died of wounds sustained in a struggle for liberty, had brought him up to admire and reverence the names of Sophocles and Milton, Locke and Pope. He took care of his early widowed mother throughout the years of his boyhood, and intensified the tradition of his puritan family when at the age of twenty-one he married a granddaughter of Washington who, as the heiress of Arlington, cherished the spirit and the memorials of her ancestors. Among the pictures of the founder of the Union there had now come to live a man who loved it no less than Lincoln, and dreaded its break-up no less, and was yet called upon by fate to lead the army which tried to destroy the Union. He was free from the self-righteousness of Davis, being a man of an extremely tolerant disposition, and as far as the question of slavery was concerned, his father-in-law (though a Southerner and a Virginian) had followed Washington's example in arranging for gradual enfranchisement within the narrow circle under his personal control, specifying in his will the year in which his slaves were to be freed.

Lee's serene and energetic nature found adequate occupation in the work of an artillery officer, in a happy marriage, and in the exemplary upbringing of his seven children. His letters to his wife became one of the treasures of the nation. The purity of his lineaments, the nobility of his demeanor, the perfect and yet virile translucency of his gaze, were characteristic of a man who was never tormented by ambition, who declared duty to be the most sublime word in the language, who always avoided the limelight, and sought happiness in the inner equipoise of the soul. As disinclined for phrase-making as Lincoln, but in temperament utterly diverse from Lincoln (who was always inclined to let things take their course, and ultimately became the instrument of destiny), Lee was from the first relegated rather to the work of the general staff officer than to that of the commander of troops in the field; rather to the training of young men at West Point than to the leading of cavalry charges; and although in the Mexican War he distinguished himself by personal courage, he really detested war quite as much as did the civilian Lincoln. "My heart bled for the inhabitants," he wrote home after taking a fortified position. "I was not so much concerned about the soldiers, but the thought of the women and children was horrible. . . . You can have no idea how ghastly the sight of a battlefield is." The greatest of American strategists was a pacifist at heart.

Into what a whirlpool of the feelings must such a man have been cast when the ground on which he had built up his life began to quake under his feet. The integrity of the Union was threatened! For Lee this was as great a shock as if he had been told that his wife had been unfaithful or that one of his sons had committed a crime. As a soldier he had not allowed himself to adopt any marked political line; in his own house, as a puritan and heir to the most liberal traditions, he had been able to exclude the vociferations of his own caste during the years when the slave conflict was becoming intensified. "In every land, slavery as an institution is a moral and political evil," he said, and he had pierced to the very heart of the problem by declaring, "I regard it as a greater evil for the whites than for the blacks." Lincoln's basic thought, in almost identical words! Still, he had described the position of the blacks here in America as preferable to their position in Africa, with the remark: "The painful discipline to which they are subjected is necessary for their further cultivation as a race, and will, one may hope, prepare them for better things. How long their enslavement will have to last must be left to the knowledge and determination of a wise providence."

With this ambiguous utterance he closed the book of politics with a bang, as it were, and turned back to his maps, his plans, and his drawings.

But the gusty winds of that epoch blew the book open once more, and when Lincoln was elected President, Lee was menaced with the need for a decision. He wrote to his son:

"I cannot imagine a worse disaster for our country than the rupture of the Union. It would signify a heaping-up of all the evils of which we complain, and I am resolved to sacrifice everything but honor to prevent it, for secession is nothing else than revolution. . . . A Union which can only be maintained by swords and bayonets, one in which contention and civil war have replaced brotherly love and kindliness, has no more charms for me. . . . Should the Union be dissolved and the government break in pieces, I shall return to my native State, share the miseries of my people, and only draw my sword for defence."

Once more an ambiguity at the close, once more a straightforward and efficient soldier's longing to avoid a conflict.

Three months later, however, Fate came knocking at his door. Lincoln, having been informed that Lee was the most capable among the officers at his disposal, offered him the command of the invading army. A dread ordeal! He had so recently stigmatized secession as revolution; now he was invited to draw the uttermost inference from this, to lead the soldiers who were to fight against, perhaps destroy, his own home! Impossible! He refused, and two days later he resigned his commission in the United States army, writing one of the finest of his letters, a missive of thanks to General Scott:

"To no one else have I been so much indebted, General, as to you for your invariable kindness and consideration. It has ever been my most ardent wish to earn your approval. I shall carry with me to the tomb the most grateful remembrance of your delicate forbearance. Your name and your reputation will always be dear to me."

With the closing words he lowered his sword before the adversary who till yesterday had been his commanding officer.

Will he now withdraw into private life, thus escaping the conflict which torments his heart? This, likewise, is impossible, seeing that he has been an officer for thirty years, and, all his life, has watched the sun rise and set behind Virginia's forests, hills, and waters. Is it not close to the frontier, open to the first brunt of the attack — Arlington, now the holy of holies of the nation, the place which he, more than all men, is called upon to defend, since he is its master? How could he look his friends and kinsmen in the face when all of them are hastening to take up arms, should he, universally regarded as supreme master of warcraft, stay at home inactive or at most care for the wounded? He has no choice but to cast logic to the winds, and to follow his natural bent. He who regards slavery as an evil, he who has spoken of the Union as the greatest good, he who has described secession as revolution, he, Robert E. Lee, takes a command in the army which is to maintain slavery, to disrupt the Union, and by means of secession to establish an independent confederacy. He is impelled by the instinctive desire to safeguard his home, which is specially endangered by its proximity to the border, and, since he knows every road and every covert, it is likely enough that he can lead better here than he would have been able to on the other side.

Yet his longing for justice is so keen, his belief in the inviolability of private judgment is so overwhelming, that, through his wife, he sends a message to their son, who is a lieutenant in the Union army.

"Let him abide by his own judgment, his own reasons, and his own conscience as to the way he proposes to follow. I do not want him to be guided by my wishes or my example. If I have made a mistake, he may be able to correct it. Every one must decide this important question for himself, and in accordance with his own principles."

What splendid Lincolnian tolerance! Aye, a year later he will outdo even this. By the terms of his father-in-law's will, his slaves were to be freed in the year 1862. As heir and as puritan, Lee obeys the behest. The commander of the army that is fighting against the liberation of the slaves writes with his own hand the passes that are to enable his own slaves to cross the Southern lines and enter the territory held by the Union forces.

The man who excelled side by side with Lee, was at once like him and unlike. Jackson, too, was of good family, poor in youth, a resolute man, and obedient to the call of duty. But he was also a man given to prayer, which he said daily at fixed hours, and which steeled him in battle. Jackson believed in fate, like Lincoln, but was, thanks to his piety, of a far more tranquil disposition; he was a devout Christian who would neither read a letter nor begin a battle on a Sunday; one who clung faster to this anchorage as the years went by, and seems in actual fact to have died with the words on his lips, "Very good; everything in order."

A sense of order, a pure love of justice, temperance in all things, and a crystal clarity of soul were characteristics he shared with Lee. It had a profoundly human as well as a military significance when Lee wrote to him after he had been wounded: "You have lost your left arm; I have lost my right." Indeed, all these men could not only fight, but on grand occasions could write in the grand style. Jackson, moreover, like Lincoln and Lee, was a pacifist, a kind of general not known in Europe. The sincerity of his Christian convictions would have alone sufficed to prevent him from desiring this war. "You do not know the horrors of war. I have seen enough of it to regard it as the climax of all evil. . . . It would be better that the South should fight for its rights within the Union than outside." Yet, as soon as the trumpets sounded and the Southern homeland issued its call, Jackson was ready and willing to fight against the liberation of the Negroes, for whom he had always shown profound sympathy.

On active service, he was very different from Lincoln, for his sense of duty made him absolutely unyielding. The chaplain came in vain to ask for clemency to four deserters. Jackson was silent.

"General," persisted the petitioner, "think of your responsibility before God!"

Thereupon the commander dismissed the parson with the rough exclamation, "That's my business. You stick to yours!"

He secured this seeming hardness at the cost of incomparable courage, and (in his own view) he owed his courage directly to the Almighty, for "my faith teaches me to feel as safe in battle as in bed. God has decided the hour of my death. I do not concern myself about the matter, but I am always ready."

This death came to him in a cruelly ironical fashion. The man who was loved by all who served under him was hit by the stray bullets of some of his own soldiers, and then they let him fall when he was being carried to hospital on a stretcher, one of the bearers being hit. Thus tortuous were the ways on which Fate displayed herself to a fervent devotee. Many believed that had Jackson survived, the war would have ended differently. In reality the issue was determined by other factors than the death or the failure of an individual leader. Superior man power and the blockade were to win the victory at last. But years were still to pass before then.

XVI

Europe stood invisible between the combatants, favorable, in the main, to the South. For two years Napoleon was disposed to intervene, and only refrained from taking a definite line against the North because his aim, the conquest of Mexico, was hazardous and irrelevant. Bismarck maintained a formal neutrality, but admitted subsequently that his sympathies had been on the side of the members of his own caste, the landed gentry of the South. Among the potentates of the Old World, the Tsar alone openly favored the North: having abolished the Russian counterpart of slavery at the moment when the war was about to begin, he found in this a convenient pretext for a pro-Union policy, and a moral mask for a policy that was fundamentally anglophobe.

For it was inevitable that England, whose attitude in case of intervention would prove decisive, should incline to the side of the South. To the business world of Britain, the North was a rival whose prosperity could not be an object of desire, whereas the South supplied various necessaries which were now held up by the blockade — chief among them cotton, the lack of which threatened Britain's premier manufacturing industry with destruction. Historians could see no reason for blaming the Southern States because they had broken away from the Union, seeing that this had itself been formed only eighty years back by a secession from the old country. Statesmen were naturally pleased to witness the break-up of a power which, if it remained united, might within half a century challenge the British command of the sea. Even the moralists were, some of them at least, champions of the South: either because this was the weaker side; or because, like Gladstone, they regarded the cause of the war as preposterous; or because, like Dickens, they held that no cause made war justifiable. Disraeli was sedulously neutral; but Darwin, Tennyson, and John Stuart Mill saved the honor of the British name by their outspoken sympathy with the slaves and the liberators; and these enlightened men were backed up, not only by part of the middle-class intellectuals, but also by the whole of the manual workers, who were reduced nearly to starvation by the closure of the factories, but realized that the claim to freedom did not rest solely upon the color of a man's skin.

Such being the general trend of British sympathies, when a bold Northern naval officer stopped and boarded a British mail packet, the *Trent*, which had recently sailed from Havana, and forcibly removed from her two Confederate commissioners to Europe, war with England became imminent, and all the enemies of the North were supplied with legal warrant for their wrath. But while London and New York were interchanging Homeric threats across the Atlantic, one side clamoring for war or demanding surrender of the envoys, and the other shouting its enthusiastic admiration of the naval hero, Lincoln remained calm. Though several of his cabinet members were foaming at the mouth, he recognized, as he had done in the John Brown affair, that exaggeration was a grave error, made due allowance for the historical situation with its reversal of rôles, and determined to brave unpopularity once more:

"I fear the traitors will prove to be white elephants. We must stick to American principles concerning the rights of neutrals. We fought Great Britain for insisting by theory and practice on the right to do exactly what Captain Wilkes has done. If Great Britain shall now protest against the act and demand their release, we must give them up, apologize for the act as a violation of our doctrines, and thus forever bind her over to keep the peace in relation to neutrals, and so acknowledge that she has been wrong for sixty years."

He toned down the most emphatic passages in Seward's diplomatic notes, being unaware that on the other side of the ocean the dying Prince Consort was doing the same thing with the notes drafted by Lord John Russell. The impression made in London by the liberation of the envoys and the apology was remarkable, for England is inclined to appreciate such conduct, and the result was that the Southern agents, when they did at length arrive, had a cool reception. Once more it had been Lincoln who had saved the country in one of the most critical moments of the war.

No less cautious was he in his management of the reconquered areas of the Union. There was to be no question of punitive measures.

"Broken eggs cannot be mended; but Louisiana has nothing to do now, but to take her place in the Union as it was, barring the already broken eggs. The sooner she does so, the smaller will be the amount of that which will be past mending. This government cannot much longer play a game in which it stakes all, and its enemies stake nothing. Those enemies must understand that they cannot experiment for ten years trying to destroy the government, and if they fail still come back into the Union unhurt. If they expect in any contingency to ever have the Union as it was, I join . . . in saying, 'Now is the time.'"

Again, he writes to the military governor of Louisiana: "In all available ways give the people a chance to express their wishes at these elections. . . . At all events get the expression of the largest number of people possible. . . . Of course the men elected should be gentlemen of character, willing to swear support to the Constitution as of old, and known to be above reasonable suspicion of duplicity."

Meanwhile Lincoln was waiting for the victory which would free the proclamation from its imprisonment in the drawer. The military situation grew more and more critical. Pope, a new general, was defeated by Lee in the end of August, once more at Bull Run, his army retreating in disorder upon the capital, to arouse panic there, while Lee was enabled to invade Maryland, part of the blame for this falling on McClellan, who seemed to want Pope to be defeated, and certainly did not march in accordance with the orders he had received. This did not lead to McClellan's dismissal, for in fact his position was strengthened in order to promote the reconstruction of the demoralized army, the change being made on Lincoln's wish and in opposition to the advice of almost all the members of the cabinet. Although McClellan did indeed excel in such organizational work, and was still beloved by the soldiers, and although, since he was a Democrat, political considerations may have made it inexpedient to cashier him, there can be little doubt that Lincoln retained him in his command too long; and it was soon to become apparent that the President was mistaken in his estimate of McClellan's moral worth.

At any rate, in these circumstances he made a vow born of faith and superstition, and disclosed the full horror of his internal perplexities; he pledged himself before God to issue the proclamation as soon as the enemy should have been driven out of Maryland. Never in his life did Lincoln own up to any other emotional act of the kind; for if on other occasions similar instinctive tendencies may have been at work, they were always veiled by his ironic humor, and hidden away behind a smoke screen of anecdote. Yet when we recall the attention he paid to signs and portents, his fondness for interpreting dreams, his bent towards fatalism, and his melancholy remark about renouncing visions of Elysium, we cannot but infer that, like all great men, at decisive moments and in desperate emergencies he was prone to guide his footsteps through the confusion of events by secret directives, pointers, and stars. He may have called them "God" or "Christ"; he may have made the aforesaid oath to God, or to himself, or (as he himself declared) to both at once. The name matters nothing.

Inclined by temperament to listen, to hesitate, to await developments, he was now for the second time in his life being forced into an impatience uncongenial to his nature. The first time had been at Springfield (was it really two years ago?) when he was President elect, but powerless to interfere. Now again, as commander, he was powerless, and could only hope for a victory which would release the proclamation from its drawer. All sorts of outside influences were at work, urging him more and more impetuously to utter, at length, the word of emancipation — and yet his judgment and his vow forbade him to declare that this word had long since been made ready!

Ministers enter his room, notable fighters in the abolitionist struggle. "When the hour comes for dealing with slavery," he says to them, "I trust I shall be willing to do my duty, though it costs me my life. And, gentlemen, lives will be lost." According to the report of the interview, these last words were said in a sad and weary tone, and yet with a smile. One day a number of Quakers came to see him, and quoted his own speeches against him, forcing him on the defensive. When another visitor remarked that he seemed to have changed his mind, he had an effective answer. "Yes, I have, and I don't think much of a man who isn't wiser to-day than he was yesterday." To an enthusiast he says, in true farmer style, "Sir, the slaves will not be freed merely by passing a decree to that effect. You may call a calf's tail a leg, but that doesn't really give the calf five legs!"

Sometimes he spices his soft words with so much secret irony, that certain delegates from the religious denominations of Chicago can hardly have failed to notice it.

"I am approached with the most opposite opinions and advice, and that by religious men, who are equally certain that they represent the divine will. I am sure that either the one or the other class is mistaken in that belief, and perhaps in some respects both. I hope it will not be irreverent for me to say that if it is probable that God would reveal His will to others, on a point so connected with my duty, it might be supposed He would reveal it directly to me; for unless I am more deceived in myself than I often am, it is my earnest desire to know the will of Providence in this matter. And if I can learn what it is, I will do it! These are not, however, the days of miracles, and I suppose it will be granted that I am not to expect a direct revelation. I must study the plain physical facts of the case, ascertain what is possible, and learn what appears to be wise and right. . . .

"What good would a proclamation of emancipation from me do, especially as we are now situated? I do not want to issue a document that the whole world will see must necessarily be inoperative, like the Pope's bull against the comet! Would my word free the slaves, when I cannot even enforce the Constitution in the rebel States? . . . And what reason is there to think it would have any greater effect upon the slaves than the late law of Congress — which offers protection and freedom to the slaves of rebel masters who come within our lines? Yet I cannot learn that that law has caused a single slave to come over to us. . . . For instance, when after the late battles at and near Bull Run, an expedition went out from Washington under a flag of truce to bury the dead and bring in the wounded, and the rebels seized the blacks who went along to help, and sent them into slavery.

"I view this matter as a practical war measure, to be decided on according to the advantages or disadvantages it may offer to the suppression of the rebellion. . . . I am not so sure we could do much with the blacks. If we were to arm them, I fear that in a few weeks the arms would be in the hands of the rebels; and, indeed, thus far we have not had arms enough to equip our white troops

. . . There are fifty thousand bayonets in the Union armies from the border slave States. It would be a serious matter if, in consequence of a proclamation such as you desire, they should go over to the rebels. . . . Whatever shall appear to be God's will, I will do. I trust that in the freedom with which I have canvassed your views I have not in any respect injured your feelings."

Thus ruthlessly does he strip these pastorally minded delegates of the illusion that human happiness is the only thing at stake. It seems as if the melodramatic scene of these men who ask instead of reckoning had made him more of a realist than ever; and though he begins and ends with God, nothing could be further from God than the intervening substance of his speech. Can we be surprised that from preachers, pamphleteers, and newspaper writers there should come denunciations of the cold-blooded slavophobist President? Can we be surprised that he is blamed for speaking of the "nigger question", and for his avoidance of the sentimentalism beloved of the crowd? That in various State elections the Republicans should sustain formidable losses? That Greeley, the influential editor of the *New York Tribune*, should, in an open letter, blame the President for a lack of energy in Louisiana? Lincoln, he said, was "unduly influenced by the counsels, the representations, the menaces, of certain fossil politicians hailing from the border slave States. . . . We complain that a large proportion of our regular army officers, with many of the volunteers, evince far more solicitude to uphold slavery than to put down the rebellion."

Will Lincoln, with a dignified gesture, wrap himself in his toga, and instruct a subordinate to send a semi-official answer? The very day on which he receives the newspaper, he replies with his own hand, using the identical method of an open letter, which, Socratic in its style, must rank as one of his most brilliant documents:

"I have just read yours of the 19th. . . . If there be in it any statements, or assumptions of fact, which I may know to be erroneous, I do not, now and here, controvert them. If there be in it any inferences which I may believe to be falsely drawn, I do not, now and here, argue against them. If there be perceptible in it an impatient and dictatorial tone, I waive it in deference to an old friend, whose heart I have always supposed to be right. . . .

"I would save the Union. I would save it the shortest way under the Constitution. . . . If there be those who would not save the Union unless they could at the same time save slavery, I do not agree with them. . . . My paramount object in this struggle is to save the Union, and is not either to save or to destroy slavery. If I could save the Union without freeing any slave, I would do it; and if I could save it by freeing all the slaves, I would do it; and if I could do it by freeing some and leaving others alone, I would also do that. What I do about slavery and the colored race, I do because I believe it helps to save the Union. . . . I shall do less whenever I shall believe what I am doing hurts the cause, and I shall do more whenever I shall believe doing more will help the cause. I shall try to correct errors when shown to be errors, and I shall adopt new views so fast as they shall appear to be true views. I have here stated my purpose according to my view of official duty; and I intend no modification of my oft-expressed personal wish that all men everywhere could be free.

"Yours, A. Lincoln."

Never in Europe has such a document been published by the chief of a State, not even in peace time nor in the form of an official decree. But even in America it is unique, for what other President has answered opinionated newspaper criticism in this way, answered it by return of post so that deliberation was impossible, answered it also in a newspaper where all (including the enemy) could read it, in phraseology equally intelligible to the most uncultured farmer of the West and to the shrewdest lawyer of the East, and in a document both logical and political, both matter-of-fact and in the highest sense of the word moral? Having done so, indeed, he gives vent to his feelings, saying to his friends apropos of Greeley's onslaught: "It reminds me of the big fellow whose little wife was wont to beat him over the head without resistance. When remonstrated with, the man said, 'Let her alone. It don't hurt me, and it does her a power of good.'"

XVII

And all this with the proclamation lying in the drawer! No, the President, a fighter and much fought over, was not a sentimentalist; everything in him was alert and ready for action, and even if in secret he believed he had a mission, at this period he was inclined more and more to make short work of feelings. That he valued liberty more than he loved the blacks, and that he would not allow even his love of liberty to interfere with his devotion to the Union, he proved by his behavior during all the years of his government. Yet his feeling towards the Negroes was shown by the way in which he addressed them.

Here are some of them in his room, a committee of leaders, headed by a black minister. They have come to ask his opinion about foreign colonization schemes for those of their brethren who may be freed from slavery. He invites them to be seated, tells them that a sum of money has been voted by Congress for the purpose in question and placed at his disposal, and he goes on to talk frankly of generalities:

"Your race suffer very greatly, many of them, by living among us, while ours suffer from your presence. In a word, we suffer on each side. If this is admitted, it affords a reason, at least, why we should be separated. You here are free men, I suppose."

"Yes, Sir."

"Perhaps you have long been free, or all your lives. Your race are suffering, in my judgment, the greatest wrong inflicted on any people. But even when you cease to be slaves, you are yet far removed from being placed on an equality with the white race. You are cut off from many of the advantages which the other race enjoys. The aspiration of men is to enjoy equality with the best when free, but on this broad continent not a single man of your race is made the equal of a single man of ours. Go where you are treated the best, and the ban is still on you. . . . I cannot alter it if I would. It is a fact about which we all think and feel alike, I and you. . . . Without the institution of slavery and the colored race as a basis, the war could not have an existence. It is better for us both, therefore, to be separated. I know that there are free men among you who, even if they could better their condition, are not as much inclined to go out of the country as those who, being slaves, could obtain their freedom on this condition.

"There is an unwillingness on the part of our people, harsh as it may be, for you free colored people to remain with us. Now, if you could give a start to the white people, you could open a wide door for many to be made free. If we deal with those who are not free at the beginning, and whose intellects are clouded by slavery, we have a very poor material to start with. If intelligent colored men, such as are before me, would move in this matter, much might be accomplished. . . . General Washington himself endured greater physical hardships than if he had remained a British subject, yet he was a happy man because he had engaged in benefiting his race, in doing something for the children of his neighbors, having none of his own. . . . I do not know how much attachment you may have toward our race. It does not strike me that you have the greatest reason to love them. But still you are attached to them, at all events. . . . We have been mistaken all our lives if we do not know that whites, as well as blacks, love their self-interest. . . . I ask you, then, to consider it seriously, not as pertaining to yourselves merely, nor for your race and ours for the present time, but as one of the things, if successfully managed, for the good of mankind — not confined to the present generation."

Lincoln in the seducer's rôle! Or perhaps we should rather compare him to Don Juan trying to persuade Doña Elvira, after he has loosed her from love's chains, that it is really better for them to part. Note the psychological subtlety with which he brings it home to the Negroes that they will do well to make up their minds to emigrate — for otherwise it will be necessary to force exile upon them. True that slavery has been the greatest of injustices — but does its removal imply that we are all to love one another?

"I deny," he had exclaimed in the Douglas debates, "that because I do not want a negro woman for a slave, I do necessarily want her for a wife."

But to-day they are sitting around him in a circle, and he is alone

LIBERATOR

LIBERATOR 367

with them for the first time in his life, Lincoln the only white man in a room full of blacks; and, however well-behaved and well-educated they may seem, however much he may feel them to be entitled to equal rights with himself, yet with all his senses he is aware of their differences from members of his own race. They sit there, looking at him pleadingly out of their dark and mournful eyes, and when he puts a question there comes a prompt answer from black lips, "Yes, Sir." Is he not "sir", "seigneur", "lord", in the double sense of the term? Is not their hesitant, perhaps subservient tone reminiscent of the chains which the fathers of all these men wore? Can the spell of those bonds ever be broken? "I cannot alter it if I would." "It does not strike me that you have the greatest reason to love us." Then he ventures to conjure up the shade of Washington, in order to show them why they ought to sacrifice themselves on behalf of their less instructed brethren.

Still the proclamation rustles in its drawer, waiting for a victory. Every morning, and often in the evening as well, he goes to the War Office, and reads the latest telegrams. "I come here," he once said to the officials, "to escape my persecutors. Many people call and say they want to see me for only a minute. That means, if I can hear their story and grant their request in a minute it will be enough." He looks through all the messages, that he may get his news from the most recent sources, and may feel sure that nothing is being kept from him. Then he writes his own dispatches slowly and thoughtfully, looking out of the window, left elbow on the table, forehead resting in his hand, moving his lips and muttering each sentence over to himself before he commits it to paper — just as he used to in his young days. As soon as he has composed it to his satisfaction, he writes it out, and hardly ever needs to correct it afterwards. Is it a generation since, in the Indiana cabin, he used to rough-draft in charcoal on a board that which was not until after due deliberation transferred to the costly medium of paper? Were it three generations, no method, no dignity would change the slow and heavy rhythm of this bony man.

It meant still more for him, this little telegraph room at the War Department. It was a substitute for the store where, only a few

years back, he had loved to sit on a keg of nails, listening, and
spinning yarns; it was a kind of hermitage with congenial company,
a convenient neutral spot where intrusive callers could not come
to worry him.   As of old he would sit on the edge of his chair, with
his right knee dragged down to the floor, and in this curious position
slowly read one telegram after the other and then again the whole
lot from the beginning.   "Well, I guess I have got down to the
raisins," he once said.   The officials look at him wonderingly.   "I
used to know a little girl out West who sometimes was inclined to
eat too much.   One day she ate a good many more raisins than she
ought to, and followed them up with a quantity of other goodies.
It made her very sick.   After a time the raisins began to come.
She gasped and looked at her mother, and said: "Well, I will be
better now, I guess, for I have got down to the raisins.'"

His impatience for the victory is growing.   In the summer he and
his family had gone to a simple little house, a few miles out of the
city, near to a place used as a home for old and disabled soldiers.
On his way thither, he often passed long lines of ambulances, laden
with the victims of a recent battle.   A friend who was with him on one
of these occasions reports: "His attitude and expression spoke the
deepest sadness.   He paused, and, pointing towards the wounded
men, said, 'Look yonder at those poor fellows.   I cannot bear it!
This suffering, this loss of life, is dreadful.'"   The friend reminded him
how he had once said, "Never fear.   Victory will come."   Lincoln answered with a sigh, "Yes, victory will come, but it comes slowly."

When he learns that some young Quakers have been forcibly
enrolled, and compelled to bear arms in defiance of their principles,
he orders that they shall be dismissed and sent home.   Stanton
objects, on disciplinary grounds.   Lincoln replies, "It is my urgent
wish."   Another time, twenty-four deserters have been sentenced
to be shot.   Lincoln refuses to countersign the order for their execution.   The general says, "Mr. President, unless these men are
made an example of, the army itself is in danger."

Lincoln: "Mr. General, there are already too many weeping
widows in the United States. . . . Don't ask me to add to their
number, for I won't do it!"

When he visits the front, he is more modest than the most callow lieutenant, for he says to himself that he holds no army rank. "I am surrounded by soldiers, . . . and it is not proper for me to make speeches in my present position."

To a regiment : "Your colonel has thought fit, on his own account and in your name, to say that you are satisfied with the manner in which I have performed my part in the difficulties which have surrounded the nation. For your kind expressions I am extremely grateful, but on the other hand I assure you that the nation is more indebted to you, and such as you, than to me."

At other times his wit enables him to deal effectively with fools. At a review, an officer forced his way to the President's carriage and complained of a grievance. He declared that his general (who was present) had threatened that morning to shoot him. Lincoln looked quizzically at the pair of them, and then said to the complainant in a stage whisper : "Well, if I were you, and he threatened to shoot me, I would not trust him, for I believe he would do it !"

Describing the consecration of a flag, a witness of the ceremony says that Lincoln showed two faces on the occasion : one was that of a statesman and sage looking out into the distance; the other that of a shrewd observer, when he was measuring with his eye the thickness of the flagstaff, and finding it too thin — as it proved to be ere long.

"How many men have the rebels in the field?" asked a visitor.

"Twelve hundred thousand," answered the President.

"Good heavens, you don't say so?"

"Yes, Sir, twelve hundred thousand — not a doubt of it. You see, all of our generals, when they get whipped, say the enemy outnumbered them from three or five to one, and I must believe them. We have four hundred thousand men in the field, and three times four makes twelve."

Once, however, the only time on record during this period of restless expectancy, Lincoln's nervous irritability was too much for him. After one and a half years of daily and hourly personal exertion, fatigue overcame him. It was in the evening, after a heavy day, when a colonel who was only just off the sick list came to see the President. His wife, said the visitor, had been nursing him in hospital, then, when she was on her way home, there had been a steamboat collision, and she had been drowned. Now he learned that her body had been recovered, and he begged leave of absence to fetch it. Owing to the imminence of a battle, the Secretary of War had refused this application, so he had come to the chief. Lincoln, whom the applicant found sitting alone in his room, coat off, surrounded by papers, lost in thought, listened in silence, and then answered with an outburst:

"Am I to have no rest? Is there no hour or spot where I may escape these constant calls? Why do you follow me here with such business as this? Why do you not go to the War Office, where they have charge of all this matter of papers and transportation? The Secretary of War has refused? Then probably you ought not to go down the river. . . . You should remember that I have other duties to attend to. . . . Why do you come here to appeal to my humanity? Don't you know that we are in the midst of war? That suffering and death press upon all of us? That works of humanity and affection, which we would cheerfully perform in days of peace, are all trampled upon and outlawed by war? That there is no room left for them? There is but one duty now — to fight. . . . Your wife might have trusted you to the care which the government has provided for its sick soldiers. At any rate you must not vex me with your family troubles. Why, every family in the land is crushed with sorrow; but they must not each come to me for help. I have all the burden I can carry."

The alarmed officer, who had heard so many tales of Lincoln's kindliness, withdrew, overwhelmed with disappointment. He reached his hotel. Early next morning came a knock at his door. When he opened it, there stood the President, who grasped his hand impulsively. "My dear Colonel, I was a brute last night. I have no excuse for my conduct. Indeed I was weary to the last extent; but I had no right to treat with rudeness a man who had offered his life for his country, especially a man who came to me in great affliction. I have had a regretful night, and now come to beg your forgiveness." Everything had been arranged, he had just seen Stanton, here was the pass, there was a carriage below, they would drive together to the wharf, and the colonel could leave by the next steamer.

XVIII

At length, in the middle of September, came the victory. McClellan, having finally made up his mind to advance, defeated General Lee at Antietam. Though the battle was not decisive, Lee was forced to withdraw, and in this restricted eastern theater of war a few miles were important, while more important still was the effect of the news upon the wearied North and upon a skeptical Europe. "Please don't let him get off without being hurt," Lincoln wired to McClellan, and reinforced this urging in a personal visit to the camp; but McClellan was inert, and failed to follow up the enemy.

For the moment it was more important to turn the success to account in the political field, for England, which had been on the point of recognizing the South as an independent power, was now given cause to reconsider her attitude.

Lincoln's restlessness was greatly intensified by the victory. His moment had come, and he must take action as he had vowed. At about this time, just before or just after the battle of Antietam, he wrote the following memorandum: "The will of God prevails. In great contests, each party claims to act in accordance with the will of God. Both may be, and one must be, wrong. God cannot be for and against the same thing at the same time. In the present civil war it is quite possible that God's purpose is something different from the purpose of either party; and yet the human instrumentalities, working as they do, are of the best adaptation to effect His purpose. I am almost ready to say that this is probably true; that God wills this contest, and wills that it shall not end yet. By His mere great power on the minds of the now contestants, He could have either saved or destroyed the Union without human contest. Yet the contest began. And having begun, He could give the final victory to either side any day. Yet the contest proceeds."

The value of this written monologue is intensified in Lincoln's case by its rarity, and by the critical character of the hour when it was penned. We look into his heart, the heart of a philosopher. There is no word of self-justification, no railing against the enemy, not even a tranquil conviction of agreement with God's purpose — this being in his later years Lincoln's term for destiny. There is no evidence that he really believes in a personal God, or in the Son of God. On the other hand, his thorough-going fatalism leads him to assume that destiny may have other determinants, and determinants that are beyond his ken, for why else does God not end the war? The whole memorandum is one long question, to which no answer is forthcoming. It is instinct with skepticism against all that happens; against all the things to which he is devoting his energies by day and by night; and it is thrice interrupted by the "and yet" which was characteristic of Lincoln's speeches and writings since early youth, and which drops all the virility of a major common chord into the minor realm of his melancholy.

With such an "and yet" he now rallies his energies, for, no matter what may be the will of destiny or what may be the guiding idea of the struggle, of this, at least, he is convinced, that slavery is an injustice and ought to be abolished. Five days after the victory of Antietam, he summons a cabinet council, without acquainting its members with its specific purpose. Lincoln, who after the loss of a battle and when the safety of the capital was threatened, had always remained calm, however agitated his advisers might be, is to-day, when there is no danger, greatly excited. He is going to make the great proclamation public, and at the same time reveal the inner promptings of his heart to collaborators who have not hitherto been acquainted with his hidden motives. For twenty years he has eagerly longed for this act, and for a year half the country has been urging him to take the decisive step, but the complications of the issue have made him hold his hand. Now he is going to act on his own initiative, and this without any immediate compulsion. The hesitations of the statesman who doubts the results of the measure unite with his temperamental shrinking from irrevocable decisions — the hesitancy which has underlain his vagrant and irregular way of living has twice interfered with his marital schemes, once actually leading him to turn tail on the day fixed for his wedding. Everything combines to increase his embarrassment when he now confronts the expectant glances of his colleagues. What does he do? He picks up the latest issue of a comic paper, and reads them a satirical effusion by Artemus Ward, a man whose wit he greatly admires.

Is there any one in this circle who can understand him? Some of them, beyond question, are censorious, and all the more when they learn the gravity of the purpose for which they have been summoned. Is the President such an inveterate Bohemian that even in the most serious moments of his life and at the most serious crises in his country he cannot refrain from witticisms and anecdotes? But at length he lays the paper down, and says:

"I have, as you are aware, thought a great deal about the relation of this war to slavery. . . . When the rebel army was at Frederick, I determined, as soon as it should be driven out of Maryland, to issue a proclamation of emancipation. . . . I made the promise to myself and" — hesitating a little — "to my Maker. The rebel army is now driven out, and I am going to fulfill that promise. . . . I do not wish your advice about the main matter, for that I have determined for myself. This I say without intending anything but respect for any one of you. But I already know the views of each on this question. . . . If there is anything in the expressions I use, or in any minor matter, which any of you thinks had best be changed, I shall be glad to receive the suggestions. . . . I know very well that many others might, in this matter as in others, do better than I can; and if I was satisfied that the public confidence was more fully possessed by any one of them than by me, and knew of any constitutional way in which he could be put in my place, he should have it. I would gladly yield it to him. But though I believe that I have not so much of the confidence of the people as I had some time since, I do not know that, all things considered, any other person has more; and, however this may be, there is no way in which I can have any other man put where I am. I am here; I must do the best I can, and bear the responsibility of taking the course which I feel I ought to take."

Do we not hear the hesitation, the perplexity? Do we not see the rigid, unanimous silence of the lips and the eyes of those who surround him? Do we not feel this atmosphere of monologue? Why does he mention the possibility of his yielding up his place to another? Why does he insist, almost churlishly, that he does not seek their counsel? Because he has had to call upon all his virile energy to brace himself to this great resolve, and still trembles now that the decisive moment has come, as a reserved youth trembles when the moment has come for him to make a long deliberated and frequently postponed avowal of love. Because he, having a poet's nature, is always restrained from impetuous action by his tendency to weigh opposing considerations, and would now, at the eleventh hour, gladly find a substitute to act in his place. Still, he says to himself, "I am here, and I have to act as best I can." Or as he actually says shortly afterwards, "I can only trust in God that I have made no mistake."

Now the secretaries seem to have understood him. They even noticed, according to their reports, his delicate hesitation before he uttered the words "my Maker." The greatness of the occasion, and the impressive figure of this poor Western lawyer who had set forth to free the slaves, would appear to have touched their common humanity; for, after a brief discussion, he tells them, in a lighter tone, how, in his trouble and anxiety, he had dropped on to his knees like a child and had vowed that if the enemy was driven out of Maryland he could take this as a sign that he was to issue the proclamation.

And, as if wishing to commit himself beyond the possibility of recall, the selfsame day Abraham Lincoln made the Emancipation Proclamation known to the world.

XIX

The effect was catastrophic. Confusion was widespread throughout the North, there was a slump on the stock exchange; the elections were adverse; the Democrats declared that thousands of whites were being forced to give their blood in order that their fellow countrymen might be illegally deprived of property. In the South, no one moved a finger; not a soldier had to be withdrawn from the front in order to keep watch on the freed slaves; these latter went on quietly toiling in the fields; and the Southern newspapers could point triumphantly to the fact, declaring the slaves to be so happy that none of them wanted freedom. From Europe came threats in plenty, and only one congratulatory voice to break the chorus of disapprobation. Thousands of Lancashire workers, unemployed and starving because the spinning mills were closed for lack of cotton, thanked Lincoln for his services to the cause of humanity. They alone understood this man who was one of their own kind, and one after their own heart, the man who had said, "Wealth is a superfluity of things we do not need."

He is not seriously perturbed. "It is six days old," he writes to the Vice President, "and while commendation in newspapers and by distinguished individuals is all that a vain man could wish, the stocks have declined, and troops come forward more slowly than ever. This, looked soberly in the face, is not very satisfactory. We have fewer troops in the field at the end of the six days than we had at the beginning. . . . The North responds to the proclamation sufficiently in breath; but breath alone kills no rebels. I wish I could write more cheerfully."

New convulsions in the interior of the parties resulted, for these divisions of political party persisted within the belligerents. Only the convinced abolitionists were satisfied with the new line, for even old friends and fellow members of his own party, like Carl Schurz, were critical. Lincoln's reply to Schurz throws light on some of his difficulties:

"I ought to be blamed if I could do better. . . . I think I could not do better, therefore I blame you for blaming me. I understand you now to be willing to accept the help of men who are not Republicans, provided they have 'heart in it.' Agreed. I want no others. But who is to be the judge of hearts, or of 'heart in it'? If I must discard my own judgment and take yours, I must also take that of others; and by the time I should reject all I should be advised to reject, I should have none left, Republicans or others —

not even yourself.   For be assured, my dear Sir, there are men who
have 'heart in it' that think you are performing your part as poorly
as you think I am performing mine.

"I fear we shall at last find out that the difficulty is in our case,
rather than in particular generals.   I wish to disparage no one —
certainly not those who sympathize with me; but I must say I need
success more than I need sympathy, and that I have not seen
so much greater evidence of getting success from my sympathizers
than from those who are denounced as the contrary.   It does seem
to me that in the field the two classes have been very much alike
in what they have done and what they have failed to do.   In seal-
ing their faith with their blood, Baker ' and others', Republicans,
did all that men could do; but did they any more than . . .
Stevens 'and others', none of whom were Republicans, and some
at least of whom have been bitterly and repeatedly denounced to
me as secession sympathizers?"

So embarrassing, so troublesome, was the attitude of the political
leaders throughout the war, that even so devoted a collaborator as
Carl Schurz could blame, or at least complain of, the President;
and reproach from his most trusted friends was doubly wounding.
But nothing could alienate him from tried intimates.   Within a
day or two of sending this outspoken letter, he asked Schurz to
call, received the visitor at seven in the morning by the fireside, in
his gigantic house slippers, slapped him in friendly fashion on the
knee, and said, "Now, young man, tell me frankly whether you
really regard me as such a poor sort of cuss as you made out in your
letter. . . .   Did I trounce you in my answer?   I didn't mean to
hurt your feelings.   I think we really understand one another, and
if so it will be all right."   Then Lincoln went on to explain his
reasons in the matter of the new generals.

And, to crown all, once again the victory had not been followed
up by an advance against the enemy capital, now so close at hand,
as Lincoln had urged in his peremptory telegram, and the nation
had expected.   In vain McClellan, when Lincoln came to review
the troops, had provided a fiery steed for the President.   Being a
good rider, he had hoped that the lanky civilian would discredit

himself before the soldiers. When the general, attended by his glittering staff officers, galloped along the front to the accompaniment of rattling drums, blaring bugles, and mortar fire, the civilian President made just as good a showing as he, in spite of having to hold a tall hat in one hand.

But by this time the purport of McClellan's obscure machinations was becoming plainer. On the peninsula, even before the battle of Antietam, he had received an emissary from the Democratic Party, the mayor of New York, who had come to offer him the presidential nomination for 1864. In return, he was only to pledge himself to carry on the war in such a way as to conciliate the South. After thinking the matter over, McClellan accepted the offer in writing, but, acting on the advice of one of his generals, destroyed this document. When, after the battle, the compromising visitor returned, and succeeded in getting a letter of acceptance, several of the generals who got wind of the matter and had long been vainly urging an advance threw up their commissions. How far McClellan's behavior when the Civil War was in progress was to be regarded as high treason, is not easy to decide, but at any rate Lincoln made up his mind to get rid of this Napoleon if Lee were allowed to escape from the trap, and he declared that McClellan really did not "want" to damage the enemy. At about this time, when Lincoln had spent a night in the camp, he rose at dawn and went for a walk with an old friend to watch the sunrise and the awakening of the soldiers to activity. Looking down over the scene, and waving his hand, he said:

"What is all this?"

"Why, what is it but the Army of the Potomac?" rejoined the other.

"No," said Lincoln, "no, this is General McClellan's bodyguard."

When five weeks had elapsed, and McClellan was still inactive, saying that he could not move because the horses were tired, Lincoln telegraphed to him laconically, "Will you pardon me for asking what the horses of your army have done since the battle of Antietam that fatigues anything?" Again: "The enemy's route is the arc of a circle, while yours is the chord. The roads are as good on your side as on his. . . . I would press closely to him, . . . and at least try to beat him in Richmond. . . . If we never try, we shall never succeed." Having written thus ironically, he ends his dispatch with the words: "This letter is in no sense an order."

But at the same time, through Halleck, he sends McClellan strict injunctions to advance. Immediately after this, "I ask a direct answer to the question, Is it your purpose not to go into action again until the men now being drafted in the States are incorporated into the old regiments?"

At length in November he comes to a belated resolution, removes McClellan, the Democrat, from command, and replaces him by Burnside, a Republican, though at rather an unlucky moment, for meanwhile the enemy has been strengthening his position, and in December Burnside sustains a defeat at Fredericksburg.

For the further complication of Lincoln's and the country's situation, there simultaneously occurred a cabinet crisis. In Congress a strong feeling had developed against Seward's lukewarm policy; and this culminated in the appointment of a Senate committee to wait upon the President and request Seward's removal. Thereupon Seward tendered his resignation. Quarrels with Seward had also led Chase and Stanton to talk of resigning. Lincoln, unwilling to lose at one blow three of his most important coadjutors, of whom Stanton and Chase, at least, seemed to him irreplaceable, took the matter in hand, and was able to conduct it to a successful issue. For when the nine senators appeared to lodge their complaint against Seward, they found themselves, to their great surprise, faced by the whole cabinet with the exception of Seward, and they had in turn to state their grievances before the assembly, Chase finding it necessary to take up the cudgels on behalf of Seward, whom Lincoln also defended.

Shortly afterwards he dispatches Welles to Seward to ask the latter not to press his resignation; Welles is to come back and report. At the same time he sends for Chase and Stanton. The adversaries meet at the President's, and very soon Welles joins the company.

"Have you seen the man?" asks Lincoln, who is sitting by the fire, and wishes for speedy news of Seward, without naming him before Chase.

"Yes, he has agreed."

When Chase now says that he has prepared his resignation, since he must really be regarded as the root-cause of the crisis, Lincoln's eyes light up, and he asks quickly, "Where is your tender of resignation?"

"I brought it with me," answers Chase, taking a paper from his pocket. "I wrote it this morning."

"Let me have it," rejoins the President, reaching his long arm and fingers towards Chase, who hesitates to surrender the document. But Lincoln takes it from him, and opens it at once, saying, "This is the solution of the Gordian knot!" Thereupon Stanton, who is standing in front of the fire, and does not want to be backward in the chivalrous contest, intervenes:

"I informed you the day before yesterday that I was ready to tender you my resignation. I wish you, Sir, to consider my resignation at this time in your possession."

"You may go to your department," answers the President; "I don't want yours. This," holding out Chase's letter, "is all I want; this relieves me; my way is clear; the trouble is ended. I will detain neither of you longer."

A few days later, Lincoln wrote a duplicate letter to Seward and Chase:

"Gentlemen, you have respectively tendered me your resignations. . . . I am apprised of the circumstances which may render this course personally desirable to each of you; but after most serious consideration my deliberate judgment is that the public interest does not admit of it. I therefore have to request that you will resume the duties of your departments respectively.

"Your obedient servant."

A farmer, a raftsman, afterwards indeed a lawyer, but above all one who knows men's hearts, understands their weaknesses and susceptibilities! Thus Lincoln was as well able to deal with this dangerous crisis as if he had been Talleyrand or another of those diplomats of the Old World whose nature and activities were so uncongenial to him.

XX

Disappointment gradually made Lincoln stricter in matters of discipline. When a young brigadier, through carelessness, was taken prisoner, with the squadron of cavalry under his command, Lincoln said, "Sorry to lose those horses. I can make a brigadier any day, but horses cost the government a hundred and twenty-five dollars a head!"

To a Western official he wrote:

"You cannot have reflected seriously when you ask that I shall order General Morgan's command to Kentucky as a favor because they have marched from Cumberland Gap. The precedent established by it would evidently break up the whole army. . . . I sincerely wish war was an easier and pleasanter business than it is; but it does not admit of holidays."

When a certain major was reported to him as having said that neither army should get much advantage of the other, but that both should be kept in the field until they were exhausted, when a compromise could be made and slavery saved, he endorsed a report of the inquiry as follows (though the officer was described as loyal).

"In my view it is wholly inadmissible for any gentleman holding a military commission from the United States to utter such sentiments. . . . Therefore let Major John J. Key be forthwith dismissed from the military service of the United States." But when he refused to pardon a convicted slave dealer, and countersigned the death sentence, he probably felt nearly as sick at heart as the condemned man.

On the other hand his inborn sympathies went out to the Negroes, and to the Indians as well. In the racial struggle, as in the class struggle, Lincoln always wanted to espouse the cause of the weaker, and may therefore be regarded, his skepticism notwithstanding, as a better Christian than many who were regular attendants at church. When it was proposed to execute three hundred Indians who had participated in a rising in Minnesota, he demanded a special report. "If the record does not fully indicate the more guilty and influential of the culprits, please have a careful statement made on these points and forwarded to me"; and three weeks later he asked the judge-advocate-general for a legal opinion "whether, if I should conclude to execute only a part of them, I must myself designate which, or could I leave the designation to some officer on the ground?"

Later still, when the matter was being considered by the Senate, he wrote that body: "Anxious to not act with so much clemency as to encourage another outbreak on the one hand, nor with so much severity as to be real cruelty on the other, I caused a careful examination of the records of trials to be made, in view of first ordering the execution of such as had been found guilty of violating females. Contrary to my expectation, only two of this class were found." In the end, thirty-nine of the culprits were executed. When the youthful Lincoln had fought the Indians, he had not killed any of them, and had saved one from death; now the aging Lincoln, as supreme commander, saves two hundred and sixty-one Indians, and must have been happier in doing so than on the day when he had been forced to uphold the death sentence on the slave dealer.

When Congress was sitting in December, the President's unceasing personal struggle on two fronts, the near approach of the momentous date fixed for the enforcement of the proclamation, the varying and for the most part unfavorable fortunes of the war, the skepticism of friends regarding the new measure and the scorn in which it was held by enemies, made him weary and dispirited. An old acquaintance who had not seen him for six years was shocked at his appearance.

"The change . . . was simply appalling. His whiskers had grown and had given additional cadaverousness to his face. . . . The light seemed to have gone out of his eyes, which were sunken far under his enormous brows. . . . There was over his whole face an expression of sadness, and a far-away look in the eyes, which were utterly unlike the Lincoln of former days."

But time presses, and, while the war stagnates, the sands of this agitated year are running out. Many declare that he will not dare to enforce the proclamation. In actual fact, he is preparing the details of its enforcement. Little areas of the South which have not made common cause with the secessionists are being excepted, so that the whole may give a more definite impression of being a punitive measure. At the same time he is considering new difficulties that will have to be faced, is making provision for those who are about to be freed. How can they best be enrolled in the army, and how can he make sure that the officers will treat them as well as the whites? He interests himself in the "jigger", which burrows into the skin of the feet, and caused much lameness and suffering among the Haitian Negroes. What remedies can be found for this affliction? How can the pests be exterminated? A black preacher, whom he consults on various points, goes into ecstasies about him. "He treated me as a man. He did not let me feel for a moment that there was any difference in the color of our skins."

Naturally he was well aware of the paradoxical character of the proclamation. It must have been bitter to him to read the mocking comments of the British press, to the effect that Lincoln was abolishing slavery in the States where his writ did not run, while leaving the institution untouched in those he could effectively rule. No one saw the dangers more plainly than he, who had hesitated so long before facing up to them, and he said with one of his expressive smiles, "We are like whalers who have been long on a chase; we have at last got the harpoon into the monster, but we must now look how we steer, or with one flop of his tail he will send us all into eternity."

Inasmuch as he was determined to enroll the freed blacks in an army that had been created to free the blacks, inasmuch as he was thus forced to confuse means with ends in the strangest way possible, and was in many instances setting them free only that after a little while they might perish on the battlefield, he was able in a wonderfully apt and moving phrase to enshrine the pathos of the situation. After the victory there would be "some black men who will remember that with silent tongue and clenched teeth and steady eye and well-poised bayonet they have helped mankind on to this great consummation."

But for all his seriousness, his Puckish humor is never far away. When a clergyman, a doctor of divinity, comes to him just before the New Year to ask him with great solemnity whether he intends to enforce the proclamation on the due date, Lincoln answers, with a twinkle in his eye, "Well, Doctor, you know Peter was going to do it, but when the time came he didn't."

A little later: "God has allowed men to make slaves of their fellows. He permits this war. He has before Him a strange spectacle. We, on our side, are praying Him to give us victory, because we believe we are right; but those on the other side pray Him, too, for victory, believing they are right. What must He think of us? . . . As for the negroes, . . . what is going to become of them? I . . . think of a story I read in one of my first books, 'Aesop's Fables.' It was an old edition, and had curious rough woodcuts, one of which showed four white men scrubbing a Negro in a potash kettle filled with cold water. The text explained that the men thought that by scrubbing the Negro they might make him white. Just about the time they thought they were succeeding, he took cold and died. Now, I am afraid that by the time we get through this war the Negro will catch cold and die."

Thus skeptical was Lincoln, who just now had showed so emotional an enthusiasm and who, when New Year's Day came, was keenly alive to the far-reaching import of the document to which he was attaching his signature. His proclamation which was only a frame around the one of September, read:

"Whereas on the twenty-second day of September, in the year of our Lord, one thousand eight hundred and sixty-two, a proclamation was issued . . . containing, among other things, the following, . . . Now I, Abraham Lincoln, President of the United States, by virtue of the power in me vested as Commander-in-Chief of the Army and Navy of the United States in time of actual armed rebellion against the authority and government of the United States, and as a fit and necessary measure for suppressing said rebellion, do, on this first day of January, in the year of our Lord, one thousand eight hundred and sixty-three, . . . designate as the States and parts of States . . . in rebellion . . ." (list follows).

". . . all persons held as slaves within said designated States, and parts of States, are, and henceforward shall be, free; and that the Executive government of the United States, including the military and naval authorities thereof, will recognize and maintain the freedom of said persons.

"And I hereby enjoin upon the people so declared to be free to abstain from all violence, unless in necessary self-defence; and I recommend to them that, in all cases when allowed, they labor faithfully for reasonable wages.

"And I further declare and make known, that such persons of suitable condition, will be received into the armed service of the United States to garrison forts, positions, stations, and other places, and to man vessels of all sorts in said service.

"And upon this act, sincerely believed to be an act of justice, warranted by the Constitution, upon military necessity, I invoke the considerate judgment of mankind and the gracious favor of Almighty God.

"In witness whereof, I have hereunto set my hand and caused the seal of the United States to be affixed.

"Done at the city of Washington, this first day of January, in the year of our Lord, one thousand eight hundred and sixty-three, and of the independence of the United States of America the eighty-seventh."

When Lincoln read this document drafted by himself, with the exception of the paragraph preceding the last one, to his cabinet on *old* year's eve, the suggested emendations were, in general, matters of little moment. Chase, however, pointed out that on an occasion like this a reference to the deity would be appropriate.

"Yes, I had forgotten that," assented Lincoln, adding the relevant paragraph.

In the afternoon, and on New Year's morning, he made a fair copy of the document. He was so much excited that he wrote to General Halleck, the commander in chief, a crustily worded epistle concerning disputes among the military leaders.

"If in such a difficulty as this you do not help, you fail me precisely in the point for which I sought your assistance. . . . Your military skill is useless to me if you will not do this." But when Halleck protested, Lincoln canceled the letter the same day, endorsing it with the splendid words: "Withdrawn because considered harsh by General Halleck."

He had to leave his writing table because hundreds of visitors were flocking to the White House to wish him a happy New Year. Not until the middle of the afternoon did he get back to his study and said to Seward's son who was waiting to get his signature, while dipping his pen:

"I never in my life felt more certain that I was doing right, than I do in signing this paper. But I have been receiving calls and shaking hands since eleven o'clock this morning, till my arm is stiff and numb. Now, this signature is one that will be closely examined, and if they find my hand trembled, they will say, 'He had some compunctions.' But, any way, it is going to be done!"

Thus at the very last moment did his shrewdness blend with the conviction of his historical mission, but he knew that the former was transitory, whereas the latter was eternal. He foresaw that out of this war measure there would soon emerge a new general formula of equality, as a complement to the basic ideas of the fathers of the country. He felt that these strokes of the pen would bring freedom to the last among innocent men who suffered under the curse of slavery, that it would break the chains of all the Negroes and of all such as the young mulatto woman he had seen long ago in the Southern slave market, and so, slowly and firmly, he wrote at the foot of the proclamation:

ABRAHAM LINCOLN

BOOK FIVE

FATHER

I

That November day in 1860, when the whole country, in great excitement, was voting for or against Lincoln, there was a shop assistant in a small Illinois town, a slightly built man of medium height and about forty years of age, selling hides to saddlers and cobblers who, likely enough, did not trouble to leave their jobs in order to go to the poll; the leather seller himself had no vote, not having yet been long enough in Illinois. The house and the business belonged to his father and his brothers, whom he had recently come to join, having for the last six years been wandering hither and thither in an unsuccessful quest for an adequate means of livelihood to support himself, his wife, and his four children.

In his twenties, he had been better off, having got on well enough in war and peace as lieutenant and then captain, usually on good terms with his superiors. But he had never had much enthusiasm for a soldier's life. Not that he had lacked courage, for as a boy of eight he had helped his father in the farm work, and while at the military academy and afterwards in the Mexican War he had been famed for his horsemanship. Nevertheless, shooting, slaughter, and victories were little to his taste; a dislike for firearms and an affectionate disposition, especially toward animals, made warfare repugnant to him; so did an almost feminine shyness, which rendered him throughout life unwilling to show himself naked before any one; so did the possession of hands which were too fine for the rough work of campaigning, and had won for him the nickname of "Little Beauty."

Speaking generally, he was not inclined toward activity. Trust in God, which he may have inherited from his mother, a pious Methodist, disposed him to confide in chance rather than in destiny. He had even started in life without a name, for not until he was six weeks old had his parents given him one, drawing lots, and happening on the remarkable appellation of Ulysses and Hiram. When, at seventeen, he was entered at West Point, the Congressman responsible for his appointment gave his name as Ulysses Simpson. He accepted the modification, his Solomonic patron saint being thus transformed.

His only weakness was drink. Perhaps his trouble in this direction had begun when he was twenty-five, and, as quartermaster during the Mexican War, was brought into more intimate contact with liquor than was safe for him. Certainly thenceforward only with great difficulty could he free himself from the passion for it, though he once founded a temperance society. The trouble grew on him so much that at thirty-two, being a captain whose record was in other respects unblemished, he had to leave the army. He made his way home with money borrowed from a comrade, and his father vainly wrote to the Secretary of War to implore leniency and reinstatement. Ten years later perhaps, the chief, whose name was Jefferson Davis, may have regretted having cashiered this captain, for an act of clemency might have bound to him for life the man who, as things turned out, was to smash the Southern Confederacy.

However that may be, the broken officer, uprooted and given to drink, spent the next few years vainly exploring all kinds of possibilities. He became a farmer, and then abandoned the calling; in or near St. Louis, he carted wood to market; became by turns a house agent, a district engineer, and a debt collector; struck root nowhere, was shunned by old friends whom he encountered in the street, for they were afraid he would ask them to lend him money. Now he was working in his father's leather business, and, had it not been for a strange turn of fortune, might have continued this occupation for the rest of his life, distinguished only by the possession of two unusual Christian names.

But the war hammered a new name out for him. Within a few days of Lincoln's first appeal for volunteers, this ex-officer helped to get a company together. When, however, he brought his men to Springfield, to have them enrolled there, he handed over the command to a captain he had trained, and himself stumbled along in the rear, dressed in mufti, gripsack in hand and cigar in mouth. This was Grant, who promptly answered the call to the colors because the old melody appealed to him; but he was not ambitious and he had no taste for display. And as he made his modest entry into Springfield on the day he began his fortieth year, he faintly reminds us of that other man who, though already President, had a few weeks before wandered through these very streets, so unceremoniously and so ill attired. No doubt, Grant's reputation was not so good as that other man's, for he had not found it easy to get back into the service, and had had to borrow money before he could buy a uniform and a mount — so ludicrous were the conditions under which the man who was to decide the issue of the war made his entrance.

Now he made a great effort. Thanks to his earnestness and experience, he soon became indispensable, secured rapid promotion, was within two months in command of a volunteer regiment containing a thousand men, and ere long in charge of southeastern Missouri and the adjoining regions. The scarcity of officers was bringing about the speedy advancement of every efficient soldier, and no one as yet regarded Grant as more than this. Even his first success in the field, the taking over of the little town of Paducah, was not so remarkable as a military exploit as because of the issue of a document which acquainted the possible reader with the firm and simple tone of one of its new generals. But Lincoln was prompt to recognize that there must be rare qualities in the man who had penned the following proclamation to the inhabitants of the conquered town:

"I am here to defend you against the enemy, to support the authority and liberty of your government. I have nothing to do with opinions, only with rebellion and its helpers. The strong arm of the government is here to protect its supporters and to punish its adversaries. I shall withdraw my troops as soon as it becomes plain that you are in a position to defend yourselves, to safeguard the power of the government, and to protect the rights of citizens."

This man's tone and demeanor impressed the Kentucky legislature, so that it decided to stand by the Union. Lincoln said,

"A man who can write like this seems fitted to take command of the West."

Shortly afterwards, the nation, too, heard of the new leader, for when he took the powerful Fort Donelson, and the enemy general asked for terms, he wrote back: "No terms except unconditional and immediate surrender can be accepted. I propose to move immediately upon your works." This impressed people, and play was made with the initials of his Christian names, so that he was spoken of as "Unconditional Surrender Grant." In twelve months the tanner's assistant, who had hitherto failed at everything he had tried, had become a major general, with the most noted victory of the war to his credit. Despite the sharply worded complaints of his superior officers (and probably Grant, as of old, really did drink now and again), Lincoln, who had never seen him, stood by him, and made him commander in Tennessee. Now there came reiterated complaints, from Halleck, from members of Congress, and in the press; and once when he wrote a sharp answer to his chief, he fully expected arrest. As far as the general public was concerned, his answer was silence, and although headquarters sometimes ignored him, sending orders direct to his subordinates, and although these latter acted at times on their own initiative, he never uttered any complaints either against them or against Halleck. This policy of silence, together with his aloofness in political matters and his sedulous avoidance of theatrical demonstrations, tended to confirm the prevailing belief that he was nothing more than an officer of average ability who had made a couple of lucky hits. An officer who rode into battle wearing a civilian's cloak, and who never put on gloves, must seem as queer a customer among generals who liked to show off and to ride at the head of brilliant staffs, as the President with unpressed trousers seemed among elegantly dressed diplomats. These very characteristics met with the approval of Lincoln, who replied to all criticisms by saying, "We'll go on trying him a while yet."

Lincoln and Grant, who had grown up under similar conditions in the wilds, had both of them been thrown on their own bodily resources very early in life, so that while the former had been able at sixteen to fell the tallest trees, the latter had at ten been sent to the town forty miles away in sole charge of a wagon. But both men were less disposed to rely on physical strength than on the common sense which had been developed by poverty and solitude, and their native simplicity was so overwhelming that Grant did not even lose it in the strange atmosphere of West Point. Indifferent to display, both of them unsystematic in their mode of living, and both of them timid where women were concerned, they were more exposed than most of their companions to the vicissitudes of environment and daily happenings. Suddenly uplifted into positions where they had to work in the grand style, they continued to depend, before all, on common sense; and, amid the complexities of politics and war, they still made, as a rule, exceedingly simple decisions, this accounting for the clear and virile nature of their public appeals.

But Lincoln was in every respect moderate, whereas in one point Grant was the reverse. By his inclination, from time to time, to put his reserved and comparatively passive nature under the influence of liquor, he showed that his character was not so well balanced as Lincoln's, and he thus ruined his youth, while later this weakness postponed the public recognition of his successes. In Lincoln, who much excelled Grant in culture, force of mind, and philosophical grasp, the excess of unutilized energies manifested itself as spiritual preëminence, which brought him forth out of obscurity, and enforced recognition. For Lincoln, too, imagination, which Grant lacked, provided an infallible key to the understanding of his fellows, and became a guiding force. That was why, while Grant was only able to get into touch with Lincoln through personal contact, Lincoln was able to discern Grant's abilities from afar, and, in the decisive year now beginning, to single him out from among all the other generals. Had it not been for Lincoln's powers of imagination and judgment, Grant would never have gone forward to victory, and would never have become a popular hero.

II

Had the war been nothing more than a duel between the adversaries, the South would probably have been invincible, or could only have been defeated in the course of many years' campaigning by the attrition of its forces through the man power of the North. The decisive factor was the blockade, which made it impossible for the South to procure raw materials and weapons from Europe, and also prevented export, with the result that after a time there were only two or three sea harbors, at which, despite the vigilance of the North, a certain amount of incoming and outgoing of goods remained possible. But so long as the Mississippi route was still available for rebel traffic, there was a way by which the South could procure flax and wheat from Europe through Texas and Mexico; that was why it was so important to deprive the enemy of the key position of Vicksburg.

As in the taking of New Orleans, it was necessary to operate simultaneously by land and water, using gunboats on the river. Grant ventured to sever himself from his Northern communications. Like Bonaparte in the first Italian campaign, he defeated two hostile armies successively in several engagements, invested the town, cut off its food supply, bombarded it fiercely, and compelled it to surrender on Independence Day, thirty thousand men laying down their arms. When, just afterwards, Port Hudson likewise capitulated, and, after two years' suspension of traffic, the first ship made its way from St. Louis to New Orleans, Lincoln, with a poetical figure of speech, was able to say, "The signs look better. The Father of Waters again goes unvexed to the sea."

During these same weeks, another Northern general was, with the strong hand, compelling fortune to favor the Northern cause. Hooker, who in January had replaced the defeated Burnside, had been over-impetuous, and in May, at Chancellorsville, had sustained a reverse which enabled Lee to make a third and last attempt to advance into Northern territory. The Southern commander had forced his way through Maryland to the boundary of Pennsylvania; panic had ensued, people had clamored for the reinstatement of McClellan, but Lincoln, hard hit by Hooker's failure, had appointed Meade, a lean, stiff-necked, schoolmastery kind of man, endowed with all the expert's virtues appropriate to such characteristics.

When the new commander now faced Lee, both generals felt, and the world at large felt, that the fate of the war hung in the balance, for another Southern victory here and at this time might have led the European powers to recognize the independence of the South, and might have ensured a political success for the war-weary Northern Democrats.

But on the third day of battle, Meade defeated Lee at Gettysburg, simultaneously with Grant's taking of Vicksburg, and by these two victories in the beginning of July, 1863, the issue of the war was really settled. Had the great success at Gettysburg been resolutely followed up, the campaign might speedily have been brought to a conclusion; the North was cleared of the enemy, the capital was no longer in danger, the Southern strength was almost confined to the Atlantic region, the blockade became thoroughly effective, and Jackson had fallen at Chancellorsville. If the South was nevertheless able to carry on the war for the best part of another two years, this shows the weakness of the North, and redounds to the credit of Lee.

Lincoln, now that he had found Grant, ceased to spend much time over the war map. Not from any love of autocracy, not from excessive self-esteem, had he been led to occupy himself with strategy, but only from sheer necessity and the loneliness of his position; and even then he had always accompanied his military proposals with the remark that they were recommendations, not orders. The knowledge he at length acquired might have given things another turn; thus, he had warned Hooker against crossing the river, at the risk of being entangled there "like an ox jumped half over a fence and liable to be torn by dogs front and rear without a fair chance to gore one way or to kick the other." Again: "If the head of Lee's army is at Martinsburg and the tail of it on the plank road between Fredericksburg and Chancellorsville, the animal must be very slim somewhere. Could you not break him?" The opinionated general might well be inclined to deride the lay adviser whose metaphors, however picturesque, were so obviously those of a farmer; but posthumous criticism has justified the amateur as against the professional expert.

For the rest, Lincoln had only been mistaken as to Hooker's capacity, having rightly appraised the man's character; for when he put the general in command of the Army of the Potomac the news of the appointment was conveyed in a letter so intensely skeptical that it might well have been one of dismissal rather than of promotion:

"I think it best for you to know, that there are some things in regard to which I am not quite satisfied with you. I believe you to be a brave and skillful soldier, which, of course, I like. I also believe you do not mix politics with your profession, in which you are right. You have confidence in yourself, which is a valuable if not an indispensable, quality. You are ambitious, which, within reasonable bounds, does good rather than harm; but I think that during General Burnside's command of the army, you have taken counsel of your ambition, and thwarted him as much as you could, in which you did a great wrong to the country and to a most meritorious and honorable brother officer.

"I have heard, in such a way as to believe it, of your recently saying that both the army and the government needed a dictator. Of course, it was not for this, but in spite of it, that I have given you the command. Only those generals who gain successes can set up dictators. What I now ask of you is military success, and I will risk the dictatorship. . . . I much fear that the spirit, that you have aided to infuse into the army, of criticizing their commander and withholding confidence from him, will now turn upon you. I shall assist you as far as I can to put it down. Neither you nor Napoleon, if he were alive again, could get any good out of an army while such a spirit prevails in it. And now beware of rashness. Beware of rashness, but with energy and sleepless vigilance go forward and give us victories."

This is Lincoln's new tone; we shall hear it again and again when he is holding converse with generals and civil servants, with soldiers and office seekers. It is no longer the tone of one who is learning, questioning, and inciting; it is the tone of an experienced man, getting old: it is the tone of a father. In this case he is severe, because he has to do with a man in a leading position, weaknesses notwithstanding. But through these austere and manly harmonies there sounds the silver bell of humor. The note is one of self-sufficient irony, characteristic of him who knows his fellows through and through, and who, notwithstanding all disappointments, is still a lover of mankind.

Yet with every nerve fiber he remains in close contact with the gains and losses of the war. When, a few months later, this same Hooker is defeated, an eyewitness describes the President as utterly prostrated by the evil tidings:

"About three o'clock in the afternoon, the door opened, and Lincoln came into the room. I shall never forget that picture of despair. He held a telegram in his hand. . . . His face, usually sallow, was ashen in hue. The paper on the wall behind him was of the tint known as 'French gray', and even in that moment of sorrow and dread expectation I vaguely took in the thought that the complexion of the anguished President's visage was almost exactly like that of the wall. He gave me the telegram and, in a voice trembling with emotion, said: 'Read it — news from the army.' . . . It was to the effect that the army had been withdrawn from the south side of the Rappahannock and was then 'safely encamped' in its former position. The appearance of the President, as I read aloud these fateful words, was piteous, . . . ghostlike. Clasping his hands behind his back, he walked up and down the room, saying, 'My God, my God, what will the country say?'" At once he ordered a steamer to be made ready, that he might take Halleck with him to the army headquarters.

When, shortly afterwards, Meade has become a person of influence through winning his great victory, we hear all the President's reserve in the tone in which the general is asked whether it will be agreeable to him to have his unlucky predecessor Hooker appointed to a subordinate command in his army: "Write me in perfect freedom, with the assurance that I will not subject you to any embarrassment by making your letter or its contents known to any one. I wish to know your wishes before I decide whether to break the subject to him. Do not lean a hair's breadth against your own feelings, or your judgment, . . . on the idea of gratifying me."

Among these army leaders, Grant was, for Lincoln, the only one worthy of complete confidence. At first, the President had asked for confidential reports about the general, and after a while had said, "I can't spare this man; he fights." When people complained that Grant drank, Lincoln (to whom topers were uncongenial) made a reply recalling that which George II is said to have made when a similar charge was brought against General Wolfe: "Can you tell me the kind of whisky? I should like to send a barrel to some of my other generals."

When he had taken Vicksburg, Grant received the following letter:

"My dear General: I do not remember that you and I ever met personally. I write this now as a grateful acknowledgement of the almost inestimable service you have done the country. I wish to say a word further. When you first reached the vicinity of Vicksburg, I thought you should do what you finally did — march the troops across the neck. . . . When you turned northwards . . . I feared it was a mistake. I now wish to make the personal acknowledgement that you were right and I was wrong.

"Yours very truly, A. Lincoln."

One of Lincoln's great moments. No one knows what he has been thinking, what his doubts have been; no one is urging him to confess his error, least of all the victorious general. But he has pricks of conscience, and feels that he must atone for his fault. His doubt in the soundness of Grant's military judgment was an injustice, and, now that the general has made so brilliant a showing, he must relieve his mind and he can only do this by an avowal which no one is demanding of him, and which, should it be misunderstood, can only damage his prestige. But his poetic temperament makes him a shrewd judge of character, and he knows with whom he can venture so candid an admission.

In this gradation of estimates and shading of tones, Lincoln showed a knowledge of the human heart which was flawed only by his occasional inclination to take too kindly a view.

III

"With public sentiment, nothing can fail; without it, nothing can succeed. Consequently, he who molds public sentiment, goes deeper than he who enacts statutes or pronounces decisions. He makes statutes and decisions possible or impossible to be executed." With the utterance of this typically American idea, in which the man of the forest declared his independence of the man of the street, Lincoln also disclosed the source of his most arduous struggles. For the more the rivalries between the generals at the front were subdued, or were at any rate lifted out of the domain of party conflicts, the more furiously did the political parties rage one against another; for the seeming interminability of the war made not only the Democrats, but also the radicals, clamor for an end, which the former hoped to reach by a general compromise, and the latter by a more vigorous prosecution of the fight. In this war, as in others, martial law and conscription were the main points around which opposition to the government became concentrated.

The extensive way in which Lincoln interpreted and exercised his rights as commander in chief could not fail, in the United States, to arouse more adverse feeling than similar measures arouse in the militarist States of Europe; and when he asked a great law authority for an opinion on the bearing of a precedent of the Revolution which was in his favor, we recognize that considerable uncertainty existed in matters of practice. The question whether it was permissible for the military authorities to arrest people for political reasons, and, if so, what sort of utterances would justify such an arrest, was a political one. The question how far the "necessities of war" extend, and what can be regarded as suspicious activity in the case of a political party, was another one. Lincoln had an indemnity law approved by Congress, and secured an extension of his powers, which in accordance with an old statute allowed him to appoint certain officials in the event of death or illness. But here, likewise, the decisive point was, not the laws, but daily practice, and during the latter half of the war he found it necessary to stiffen this more and ever more; the man who pardoned numberless soldiers condemned for isolated offenses, had scores of civilians jailed for agitation which tended to promote war weariness. Lincoln was attacked on both counts; on the former as a weakling, and on the latter as a tyrant.

But the complaints of tyranny were louder, for the cases of imprisonment on account of political agitation became more frequent, and the complainants were more widely known. Towards the end of the war, Seward and Stanton employed a sort of *lettre de cachet* to put spies, secret agents, and defeatists out of action. Though the President had a temperamental dislike for such measures, he had to countenance them if he was to win a war to which half the people in the country were openly opposed. In Congress a representative would exclaim within hearing of the rebels as well as of the North, that his sympathies were with the South, and that under President Lincoln there was dominant an overbearing spirit whose children were contention and murder. "I believed, what you all in your hearts believe to-day, that the South could never be conquered — never."

The man who said that was named Vallandigham, and though he lost his seat shortly afterwards, his position in Ohio was strong enough for him to be able to lead the opposition against an order issued by the military governor, to the effect that persons who did anything advantageous to the enemy would be accused as traitors or spies and sentenced by court-martial. At great public meetings, directly aimed against the President, Vallandigham fostered excitement, and described the order as a clandestine electoral intrigue upon which he would spit and trample; free men must not put up with anything of the kind, which was the work of "King" Lincoln! He announced that half a million Northerners were already enrolled in secret societies, and it was true that thousands favored the cause of the enemy. "Jefferson Davis," one such partisan exclaimed, "is a gentleman, which was more than Lincoln is!" Thereupon the governor, though himself a Democrat, took action without instructions from Washington, had Vallandigham arrested, and tried by a military commission, which sentenced him to confinement in a fortress.

Lincoln was startled by the coup — not because he disapproved of it on principle, but because he would have preferred that it should be carried out more discreetly. What must he feel, however, when in this attack the paradox of his position was made more salient than ever? Although in lonely hours he was fully aware of the inadequacy of the best he could do, although he was disheartened by internal and external conflicts and was continually wondering whether another could have done and how he himself could do better, he had hitherto always been able to take refuge in the conviction that he was a son of the people, and immune to the temptations of pride and self-glorification. Now he read in the reports that he was being stigmatized as "King Lincoln." What was he to do?

He did something novel. Canceling the sentence, he had the zealot taken out of prison and handed over to the enemy! A Northern soldier conducted this gentleman between the lines, and (the Southerners having agreed to receive him) entrusted him to the care of a rebel soldier. The effect of this humorous device was tremendous. In the South there was loud rejoicing: at length the counter revolution had begun! In the North, at first, criticism and adverse comment were rife: the man had been a State and not a war prisoner; his treatment was a dishonor to the country. Lincoln's withers were unwrung, for he knew that he had a stronger ally than lawyers or moralists — the American sense of humor. He had been able to make Vallandigham ridiculous.

The latter, now among his beloved enemies, was in an embarrassing situation. If he advised them to compromise, as he himself wished, he was afraid that his party would lose influence in the North because of the disappearance of the enemy, but if he recommended an invasion of Pennsylvania, the alarmed North would once more consolidate its forces. He had therefore to content himself with the vague counsel to hold on for another year, when the Lincoln dynasty would be beaten at the polls. The Southern president, who gave him a friendly enough reception, did not take the man seriously, so our knight errant made his way to Canada in a blockade runner, writing there an open letter in which he declared that

the South was resolved to fight to the last man, and when he got
home again Lincoln did not even pay him the compliment of ordering his rearrest, for his influence had been completely undermined
by the joke of his deportation.

Thus, in this matter likewise, Lincoln showed himself a shining
exception among statesmen, in that he did not insist upon his rights,
but discussed the pros and cons of the problem with the people.
He did so, immediately after the arrest, in one of his most notable
letters which was published. There we read of Vallandigham :

"He was not arrested because he was damaging the political prospects of the Administration, or the personal interests of the commanding general, but because he was damaging the army, upon the
existence and vigor of which the life of the nation depends. . . .
And yet let me say that in my own discretion I do not know whether
I would have ordered the arrest of Mr. Vallandigham.   While I cannot shift the responsibility from myself, I hold that, as a general
rule, the commander in the field is the better judge of the necessity
in any particular case. . . .   It gave me pain when I learned that
Mr. Vallandigham had been arrested — that is, I was pained that
there should have seemed to be a necessity for arresting him — and
it will afford me great pleasure to discharge him so soon as I can, by
any means, believe the public safety will not suffer by it.   I further
say that as the war progresses it appears to me opinion and action,
which were in great confusion at first take shape and fall into more
regular channels, so that the necessity for strong dealing with them
gradually decreases."

Thousands of those who read this letter flocked once more to the
support of the man whose fairness was admitted even by his adversaries.

Whenever, in individual cases, there was a conflict between policy
and justice, Lincoln was guided by his sense of justice.   In Missouri
the general in command wishes to exile a minister, the President
examines the man personally, and writes :

"Now, after talking with him, I tell you frankly I think he does
sympathize with the rebels, but the question remains whether such
a man, of unquestioned good moral character, who has taken such

an oath as he has, and cannot even be charged with violating it, and who can be charged with no other specific act or omission, can, with safety to the government, be exiled upon the suspicion of his secret sympathies." As in his law practice, Lincoln continues to display that inviolable regard for justice, which here and now, as formerly in Springfield, makes him protect a man of little account, while refraining from interference with the condemnation of a noted leader.

The letter just quoted was intended as a reply to the sentiments expressed, among others, by Governor Seymour, of New York, one of the most powerful of Lincoln's enemies, the two men having come into sharp conflict over the question of conscription. Not until the war had been going on for nearly two years, and only after a fierce struggle in Congress, where many of the representatives regarded the introduction of compulsory service as a despotic infringement of the rights of citizens, had the law for enforced drafts been passed, and fresh disputes were continually arising over the credits of men previously enlisted, assignable to the individual States. Inasmuch as the new law promised compensation after the war to volunteers only, the majority of those enrolled were lured to join up as free levies, and only those who comprised the residue were compulsorily drafted, while these latter were allowed to provide substitutes, if they could find them on payment of a few hundred dollars. Many of the substitutes, having taken the money, and presented themselves for training, deserted at the first opportunity.

Seymour, who was interfering with the operation of the compulsory service law in the largest city of the Union, when asked by Lincoln to come and see him, answered three weeks later that he would write about the matter, but omitted to do so, not wishing to compromise himself by entering into relations with the President of the United States; nor did he reply to an invitation from Stanton. When, that summer, there was a great rising in New York, led by foreigners, to resist the draft, when for several days murder and arson were rife in the town, when Negroes were lynched by the mob and an orphan asylum for colored children was burned to ashes, the governor spoke soft words to the rioters, merely advising them to behave themselves, and then he would help them to get what they wanted.   In face of such a mood in the business metropolis of the North, Lincoln had to carry on the war.

At other times discontent and anger burst from him with all the fierceness of a mountain torrent. When, a year later, Chicago demurred against a new draft, the citizens sent the editor of the *Chicago Tribune* and two other persons to Stanton and then to the President to protest. Lincoln listened silently for a time to the arguments that were being exchanged. Then "he suddenly lifted his head, and turned on us a black and frowning face. 'Gentlemen,' he said, 'after Boston, Chicago has been the chief instrument in bringing this war on the country. The Northwest has opposed the South as New England has opposed the South. It is you who are largely responsible for making blood flow as it has. You called for war until we had it. You called for Emancipation, and I have given it to you. Whatever you have asked you have had. Now you come here begging to be let off from the call for men which I have made to carry out the war you have demanded. You ought to be ashamed of yourselves. I have a right to expect better things of you. Go home and raise your six thousand extra men. And you, Medill, you are acting like a coward. You and your *Tribune* have had more influence than any paper in the Northwest in making this war. You can influence great masses, and yet you cry to be spared at a moment when your cause is suffering. Go home and send us those men.'"

The impression produced by this rare outburst, such as no one ever expected from Abraham Lincoln, was so powerful, the fundamental honesty of this wrath and the moral fervor that animated these invectives were so overwhelming, that the member of the deputation who reports the incident tells us how he himself was convinced of his error by the thundering Jupiter into whom the gently ironical lover of his fellows seemed to have been suddenly transformed.

IV

The South had become a fortress. Now that the last corridor leading to neutral lands had been closed, and now that few merchant captains were bold and skillful enough to run the blockade, there had set in a general lack of food, clothing, and munitions of war. It was a land almost deprived of salt; in winter there was no coal, in summer no ice; wood had to be used for shoes instead of leather; there was no suitable diet for the sick, and there was a shortage of drugs — a country where hunger gnawed and the wastage of men was irreplaceable, one in which nothing but dictatorship and harsh measures could prevent revolts. Here, likewise, compulsory service, which was ultimately extended to all males between seventeen and fifty, allowed a paid substitute to be provided, so that in the South no less than in the North people grumbled that it was a rich men's war in which the poor men had to fight the battles; but these complaints were voiced under the rose, for the critics and the press were muzzled by Draconian edicts, and if one should wish to form a true estimate of the moderation of Lincoln's measures, one need merely compare them with Jefferson Davis' extension of martial law.

Only in one matter, during this latter half of the war, was the South in a comparatively advantageous position; there was a passionate determination to continue the struggle, and opposition to it was almost unheard, whereas in the North the adversaries of the war raised an unceasing hubbub; the obstinate spirit of defiance which in the South had replaced the proud enthusiasm of the early days was still unbroken, and indeed went so far that there was no eagerness to effect exchanges of prisoners, and often enough the obligations implied in such exchanges were evaded. For thousands of Southerners who had been taken prisoners by the North, or had been living in the North when the war began, and had been allowed to return home on pledging themselves not to bear arms against the Union, had after their return been officially exempted from their oath and enrolled or reënrolled in the ranks; but when the like procedure was advocated in the North, Lincoln rejected the plan as an infringement of the elementary principles of morality. Was it to be wondered at that the growing hatred should be turned against the prisoners? The cruelties inflicted on them were so abominable that the North shrank from retaliation. Especially ruthless was the treatment of recaptured Negroes, one group of whom was massacred without trial, in the design of suffocating this greatest of all dangers by terrorist methods. Inflamed by the news of such atrocities, however, some of the Northern generals, like Butler in New Orleans, were brutal in their treatment of conquered States, and the behavior of Sherman's army in its march from Atlanta to the sea went beyond retaliation in its excesses.

The nature of this struggle as a civil war grew plainly more paradoxical as the years went by. Secret societies, passing by such names as Sons of Liberty, Knights of the Golden Circle, Order of the American Knights, and so on, were, with their indeterminate moral foundation, attractive chiefly to the uneducated — but, since their members were armed, and because they were spies, they were a serious factor which had to be reckoned with. Lincoln kept himself and the government informed, had his own spies in the societies and arrested a leader now and again, but refrained from making a sweeping attack. He still tried to attain his ends by wisdom, patience, and irony, usually spoke of the enemy as "these Southern gentlemen", and was ever on the alert to insist that the South must not be regarded as a foreign country. He had been most unfavorably impressed by the phrase: "Drive the invaders from our soil." Upon reading it, he said, "Will our generals never get that idea out of their heads? The whole country is our soil."

But this twofold character of the Civil War could not fail, often enough, to inspire Lincoln with grievous suspicions. When McClellan, having defeated his enemy and teacher Lee, had refrained from following up the advantage, wasting a year and more in futile hesitations, Lincoln had confided his doubts in private conversations. Now, when Meade, who had been reproached with inactivity after his victory, begged to be relieved of his command, the President wrote to him as follows:

"I am sorry now to be the author of the slightest pain to you. But I was in such deep distress myself that I could not restrain some expression of it. I have been oppressed nearly ever since the battles of Gettysburg by what appeared to be evidences that yourself and General Couch and General Smith were not seeking a collision with the enemy, but were trying to get him across the river without

another battle. What these evidences were, if you please, I hope
to tell you at some time when we shall both feel better." Then
come various details, and an enumeration of unutilized possibilities.
The writer goes on :

"Again, my dear general, I do not believe you appreciate the
magnitude of the misfortune involved in Lee's escape. He was
within your easy grasp, and to have closed upon him would, in
connection with our other late successes, have ended the war."

Lincoln probably took the wiser course when he determined not
to send this letter, but the decision to withhold it did not imply any
change in his inner conviction that the country was being injured
by his leading generals' mistaken notions of honor or other wrong-
headed sentiments. When a man as just as he speaks of proofs,
we may be sure that he would have destroyed the draft of his letter
had he subsequently come to recognize that the proofs were not
convincing; but since, year after year, the same suspicions recur
as regards different persons occupying similar posts, we may assume
that nothing but a desire to retain the victorious general's services
for the country can have led him to keep them to himself on this
occasion.

How poignant must be the feelings in the heart of this ruler who
regards "the whole country as our soil", this man whose brother-
in-law is fighting for the South, who has the tragical nature of the
Civil War forced upon his attention day by day, both officially
and personally, who is himself conscious of being partly a Southerner
because of his descent from that unknown grandfather — and now
detects the same conflict in the feelings of his own generals, each
one of whom is urged towards victory by the promptings of ambition, but whom a persistent and ineradicable sense of chivalry keeps
from attempting the final destruction of their comrades in the
South. A great game of hazard is here being played, and to Lincoln,
the philosopher, must it not sometimes really seem like a game, one
whose rules are uncertain and whose end is obscure?

He therefore never put any formal obstacles in the way of would-
be negotiators. He was not afraid to allow two of the leaders of the
Northern opposition to the war to pass the lines in order to talk

matters over with Jefferson Davis; but, after a discussion limited
to the topics of religion and war with France, they came back con-
verted. Greeley, who in the perpetual modifications of his policy
was always consistent in the way he worked against Lincoln, had,
at first, been dissatisfied with the President's hesitation in the matter
of abolition, and was now dissatisfied with resoluteness, wanted a
compromise, and wrote to inform him that two emissaries with
letters from Davis were waiting on the Canadian frontier. Lincoln,
esteeming the influence of the *New York Tribune* more highly than
its editor's motives, had recourse once again to the shrewd device
of burdening men who wanted to make themselves important with
responsibility for what they proposed, and sent Greeley to Niagara
— where the editor found that the emissaries had no authority to
treat. Greeley, mortified by this ironical handling, and eager to
get his own back, renewed his furious onslaughts on the President.
The latter was unperturbed, saying that when he had been a lad in
the West they had gone on cobbling their boots over and over again
until the leather was too rotten to hold the stitches — like Greeley.

Just before Greeley went to Niagara, Lincoln had issued an open
letter "to whom it may concern":

"Any proposition which embraces the restoration of peace, the
integrity of the whole Union, and the abandonment of slavery, and
which comes by and with an authority that can control the armies
now at war against the United States, will be received and considered by the Executive Government of the United States; . . .
and the bearer or bearers thereof shall have safe conduct both
ways."

This offer was really a disavowal of all agents who might attempt
to negotiate between North and South. When Lincoln's old friend
Stephens, now Vice President of the Confederacy and leader of the
moderates, basing himself on Vallandigham and furnished with
letters from "President Jefferson Davis", wanted to come to Washington in order to negotiate, Lincoln's answer was a curt refusal:
"The request of A. H. Stephens is inadmissible. The customary
agents and channels are adequate for all needful communication
and conference between the United States forces and insurgents."

V

"God must like the common people, or he would not have made so many of them." Such were the splendid words, that would never have occurred to a rich man or to one who had grown up in a study, in which Lincoln once expressed his feelings in favor of white and colored labor. Another time, he said, "I hold that if the Almighty had ever made a set of men that should do all the eating and none of the work, he would have made them with mouths only, and no hands; and that if he had ever made another class, that he had intended should do all the work and none of the eating, he would have made them without mouths and with all hands."

Living though he was under the pressure of daily cares, of petty successes and failures, in the midst of party struggles, earthbound, he never lost sight of the guiding star of his endeavor, but, directing his gaze more and more fervently upward, realized the need, among concrete figures and positions, for stressing ever more insistently the moral law of the struggle. In a speech delivered toward the close of the war, he said: "The world is in want of a good definition of the word liberty. We all declare ourselves to be for liberty, but we do not all mean the same thing. Some mean that a man can do as he pleases with himself and his property. With others it means that some men can do as they please with other men and other men's labor. Each of these things is called liberty, although they are entirely different. To give an illustration: A shepherd drives the wolf from the throat of his sheep when attacked by him, and the sheep of course thanks the shepherd for the protection of his life; but the wolf denounces him as despoiling the sheep of his liberty — especially if it be a black sheep."

Here, once more, we have one of those images in which the farmer becomes a logician, while the statesman enters into the outlook of the farmer, and thus is able to create immemorable parables for the people.

He is especially successful with such parables in dealing with the main problem of his career, the simplicity of his utterances giving them the force of proverbs: "Whenever I hear any one arguing for

slavery, I feel a strong impulse to see it tried on him personally."
Two ladies come from Tennessee, to beg for the freeing of their
husbands, who are prisoners of war, and when one of them, who pays
three visits, insists with unwearied emphasis that her husband is a
very religious man, Lincoln, granting her request, delivers himself
as follows:

"You say your husband is a religious man; tell him when you
meet him, that I say I am not much of a judge of religion; but that,
in my opinion, the religion that sets men to rebel and fight against
their government, because, as they think, that government does
not sufficiently help some men to eat their bread in the sweat of
other men's faces, is not the sort of religion upon which people can
get to heaven."

He spoke of this afterwards as his shortest and best speech.
Again, writing in an autograph album: "I never knew a man who
wished himself to be a slave. Consider if you know any good thing
that no man desires for himself."

But the problem had not been solved by the issue of the proclamation. No one overlooked its historical value; a big picture was
painted, showing the cabinet in the momentous session, and Lincoln,
when sitting for his portrait, discussed the details with the painter,
as if it had all happened a hundred years before, instead of only
two. Yet the extremists still mistrusted him; Sumner wanted in a
speedy and radical fashion to get to work with the formula of the
French Revolution: All citizens are equal before the law. Nevertheless a bill which proposed a simple prohibition of slavery in the
United States, as an addendum to the Constitution, while it passed
the Senate, was rejected by the House as late as the summer of 1864.
Lincoln, who regarded his proclamation as a war measure which
would be invalidated by the end of the war, wanted to leave it to
the electors, by an addendum, to free the Southern Negroes, or,
preferably, the black soldiers.

For meanwhile, as Lincoln had foreseen, the main purpose of the
proclamation had been fulfilled. At the beginning of the last year
of the war, one hundred thousand Negroes had been enrolled; and
by the end of the war, one hundred fifty thousand were fighting

under the banner of the Union. "What a disgrace for their white fellow soldiers," exclaimed the Southerners, and to some extent public opinion in Europe followed the same trend, ignoring the fact that the South had unhesitatingly enlisted other men of color, the Indians, and never anticipating the grotesque expedient to which the Southerners would have recourse in the closing weeks of the struggle, reducing their previous contention to absurdity. The Democrats, on the other hand, were imploring or angrily urging Lincoln to revoke the proclamation, and thus to secure a speedy though mediocre peace. His answer was : "I shall not, in any event, . . . as Executive, ever return to slavery any person who is freed by the terms of that proclamation, or by any of the acts of Congress. . . . I wish to see in process of disappearing that only thing which could ever bring this nation to civil war."

All the same, the first enfranchisement had brought new difficulties in its train. Lincoln's fundamental idea of freeing the Negroes while simultaneously sending them out of the country, this premonition of the disaster in which a mingling of the races might one day involve America, had induced him to found an experimental colony on the coast of San Domingo, but he had handed over the Negroes to a swindling agent, whose contracts he had only been able to cancel on the formal ground that they had not been properly sealed. Now the protection of the State and Lincoln's personal intervention made it possible to ship the discontented Negro colonists back to Washington, where they could be given useful work to do in the camps.

At first only a few of the governors of the border States would risk a trial of Negroes in the army. To one of these, Johnson, Governor of Tennessee, who was to succeed him in the presidential chair, Lincoln wrote encouragingly, saying that a man of so much ability and in so favorable a position should undertake the formation of Negro corps :

"When I speak of your position, I mean that of an eminent citizen of a slave State and himself a slaveholder. The colored population is the great available and yet unavailed-of force for restoring the Union. The bare sight of fifty thousand armed and drilled black soldiers upon the banks of the Mississippi would end the rebellion at once. And who doubts that we can present that sight if we but take hold in earnest."

He also insisted upon the need for treating black prisoners exactly like white ones. But soon there were setbacks. On the landing stages in a Maryland river, the black troops disseminated alarm and disorder among the whites, an officer was killed, there was rioting and murder in Missouri, and complaints arrived from Kentucky that the militia was simply impressing Negroes without their consent or any legal warrant.

Incidents of this kind gave rise to numerous attacks on Lincoln, which he never warded off more effectively than in an open letter he sent to a loyalist mass meeting in Springfield, to debate therein with an absent opponent:

"There are those who are dissatisfied with me. To such I would say: You desire peace, and you blame me that we do not have it. But how can we attain it? There are but three conceivable ways: First — to suppress the rebellion by force of arms. This I am trying to do. Are you for it? If you are, so far we are agreed. If you are not for it, a *second* way is to give up the Union. I am against this. Are you for it? If you are, you should say so plainly. If you are not for *force*, nor yet for *dissolution*, there only remains some imaginable *compromise*. . . .

"You say you will not fight to free negroes. Some of them seem willing to fight for you; but no matter. Fight you, then, exclusively to save the Union. I issued the proclamation on purpose to aid you in saving the Union. I thought that, . . . to whatever extent the negroes should cease helping the enemy, to that extent it weakened the enemy in his resistance to you. Do you think differently? I thought whatever negroes can be got to do as soldiers, leaves just so much less for white soldiers to do in saving the Union. Does it appear otherwise to you? But negroes, like other people, act upon motives. Why should they do anything for us, if we will do nothing for them? If they stake their lives for us, they must be prompted by the strongest motive, even the promise of freedom. And the promise, being made, must be kept."

Such is the Socratic method which Lincoln, as late as the third year of the struggle, uses when discussing with his people the motives, aims, and prospects of a war which he can only hope to win if the people have a thorough understanding of its intellectual basis. For there are millions of farmers and business men, and there are other millions of fathers, women, and soldiers, who can grasp this bold logic, this clear method of exposition; and precisely because his discourse contains no superlatives, because it is devoid of phrase making, they can follow a train of thought that could never have been thus formulated by a man of the Douglas type, but only by one who had lived for many years the life of the common people.

Yet this is the same man who, speaking with the voice of a wise old father, refers to the matter in another speech thus: "Upon a clear conviction of duty, I resolved to turn that [the negro] element of strength to account; and I am responsible for it to the American people, to the Christian world, to history, and in my final account to God."

VI

The White House is brilliantly illuminated, and Washington is thronged with strangers, for Grant is coming to-day to take over the supreme command of all the armies, with the rank of lieutenant general, which before him in this country none but Washington has held. The streets are filled with carriages and riders, the rooms of the executive mansion with officers, diplomats, and smartly dressed women, for it is March, 1864, Grant has captured Vicksburg, Meade has defeated Lee at Gettysburg, everything is taking a favorable turn, the multitude has received an answer to the refrain which has been voiced all over the country: "Abraham Lincoln, give us a man."

But, like Lincoln three years earlier, Grant had made an unobtrusive entry into the capital, turning up that evening accompanied by his little boy, whom he always had with him in the field, and now, quitting his hotel unnoticed, one officer among many, he made his way to the White House, which he was entering for the first time. A vague dread of intrigues and scandals, and, above all, a fear that the politicians would try to influence him, had kept this soldier away from Washington. Nor, now, does he have himself announced; he will find tall Father Abraham for himself; it is only half-past nine, and there is plenty of time. One comfort is that his wife need not thrust her way into this turmoil! In a few moments, however, Lincoln's sharp eyes have picked him out; soon they are both ringed round and can no longer move — the rather small, bronzed officer beside the long-armed giant in a swallow-tail, the two men united by their intrinsic seriousness and by a diffidence they have never been able to shake off, though both of them have long been accustomed to command.

At length they are able to get away from the press of people, and take refuge behind a sofa. Grant is introduced to Mrs. Lincoln and to the cabinet members, but the crowd wants to see him, and with internal trepidation the fearless general has to stand on the sofa and allow himself to be clapped — saying afterwards, "This has been the warmest campaign I have witnessed during the war." To prepare Grant for the ceremony of conferring the new commission, the President gave him a copy of the speech he himself proposed to make on that occasion, saying, "you are, perhaps, not so much accustomed to public speaking as I am", and asking him to stress two points in an answer of equal brevity — a word or two which might tend to minimize the jealousy of the other generals, and something about kindly feelings towards the Army of the Potomac. But when, next day, the ceremony took place in the presence of the cabinet, Grant, reading aloud the little address he had penciled on half a sheet of notepaper, had to contend with difficulties like those General Washington had encountered when delivering his first official speech; and the three well-formed sentences did not contain a single word about the two matters for which Lincoln had stipulated. Nothing but the general's determination to remain independent of the politicians can account for this little difference with the President.

It remained the only one. For though Stanton and Halleck had warned Grant not to tell Lincoln too much about his plans, the general found that Lincoln did not even ask about them. After

their short, matter-of-fact conversation, they had taken to one
another, but Grant felt ill at ease in this city, and refused Mary's
invitation to a banquet :

"I must be in Tennessee at a given time."

"Mrs. Lincoln's dinner without you would be 'Hamlet' with
Hamlet left out."

"I appreciate the honor, but time is very important now. I
ought to be at the front, and a dinner to me means a million dollars
a day lost to the country."

When he had gone, Lincoln said, "I hardly know what to think
of him. He's the quietest little fellow you ever saw. He makes
the least fuss of any man I ever knew. I believe on several occasions
he has been in this room a minute or so before I knew he was here.
It's about so all around. The only evidence you have that he's in
any particular place is that he makes things move. . . . As soon as
I put a man in command of the army, he'd come to me with the plan
of a campaign, and about as much as to say, 'Now I don't believe
I can do it, but if you say so I'll try it on', and so put the responsibility of success or failure on me. They all wanted *me* to be the
general. Now it isn't so with Grant. He hasn't told me what
his plans are. I don't know, and I don't want to know. I am glad
to find a man who can go ahead without me. When any of the rest
set out on a campaign they'd look over matters and pick out some
one thing they were short of and they knew I couldn't give them,
and tell me they couldn't hope to win unless they had it — and it
was generally cavalry. Now when Grant took hold I was waiting
to see what his pet impossibility would be, and I reckoned it would
be cavalry, of course, for we hadn't horses enough to mount what
men we had. There were fifteen thousand men, or thereabouts, up
near Harper's Ferry, and no horses to put them on. Well, the
other day Grant sent to me about those very men, just as I expected ;
but what he wanted to know was whether he could make infantry
of 'em or disband 'em."

Thus at length had Lincoln, towards the end of the war and his
life, found a man of his own caliber, a man equal to himself in simplicity, straightforwardness, and insight. Since Grant now took

charge at the center (where, by the way, he retained Meade in a post of honor and full responsibility), he appointed to his former command his friend, the swiftly moving and clear-sighted Sherman, an officer who was as strict with his subordinates as he was gentle and friendly toward every one, toward animals and children, and who continued, even when winning splendid victories in the later months of the year, to look upon Grant as his master. Now Sherman, with a superior force, began to push back his adversary Johnston upon Atlanta, and finally, in September, achieved the conquest of this leading position well within enemy territory, which thus became the base for further operations.

Grant, the first officer to ask nothing of the President, because he expected nothing, found that Lincoln, in return, asked nothing from him — because he expected everything.

"Not expecting to see you again before the spring campaign opens, I wish to express in this way my entire satisfaction with what you have done up to this time, so far as I understand it. The particulars of your plan I neither know nor seek to know. You are vigilant and self-reliant; and, pleased with this, I wish not to obtrude any constraints or restraints upon you. . . . If there is anything wanting which is within my power to give, do not fail to let me know it. And now, with a brave army and a just cause, may God sustain you." Once more we have Lincoln's last and finest style. The tone of the father.

According to military experts, as a commander Grant was outmatched by his opponent Lee. In the former's own words, his tactics were to keep on hammering, to seek out and destroy the enemy whenever and wherever he could; for the enemy was no longer in a position to replace his losses; the more territory the Northerners occupied, the wider the area from which they could recruit, whereas the Southerners were losing all the time. Nevertheless, Lee was able again and again to slip out of the noose. In the end, the duel came to resemble a game of chess in which one player still has nearly all his pieces, while the other, with very few left, can put up a good fight, being the better player. Thus in the spring there was an indecisive struggle on last year's battlefields;

Northern reverses in June, threatening Grant's position, but not causing Lincoln serious alarm; and finally in July, when Grant with one hundred fifty thousand men was already close to Petersburg and Richmond, Washington was actually threatened by one of Lee's generals, just as it had been three years earlier.

The enemy was so near that he was able to attack one of the forts of the capital, the town was practically undefended, being manned almost exclusively by raw recruits, the Southerners had crossed the Potomac, and with a bold coup they might have seized President and cabinet, even as they might have done at the outset of the war. A steamer was kept in readiness to carry the heads of the government to some safer place, should there be need. Lincoln was too much of a fatalist, and too weary, to be afraid of death. He visited the forts, heard the bullets whistling, remained perfectly calm, wired to the general: "Let us keep on the alert, but let us keep cool." Welles describes him as sitting at noon in the shade, leaning against the breastwork of a fort, his back towards the enemy. In this comfortable attitude, he is obviously much more at home than Grant was at the White House.

The troops sent by the latter to relieve the capital arrived in time to drive away the enemy, who was, however, able to withdraw unmolested across the Potomac.

VII

The fate of the country turned on the next presidential election. Though the last election had intensified the conflict, none the less that conflict might have been avoided had the South shown a little moderation. Now the struggle was raging, and a decision was at hand, but this decision depended far more on the next election than the outbreak of the war had depended on the former one. If a Democrat were returned to head the administration, he would not need, as Lincoln had needed, to wait until March before making his presence felt; his mere election in the beginning of November would suffice to paralyze the Northern forces and to invigorate the declining strength of the South, for both sides knew that the Democrats aimed at peace without victory; and, on the other hand, the election of a Republican President would mean a fight to a finish.

For Lincoln this alternative was complicated by the fact that his own party was hostile. The radicals detested him because his hesitation at the outset had prevented his taking a clear line upon the slavery question, and because, when he subsequently decided for abolition, he had done so only as a war measure; the members of the Greeley clique had personal reasons for wanting another than Lincoln as President, negotiating at first with General Butler and General Rosecrans, but inclining at last to unite in support of Frémont. Of these factions in Missouri, Lincoln said, "Either party would rather see the defeat of their adversary than that of Jefferson Davis. You ought to have your heads knocked together."

But Lincoln's most troublesome opponent was not at the front, like these generals; he was in the cabinet, and in daily converse with the President. This was Chase, who had done the State invaluable service as a financier, but had never been personally loyal to his chief, and, under the promptings of ambition, had already in the winter been inconspicuously putting himself forward as a possible candidate — doing so primarily as a critic of the President. In the beginning of the fourth year of Lincoln's term he wrote to a newspaper editor: "Had there been here an Administration in the true sense of the word — a President conferring with his Cabinet and taking their united judgments, and with their aid enforcing activity, economy, and energy in all departments of the public service — we could have spoken boldly and defied the world. But our condition here has always been very different. I preside over the funnel; everybody else, and especially the Secretaries of War and the Navy, over the spigots — and keep them well open, too. Mr. Seward conducts the foreign relations with very little let or help from anybody. There is no unity and no system, except so far as it is departmental. . . . How, under such circumstances, can anybody announce a policy which can only be made respectable by union, wisdom, and courage?"

He wrote in like terms to another correspondent: "The Administration cannot be continued as it is. There is, in fact, no Administration, properly speaking. There are departments and there is a President. This latter leaves administration substantially to the heads of the former, deciding himself comparatively few questions. These heads act with almost absolute independence of each other."

Inasmuch as Chase thus criticized the cabinet from two conflicting outlooks, he charged the President at one and the same time with being too dictatorial and with not being dictatorial enough, and was only right to this extent, that Lincoln, as his faithful adherent Welles recognized, was by temperament disinclined for systematized work, preferred to talk matters over with one person at a time, and therefore did actually neglect on occasions to keep some of the cabinet members properly informed. It was permissible to write such criticisms in a diary, as Welles did; but it was an outrage to do what Chase did, to write them, a year before the expiration of the presidential term, to strangers who would certainly pass them on, and to use the tone proper to a discussion of events long past when speaking of a man with whom he was then actually collaborating from day to day. When he was subsequently, in a party document, spoken of as a presidential candidate, he assured Lincoln that he had made no move in the matter, and, as so often before, tendered his resignation.

"My friends," rejoined Lincoln, "bring the documents to me, but I do not read them; they tell me what they think fit to tell me, but I do not inquire for more. . . . Whether you shall remain at the head of the Treasury Department is a question which I will not allow myself to consider from any standpoint other than my judgment of the public service, and, in that view, I do not perceive occasion for a change."

The writer's coldness was unmistakable. Lincoln fully understood the situation.

"I have determined to shut my eyes as far as possible to anything of the sort. Mr. Chase makes a good secretary, and I shall keep him where he is. If he becomes President, all right. I hope we may never have a worse man. I have observed with regret his plan of strengthening himself. Whenever he sees that an important matter is troubling me, if I am compelled to decide in a way to give offence to a man of some influence, he always ranges himself in opposition to me and persuades the victim that he has been hardly dealt with, and that he would have arranged it very differently. . . . Ordinarily he discharges the duties of a public office with greater ability than any man I know. Mind, I say 'ordinarily', but he has become irritable, uncomfortable, so that he is never perfectly happy unless he is thoroughly miserable, and able to make everybody else just as uncomfortable as he is himself."

The relations between the two men fluctuate for several months. Sometimes Lincoln is really pleased to know that Chase is put out. "You were brought up on a farm, were you not?" he asked an acquaintance. "Then you know what a 'chin-fly' is? My brother and I were once ploughing on an Illinois farm. I was driving the horse and he was holding the plough. The horse was lazy; but on one occasion he rushed across the field so that I, with my long legs, could scarcely keep up with him. On reaching the end of the furrow, I found an enormous chin-fly fastened on him and knocked it off. My brother asked me what I did that for. I told him I didn't want the old horse bitten in that way. 'Why,' said my brother, 'that's all that made him go!' Now if Mr. Chase has a presidential chin-fly biting him, I'm not going to knock it off, if it will only make his department go."

There he sits in his armchair, the President of the United States, and when he speaks of his youth, of how "my brother and I were once ploughing", the romance of his life is suddenly revealed, and also the simple greatness of a people in which such an ascent has more than once been possible, to the signal advantage of the community. This it is, the aura of the common man from the West, an aura that never leaves him, and the innate slowness of his nature, which in decisive hours make even the doubters rally to his side — for, whatever they may say or feel against him, the straightforward seriousness, the shrewd reflectiveness, to which his ever more deeply furrowed countenance bears witness, the paternal look and tone with which he contemplates and in which he addresses men, his art of parable which always pierces to the core of people's lives, combine to rivet his faithful adherents to his cause, and to ensnare the waverers.

This man whose actions were resisted, misunderstood, or at best a topic of controversy — what enshrined his name, throughout these years, in the hearts of the people? His answers, his speeches, and the open letters in which he seems to take counsel with the nation. That was why his friends began the campaign with two columns of "Lincoln Stories" in the newspapers; and that was why nothing helped him more effectively than his remark to a delegation : "I have not permitted myself, Gentlemen, to conclude that I am the best man in the country; but I am reminded in this connection of a story of an old Dutch farmer, who remarked to a companion once : 'It is not best to swap horses when crossing a stream.'" The phrase is overwhelming in its brevity and force, intelligible to any farmer's wife, and withal pointed enough to down a lawyer.

Thus it happened that, when the convention met at Baltimore in June, the generals and Chase were out of the running, and it was resolved : "That we approve and applaud the practical wisdom, the unselfish patriotism, and the unswerving fidelity to the Constitution . . . with which Abraham Lincoln has discharged . . . the great duties and responsibilities of the presidential office; . . . that we approve, especially, the proclamation of emancipation."

At Lincoln's desire, the legitimation of this act by an amendment to the constitution was made a cardinal point of the program. This was a very dangerous feature from the campaigning point of view, but he insisted on clarity. All the Republicans nominated him for a second term, with the exception of the delegate from Missouri, the slave State which produced the largest number of radicals.

The wording of his acceptance was remarkably cool. "I regard this nomination for a second term of office, by no means as a personal compliment, but only as an expression of the general view that I am perhaps better fitted to carry a difficult task to a conclusion than might be one who had not been so severely trained for it." He adds : "The nomination is gratefully accepted, as the resolutions of the convention, called the platform, are heartily approved."

This time he had not asked the schoolmaster to help, as he had when accepting the nomination four years earlier. Had he done so, his friend would certainly have advised him against using the third person in this chilly way, which can only be explained as a further expression of the reserve that had already made him avoid any sort of canvassing for the nomination. In this matter Lincoln, though in general he groaned under formalities, from the wearing of a collar, down to the assumption of an official manner, stood upon his dignity as President, and would not on any account lower it by showing the eagerness of a candidate.

There were dissensions among the Democrats as well. Some of them, like Vallandigham, wanted peace at any price; others, like Seymour, wanted to continue the war. The only declaration on which they could agree was "that the war is a failure." Thus neither a defeatist nor a hotspur would serve their turn as presidential candidate. The best would be a cashiered general, for whom one faction could vote on the ground that the war had been badly waged, and the other on the ground that it must be speedily ended. Who was the heaven-sent person to fill this rôle? McClellan obviously. Had he not been the most conspicuous victim of the party now in power? In his speech, he did not go so far as to declare that the war had been a failure, but he allowed glimpses of his opinion that he could have made a better job of it. In this dilemma he and his party tried to minimize the victories of the last twelve months; and since, as luck would have it, Grant made a further advance at this juncture, they did their best to ignore it. On the other hand, the Southerners' raid on Washington, the unsuccessful siege of Petersburg, the heavy losses and desertions, suited their book admirably, for it was their strange fate to have, in the midst of a war, to hope for a weakening of the national will to fight.

"This convention does explicitly declare . . . that, after four years of failure to restore the Union by the experiment of war, . . . justice, humanity, liberty, and the public welfare demand that immediate efforts be made for a cessation of hostilities, with a view to an ultimate convention of the States or other peaceable means, to the end that at the earliest practicable moment peace may be restored on the basis of the Federal Union of the States."

The danger of this formula lay in its implication that Lincoln did not want peace, whereas it was Jefferson Davis who did not want a Federal Union of the States. As regards future possibilities, the formula left the main question undecided, and the door open for decades of new disturbances, for on such a basis no one could say whether a State belonging to a Federal Union was entitled to withdraw from it — a right which the Democrat Jackson had denied. The opposing party was shocked both by the formula and by the choice of a candidate, for in the event of McClellan's election, Lincoln would have had to make peace though the war had not been fought to a finish, and it would have been almost impossible for him to constrain himself to such a course.

As had happened four years before, the real hubbub did not begin till after the nominations, and these months during the last summer of his life were probably more exciting than any others of his life; indeed, he received a number of urgent demands to withdraw before the election. Weed, the greatest of party managers, declared that he had no chance of success, and formed a cabal with Greeley; the chairman of the central Republican committee advised him to make overtures for peace, as a means for saving himself at the polls; two leading abolitionists described him in a manifesto as a usurper driven onward by the lust for power; in the Northwest, a rising was planned for August, to put an end to the war; and committees came to him with a request that he would make way for another Republican candidate. The name of this candidate was Grant.

The previous year, some of the newspapers had already referred to Grant as the coming man. When a friend had asked him what was his attitude toward such promptings, he had replied that he had as big a job on hand as one man need desire, and that even if he might become President some day, it would not be in Lincoln's time. At this very moment, Grant's friend was summoned to Washington to see Lincoln. Only after a discussion of the political situation did this friend show the President Grant's letter. Lincoln said, "My son, you will never know how gratifying that is to me. No man knows, when that presidential grub gets to gnawing at him, just how deep it will get until he has tried it; and I didn't know but what there was one gnawing at Grant." Not until afterwards did the visitor learn that Lincoln's real reason in sending for him had been to inquire about this very matter.

When in June a gathering was held to do honor to Grant — with the thinly disguised object of running him for the presidency — Lincoln, invited to participate, wrote:

"It is impossible for me to attend. I approve nevertheless of whatever may tend to strengthen and sustain General Grant and the noble armies now under his command. He and his brave soldiers are now in the midst of their great trial, and I trust that at your meeting you will so shape your good words that they may turn to men and guns, moving to his and their support."

In this priceless comment, which refers Grant to his work on the edge of things, Puck once more sits beside the mentor, and the roguishness of the writer's humor must have been obvious.

For even now Lincoln is not quite certain how deep this grub, that is nourished on longing for fame and love of popular acclamation, may have gnawed in Grant; he is afraid lest it may have distracted the general's thoughts from the army, and he therefore sends a confidant to the front to make inquiries. At the first question with regard to designs of running him for the presidency, Grant says, striking his fists hard on the strap arms of his camp chair, "They can't compel me to do it." So emphatic a gesture was rarely seen from General Grant.

"Have you said this to the President?" asks the visitor.

"No, I have not thought it worth while to assure the President of my opinion. I consider it as important for the cause that he should be elected as that the army should be successful in the field."

Lincoln was greatly relieved at the news. "I told you they could not get him to run till he had closed out the rebellion." But he had wanted confirmation of this presentiment. Earlier he had said of Grant, "If he takes Richmond, let him have the presidency," and this was Lincoln's true feeling. He had no hesitation about fighting McClellan, whom he felt to be his inferior; but Grant was as important as a soldier as he himself was as a statesman, and was in addition the arm which his head now needed; besides, any rivalry there had been, had been purely behind the scenes, and never a public matter of the electoral struggle, and so far as Grant had political aims they were those which Lincoln had been fulfilling for three years past.

Hence the latter's uneasiness when he feared that the commander might be going to enter the field against him; hence the relief when he found that Grant intended to stick to the job with the army.

How different must be his feelings towards Chase, who had forfeited his confidence through the before-mentioned intrigue. Now Lincoln took the Secretary of the Treasury at his word, accepted the resignation that had been tendered so frequently, and let him go at a moment when such action in the case of so prominent an abolitionist could not fail to have an unfavorable reaction upon the electoral struggle. He even ventured to call for new levies at the most difficult moment in that struggle. His friends urged him against the step, but he said, "I am quite willing the people should understand the issue. My reëlection will mean that the rebellion is to be crushed by force of arms. We must lose nothing even if I am defeated." It was in this magnanimous spirit that he approached the struggle at home as well as the struggle against the enemy, saying in a public address, "We accepted this war; we did not begin it. We accepted it for an object, and when that object is accomplished the war will end, and I hope to God that it will never end until that object is accomplished."

In this manly tone we hear once more the voice of the fighter, whose rôle Lincoln the father has still to play for a few months.

For the calling up of new levies had aroused a storm from both sides. "The arbitrary act of a tyrant!" exclaimed the newspapers. "He has violated personal liberty, the freedom of the press, the Constitution, the right of asylum; he has frustrated his opponents' will to peace; has within a brief period misused every power put into a dictator's hands in war-time. If Lincoln is not elected, he will do everything he can, at the eleventh hour, to ruin the government." His old friend Swett writes home from New York:

"The malicious foes of Lincoln are calling . . . a Buffalo convention to supplant him. They are . . . Sumner, Chase, Frémont, Wilson, etc.

" The Democrats are conspiring to resist the draft. We seized this morning three thousand pistols going to Indiana for distribution. The war Democrats are trying to make the Chicago nominee a loyal

man. The peace Democrats are trying to get control of the government and, through alliance with Jefferson Davis, to get control of
both armies and make universal revolution necessary.

" The most fearful things are probable."

The most fearful things, conspiracy — why not assassination?
"If they kill me," said Lincoln calmly, "the next man will be just as
bad for them. In a country like this, where our habits are simple,
and must be, assassination is always possible, and will come if they
are determined on it."

At this time of crisis, when bitterness of feeling was at its climax,
in the middle of August, the landlord of an inn in a little Pennsylvania town found one morning an inscription on a window pane,
scratched with a diamond. The words ran : "Abe Lincoln departed
this life Aug. 13th, 1864, By the effects of Poison."

The finder paid little attention to the matter, for the date mentioned was already past, and the style of the inscription suggested
that it must be the work of a lunatic. Not until eight months afterwards, when the whole country was ringing with the name of an
assassin, did he recall that at the time in question the room had been
tenanted by an actor named Booth.

VIII

In the scantily furnished room of the home for convalescent
soldiers where the President lived in the summer, Carl Schurz sat
opposite him one evening, and listened as he soliloquized.

"He spoke like a man who needed to pour his heart out, who
wanted to give vent to melancholy thoughts. . . . Was it necessary, was it magnanimous, was it merely just to impugn the honesty
of his motives? He said, 'People are urging me, even vituperatively,
to withdraw in favor of some one else, and this though I was nominated unanimously. I should be glad enough to do so, and I could.
I don't deny that some one else might not make a better job of the
business than I am doing. That's quite possible. But here I am,
and the better man has not turned up. If I were to withdraw in
favor of a better man, it is not certain, nay it is unlikely, that a better

man would step into my shoes. It is far more probable that my
enemies would fall out among themselves, and that those who want
to get rid of me would in the end get some one by no means to their
liking. In that case my retirement would only intensify the confusion. God knows I have tried to do my duty as best I could, to
be just to every one and unjust to nobody. Now people who have
been my friends, and ought to know me, declare that I am inspired
with dictatorial lusts, that I have done this or that unprincipled deed,
inflicted this wrong or that upon the community, with the object of
keeping myself in office. Are those who wish to unseat me thinking
of nothing but the common welfare? I hope so, I hope so!'"

While he had been speaking, night had fallen. When lights were
brought in, Schurz saw that Lincoln's eyes were moist.

A little later, a State governor advised him to take a fortnight's
holiday, since he was overworked. "Ah," said the President, "two
or three weeks would do me no good; I cannot fly from my thoughts
— my solicitude for this great country follows me wherever I go.
I do not think it is personal vanity or ambition, though I am not
free from these infirmities, but I cannot but feel that the weal or woe
of this great nation will be decided in November. There is no
programme offered by any wing of the Democratic party but this
must result in the permanent destruction of the Union."

"But McClellan is in favor of crushing out this rebellion by force."

"The slightest knowledge of arithmetic will prove to any man that
the rebel armies cannot be destroyed by Democratic strategy. It
would sacrifice all the white men of the North to do it. There are
now in the service of the United States nearly one hundred and fifty
thousand able-bodied colored men, most of them under arms. . . .
The Democratic strategy demands that these forces be disbanded, and
that the masters be conciliated by restoring them to slavery. The
black men who now assist Union prisoners to escape are to be con-
verted into our enemies, in the vain hope of gaining the good will of
their masters. We shall have to fight two nations instead of one . . .
Will you give our enemies such military advantages as insure success,
and then depend on coaxing, flattery, and concession to get them
back into the Union? Abandon all the posts now garrisoned by

black men, take one hundred and fifty thousand men from our side and put them in the battlefield or cornfield against us, and we would be compelled to abandon the war in three weeks. . . . There have been men base enough to propose to me to return to slavery the black warriors of Port Hudson and Olustee, and thus win the respect of the masters they fought. Should I do so, I should deserve to be damned in time and eternity."

Such are the doubts which, in these August weeks, trouble the aging heart of the friend of the people. He has to pass through the terrible moments of despondency which no prophet can escape; the hours in which even a man who feels himself inspired with the divine fire has a sense that he is banned because all shun him, and begins to wonder whether it is not time for him to get rid of himself. Yet if he were to withdraw, would he not, in the best possible event, only be evacuating the field in favor of a radical or lukewarm successor, who would split the nation anew, or would try to make peace without any guarantees? Was there not a likelihood of McClellan's election on the Democratic ticket even if Lincoln should himself persist in his candidature? Would not McClellan, a patrician, a friend of capitalists and the master class, be also impelled by his inclinations and his political program to return the Negroes to slavery and thus at one and the same time lose the war and sacrifice the ideas for which it had been fought? It was rumored that McClellan intended, if elected, to seize the reins of power at once, instead of waiting till next March. Lincoln, on the other hand, had announced that in any event he would stick to his post until the last day permitted by the law.

But what if McClellan should be elected, and thereafter there should arise the duplex governmental situation which Lincoln had himself experienced from autumn to spring four years earlier — a condition of affairs which had reduced him almost to despair? Was the country once again to be dragged this way and that, during a period of interregnum, by refractory members of the cabinet; was the government to be deprived of its most essential characteristic — unity? On the other hand, would it not be possible to turn McClellan's faculty for recruiting to account during the winter months, which was usually a slack time for fighting? Turning over such thoughts in his mind, Lincoln decided to bind his secretaries, in a very unusual way, for a possible interregnum. They were to sign the following declaration:

"This morning, as for some days past, it seems extremely probable that this administration will not be reëlected. Then it will be my duty to so coöperate with the President-elect as to save the Union between the election and the inauguration; as he will have secured his election on such ground that he cannot possibly save it afterward."

He explained later, confidentially, that his intention had been to make the best possible use of McClellan after his election. In this way he would be able to restrain the latter from yielding to an impulse towards illegal usurpation of authority, and thus only could he make sure of his sometime collaborator during these four months.

But how could he get his cabinet to give such a promise? Had they become his friends during the years in which he and they had worked together? Welles and Stanton were loyal to him, though jealous of one another, as navy and army are apt to be. "Did Stanton tell you I was a damned fool? Then I expect I must be one, for he is almost always right, and generally says what he means." He had just got rid of the influential Blair, and at a very unfavorable moment. Seward, who had at first been jealous of the President and now relied on Lincoln's favor for support against his colleagues, was not of a type to feel affection for any one. Finally Lincoln himself, being of so anomalous a type, was not the man best fitted to compact a number of individualities into a whole, and his cabinet had therefore remained an amorphous structure. Was he to disclose the dangerous signs of his own sense of weakness to these men, especially now, when two new and untried cabinet members had come to join them? Yet he needed their signatures. What did he do? He came to the cabinet meeting, laid the before-mentioned declaration on the table folded so that they could not read it, and asked them to sign it unread. When they had done so, he sealed it and took it away with him.

The fact that they complied, amazed but not unperturbed, bears the strongest possible witness to the force of moral suasion Lincoln could exercise.　He was not among friends, only among officials, no more than two of whom had any personal affection for him, when he passed this folded paper around the table for signature; and if history ever should assemble the important documents in which Lincoln's character displayed itself, this one should be among them — a document in which an experienced father was merely trying to make wise provision for the future.

Suddenly the popular mood changed.　A few days after the signing of this mysterious document news came that Sherman had made his victorious march through Georgia, had conquered Atlanta, and Lincoln was able, as a rejoinder to the convention of the war-weary Democrats, to order a day of prayer and thanksgiving in commemoration of the latest victories.　Now, when the Army of the West was able to penetrate farther into the enemy land, hope revived in the North, and therewith Lincoln's chances of election improved.　Raids on banks, robbery, and murder, on the Canadian frontier, showed American citizens what might be the outcome of a revolution in war time.　Schurz threw up his position as general to speak for Lincoln as he had done four years earlier; and even Chase, after several months of enmity, decided to campaign on behalf of the President's reëlection.　Since this was the prevailing sentiment, the Democrats only harmed their own cause when, on public platforms, they continued to speak of the war as a failure, and the party leaders became still more uneasy when even McClellan advocated a fight to a finish. The South, too, contributed indirectly toward Lincoln's reëlection by asking prisoners it was proposed to exchange, for whom they intended to vote, and allowing none but Democrats to return to the North, naturally compromising those who came back on such terms. The soldiers, above all, were eager to vote for Father Abraham.

Lincoln knew, indeed, how to appeal to them, as when he spoke to an Ohio regiment: "I happen, temporarily, to occupy this big white house.　I am a living witness that any one of your children may look to come here as my father's child has.　It is in order that each one of you may have, through this free government which we have enjoyed, an open field and a fair chance for your industry, enterprise, and intelligence — that you may all have equal privileges in the

race of life with all its desirable human aspirations — it is for this that
the struggle should be maintained, that we may not lose our birthright."

On the election day he was sitting, as his custom was in the afternoon, with a few acquaintances in the telegraph room of the War
Department, this time not to get the latest news of the advances
made by his generals, but to learn the progress of the voting. His
mind may well have gone back to that day four years earlier when
he had been sitting in his little house in Springfield awaiting the news
from the remote States and the great cities. Now he was in the heart
of the capital, and once again, after an exciting six months, he felt
that there was no occasion for excitement on this concluding day.
Stanton read the telegrams aloud, Lincoln glanced at them and made
comments, until there was a lull, and he called one of the assistant
secretaries of State to ask:

"Have you ever read any of the writings of Petroleum V. Nasby?"

"I have only looked at some of them," was the answer, "and they
seemed to me funny."

"Well," said the President, "let me read you a specimen," and,
pulling out a thin yellow-covered pamphlet from his breast pocket,
he began to read aloud. Stanton was shocked, but Lincoln continued to read till new telegrams came in. After these had been
considered, he resumed his reading aloud from the pamphlet. This
was one of the moments in which the man who never used ordinary
stimulants or narcotics wanted to relieve tension by indulging in
witticisms. The trait was a great annoyance to well-brought-up men
and women among his acquaintance, but for us after the lapse of
more than half a century it gives a clue to the heart of this most
natural of all the men who have ever held sway over their fellows.

Lincoln was reëlected by an overwhelming majority of 212 electoral votes out of 233, only three of the participating States having
voted against him, among them Kentucky. The great difference
between the figures in 1864 and 1860 was due to the secession of the
South.

Next evening he exclaimed to a gathering, "I am thankful to God
for this approval of the people; but, while deeply grateful for this

mark of their confidence in me, if I know my heart, my gratitude is free from any taint of personal triumph. . . . It is no pleasure to me to triumph over any one."

An evening later, in response to a serenade, he returned to an old problem, summarizing as follows his ideas on the problem of the State:

"It has long been a grave question whether any government not too strong for the liberties of its people can be strong enough to maintain its existence in great emergencies. . . . What has occurred in this case must ever recur in similar cases. Human nature will not change. In any future great national trial, compared with the men of this, we shall have as weak and as strong, as silly and as wise, as bad and as good. Let us, therefore, study the incidents of this, as philosophy to learn wisdom from, and none of them as wrongs to be revenged. But the election . . . has demonstrated that a people's government can sustain a national election in the midst of a great civil war. Until now, it has not been known to the world that this was a possibility. It shows, also, how sound and strong we still are . . . it adds nothing to my satisfaction that any other man may be disappointed or pained by the result.

"May I ask those who have not differed with me to join with me in this same spirit towards those who have? And now let me close by asking three hearty cheers for our brave soldiers and seamen, and their gallant and skillful commanders."

Not a word of triumph, not a gesture of victory, nothing but a simple expression of gratitude, and the thoughts of a skeptic who does not for a moment except himself from human imperfection. He appends a request, delicately uttered, spoken almost with embarrassment — a request that, in view of the common peril, his hearers shall cease to quarrel one with another.

From the mood that animates the victor in the electoral struggle, we may infer the friendliness and wisdom Lincoln would have displayed in his attempts, as victor in the war, to conciliate and reconstruct the South. He had already begun to work towards these ends.

IX

"I desire to so conduct the affairs of this administration that if, at the end, when I come to lay down the reins of power, I have lost every other friend on earth, I shall at least have one friend left, and that friend shall be down inside of me." Because he carried on the government in accordance with this principle, he was fiercely attacked, and it is unlikely he would have been reëlected had not recent victories in the field given practical demonstration of the soundness of his policy; and because he held fast to this principle, he was, even in Congress during the last year of his life, accused of having exceeded his rights and arrogated powers to himself in connection with the thorny problem of reconstruction.

His opinion did in fact vacillate as to whether and to what extent Congress would be justified in refusing to accept new or returning senators and representatives from the reconquered States, and the problem was even thornier as regards the border States. In Missouri, this year, it had been found necessary to take a side, neutrality was suspect, property insecure. He had therefore given a piece of advice to General Schofield, one which it would still be wise to impress as a golden rule upon every neutral soldier: "Let your military measures be strong enough to repel the invader and keep the peace, and not so strong as to unnecessarily harass and persecute the people. It is a difficult rôle. . . . If both factions, or neither, shall abuse you, you will probably be about right. Beware of being assailed by one and praised by the other."

When, from 1863 onwards, Louisiana and Tennessee were discussing the possibility of forming new governments in order to reënter the Union, and were actually taking steps towards this end, there was still lacking any definite proposal as to the way in which the broken threads might be retied, and Lincoln — cautiously, that he might avoid all semblance of the authoritarianism of which the individual States and the Congress of the Union were apt to complain — set to work wherever he could, advising and mediating, like a father dressed up as a diplomat. In the summer of that year, he wrote to a general in Louisiana:

"While I very well know what I would be glad for Louisiana to do, it is quite a different thing for me to assume direction of the matter. I would be glad for her to make a new constitution, recognizing the emancipation proclamation, and adopting emancipation in those parts of the State to which the proclamation does not apply. And while she is at it, I think it would not be objectionable for her to adopt some practicable system by which the two races could gradually live themselves out of their old relation to each other, and both come out better prepared for the new."

When matters had advanced a stage, he wrote to the governor: "Now you are about to have a convention, which, among other things, will probably define the elective franchise. I barely suggest, for your private consideration, whether some of the colored people may not be let in, as, for instance, the very intelligent, and especially those who have fought gallantly in our ranks. They will probably help in some trying time to come, to keep the jewel of liberty within the family of freedom."

So uncertain was the position as to the fundamental problems of the nation. But at about the same date, filled with an impatience and an uneasiness that were rare in him, he wrote to Johnson, military governor of Tennessee, with an urgency quite foreign to his usual style:

"All Tennessee is now clear of armed insurrectionists. You need not to be reminded that it is the nick of time for reinaugurating a loyal State government. Not a moment should be lost. You and the coöperating friends there can better judge of the ways and means than can be judged by any here. I only offer a few suggestions. The reinauguration must not be such as to give control of the State, and its representation in Congress, to the enemies of the Union, driving its friends there into political exile. The whole struggle for Tennessee will have been profitless to both State and Nation if it so ends that Governor Johnson is put down and Governor Harris put up. It must not be so. You must have it otherwise." For the one and only time in his life, Lincoln uses the Napoleonic catchword, "not a moment should be lost." It would seem he feels himself driven.

At the same time voices were raised in Congress advocating new schemes of reconstruction in opposition to the President's. Lincoln, moreover, alienated half the Congressmen by issuing, before his re-election, a proclamation associating reconstruction with a general amnesty. According to this proclamation, politically accused persons in the reconquered States would merely have to swear that thenceforward they would comply with the Constitution, the laws, and the demand for the abolition of slavery. Further, any State government was to be recognized as valid if it had been reconstituted by not less than one tenth of the electors who had been on the register in 1860, and who should have taken the before-mentioned oath. Both of these concessions were regarded by the majority in Congress as going too far. Lincoln's clemency was ridiculed as weakness, and was probably too far-reaching. But, as if he foresaw that he would not be granted time to complete reconstruction when the war was ended, he pressed onward toward the realization of what he had most at heart, the ending of slavery:

"The war is nearly over. . . . Then the government forces must be withdrawn from all the southern States. Sooner or later we must take them all away. Now, what I want you to do is this: do all you can, in any and every way you can, to get the ballot into the hands of the freedmen! We must make voters of them before we take away the troops. The ballot will be their only protection after the bayonet is gone, and they will be sure to need all they can get. I can see just how it will be." Thus vigorously is he already steering towards the epoch of peace, which is natural to him; thus forcibly does this heart filled with a great sense of responsibility beat when it feels called upon to ensure peace among men.

This subtle sympathy, the source of his power, which perforce during the first years of the war had seemed to flow less strenuously or at any rate less audibly, now, in the last year of the struggle, was displayed more abundantly than ever; and now, too, as in his youth, it was shown just as warmly toward whites and toward blacks, with the result that no class understood him better than the working class. In a splendidly phrased letter, he promptly replied to a congratulatory address from the trade unionists of Manchester — one of those letters in which he held converse with the world at large:

"One duty, paramount to all others, was before me, namely, to maintain and preserve at once the Constitution and the integrity of the Federal Republic. A conscientious purpose to perform this duty is the key to all the measures of administration which have been and to all which will hereafter be pursued. . . . It is not always in the power of governments to enlarge or restrict the scope of moral results which follow the policies that they may deem it necessary for the public safety from time to time to adopt. . . . A fair examination of history has served to authorize a belief that the past actions and influences of the United States were generally regarded as having been beneficial towards mankind. I have therefore reckoned upon the forbearance of nations. . . . Through the action of our disloyal citizens, the working men of Europe have been subjected to severe trials, for the purpose of forcing their sanction to that attempt. Under the circumstances, I cannot but regard your decisive utterances upon the question as an instance of sublime Christian heroism which has not been surpassed in any age or in any country. It is indeed an energetic and reinspiring assurance of the inherent power of truth and of the ultimate and universal triumph of justice, humanity, and freedom."

If we are to see these words in all their ancient splendor, we must blow away from them the dust that has gathered on them after thousands of street fights; then we shall see them once more as Lincoln saw them, for, while throughout these years he had had, day after day, to keep his gaze fixed on the earth, he could find an evening hour now and again to lift his eyes to the stars. For him the reconciliation of the classes was an attainable ideal. When the Workingmen's Association of New York made him an honorary member of that body, he said to the delegates who came to inform him of the fact:

"You comprehend, as your address shows, that the existing rebellion means more and tends to more than the perpetuation of African slavery — that it is, in fact, a war upon the rights of all working people. Partly to show that this view has not escaped my attention, and partly that I cannot better express myself, I read a passage from the message to Congress in December, 1861." Follow the

LINCOLN IN 1865

His last picture, taken April 10, by Alexander Gardner, Washington

remarks on capital and labor already quoted in this work on page 281. Thereafter, he continued :

"None are so deeply interested to resist the present rebellion as the working people. Let them beware of prejudice, working division and hostility among themselves. The most notable feature of a disturbance in your city last summer was the hanging of some working people by other working people. It should never be so. The strongest bond of human sympathy, outside of the family relation, should be one uniting all working people, of all nations, and tongues and kindreds. Nor should this lead to a war upon property, or the owners of property. Property is the fruit of labor; property is desirable; is a positive good in the world. That some should be rich shows that others may become rich, and hence is just encouragement to industry and enterprise. Let not him who is houseless pull down the house of another, but let him work diligently and build one for himself, thus by example assuring that his own shall be safe from violence when built."

Here, once again, is Lincoln's art of forming thoughts as if he were quarrying his words out of the granite rock of reason; but in truth this art is an expression of his character, which embraces both heart and head. Never has the thorny problem been solved by simpler means, and after the lapse of sixty years, after a spate of books and discussions, what he said seems all the fresher to-day, because it was not the utterance of a thinker or statesman who mounts a pedestal to talk down to the intelligence of the man in the street, but because a man has come from out of the woods and the streets who, having become a statesman, retains the primal simplicity which we recognize in his deeply furrowed visage.

X

For him, private life had ceased to exist. Work, agitations, enemies at home, reverses abroad, danger threatening to undo the work done by the fathers of the country and to frustrate the activities of his own career; such had been his lot for three or four years, almost without cessation. The tree-feller's tall body had been attacked from

within, mined as it were and weakened here and there; he was laid up
for a while by a modified smallpox, caught in a visit to the front; he
complained that his legs were always cold, but he would not give way;
very rarely indeed, after a sleepless night, would he lie down on
Welles' sofa, or say that he was too tired to receive visitors. "I
hardly know how to rest. It may be good for the body. But what
is tired in me lies within, and can't be got at."

As the years went by, the tensions increased rather than dimin-
ished. If things were going well in the field, he would be harassed
by the violence of the political factions; when all was quiet in that
quarter, the result would be a decline in recruiting; and if, for a
moment, matters really seemed to be making progress everywhere,
he would still be perturbed by the mutual jealousies of the members
of the cabinet or the governors. In addition he was distressed by
the daily sight of the sufferings caused by the war, for hospitals
abounded in Washington, and the surrounding hills were sprinkled
with tents for the temporary accommodation of the sick and
wounded, while the stretchers seemed to pass in unending succession
whenever the President went out for air and exercise.

Riding was about his only exercise. He had a good seat, but was
a hard rider, so that he tired out a lot of horses, and on his rides
and drives he had to put up with the precautions of Stanton, who
insisted on his being accompanied by a bodyguard. Sometimes,
however, when the military situation was causing him great anxiety,
or when the receipt of a disturbing telegram had made it impossible
for him to sleep, he would — in summer, when he was staying at
his country quarters — get up in the middle of the night and ride
off unattended to the War Department. On such occasions, he
was always exposed to the risk of assassination. One night in
August, at about eleven o'clock, the sentinel at the Soldiers' Home
heard a rifle shot, and soon afterwards approaching hoof beats.
In two or three minutes a horse came dashing up, and the man
recognized the President, arriving thus belated, and bareheaded.
To the sentry, who took the horse's bridle, Lincoln said, "He came
pretty near getting away with me, didn't he. He got the bit in
his teeth before I could draw the rein." The man asked him where

his hat was. "Somebody fired down at the foot of the hill. The horse bolted, and my hat was jerked off." The sentry and a corporal went off in the direction of the shooting, and found the President's hat, with a bullet hole through the crown. Next morning, when Lincoln saw the hat, he joked and made light of the occurrence, but added that he wished to have it kept quiet. Thenceforward he never rode alone.

Sometimes, after riding into Washington in the small hours, he would spend the rest of the night at the White House, writing or reading, and would ride back to the Soldiers' Home when morning came, depressed in mood. Such depression was common enough, for Lincoln was incapable of taking much delight in victory or of feeling hatred for the enemy, and civil war was doubly distressing to him, since the enemies were his brothers. "The war," he said in a speech during the last year of his life, "has carried mourning to almost every home, until it can almost be said that 'the heavens are hung in black'!"

Yet his very loneliness, his temperamental melancholy, made him refractory to a perennial gloom, for hitherto he had always been accustomed to find distraction in the world of his fellows, and thus, as it were, to secure release from himself. Now, however, the shadows were thickening around him, as if tending, day by day, to reproduce for him objectively the dark imagery of his own subjective world. And he was being held responsible for all this! What could he do but persist more and more resolutely in seeking within his own self the sanction for his activities: "I do the very best I know how, the very best I can; and I mean to keep doing so until the end. If the end brings me out all right, what is said against me won't amount to anything. If the end brings me out wrong, ten angels swearing I was right would make no difference." Moving words of this kind would be said quietly to an intimate, much as if he were soliloquizing; but at times he would say the same sort of thing openly, in a more strenuous formulation.

Here is a delegation of radicals from Missouri, threatening to make a revolution if he does not put an end to the system of strict government by martial law. When he refuses, one of them tells him point-blank that there will be bloodshed, and that he will be responsible. Will he fire up, and show the offender the door? While the delegate is speaking, the President stands, the tears flowing down his cheeks. Then, pulling himself together, he says, "You appear to come before me as my friends if I agree with you, and not otherwise. . . . I am well aware that by many, by some even among this delegation — I shall not name them — I have been in public speeches and in printed documents charged with tyranny and willfulness; with a disposition to make my own personal will supreme. I do not intend to be a tyrant. At all events I shall take care that in my own eyes I do not become one."

Immediately afterwards, when he has discovered a couple of old acquaintances among the delegation, and has kept these for a private talk, the others, as they leave, hear his hearty laughter echoing through the room. Thus quickly could Lincoln's moods change; thus quickly, indeed, had they to change, if he were to be able to bear his heavy burden.

A Congressman comes to talk over important affairs. Before getting down to business, the President tells a humorous anecdote. The visitor protests, gets up, saying that he has not come to listen to stories, that the times are too serious for that sort of thing. Lincoln, changing his tone, rejoins, "Sit down, please. I respect you as an earnest and sincere man. You cannot be more anxious than I have been, constantly, since the beginning of the war; and I say to you, now, that were it not for this occasional vent, I should die." Down to the very tone of his voice, we seem to hear his animus, his repression, his recognition of the other's earnestness, and his strong desire to make himself understood as between man and man.

Again, when he is in a condition of tense anxiety because Burnside has been hemmed in, has been unable to send news for a long time, and may have had to surrender, there comes a telegram saying that gunfire has been heard from the direction of Knoxville. "Glad of it," says Lincoln. "It reminds me of Mrs. Sally Ward, a neighbor of mine. She had a very large family. Occasionally one of her very numerous progeny would be heard crying in some

out-of-the-way place, and she would exclaim, 'There's one of my
children that isn't dead yet '!"

He seldom has time for reading. When he can spare a moment
to look at a book, what he likes best is to do this in the company
of his son Tad. If he quotes Shakespeare nowadays, it is in the
vein of political irony, as so often when he repeats the lines from
"King Richard the Second": "For God's sake let us sit upon the
ground and tell sad stories of the death of kings." He writes in a
private letter, "Some of Shakespeare's plays I have never read,
while others I have gone over perhaps as frequently as any unprofessional reader. Among the latter are 'Lear', 'Richard III',
'Henry VIII', 'Hamlet', and especially 'Macbeth.' I think
nothing equals 'Macbeth.' It is wonderful. Unlike you gentlemen of the profession, I think the soliloquy in 'Hamlet' commencing 'Oh, my offence is rank', surpasses that commencing
'To be or not to be.' But pardon this small attempt at criticism."

What a wealth of substance there is in these fugitive lines! How
modest he is; how frankly he admits the limitations of his knowledge; how amazing and yet how comprehensible it is that he,
ringed in by ambitious politicians, always on the edge of an abyss,
should not want to contemplate likenesses of himself, but should
have a natural inclination to look at his counterparts, and should
therefore have a special love for "Macbeth."

On the other hand, precious ideas come into his mind and find
utterance, to be preserved only by a lucky chance. Once when
some ladies were with him in his carriage as he drove to the Soldiers'
Home, there was a discussion as to the trees they were passing.
"Let me discourse on a theme I understand," said the President.
"I know all about trees, by right of being a backwoodsman. . . .
Trees are as deceptive in their likeness to one another as are certain
classes of men, amongst whom none but a physiognomist's eye
can detect dissimilar moral features until events have developed
them. Do you know it would be a good thing if in all the schools
proposed and carried out by the improvement of modern thinkers,
we could have a school of events? . . . It is only by that active
development that character and ability can be tested. Under-

stand me, I now mean men, not trees; they can be tried, and an analysis of their strength obtained less expensive to life and human interests than man's. What I say now is a mere whim, you know; but when I speak of a school of events, I mean one in which, before entering real life, students might pass through the mimic vicissitudes and situations that are necessary to bring out their powers and mark the caliber to which they are assigned. Thus one could select from the graduates an invincible soldier, equal to any position, . . . a politician too cunning to be outwitted, and so on. These things have all to be tried, and their sometime failure creates confusion as well as disappointment. There is no more dangerous or expensive analysis than that which consists of trying a man."

Of course many of these improvisations must have been lost because those who heard them omitted to write them down. From this instance, and noting the general course of his mental development, we may argue as to others, and may perhaps infer that Lincoln, whose healthy but slowly moving nature was designed by God for the attainment of a great age, would in later years have inclined more and more to unfold a didactic wisdom.

Only at considerable intervals, now, has he still time to give himself up lovingly to the careful elaboration of a speech, and this is one of the ways in which he finds relaxation. Here the poet in him is seeking an outlet, in conjunction with the natural desire to express in words the feelings of his big family. Apart from the inaugural address, and the proclamation, Lincoln probably never took more pains in the preparation of a brief speech than he did over the wording of the address he made at the consecration of a cemetery in Gettysburg. In the open air, there had spoken before him, to an audience of many thousands, the most famous orator in the country, the handsome and highly respected Everett, whose method was classical. Then, amid the general tension, the President mounted the rostrum, took a document out of his coat pocket, selected one sheet from it, put on his glasses with an unceremonious gesture, and, in his high tenor voice, read aloud a few sentences, making too quick a job of it to give the photographers stationed in front of him time to do their work. He said:

"Four score and seven years ago our fathers brought forth on this continent, a new nation, conceived in liberty, and dedicated to the proposition that all men are created equal.

"Now we are engaged in a great civil war, testing whether that nation, or any nation so conceived and so dedicated, can long endure. We are met on a great battlefield of that war. We have come to dedicate a portion of that field, as a final resting place for those who here gave their lives that that nation might live. It is altogether fitting and proper that we should do this.

"But, in a larger sense, we cannot dedicate — we cannot consecrate — we cannot hallow — this ground. The brave men, living and dead, who struggled here have consecrated it, far above our poor power to add or detract. The world will little note, nor long remember, what we say here, but it can never forget what they did here. It is for us, the living, rather, to be dedicated here to the unfinished work which they who fought here have thus far so nobly advanced. It is rather for us to be here dedicated to the great task remaining before us — that from these honored dead we take increased devotion to that cause for which they gave the last full measure of devotion — that we here highly resolve that these dead shall not have died in vain — that this nation, under God, shall have a new birth of freedom — and that government of the people, by the people, for the people, shall not perish from the earth."

The words seemed to make little impression. Even among the masters of language the chorus of approval was reserved for Everett. But the latter wrote to the President, saying that his own long speech had been put in the shade by Lincoln's pithy words.

And what Lincoln, with honest conviction, had denied, did after all happen. The name of Gettysburg is merely the name of one among numberless battles, of which few in Europe have ever heard or troubled to remember which side was victorious; and even in the United States it would have become a mere fact among others taught to children in schools but for these few words uttered by a man in civilian attire, dying away down the wind when they were spoken, that have made the name immortal, showing once again that Homer can be productive without Achilles, but that Achilles cannot win immortality without Homer.

XI

Mary's disappointments grew. The glamour of the White House, the splendors of which she had fondly dreamed, could rarely shine forth in this time of war, and once when she held a great gathering, she earned scant approval. Her nervous temperament and her husband's unceremonious ways made the pair of them ill-suited for the elaborate and tasteful reception of several hundred guests, and even their intimates described the affair as a muddle. Yet what, throughout these years, was there to satisfy her beyond the display of a power which really belonged to her only as a shadow without substance? Had she been a devoted wife with no thought beyond the endeavor to relieve her husband of the cares which weighed upon him as if he had had to carry the whole burden of the war, or had she been a shrewd helpmate from whom now and again he could seek counsel, she could in such ways have found more satisfaction than in the ostentations of an existence which lacked the solid foundation of a well-established "society life."

Furthermore, she was a woman from the South, and was therefore open to the suspicion, however foolish, however unwarranted, of treasonable practices, or at least of lending aid to espionage. Thousands upon thousands, not only at Washington but in widening circles, knew that the President's lady had brothers and other kinsmen in the rebel army, and if the soldiers strung together malicious rhymes about her, if they invented fables about Mary's quite imaginary lovers, if they coupled her name with that of Jefferson Davis, these expressions of the popular mood must be regarded as symbolic of her estrangement from the common folk — an estrangement contrasting so signally with Lincoln's fundamental oneness with the people.

When her brother was killed in the war, she could not wear mourning for him, and she had outwardly to rejoice over the conquest of Southern States, although at Vicksburg a second brother had been fatally wounded. A third Northern victory cost the life of a third of her brothers. Her brother-in-law, too, who at the outset of the war had rejected Lincoln's offer and had thrown in his lot with the South, was killed, and this man's widow, Mary's half sister, wishing to visit her mother in Kentucky, and receiving a pass from Grant, refused to take the necessary oath. The President wired: "Send her to me." She came to Washington, and the sisters met, after losing three brothers in the war and after their respective families had been in arms against one another for nearly three years. In the end, Lincoln let her return South without having taken the oath.

Next summer, her behavior in Kentucky was open to suspicion, and Lincoln had to wire to the major general in command: "I hear a rumor to-day that you recently sought to arrest . . . General Helm's widow, . . . but were prevented by her presenting the paper from me. I do not intend to protect her against the consequences of disloyal words or acts, spoken or done by her since her return to Kentucky, and if the paper given her by me can be construed to give her protection for such words and acts, it is hereby revoked *pro tanto*. Deal with her for current conduct just as you would with any other."

Another of Mary's Southern sisters who was likewise equipped with a pass from Lincoln was officially charged with importing goods under cover of this document. Mary broke off communications with her, Lincoln would not receive her, and refused her the pass she needed for her journey. When subsequently in her hotel she let her tongue wag in favor of the South, the President sent her a message to the effect that if she was still within the city limits when twenty-four hours had elapsed, she would find herself in the capital prison.

As an outcome of these incidents and suspicions, and also to save Mary from abusive letters, it was arranged that all her correspondence should be opened by one of the President's secretaries, but even though this was the outcome of his considerateness, was done to protect her against her accusers, and was in no sense due to suspicion on his part, it could not fail to arouse a disagreeable feeling in her mind, and thus to darken a household atmosphere that was in any case murky. The missives exchanged between husband and wife, in so far as they have been made accessible, manifest a cool tone: "It is a matter of choice with yourself whether you come home. There is no reason why you should not, that did not exist when you went away." On another occasion he wires to her just as frigidly to New York that she can decide for herself whether she shall come back or stay where she is; but next day he telegraphs, "I would be glad for you to come." A day later still, and he has to clear up an ambiguity in the first message of the series, which she has interpreted unfavorably and has obviously answered skeptically. He wires: "It was never healthier, and I really wish to see you."

A lad, Welles' son, was once standing close by the carriage when Lincoln and Mary were getting in. He heard Mary expressing an urgent desire for a certain officer's promotion. The President refused, and repeated the refusal when his wife reiterated her wish. Then she said, "If you don't promise to let me have my way, I'll throw myself down here in the mud." Thereupon Lincoln yielded. Though we have not much information on the subject, this example of Mary's lack of mental balance does not stand alone. After her boy's death, she was almost crazy for a time; she never again entered the room where he died; and once she was so extravagant in her expressions of sorrow that Lincoln, pointing to a lunatic asylum, said in a fatherly way, and as if prophetically, "Mother, do you see that large white building yonder? Unless you control your grief, I am afraid we shall have to send you there."

She saw visions. Her dead son and her slain brothers (so she told her sister) appeared to her at the foot of her bed; and she was anxious about Lincoln, partly from superstitious foreboding, and partly through a reasonable dread that attempts would be made to assassinate him. Once when, accompanied by some guests, she was driving to the Ford Theater (whither Lincoln occasionally went for relaxation), and the carriage jolted against some obstacle or other, she fancied that an attack was being made.

The lady who was with her spoke tranquilizing words, and then asked the President whether the eight cavalrymen of the body-guard were not a perfect protection. "Not much," he rejoined. "I believe when my time comes there is nothing that can prevent my going. But the people will have it so." When they reached the theater, a way had to be made for them through the crowd, and it occurred to the lady how easily something might happen there.

The amazing thing was, indeed, that during four years, and when his enemies had so many excellent opportunities, nothing happened. Mary saw the risks with her eyes and felt them with her nerves. Credulous of dream warnings as she was, how could she forget that vision he had had after his first election, the reduplicated image with a second and fainter head, which she had interpreted as a sign that he would die during his second term? If she re-membered it, why did not she seize upon the moments during which he doubted, the moments when her husband was inclined to withdraw from the struggle, that she might strengthen him in this resolve? There is no evidence that she believed in his genius. Why, then, should she want to stay in this house that was so grimly haunted, for all its splendors, were it not the splendors that allured her? In Lincoln's hours of self-communing, the lonely man might have been much influenced by the promptings of a beloved wife, might perhaps have been induced to abandon the political field.

But the connubial atmosphere surrounding Lincoln was a chilly one, here in the great mansion, as formerly in the small house: his children were the only gifts his wife had ever brought him. One evening when he was reading "King John" aloud to a friend, and came to the passage where the king says he will see his good boy again in heaven, the President broke off and covered his eyes with his hand. Of the two remaining sons, Robert was at the university, and Tad was his darling. It might almost be said that the lad had become one of the bodyguard, he told his father the story of the men's lives, made them come with him to feed his goats, donned a uniform to ride his pony beside them, let their tricks impose upon himself and his father (as when two of the men would masquerade as an elephant). When Tad was away, the old man was uneasy, wiring to his wife on one occasion : "Tell Tad the goats and father are very well, especially the goats."

Former friends are dead or have fallen away. Only three remain. He writes to Weed in New York : "I have been brought to fear recently that somehow, by commission or omission, I have caused you some degree of pain. I have never entertained an unkind feeling or a disparaging thought toward you ; and if I have said or done anything which has been construed into such unkindness or disparagement, it has been misconstrued. I am sure if we could meet we would not part with any unpleasant impression on either side. Yours as ever."

Herndon and Speed, who never ask anything of him, are devoted to him, but they are far away. After his reëlection he appoints Speed's brother Attorney General. Once, amid the press of business, he telegraphs to Hannah Armstrong : "I have just ordered the discharge of your boy William, as you say, now at Louisville, Kentucky." Thus remote sound the names of his oldest friends, and of the State in which he had been born, now fighting against him.

If he wants to help an acquaintance, he does it through an intermediary. An agent has been removed from his position, on a charge of having sold State timber and stone for his private benefit. Lincoln writes to the postmaster of the place, not to the governor : "He is an old acquaintance and friend of mine, and I will thank you, if you will, to set a day or days and place on and at which to take testimony on the point. . . . Please do this for me."

Seldom does the manly humor of the former time show through in one of the many letters to which he affixes his signature day after day : "My dear Colonel Dick," he writes to an old friend, "I have long determined to make public the origin of the greenback and tel¹ the world that it is Dick Taylor's creation. You had always been friendly to me, and when troublous times fell on us, and my shoulders, though broad and willing, were weak, and myself surrounded by such circumstances and such people that I knew not whom to trust, then I said in my extremity: 'I will send for Colonel Taylor; he will know what to do.' I think it was in January, 1862, on or about the 16th, that I did so. You came, and I said to you: 'What can we do?' Said you: 'Why, issue treasury notes bearing no interest, printed on the best banking paper. Issue enough to pay off the army expenses and declare it legal tender.' Chase thought it a hazardous thing, but we finally accomplished it, and gave the people of this republic the greatest blessing they ever had — their own paper to pay their own debts. It is due to you, the father of the present greenback, that the people should know it, and I take great pleasure in making it known. How many times have I laughed at you telling me plainly that I was too lazy to be anything but a lawyer? Yours truly."

Why does he write this, if not to listen to his own voice once more, singing in the familiar tones? Why does he draw this unknown adviser forth into the limelight to make even a grumpy old man smile? All this, too, in the manner of one whose love of mankind is invincible, despite the enmity of some and the suspicion of others? Nothing but an imperturbable conviction that he is on the right path, nothing but a tranquil certainty, could keep this feeling alive in him.

And yet this certainty is sustained by another, credulously fatalistic, a conviction that there is a predestined equipoise in the human heart. Sometimes he formulates his sense of destiny in a religious fashion; and, indeed, during these last years, he uses the name of God more frequently than of yore. He writes to a clergyman: "If it were not for my firm belief in an over-ruling providence, it would be difficult for me, in the midst of such complications of affairs, to keep my reason in its seat. But I am confident that the Almighty has His plans and will work them out; and whether we see it or not, they will be the wisest and best for us." When another minister expresses the hope that the Lord is on the side of the North, Lincoln gives the magnificent Protestant answer: "I am not at all concerned about that, for I know the Lord is always on the side of the right. But it is my constant anxiety and prayer that I and this nation should be on the Lord's side."

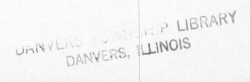

The name we give to such outlooks is of little moment. He himself uses various terms. He says on another occasion: "I have had so many evidences of God's direction, so many instances when I have been controlled by some other power than my own will, that I cannot doubt that this power comes from above. I frequently see my way clear to a decision when I am conscious that I have no sufficient facts upon which to found it. But I cannot recall one instance in which I have followed my own judgment, founded upon such a decision, where the results have been unsatisfactory; whereas, in almost every instance where I have yielded to the views of others, I have had occasion to regret it. I am satisfied that when the Almighty wants me to do or not to do a particular thing, He finds a way of letting me know it." Here he gives a clear formulation of the manner in which self-reliance and fatalism are complementary elements in a resolute character, and how each reinforces the other. This conviction of guidance from above, which Lincoln shares with all great men, leads him to the utterance: "I am not bound to win, but I am bound to be true. I am not bound to succeed, but I am bound to live up to the light I have."

Another influence which was still alive in Lincoln as of old, was superstition — not in conflict with his fatalism, but amplifying it. After a defeat, he said he had had a foreboding of it, adding, "I believe I feel trouble in the air before it comes." In a speech to explain how it was that the Fourth of July, the birthday of the United States, had acquired so much significance, he said: "The two men most distinguished in the framing and support of the Declaration were Thomas Jefferson and John Adams, . . . the only two of the fifty-five who signed it and were elected Presidents of the United States. Precisely fifty years after they put their hands to the paper, it pleased Almighty God to take both from this stage of action. . . . Another President, five years after, was called from this stage of existence on the same day and month of the year; and now, on this last Fourth of July just passed, . . . we have the surrender of a most powerful position and army on that very day."

Sometimes, too, as in former days, he will still be alarmed by a dream. One morning he sends his wife a telegram containing no more than the sentences: "Think you had better put Tad's pistol away. I had an ugly dream about him." Mary takes away the pistol, and leaves it in the hotel when she returns with the boy to Washington. Soon afterwards the President wires to the hotel keeper: "Tad is teasing me to have you forward his pistol to him." We see Lincoln torn between superstition and paternal love, between premonition and tenderness. If, in the end, the youngster gets back his pistol, this too, perhaps, is God's will.

XII

The greatest relief of tension that came to Lincoln during these four years was to be found in one of the most arduous of his duties, and was the outcome of his wish to temper justice with mercy, for in him compassion predominated even over his craving for justice.

Never in history has any other ruler, within so short a time, so often granted clemency. Most of the offenders were men who had deserted the colors, some from cowardice, some from war weariness, and some as practitioners of the industry of enlisting as substitutes or to earn the handsome bounty that was payable to volunteers and then deserting in order to play the same game once more, perhaps several times. Desertion in war time is a capital offense. But there is always Father Abraham who would not hurt even a cat! Appeal to the President, and he will look into the matter. Every one of these cases was, in fact, carefully studied by him, with the result that during the last two years of the conflict there were filed in the War Department hundreds upon hundreds of telegrams containing the phrase "Suspend execution of so-and-so." Sometimes he would send an additional docket to the director of telegrams: "Please send above dispatch." Or "Will you please hurry off the above. To-morrow is the day of execution."

Disciplinary considerations, which the angry generals were apt to adduce as reasons against all this leniency, left him cold. Cowardice? "I never felt sure but I might drop my gun and run away if I found myself in line of battle." Another time: "If God has given a man cowardly legs, how can the fellow help it if they run away with him?" In a message to Congress: "The severest justice may not always be the best policy." He is especially keen on protecting the younger soldiers: "I think the boy can do us more good above ground than under ground." Or he would probe to discover the indirect causes of desertion: "Must I shoot a simple-minded soldier boy who deserts, while I must not touch a hair of a wily agitator who induces him to desert? . . . I think that in such a case, to silence the agitator and save the boy is not only constitutional, but withal a great mercy." An old man whose only son has been sentenced to be shot comes to beg for mercy. Lincoln shows him a wire from General Butler: "Urgently beg you not interfere with court-martial procedure, for this completely destroys discipline of troops." The old man, having read the telegram, sits weeping. Suddenly Lincoln says, out loud, "To the devil with this Butler", seizes his pen, and writes: "Job Smith is not to be shot until further orders from me." The father remains uneasy. What will happen when "further orders" are sent? "I see," said Lincoln, "that you are not very well acquainted with me. If your son never looks on death till further orders come from me to shoot him, he will live to be a great deal older than Methuselah."

Another man had been sentenced for going home from the front without leave — the reason being that he wished to secure his girl's position by marrying her. Lincoln, having heard the whole story, signed a reprieve, but, while writing it, said to his secretary: "I hope this soldier won't have good reason, a year hence, to regret that I did not let him be shot."

A lad, William Scott by name, having gone to sleep at his post, is under arrest. The President, in the course of an inspection, sees him and says: "My boy, you are not going to be shot. I believe you when you tell me that you couldn't keep awake. I shall send you back to the regiment. But I have been put to a great deal of trouble on your account. What I want to know is, how are you going to pay my bill?"

LINCOLN IN 1864

From a photograph by Brady, Washington

The youngster, much perplexed, said in his embarrassment that it might be possible to raise as much as six hundred dollars on a mortgage.

"No, that won't do. You must pay the debt yourself, by doing your duty as a soldier."

Sometimes the only excuse he can find for extending clemency to a deserter (and he has always to justify himself to the generals) is the offender's youth. "I am opposed to the shooting of a young fellow under eighteen." The news of this having gone round, every mother who comes to him in tears makes a point of understating the age of her erring son. There are cases where no other excuse than youth can be found for granting a reprieve. Soldier so-and-so "writes that he is to be shot for desertion on the 6th instant. His own story is rather a bad one, and yet he tells it so frankly, that I am somewhat interested in him. Has he been a good soldier except the desertion? About how old is he?" Or the President is content to exaggerate, telegraphing: "He is the son of so close a friend that I must not let him be executed." Another time, ordering the postponement of an execution, he wires to the general: "I understand you have under sentence of death a tall old man, by the name of ——. I personally knew him, and did not think him a bad man." At length, after three years, he issues a general order that men found guilty of desertion are for the time being to be imprisoned.

All these services, and hundreds of lesser ones, signify that an appeal has been made to him in the last resort, after his subordinates, and especially the Secretary of War, have refused aid. People even wire petitions to him, and he answers with inexhaustible patience. "I cannot postpone the execution of a convicted spy on a mere telegraphic dispatch signed with a name I never heard before. General Wallace may give you a pass to see him if he chooses." Others come to visit him, and, in their anxiety, forget to give him essential data. When they have gone, the President wants to help, but does not know how.

Telegram: "An intelligent woman in deep distress called this morning, saying her husband, a lieutenant in the Army of the

Potomac, was to be shot next Monday for desertion, and, putting a letter in my hand, upon which I relied for particulars, she left without mentioning a name . . . by which to identify the case. On opening the letter, I found it equally vague, having nothing to identify it, except her own signature, which seems to be ———. I could not again find her. If you have a case which you think is probably the one intended, please apply my dispatch of this morning to it."

This is the father of the nation, one who is always thinking how to help his people, even when they make it difficult for him. He does not deny that his motive is a selfish one, sublime though it may be, for "it gives me a restful feeling when, at the close of a hard day's work, I can find some excuse or other for saving a man's life." Another time he defends his clemency with the fine saying: "You do not know how hard it is to let a human being die, when you feel that a stroke of your pen will save him."

Sometimes he forces himself to be severe, but afterwards makes a last appeal to the general in command: ". . . have appealed to me for mercy, without giving any ground for it whatever. I understand these are very flagrant cases, and that you deem their punishment as being indispensable to the service. If I am not mistaken in this, please let them know at once that their appeal is denied." And when, in the end, he had felt it impossible to send a reprieve, he would say, "They are shooting a boy at ——— to-day. I hope I have not done wrong to allow it." He knows that every moment costs the life of many men, and has accepted the fact; but he cannot forget the individual whose life might be allowed to continue without interfering with the general aim.

During the last year of the war, two hundred sixty-seven were, none the less, executed by sentence of court-martial, one hundred sixty of them for murder, but about eight hundred were reprieved.

Yet Lincoln would not allow himself to be humbugged. An officer came to him complaining of being unjustly cashiered, read aloud a lengthy petition, but achieved nothing. Having pushed his request in vain, he at length burst out with, "I see that you have made up your mind against doing me justice!" The Presi-

dent's lips twitched, he laid down the petition, stood up, strode
to the officer, seized him by the collar, and ran him out of the room,
calling out fiercely in the hall, "You'd better not show yourself
here again. I can put up with criticism, but not with insult. . . .
Your papers will be sent you. I never want to see your face
again." This is the farmer and the wrestler, but also the man
with overstrained nerves and overtried patience — the man who,
after closing the door, will proceed to reproach himself for the undue
mildness which has encouraged such excesses as the visitor's.
Soon, however, he will thrust aside these feelings, like the papers on
the table, and will continue to be guided by the inner voice.

For during all these years he, the civilian, was the friend and
father of his troops. Well did they know it, and they sang, "We're
coming, Father Abraham, three hundred thousand strong!"
Every one of them knew that the President was the man to apply
to when you could not get what you wanted elsewhere — with the
result that, to all the cares of State and greater troubles with which
he was burdened, there were added these lesser concerns, which
cost him time and energy and thought, and yet did not bring him
the great compensation of saving human lives. When we read all
the documents in rapid succession, we feel, sometimes, that we
must be studying the papers of the head of a passport department
rather than those of the President of the United States.

Here is a girl from Richmond, who has for a long time been taking care of her mother in Washington and now wants to get back
to Richmond, to see her affianced there, from whom she has
been parted for two years; she wants to get married. Welles is
suspicious, thinks the girl may be a spy, but the President disre-
gards the advice of the Secretary and gives the desired pass,
saying that the war is depopulating the country, and interfering
with marriage; one must help, not hinder. Again, here is a wire
to General Meade: "Mr. —— wishes a pass from me to follow
your army to pick up rags and cast-off clothing. I will give it him
if you say so, otherwise not."

A woman has lost five sons on the field of battle. Learning this,
the President writes to her: "I feel how weak and fruitless must

be any words of mine which should attempt to beguile you from
the grief of a loss so overwhelming. But I cannot refrain from
tendering you the consolation that may be found in the thanks of
the Republic they died to save. I pray that our Heavenly Father
may assuage the anguish of your bereavement, and leave you only
the cherished memory of the loved and lost, and the solemn pride
that must be yours to have laid so costly a sacrifice upon the altar
of freedom. Yours very sincerely and respectfully, A. Lincoln."

These are the tones that will make him immortal. Then
there are hundreds of cards on which he introduces people. To the
Secretary of War: "Please see this young man from Pittsburg;
he is very young, and I should be grateful for anything you could
do for him." Such is the tone Lincoln uses in these briefest of
missives, making himself the debtor, if only a poor youngster from
Pittsburg can be helped. Paying his daily visit to the War Department, he asks the telegraph operator: "What is that woman
crying for outside?" He is told that she wants to go and see her
husband at the front, having something very important to tell
him. Recently, however, a general order has been issued that no
women are to be allowed in the fighting lines. Lincoln sits for a
while, looking moody. Then he says, "Oh, well, send her along,
all the same. Write a pass for her."

"Hadn't we better tell her to write to the colonel? Or why
shouldn't the husband be allowed to come to Washington?"

Lincoln relieved: "Yes, yes, he shall come here!" Instantly he
takes one of the long yellow forms, and, his face having cleared,
writes the telegram.

It is the son of the people, who has seen this weeping woman,
her husband, and her children, a hundred times in Illinois, has sat
at her table, has conversed with her; but it is also the poet who has
so vivid an insight, so vigorous a capacity for putting himself in
others' places, that he feels their smiles and their tears as if they
were his own, and would therefore rather see them smile than weep.
He is the man of melancholy mood, compelled to wage a terrible
war, and eager to do all in his power to reduce the suffering it causes;
and he is the practical idealist, who day after day follows the

great call of duty even in the pettiest affairs. He is the man with a supreme knowledge of his fellows, restrained by a natural sense of dignity from asking what effect his person may have. "Give yourself no uneasiness on the subject," he writes to a friend who has expressed a fear lest something that has happened may lead people to make fun of him. "I have endured a great deal of ridicule, without much malice; and have received a great deal of kindness not quite free from ridicule. I am used to it."

To keep in close touch with the people, never to lapse into the world of the politicians, to avoid surrendering to their claims even in this stony-hearted town, and, even in this palace, to keep fresh in memory the primal sounds of the forests of Illinois — these are his resolves, these are the wellsprings of his energy. When farmers and backwoodsmen come, they are always welcome, and when in Illinois they want to rid themselves of certain officials, they send along Dennis Hanks, dressed in a fine new suit, to put the matter to the President; and Hanks gets what he wants for the most part, although Stanton comes in, probably looking skeptical, so that after he has gone Hanks bluntly advises his tall cousin to rid himself of this dangerous fellow.

Of course he is often down-hearted, for the succession of petitioners is unending; but when the President is advised to receive fewer visitors he rejoins that this can't be done, because he imagines himself in the situation of those who come to ask help; and once, when there is talk of a poor man who has no friends, Lincoln says, "If he has no friends, I will befriend him." Thus he wins more abiding satisfactions than come from the votes of majorities in Congress or even from the victories won by Grant, when an old man from the highlands of New York State comes to him and says:

"Up there we believe in God and Father Abraham."

XIII

At Christmas, General Sherman had presented Lincoln with the city of Savannah "as a Christmas gift, . . . with one hundred fifty heavy guns, . . . also about twenty-five thousand bales of cotton."

His famous march through Georgia had shown the world that an army of sixty thousand men could now traverse almost unmolested the whole breadth of the South, and then form a junction with the fleet for the establishment of a new base. The terror aroused in the South by this forward movement was as great as the renown it acquired in other parts of the world. Grant, meanwhile, had held Lee so firmly in check that the latter, outnumbered, had never ventured to give battle to the Northern forces. In the middle of February, when Charleston, a cultural center of the South, fell, he and Sherman had Lee between two fires, and Grant was able to cut the main railways of the South, so that communication with the Southwest was broken off, Richmond had become untenable, and the only remaining question was whether Lee would surrender or would continue the struggle. Not until now did Jefferson Davis, who for four years had retained the supreme command, decide to give the responsibility of this position to Lee; he himself, he pathetically declared in a speech, wished to live and die with the Confederacy.

Shortly afterwards the Southern Congress passed a law enabling Negro slaves to be enrolled as volunteers, in return for the boon of freedom. This was a very difficult decision for the South to come to, and it was only arrived at by a small majority.

The resolve was, moreover, an extreme instance of the tragicomical ironies which are not uncommon in history, but are seldom so glaringly conspicuous to contemporaries and immediate posterity. As if in a fabled epigram, it showed the obsoleteness of an institution which had, in the end, to annul itself in the attempt to defend itself. The man who was willing to allow himself to be shot to death in order to maintain slavery, became free; whilst the man who stayed at home, the man who would not fight for slavery, remained a slave. Lincoln showed amazing mildness in the way he referred to this last twist of what had been the fundamental problem of a life now drawing to its close. Speaking to a regiment, he said:

"I have neither written nor made a speech on that subject, because that was their business, not mine, and if I had a wish upon the subject, I had not the power to introduce it, or make it effective. The great question with them was whether the negro, being put into the army, will fight for them. . . . I have in my lifetime heard many arguments why the negroes ought to be slaves; but if they fight for those who would keep them in slavery, it will be a better argument than any I have yet heard. He who will fight for that, ought to be a slave. They have concluded, at last, to take one out of four of the slaves and put them in the army, and that one out of the four who will fight to keep the others in slavery, ought to be a slave himself, unless he is killed in a fight. While I have often said that all men ought to be free, yet would I allow those colored persons to be slaves who want to be, and next to them those white people who argue in favor of making other people slaves. I am in favor of giving an appointment to such white men to try it on for those slaves. . . . They have drawn upon their last branch of resources, and we can now see the bottom. I am glad to see the end so near at hand. I have said more than I intended, and will therefore bid you good-bye."

This extemporized utterance was the only one in which Lincoln made any attempt to demonstrate the contradictoriness of his adversaries' last and maddest expedient. It contains no jubilation, no word of self-justification, not a single note of triumph. The same must be said of the speech with which he opened his second term of office. There were but two new features at this second inauguration: a Negro battalion formed part of the presidential escort, as a manifest sign of all that had been achieved in the interim; and the cupola of the Capitol was adorned by the new statue of Liberty, which seemed to herald a new era. But the man who, on this second occasion, administered the oath of office to the incoming President was no longer Taney, who had recently died at the age of ninety years; it was Chase, whom Lincoln, without consulting any one, had appointed chief justice. Douglas no longer sat in the first row, but there was no tiresome hat or fashionable walking-stick for any one to hold or otherwise to dispose of. Nor, to conclude, was there a lengthy oration, such as had been needed then to clarify the situation. Then, on March fourth, Lincoln delivered his famous Second Inaugural Address:

". . . The progress of our arms, upon which all else chiefly depends, is as well known to the public as to myself; and it is, I trust, reasonably satisfactory and encouraging to all. With high hope for the future, no prediction in regard to it is ventured. . . . Both [parties to the dispute] read the same Bible and pray to the same God, and each invokes His aid against the other. It may seem strange that any men should dare to ask a just God's assistance in wringing their bread from the sweat of other men's faces; but let us judge not, that we be not judged. The prayers of both could not be answered — that of neither has been answered fully. The Almighty has His own purposes. . . . 'It must needs be that offenses come; but woe to that man by whom the offense cometh.'

"If we shall suppose that American slavery is one of those offenses which, in the providence of God, must needs come, but which, having continued through His appointed time, He now wills to remove, and that He gives to both North and South this terrible war, as the woe due to those by whom the offense came, shall we discern therein any departure from those divine attributes which the believers in a living God always ascribe to Him? Fondly do we hope — fervently do we pray — that this mighty scourge of war may speedily pass away. Yet, if God wills that it continue until all the wealth piled by the bondsman's two hundred and fifty years of unrequited toil shall be sunk, and until every drop of blood drawn with the lash shall be paid by another drawn with the sword, as was said three thousand years ago, so still it must be said, 'The judgments of the Lord are true and righteous altogether.'

"With malice toward none; with charity for all; with firmness in the right, as God gives us to see the right, let us strive on to finish the work we are in; to bind up the nation's wounds; to care for him who shall have borne the battle, and for his widow and for his orphan — to do all which may achieve and cherish a just and lasting peace among ourselves and with all nations."

Such was Lincoln's address to the people when opening his second term as President. It was a father's speech. All its political elements seemed resolved into philosophy, and all philosophy was fatalism. When he was still doubtful of victory, the main purpose of his speeches and open letters was to sustain the nation's confidence. Now, when victory could only be a question of weeks, he gave all the honor to that force of destiny which he termed God, and ventured to tell his astonished auditors that God's ways were to be regarded as righteous, even if they should involve the long continuance of bloodshed. After he had for four years devoted himself to all the activities forced on him by circumstances, he was able, relieved from this burden, to resume the rôle natural to him — that of one who awaits destiny's decree, and accepts whatever fate assigns. At the same time, the speech is that of an educator, for it has the clarity of old age; it is something of a testament. Yet, broadly regarded, it is not so much a speech as an ode.

Shortly afterwards, he himself commented on it in another tone, writing to his friend Weed, in answer to a congratulation, as follows: "I expect the Inaugural Address to wear as well as, perhaps better than, anything I have produced; but I believe it is not immediately popular. Men are not flattered by being shown that there has been a difference of purpose between the Almighty and them. To deny it, however, in this case, is to deny that there is a God governing the world. It is a truth which I thought needed to be told, and, as whatever of humiliation there is in it falls most directly on myself, I thought others might afford for me to tell it."

XIV

When the war came to an end at last, once again, after a long interval, shots were fired at the foot of the Capitol. It was a salute of one hundred guns, but they were not fired to acclaim a victory in the field. The decision had been taken that Lincoln's provisional war-time decree for the liberation of the slaves should become permanent law. Four years earlier, it had been resolved in the same connection that any amendment to the Constitution for such a purpose was prohibited; and seven years farther back still, the same guns had acclaimed Douglas' negrophobist resolution in the Kansas matter. Even to-day, the vote had been regarded as uncertain, and up till noon no one had had the least idea how things were going to turn out. In the end there were one hundred nineteen for and fifty-six against. A two-thirds majority was needed, so the turn-over of three votes from yea to nay would have hung up the whole scheme once more. For a time, only, since the passing of such an amendment in due course had now become inevitable; but the great man whose life was the embodiment of the idea would not then have seen it realized before his death.

The victory was a personal one for Lincoln. Speaking to serenaders next evening, he said: "This amendment is the king's cure-all for all the evils." When three fourths of the States should have separately adopted the amendment now passed by Congress, it would definitively become law, and it was a pleasure to Lincoln that Illinois was the first State to decide in its favor. He did not live to see its final adoption.

And now at the very end of the war Lincoln, in the saloon of a river steamboat, sits face to face with the Vice President of the enemy confederation, his sometime friend of Congress days, Stephens, whom he had not seen for four years, and with whom he had exchanged warning letters shortly before the outbreak of the war. That Lincoln should be here, even though informally, to discuss possibilities of peace, was one of those improprieties through which he forfeited the confidence of politicians of his own day — and secured the common-sense approval of posterity.

Stephens, who had since the previous autumn been working for peace in the South, and had now been commissioned to negotiate, arranged through Grant to get into touch with the political chiefs of the North, though he still desired to maintain the independence of the South. Without informing his cabinet, still less consulting it, Lincoln followed his natural promptings, went on board, accompanied by Grant and Seward, and when the three received Stephens and two of the latter's friends, the fact that the negotiators were old acquaintances dispelled any embarrassment that might otherwise have ensued; and while elsewhere the advance of troops, siege, and bombardment were still going on, the men who now met were inquiring about the health of mutual friends, as if they had come together after a voyage of exploration in distant parts; then they went on to talk of the past and the future, without secretaries, without taking any notes, exchanging views uninterruptedly for four hours: a real Lincolnian proceeding, typical in its unceremoniousness.

When Stephens asked if there was no possibility of avoiding the continuance of the war, Lincoln answered that it would be enough for the South to cease its resistance. Stephens said that the settlement of the main issue might be postponed, and spoke of the likelihood that the severed States would voluntarily and freely enter into a new Union. Lincoln rejected the idea, in an indifferent sort of way, and went on to speak quite candidly of the history of his proclamation, remarking that he would not have interfered with slavery had he not been compelled to maintain the Union; and he even admitted that he was still prepared to compensate the Southern slave owners, since the people of the North were just as responsible for slavery. "I could mention persons, whose names would astonish you, who are willing to do this if the war shall now cease without further expense, and with the abolition of slavery as stated." He was not, he hastened to add, giving an assurance of anything of the kind. Congress would decide. Seward, too, pointed out that if the Southern States were to rejoin the Union immediately, they would probably be able to defeat the ratification of the amendment to the Constitution recently passed by Congress.

Thus friendly was Lincoln's attitude towards the enemy. But when Stephens tried to touch him to the quick by describing the devastation caused by the war, he found the heart he knew so well adamant. The man who formerly in Congress had shed tears during the same Southerner's speech, the man who keenly felt each successive day of warfare to be a new sacrifice of blood, was not to be diverted as much as an inch from his statesmanlike course. He bluntly refused to treat with armed rebels.

"Charles I of England," interposed one of Stephens' companions, "was willing to do so."

"I don't profess to be posted on history," replied Lincoln. "On all such matters I will turn you over to Seward. All I distinctly recollect about the case of Charles I is that he lost his head."

"Then," said Stephens, "you look upon us as rebels, who ought really to be hanged for treason?"

"Yes, that's so."

"We had supposed as much. But, to tell you the truth, we are not seriously afraid of being hanged so long as you are President."

When Stephens, in conclusion, advocates the fantastic scheme of a joint war by North and South against Mexico, where Napoleon III's adventure is in progress, Lincoln refuses to entertain it. When Stephens presses the idea, Lincoln says, shaking hands, "Well, Stephens, I will reconsider it; but I do not think my mind will change."

Has a parley to discuss the possibilities of peace ever before or since been conducted and ended in such a mood? But for Lincoln, it would have been no more than a chilly negotiation; he lifted it into the levels of human kindliness and humor. No doubt he had kept close watch on his adversary, for subsequently, describing the appearance of the small and graceful Southerner, he said, "Mr. Stephens had on an overcoat about three sizes too big for him, with an old-fashioned high collar. The cabin soon began to get pretty warm, and after a while he stood up and pulled off his big coat. He slipped it off just about as you would husk an ear of corn. I couldn't help thinking, as I looked first at the overcoat and then at the man, 'Well, that's the biggest shuck and the smallest nubbin I ever laid eyes on.'" Thus sympathetic is Lincoln's report of the meeting. All that Jefferson Davis, however, could find as a suitable epithet for Lincoln, when an account of the interview was given to him was to denounce the Northern President as "His Majesty Abraham the First."

Yet now, as always, concern for his brothers' fate weighed heavily on Lincoln; and during the return journey he was anxiously probing every possibility of inducing the South, the hopelessness of whose position was now manifest, to surrender more speedily. Might not some concession bring the war sooner to its close? How long was the struggle likely to last? A hundred days, at least. What would this cost the North? More than three hundred million dollars. What if, instead, they were to give the money to the enemy, and thus save thousands of human lives? The very next day, he drafted a message and a resolution to be submitted to Congress. Let four hundred million dollars be allotted to the South, for distribution among the slave owners in amounts proportional to their losses, owing to the liberation of the slaves; one half to be payable at once on April first, and the balance as soon as the amendment to the Constitution should have been ratified. All sequestrated property, with the exception of slaves, was to be restored, and all political offenders were to be pardoned.

When, a day later, he laid this proposal before his cabinet, enthusiastically recommending its adoption, it was unanimously rejected. "You are all opposed to me," he said with a deep sigh, and abandoned the scheme. On getting home, he endorsed the draft with the following docket: "To-day these papers, which explain themselves, were drawn up and submitted to the cabinet and unanimously disapproved by them."

Nothing in Lincoln's life shows more plainly how the lover of mankind and the statesman, the heart and the brain of this practical idealist collaborated to do what was reasonable for the moment and of profound significance for the future. He had refused to treat with the rebels as equals. Since victory was certain, why should he not await it with folded arms? The calculator was at work in him as well as the moralist, and, each supporting the other, they jointly elaborated the most effective arguments for shortening the period of mutual terrorization. The war would last a hundred days more and so it did. During these hundred days, four hundred million dollars would be blown away in the air, and, worse than this, would be used to shatter the bodies of rebels who were soon to be fellow citizens once more! What a splendid idea: no less shrewd than kindly, no less practical than moral.

XV

At length the terrible pressure from which the President had suffered throughout four long years began to slacken, and all the witnesses are agreed in declaring that there was a change in him during the last weeks of his life.

Beyond question, of late there had been an immoderate increase in tension and fatigue. "I sometimes fancy," he one day groaned, "that every one of the numerous grist ground through here daily, from a senator seeking war with France down to a poor woman after a place in the Treasury Department, darted at me with finger and thumb, picked out their especial piece of my vitality, and carried it off. When I get through with such a hard day's work there is only one word which can express my condition, and that is flabbiness."

Old acquaintances speak of finding him heavy-eyed, gray of visage, stretching out his hand to them mechanically, and listening apathetically. One describes him as looking like "a baited, cornered man, always on the defence against attacks he could not openly meet and defy or punish." The artist who is painting his portrait meets him "clad in a long morning wrapper, pacing back and forth a narrow passage leading to one of the windows, his hands behind him, great black rings under his eyes, his head bent forward upon his breast — altogether such a picture of the effects of sorrow, care, and anxiety as would have melted the hearts of the worst of his adversaries, who so mistakenly applied to him the epithets of tyrant and usurper." When his friend Swett visited the White House, in the hope of getting further help for the vast numbers of wounded, he found the President sitting by an open window, listening to a bird that was perched on a twig just outside, twittering joyously. After Swett had explained his proposals Lincoln said: "Isn't he singing sweetly?" Swett, at this, said to himself, "I see the country is safer than I thought," and moved as if to go. Lincoln stayed him, calling out:

"Here, Swett, come back and sit down. It is impossible for a man in my position not to have thought of all these things. Weeks ago, every man capable of bearing arms was ordered to the front, and everything you have suggested has been done." Thus his life was punctuated by fatigues and cares, and he said on one occasion, "I feel as though I shall never be glad again."

Now, for the first time, he takes a kind of holiday, wishing to escape the rout of place hunters who once again, just as four years earlier, are threatening to invade the White House. We are in March, the enemy capital may fall any day, Grant has invited the President to look on at the final decision of the issue, so the latter with his wife and a few intimates is going to take ten days' rest on board a river steamer in the midst of the army. Robert is there, too, the young man having been assigned to Grant's staff during the last few weeks of the war, to give him wider experience. Sherman and Sheridan have come, to hold a council of war with Grant. Even at City Point, Lincoln often passes half the day at the telegraph office, just as he does in Washington, wishing to send on Grant's reports to Stanton. He sometimes steams up and down the river accompanied by Admiral Porter, but his favorite place is among the tents, where he spends hours riding hither and thither in the camp, where the soldiers greet him with cries of "Three cheers for Father Abraham." Often he talks to the men, or, when not doing this, and not riding, he will sit for hours, chair tilted back, hand shading his eyes, watching the movements.

Refusing the admiral's bed, he has chosen for himself a small cabin in which the berth is only six feet long. When asked, next morning, how he has slept, he answers: "I slept well, but you can't put a long sword into a short scabbard." In fact, he was four inches longer than the cabin. Without telling the President beforehand, the admiral now has the ship's carpenters set to work; the room is remodeled, so that the berth can be widened, and also lengthened to suit Lincoln's stature. Next morning he says, "A miracle happened last night; I shrank six inches in length, and about a foot sideways."

Mary was the only person who was not happy these days. She was paying her first lengthy visit to the army, had a unique opportunity of showing herself off, and a pleasant excursion in the company of the French ambassador and other distinguished persons, was, of course, very much to her taste. They were going to the front of the Army of the Potomac, twelve miles from the landing stage, most of the men on horseback, but the two ladies, Mary and Mrs. Grant, driving in a sort of open carriage. They were escorted by a general seated on the box beside the coachman. In the course of the drive, this gentleman remarked that they would meet another lady, the wife of General Charles Griffin, and a personal friend of Mrs. Grant; he added that, owing to the approach of hostilities, all women had been ordered to the rear, but Mrs. Griffin had received from the President a special permit to visit her husband for a day or two.

Mary was dumbfounded. A woman had seen the President, and she had known nothing of it. "What do you mean, Sir? Did she see the President alone? Do you know, Sir, that I never permit the President to see any woman alone?" The general strove to appease her, to reassure her. "That is a very equivocal smile, Sir. Let me out of this carriage at once! I will ask the President if he saw that woman alone!" When the others arrived, she wanted to be taken to her husband immediately.

An officer grasped the situation, rode off to Lincoln, and returned with the comforting assurance that Stanton, and not the President, had issued the pass in question.

Next day the same party, arranged as before, went to visit the army which was under the command of General Ord. That officer's wife, who had remained, rode beside the President for a time. The outbreak of yesterday had warned most of the company that it would be unwise to inform Mrs. Lincoln of this, but at length one of the officers happened to mention the fact. Mary thereupon turned on him so savagely that his horse became unmanageable, and he had to back away out of sight. Soon after, when Mrs. Ord rode up to greet the ladies, Mrs. Lincoln hailed her in the most abusive terms, and asked her how she dared to run after the President. Poor Mrs. Ord retired from the scene in tears. A day or two later, on board the river steamer, when a naval captain defended Mrs. Ord's behavior, Mrs. Lincoln turned upon this champion with vituperation. Lincoln thereupon asked the captain to step up to his stateroom, in order to look at a map, obviously wishing to make amends to this gentleman.

The scenes throw a strong light on the unhappy temperament of a woman who, in truth, had never had the smallest ground for jealousy, and who, in the petty environment of Springfield, had never shown any signs of it, but now, when all her thoughts circled round the ideas of power and position, was trying to keep a tight clutch on things no one wanted to wrest from her. Nor did any one foresee how momentous were to be the consequences of these incidents. The probability is that a fortnight later they saved the life of General Grant.

XVI

A few days later, Petersburg and Richmond had fallen. Lee and Davis had fled with the remnants of the Southern army, and every one thronged to see the fortified city which had at length been taken — like Troy, much coveted, after a long siege. The river, though not yet freed of mines, was already lively with shipping, gay with bunting, and merry with music; but the ships stranded on sandbanks, and when the President on his way to Richmond, accompanied by Tad and the Admiral, was stranded with the rest, he got into a barge towed by a steam tug with a file of marines on board. No salute was fired, no triumphal entry had been prepared. Everything was extemporized, as throughout Lincoln's life. But he laughed, well-pleased, having for a week now been in the best of spirits; told an anecdote of a place hunter who had begun by asking for an appointment as ambassador but in the end had been glad to accept the gift of an old pair of trousers; and when the tug had to be cast off and dispatched to help another stranded steamer, the crew of the barge rowed on haphazard, for none of them nor yet the admiral had ever been in these waters before. They stuck fast on a rock, but managed to back off after a time; on this day of victory the sometime flatboatman was destined to be put in mind of New Salem.

At the first landing place on the steep bank there was a small house, and here they disembarked. Bedded in green were the white homes of the Southern town, well tended, but sinister and deserted, ominously quiet, the only people in sight being a dozen Negroes, digging, under the leadership of an old man. This latter now stood upright, put his hands up to his eyes, dropped his spade, and exclaimed: "Bress de Lord, dere is de great Messiah! I knowed him as soon as I seed him. He's bin in my heart fo' long yeahs, an' he's come at las' to free his chillun' from dere bondage! Glory, Hallelujah!" Thus lapsing readily into Biblical phraseology, after the manner of Christianized Negroes, he fell upon his knees and kissed the liberator's feet, the other blacks following his example.

There they lie, a dozen poor slaves, who have been digging as if nothing had happened, as if there had been no sudden change in their fate; fronting them the tall white man, lean and gray, perplexed and embarrassed. He says, "Don't kneel to me, that is not right. You must kneel to God only, and thank Him for the liberty you will hereafter enjoy. I am but God's humble instrument; but you may rest assured that as long as I live no one shall put a shackle on your limbs, and you shall have all the rights which God has given to every other free citizen of this republic." Not a brilliant oration, no more than a few deeply felt words, but the Negroes understand his glance, and when the admiral now asks them to make way, the old black assents, in the singing tone he has learned from the missionaries:

"Yes, Mars', but after bein' so many yeahs in de desert widout water, it's mighty pleasant to be lookin' at las' on our spring of life. 'Scuse us, Sir; we means no disrespec' to Mars' Lincoln; we means all love and gratitude." Then, joining hands to form a ring, they proceed with their melodious voices to sing a hymn, while the President stands in the middle and waits. About four minutes have now elapsed (so the admiral reports) since the landing, but the streets seem to be suddenly alive with the colored race. They spring from the earth. They come tumbling and shouting, from over the hills and from the water side, where no one had been visible a moment before; they flock up from all directions, for the alarm spread among them during the capture of the city has sub-sided. The little party of whites is in danger of being crushed, and the admiral orders twelve of the boat's crew to fix bayonets and form a guard round the President; but none of the Negroes are alarmed, and the press goes on increasing. Since he cannot move, Lincoln must do something. He raises his hand, and instantly there is silence. Then he begins to speak:

"My poor Friends, you are free — free as air. You can cast off the name of slave and trample upon it; it will come to you no more. Liberty is your birthright. God gave it to you as He gave it to others, and it is a sin that you have been deprived of it for so many years. But you must try to deserve this priceless boon. Let the world see that you merit it, and are able to maintain it by your good works. Don't let your joy carry you into excesses. Learn the laws and obey them; obey God's commandments and thank Him for giving you liberty, for to Him you owe all things. There, now, let me pass on; I have but little time to spare. I want to see the capital, and must return at once to Washington to secure to you that liberty which you seem to prize so highly."

Thus spake Abraham Lincoln when for the first time in his life he stood in the midst of a black multitude, thronging round him, shouting to him in a moment of fulfillment such as is vouchsafed to very few, and such as even to him had never been vouchsafed before. He spoke like a father, as one far off and yet close at hand, perhaps with an instructive mien, perhaps with one of warning, certainly with one of love; for in this hour his figure recalled that of the Teacher in whose name all these things had been done, who moved among unlettered fishermen to bring them both freedom and law. He stood there, long and lean, wearied by the struggle he had been carrying on for a decade, the struggle which, by devious paths no one had hitherto understood, and despite calumnious tongues, he had at length brought to a successful issue.

"It never struck me," says Admiral Porter, "that there was any one in that multitude who would injure Mr. Lincoln; it seemed to me he had an army of supporters there who could and would defend him against all the world. Our progress was very slow;

we did not move a mile an hour, and the crowd was still increasing. It was a warm day, and the streets were dusty, owing to the immense gathering which covered every part of them, kicking up the dirt. The atmosphere was suffocating; but Mr. Lincoln could be seen plainly by every man, woman, and child, towering head and shoulders above that crowd; he overtopped every man there. He carried his hat in his hand, fanning his face, from which the perspiration was pouring. He looked as if he would have given his presidency for a glass of water." Thus they entered the town together, the tall white man who was President and the thousands of Negroes; and when in the streets, while people threw open their casements and looked out to see the incarnation of wickedness who had been the plague of the South for four long years, it would have been easy to shoot him. After they had visited Jefferson Davis' headquarters, the State House of the Confederate Congress, and other places, and were driving back to the riverside in an open carriage, the admiral became uneasy, for in the gathering darkness what would have been simpler than for any of the vengeful Southerners to seize the chance of getting even with the arch enemy?

During these days, arrangements were made by wire to hold an anniversary celebration of the opening of the war at Fort Sumter, on April fourteenth, the day the place had been surrendered to the South. At first the President demurred at the date, saying it had been on April thirteenth. Stanton was to consult an old calendar, and make sure. But in the end he gave way, telegraphing: "I think it is little or no difference whether the Fort Sumter ceremony takes place on the 13th or 14th." There was no warning inner voice. He had no foreboding that when thus fixing the day of the festival, he was decreeing the date of his own death.

XVII

For what had not happened in Richmond, because in these days of confusion the President's visit thither had not been foreseen, might easily happen in Washington. It was to happen, and it did.

Who can be surprised? When prophets have been stoned, has

it not always been for some misconception of what they really were? Have not the martyrs of all ages invariably suffered through the misunderstanding of the crowd? Was it not inevitable that the passion of the South should be concentrated upon the man whose very name, when he was first nominated, seemed to carry with it the certainty of war? How could Southerners be expected to know that all through this last year his thoughts had turned ever towards reconciliation, and that only a week ago he had been trying to secure compensation for the defeated enemy? They looked upon him as the foe incarnate, and he should pay for his victory.

As far back as two years earlier, a secret society for the assassination of Lincoln had been financed in Richmond, by wealthy persons. A year later, there was talk of a conspiracy entered into by one hundred and fifty carefully picked young fellows, who were to assemble in Washington, kidnap Lincoln, and carry him off. An artist who was portraying Lincoln asked him if he had heard of the scheme. The President smiled, and replied: "Well, even if true, I do not see what the rebels would gain by either killing or getting possession of me. I am but a single individual, and it would not help their cause or make the least difference in the progress of the war. Everything would go right on just the same. Soon after I was nominated at Chicago, I began to receive letters threatening my life. The first one or two made me uncomfortable, but I came at length to look for a regular installment of this kind of correspondence in every week's mail. . . . It is no uncommon thing to receive them even now, but they have ceased to give me any apprehension. . . . There is nothing like getting used to things."

His general attitude towards the matter was one of incredulity. Once he protested that assassination was not an American type of crime; and, though he was willing to carry a heavy stick, as his wife advised, he often forgot to take it with him. For the rest, both as a practical man and as a fatalist, he was disinclined to take precautions. "I long ago made up my mind that if anybody wants to kill me, he will do it. If I wore a shirt of mail and kept myself surrounded by a bodyguard, it would be all the same.

There are a thousand ways of getting at a man if it is desired that he should be killed." It never seemed to occur either to him or to his friends that the dangers of his position in this respect were intensified by the victory. Besides, various sinister incidents of the last twelve months had not at this time become publicly known.

One of these was the discovery of the remarkable inscription on a window pane in a provincial inn, but neither this nor the firing at Lincoln at night near the Soldiers' Home was announced till long afterwards. Nor did any one learn at the time of a remarkable incident in a New York theater, which turned upon the utterance of three words. In the Winter Garden theater of that city, one November evening, "Julius Caesar" was being played, and in the caste were all three of the Booth brothers, two of whom lived by the fame of the third. This last, the most famous tragedian of his day, appears that night to have been playing *Caesar;* but certainly one of the brothers was playing *Marc Antony* — a man of twenty-six, exceptionally handsome, with an olive-tinted skin, classical features, a Roman nose, and flashing eyes, but (it would seem) a poor allowance of talent. In the third act comes the scene at the Capitol where Marc Antony stirs up the citizens to take vengeance on Brutus. Booth delivered the speech with increasing emphasis, as the rôle demands, coming at length to the familiar climax:

> " I am no orator, as Brutus is :
> But were I Brutus,
> And Brutus Antony, there were an Antony
> Would ruffle up your spirits, and put a tongue
> In every wound of Caesar, that should move
> The stones of Rome to rise and mutiny ! "

And here the actor strengthened the fortissimo of the conclusion by adding the words *"Sic semper tyrannis !"* — the phrase which, so the tale runs, Brutus had uttered as he thrust his dagger home in Caesar's breast. But in modern America, above all at that date, it was better known still as the motto on the Virginian coat of arms, a motto which during the war had been quoted a thousand times to intensify the martial ardor of the South.

The slip passed almost unnoticed, but one of the audience, who reported the matter long afterwards, turned to his neighbor with the skeptical inquiry, "Is that in Shakespeare?" Another, sitting behind, remarked, "It is the motto of the State of Virginia." But the man of whom the question had been asked, replied, "It's all right, he is speaking for Brutus."

At this moment there came a cry of "Fire!" Every one in the theater jumped up, and in a minute or two the place was emptied. Soon came tidings that simultaneously fires had broken out in many New York theaters and hotels, obviously the concerted work of incendiaries. It has been said that the three words "*Sic semper tyrannis!*" were a signal in the Winter Garden Theater.

However that may be, in the excitement caused by the fires, the mysterious utterance on the stage was forgotten. But there were far more obvious signs that plans for assassination were afoot. At about the same time, there appeared in an Alabama newspaper a notice asking subscriptions to a fund for the assassination of Lincoln, Seward, and Johnson before they should take office. Furthermore, shortly after Lincoln's reëlection, a lieutenant wrote to Jefferson Davis, offering to make an end of the leader of the North; the missive was passed on to the Secretary of War and other high officials "for attention."

Booth was animated by mixed motives. Sprung from a family of actors and brother of a great tragedian compared to whom he was a pygmy, spoiled and petted because of his good looks, he would probably, had the circumstances of the time been different, have followed the call of ambition in a different direction — would have become a successful lover, an adventurer in other fields. The war disclosed to him a new ideal: he had been present at the execution of John Brown; and this youth who had grown up in a stagy atmosphere needed merely to compare the rôles of Brutus and Tell with the tasks which, during these war years, had a hundred times been debated by officers and civilians for the salvation of the new confederacy. Memoranda penned by him during the last days of his life show that the heroic deed of the liberator was mingled in Booth's thoughts with the classical representations of heroic deeds. Even though mask and paint could not make him, as actor, a great Brutus, he might well desire to be one, might well think it possible to become one, in the world of fact. In real life, he could acquire more fame than would ever be acquired in the mimic world of the stage even by this idolized brother of his.

When Lincoln, the enemy of his country, was elected President for the second time, Booth went to Canada, the focus of activity for Southern conspirators and spies. There, it would seem, he hatched a plan for kidnaping Lincoln, who was to be carried off to Richmond. Getting together helpers and sympathizers, and obtaining money from unknown sources — he always insisted that he had made it himself by successful speculations in petroleum — he returned in due course to Washington, with the intention of carrying out his design on the day of the Inauguration. He tried to force his way into the eastern entrance to the Capitol, and for a moment disordered the line of police guards, but he was rebuffed, and declared later that a valuable opportunity had been missed on this occasion.

Here also was the Capitol! Would he not doubly play the part of Brutus if he were to strike down this new Caesar in full sight of the people? The deed was only postponed. As soon as Richmond fell, he hastened to organize in Washington a conspiracy, for which plans had already been made in March. Among the conspirators were Powell, formerly a soldier in the rebel army, a man named Arnold, a woman who had at one time been well-to-do in Maryland, but now kept a small boarding house in Washington, and others — Southerners one and all. Arnold lost heart, and would have liked to get out, but the ringleader had complete ascendancy over his underlings, and, himself increasingly resolute, knew how to impose his influence on them all. Each of them was assigned a specific part. Powell, a stalwart but simple-minded young Floridian, was to kill Seward; another, the comic villain of the drama, was to deal with Johnson, the new Vice President; Booth had reserved the main rôle in the tragedy for himself; a fourth conspirator, Herold by name, very young, was to function as a sort of page, and to help the arch-conspirator to escape; the boarding-house lady and her daughter were likewise in the secret. A Shakespearean exposition. The only thing still uncertain was the date; it would have to be very soon after Lincoln's return from Richmond.

Chance brought him back sooner than had originally been planned. Seward was seriously injured in a carriage accident. Lincoln, therefore, was far away when, on Palm Sunday, the day after the President had left, Lee surrendered. He did not witness the scene, when the Southern general, very much the gentleman, wearing a resplendent new uniform, met the ill-clad Grant in a little farmhouse — Grant with no insignia of rank, swordless, wearing dirty boots, to receive the vanquished warrior. A wire from the President had peremptorily forbidden the Northern commander, when agreeing to a suspension of hostilities, to decide any political issue whatever. The war was not quite finished; not until a few weeks later did Johnston surrender the remnants of the Confederate army to Sherman. More than three million men had borne arms in this war, more than six hundred thousand had perished from wounds or sickness, and the struggle had cost nearly five billion dollars; the percentage of losses had been higher in the South than in the North. The first question was whether the leaders of the rebellion were to be punished, and, if so, how. The President was asked what he was going to do with "Jeff Davis." With a twinkle in his eye, Lincoln replied:

"Well, there was a boy in Springfield who saved up his money and bought a coon, but, after the novelty wore off, it became a great nuisance. He was one day leading the beast through the streets, and had his hands full to keep clear of the little vixen, who had torn his clothes half off of him. At length he sat down on the curbstone, completely fagged out. A man passing by, noticing the lad's disconsolate appearance, stopped, and asked what was the matter.

" 'Oh,' said the boy, 'this coon's such a trouble to me!'

" 'Why don't you get rid of him, then?' asked the sympathizer.

" 'Hush,' said the boy; 'don't you see he's gnawing his rope off?

I'm going to let him do it, and then I'll go home and tell the folks he got away from me.' "

He had recovered the old tone; the nightmare had passed; as of old, Lincoln could deal with the most serious matters in light-hearted vein; nay, on this occasion he could make a matter of historical moment intelligible to the crowd, make it real and vivid, by illustrating it with one of his inimitable anecdotes. Even when he visited Seward, now confined to bed, he was in high spirits. The painter, who was present, describes him as "throwing himself, in his almost boyish exultation, at full length across the bed, supporting his head upon one hand, and in this posture relating the story of the collapse of the rebellion." It was four years now, almost to a day, since in that very room Seward had written a hostile and challenging letter to his chief, who had replied with cold self-confidence. Surely he looks younger and more lively now, as he leans forward, half recumbent, above the sick man, depicting in expressive phrases all the significance of the victory? Do we not feel, for an instant, that the terrible experiences of recent history must have vanished like an evil dream, and we are once more in Indiana, where Honest Abe had to crook up his limbs before he could find room for them, and tell one of his stories? This time he is telling history.

The capital and the whole country are jubilant throughout these days from Monday, April ninth, onward, in a frenzy of exultation which is nowise mitigated by the solemnity of Holy Week. In Washington, crowds gather, released from an evil spell, enraptured by the thought that the bad days are over. They throng the approaches to the White House, and twice the President has to address the people. What will he say to them? Retrospects are useless; the present is still confused; what invigorates him, what he wants his fellow citizens to turn their hearts towards, is the thought of the future, the rebuilding of that which has been destroyed.

"Fellow citizens, We meet this evening not in sorrow, but in gladness of heart. . . . But no part of the honor for plan or execution is mine. To General Grant, his skillful officers, and brave men, all belongs. . . . Unlike a case of war between independent nations, there is no authorized organ for us to treat with — no one man has authority to give up the rebellion for any other man. We simply must begin with and mold from disorganized and discordant elements. Nor is it a small additional embarrassment that we, the loyal people, differ among ourselves as to the mode, manner, and method of reconstruction." Then he goes on, in the course of a long speech, to explain his ideas as to the setting up of the new State government in Louisiana, as to the Negro problem, etc., discussing the matter in detail and on broad lines, as if he were talking to Congress. It is likely enough that those who came only to shout may have been somewhat bored, but they listened attentively, and some of them may have understood what he told them.

Not one among the thousands noticed the repressed passion with which two young men near the front of the gathering contemplated the speaker and listened to the following words: "It is also unsatisfactory to some that the elective franchise is not given to the colored man. I would myself prefer that it were now conferred on the very intelligent, and on those who serve our cause as soldiers."

"That is the last speech he will ever make," said the elder of the two young men to the other. They were Booth and Powell.

Suppose these two men had come from Illinois, and not from the South? Suppose this fanatical young actor had grown up among the abolitionists, instead of among the slave holders, and we cannot doubt that he would not now have had this passionate animus against the great abolitionist. Yet even as a Southerner, had Booth really known Lincoln, had he looked from close at hand into his kindly and discerning gray eyes, had he chanced to watch him riding with Tad and teaching the boy how to tell one tree from another, had he seen him writing a reprieve, or had he merely heard him telling one of his anecdotes — what then? Nay, what would this Brutus feel were he but to be made acquainted with the philosophical explanation which his new Caesar had given of Brutus' deed, describing it as a fatality which the "tyrannicide" had performed because he could not help himself? Assuredly the edifice he had constructed out of thoughts of honor and glory would have crumbled, for no one can fire a shot with passion against a breast that offers itself to the assailant's weapon.

XVIII

At the stroke of noon on April fourteenth, the guns thundered at Fort Sumter, as they had thundered there four years earlier, but this time they were Northern guns, and the charges were blank. The same Major Anderson who had then been in command of the fort, now bearing the rank of general, ran up the very Star-Spangled Banner which had then been shot down, while the band played and the crowd shouted. The orator of the occasion said: "We offer to the President of these United States our solemn congratulations that God has sustained his life and health under the unparalleled burdens and sufferings of four bloody years, and permitted him to behold this auspicious consummation of that national unity for which he has waited with so much patience and fortitude, and for which he has labored with such disinterested wisdom." Twice in this speech the orator remarks that God has let Lincoln live to see this day.

The same morning, Lincoln had been sitting in his study, surrounded by the members of the cabinet. Before the session he had refused himself to callers, and had spent an hour listening to his eldest son's report of what he had seen while with the army, being thus able to learn many confidential details regarding the surrender, and at the same time to study the capacities of his son who had been several years away from home.

When Robert showed him a picture of Lee, he placed it on the table before him, scanned it long and thoughtfully, and then said, "It is a good face. It is the face of a noble, brave man. I am glad the war is over at last."

The cabinet meeting, the first for several weeks, and the first since the Southern surrender, proceeded in a mood very different from that of previous ones for years past. Seward was absent; but, instead, Grant was there (for it was as a member of Grant's staff that Robert had arrived in Washington that morning). All joined in congratulating the victor. "The President," reports Welles, who had worked with him in this room for four years, "was more cheerful and happy than I had ever seen him before, hoping for peace, full of humanity and gentleness." This was not only because of the victory, for when Grant made no secret of his uneasiness owing to the absence of news from Sherman, Lincoln said that Sherman would get the better of Johnston, had indeed already done so. For he last night had a dream which he had dreamed several times. "It was in your department," he said, smiling to Welles, "it related to the water; I seemed to be in a singular and indescribable vessel, but always the same, that was moving with great rapidity towards a dark and indefinite shore; before landing, I awoke. I have had this singular dream before great events, before victories; preceding Antietam, Stone River, Gettysburg, and Vicksburg." "Stone River was no victory," General Grant remarked, with some acerbity.

Never before had Lincoln made so intimate an avowal to his cabinet, since that September day nearly three years before when he had read them the abolition proclamation and had told them of his vow before God. Nothing but a profound stirring of the inner self could have made this lonely man of fifty-six disclose his secret thoughts in such a way; nothing but a sincere faith in the veracity of dreams could have transformed him for the first time in his life into an optimist, and have enabled him to throw off the last of his cares. While Lincoln was talking of this dream of his which was wont to come to him before great events, a few thousand paces away the conspirators had gathered together to discuss the method and the hour of the deed by which, after their own fashion, they were to bring about its fulfillment.

The cabinet went on to consider the problem of reconstruction. Stanton had already elaborated his plans, and submitted them to his colleagues. The President said his say. He was glad, he declared, that Congress was not sitting. "If we are wise and discreet, we can reanimate the States and get their governments in successful operation, with order prevailing and the Union reëstablished, before

Congress comes together in December." He went on to speak of the prevailing desire for revenge, for the punishment of the rebels, and said he would have none of it : "No one need expect me to take any part in hanging or killing these men, even the worst of them. Frighten them out of the country, open the gates, let down the bars, scare them off," said he, throwing up his hands as if scaring sheep. "Enough lives have been sacrificed ; we must extinguish our resentments if we expect harmony and union. There is too much disposition, in certain quarters, to hector and dictate to the people of the South, to refuse to recognize them as fellow citizens. Such persons have too little respect for Southerners' rights. I do not share feelings of that kind."

Are not the assassins near? Surely they must have an ear to the keyhole, in the hope of getting a hint as to the best hour for the carrying of their scheme into effect? Had they been listening, their trigger fingers would have relaxed, for they would have known the words they heard to be those of the Father of the South. Where is Booth, that he may give heed?

Booth has just heard that the President and General Grant are going to the theater this evening. Since Grant is to be one of the victims, the chance must be seized to-night, for to-morrow he will be off again, first to pay a brief visit to his children, and then to hasten back to the front. He does not like Washington, and is uneasy about Sherman, not being a man to put any faith in Lincoln's dream. The manager of the theater has actually announced that Lincoln and the commander in chief are coming to-night, everything is being made ready for a gala performance, and the President's box has been draped with flags.

In all haste, Booth has put the last touches to his scenario. Powell is to make his way into Seward's house late that evening, under pretext that he is a messenger from the doctor and is bringing medicine. The idea of assassinating the Vice President seems to have been abandoned at the last moment, but all that is certainly known is that, the day before, Booth called at the Kirkwood Hotel and left a card for Johnson. For his own use he has hired a fine horse, has shown it with pride to his acquaintances, and has put it in charge of Herold, who is fully informed as to the plans. At noon he goes to the theater, where one of the stage carpenters, a Southerner, is perhaps privy to the plot; gets the man to place the chairs in the box the way he wants them, and in the inner door leading into the box bores a small peephole. His fervor is intensified by the chance of making an end of the two supreme criminals at the same time. Stage-struck as he was, he gave one of the actors a document in which he had penned a patriotic justification of the crime he was about to commit, with urgent instructions that it was to be published in the newspapers next day.

At this very time, Lincoln was writing his last letter. It was to one of the generals who had urged him to be on his guard. "I intend to adopt the advice of my friends, and use due precaution. . . . I thank you for the assurance you give me that I shall be supported by conservative men like yourself in the efforts I may make to restore the Union, so as to make it, to use your language, a union of hearts and hands as well as of States.

"Yours truly, A. Lincoln."

He does not want a lot of visitors to-day! Still, he cannot refuse to see the Speaker, who comes to inquire whether there is to be a summer session of Congress. No, there is not. But since the Speaker is returning to his home in the West, the President would like to send a message to the miners in that part of the world. Not necessary to write it down. Mr. Colfax will easily bear it in mind.

"I have very large ideas of the mineral wealth of our nation. I believe it practically inexhaustible. It abounds all over the western country, from the Rocky Mountains to the Pacific, and its development has scarcely commenced. During the war, when we were adding a couple of million dollars every day to our national debt, I did not care about encouraging the increase in the volume of our precious metals. We had the country to save first. But now that the rebellion is overthrown, and we know pretty nearly the amount of our national debt, the more gold and silver we mine, we make the payment of that debt so much the easier. I am going to encourage that in every possible way. We shall have hundreds of thousands of disbanded soldiers, and many have feared that their return home in such great numbers might paralyze industry, by furnishing, suddenly, a greater supply of labor than there will be demand for. I am going to try to attract them to the hidden wealth of our mountain ranges, where there is room enough for all. Immigration, which even the war has not stopped, will land upon our shores hundreds of thousands more per year from over-crowded Europe. I intend to point them to the gold and silver that wait for them in the West. Tell the miners for me, that I shall promote their interests to the utmost of my ability; because their prosperity is the prosperity of the nation; and we shall prove, in a very few years, that we are indeed the treasury of the world."

In the afternoon, he went out driving with Mary. The streets were crowded, and everywhere the carriage was hailed with accla-mation as it went by. Mary, it seems, was happy. Peace was coming at last, and would bring with it a more cheerful, a more animated life into the White House, which had been a gloomy place all these years. Such being their mood, they took rather a long drive. The conversation went back to earlier days; they talked of Springfield, and then went on to make plans for the time that would follow the second presidential term. Mary would like to spend a year in Europe, to which he good-naturedly agreed, while saying that for his own part he would have preferred a visit to Cali-fornia and other parts of the new West. As they reached home, he saw some people coming away from the door.

"Hullo, boys, do come back!" he called across the square, for he had recognized old acquaintances from Illinois, and who could be more welcome to him during these bright days of relief? He invited them in, asked them after common friends, and, since they would understand him, began to read aloud to them out of one of his favorite humorists. He was back, it seemed, in the mood that had so often been his in the old law office in Springfield, and, when repeatedly summoned to dinner, he waved the messenger away, and tranquilly went on with his reading — until at last "a sort of order" came from Mary, to say they were waiting for him. Reluctantly he stood up and bade his visitors farewell. Why should he have

LINCOLN IN 1864

From a photograph by Brady, Washington

to go to the theater, and show himself off in this way to a lot of people? Well, it is for Grant.

But meanwhile Grant had excused himself. He and his wife must start on the journey to see their children at once; they could not spare another day. They were going to quit the capital on this day of rejoicing over the victory? What could have induced them to inflict such an affront on the President and the public? Mrs. Grant explained later that after the scene Mary had made in the carriage a fortnight earlier, she was afraid of a repetition of it, and wished to avoid it at all hazards. Were she to show herself in the theater beside her husband, the famous general, and were the pair of them to be greeted with salvos of applause, who could tell but that Mrs. Lincoln might take it amiss, and, in her excitement, do something extravagant and unseemly?

Just before setting out to the theater, the President, being handed a petition from a Southern prisoner, who was prepared to take the oath of allegiance and begged for his discharge, wrote on the application, "Let it be done." Thus almost his last official act was one of clemency for the South.

The piece, "Our American Cousin", had already begun when the presidential party reached the theater. At the entry of Lincoln and his wife, there was an outburst of cheering, the acting was interrupted, every one stood, the band struck up "Hail to the Chief", the President bowed his acknowledgments, then the play went on. Since the Grants had gone, a young major and his affianced, family friends, had joined the Lincolns in their box. Nearly two hours passed.

Perhaps Lincoln may have listened, to hear what this "American cousin" had to say, but it is more likely that his thoughts wandered. A soaring mood had made the whole of this day a festal one: a dream had heralded good tidings, friends from home had told him how all was going on in that familiar little circle to which he was so much attached; Grant's trusty hand had shaken his in parting; he had told his cabinet how he was planning to heal all wounds and had banned all thoughts of vengeance, the Far West had sent its images coursing through his mind, had revealed its underground treasures to his poetic imagination, a son of his, it seemed, had ripened to manhood, and through the pictures of the day had moved, as always, the figure of the younger lad — a dream filled with tranquillity, a growing life. The general had advised precaution; well, why not?

But fate, or the rule of the unknown, which had impelled him on his amazing career toward brilliant and unanticipated goals — was it not stronger than any precaution? Had it not sent him from the wild forest to the river with its flatboats, from the river to the little country store, where he lived amid bales and crates, thence to the law office with its piles of dusty documents, and once more through the lovely, blossoming countryside serving justice and common people? There is Herndon, his true comrade, and Speed, who had been to see him recently, and, as usual, had asked for nothing. The narrow hall at Vandalia arises, where they had first tried their mettle in politics, now it is the Capitol of Springfield, all fresh and fine, and then we enter the train and ride on and on, through the land, on endless journeys by train, on to platforms, on to speeches, ever on the trail of the Little Giant. Where, now, is Douglas, who had been so full of life and activity? Where is old friend Baker? Where are his little boys, wilted and perished like half-open buds nipped by the frost?

Death was grinning at him from every corner! Would history speak of him only as the Lord of Death; would history be justly entitled to give him such a name? Looking back on this day of victory, he pondered whether he, at any turn of his life, had asked more than he should? Did not the hotspurs say he had asked too little? And yet, in the end, had not both the things he had so ardently desired in very truth come to pass? Here, where his hand touches the balustrade, it holds the Star-Spangled Banner, shot down four years ago, to wave again triumphantly to-day, while out there in the streets, as they were driving to the theater, many of those who were scanning the carriage had black faces, and all of these seemed aglow with thankfulness, painfully silent. Whither now goes the voyage of that strange ship, toward that unknown shore he had never reached in his dream, having always awakening before the landing? Towards the forests of Indiana? Towards Elysium?

Softly the assassin nears the door of the box. It is nearly ten o'clock. Having nerved himself with a drink of whisky at a neighboring saloon, he presents himself at the theater, like any quiet spectator; and no one there knows him. The play is still going on when he accosts the man who is stationed at the outer door of the box, to guard against unwarranted intrusion. He presents a card, declares that he brings news to the President, who is expecting him, and, strange to tell, is admitted. Now he is in the passageway between the two doors, and sets to work with feverish haste, locks the inner side of the outer door with a wooden bolt he has improvised in the morning. Then he goes to the inner door, and through the hole he has made there, measures the distance with his eye. Close to the door sits the President, beside him his wife, then the younger lady, and, farther to the right, the major, whom Booth does not know. Since the box actually gives upon the stage, a bold jump is all he needs to reach the boards and make his way thence to the well-known exit, where the page is waiting for him with the horse, and be gone! Courage! He will be Brutus!

Opening the inner door, before any one has time to turn round, he has his pistol at his victim's head in an instant and fires. The major springs at him, but reels back, wounded with a dagger thrust. The murderer vaults over the breastwork; but one of his spurs catches in the detested Union flag, and he falls, instead of jumping clear, breaking one of his legs; still, he gets to his feet, brandishes his dagger as he has done so often before on this very stage, and shouts his slogan: *"Sic semper tyrannis!"* Then he bursts through the terrified actors and disappears.

"He has shot the President," comes the cry; no one knows who utters it, nor, at first, are the words understood. Many are awakened out of their terror by Mary's scream, the actors do not even remember what words they had been uttering when the shot rang out, the attendants forget to lower the curtain, the major, whose arm has been badly slashed by the knife thrust, rushes to the door, finds it bolted, but manages to open it; there is general confusion

which is increased when soldiers with fixed bayonets force their way
into the theater. The President, collapsed in his chair, bleeding
from the wound in the head, unconscious, is lifted up, carried out,
but no one knows where to take him. A man from the house across
the street asks if they are carrying a sick man. They explain, he
opens his door, and the wounded President is borne to the bed
of this citizen.

At the selfsame hour, Booth's accomplice had gone to Seward's,
had forced an entry, knife in hand, had wounded four other persons, had stabbed the sick secretary in the cheek and neck, and had
then got clear off.

The bed in which Lincoln is to die is too short for him, he is so
long, and he has to be placed askew. For nine hours his vigorous
constitution struggles against the mortal injury; he lies there breath-
ing heavily till the morning. Mary is lying in the next room, the
cabinet members have assembled. Without recovering consciousness, he dies at seven o'clock; in a strange bed like a pilgrim,
slain on Good Friday like a prophet.

America buried this son of the people as in old times great kings
were brought to the grave. In a long journey, the dead man was
taken back to his home by way of all the places he had
passed through four years earlier, on his way to the capital. Count-
less numbers filed by his coffin before it was lowered into the ground
in the little cemetery at Springfield beside the grave of his little
boy — quietly, as became the man.

Over the coffin, as it moved through the country, glided the
shades of friends and foes. The assassin was hunted hither and
thither, found a hiding place for a time and was able to get his leg
set by a surgeon, was at length run to earth in a barn. He refused
to surrender, the barn was fired, and while it was burning, he was
shot. Four of his accomplices were hanged; one escaped to
Europe. The South realized what it had lost, and the crime was
called parricide.

Lee became a professor and lectured for several years. Davis
wrote memoirs, and lived peacefully for a quarter of a century
after the war ended. Grant became President. Mary lost all

her balance, sold her fine dresses, spent thirteen months in an asylum for the insane, and at last died in the house in which she had been married, her mind still clouded.

Those who mourned most deeply were the blacks; they were the ones who had blessed him so heartily as their saviour in life. They sang songs in his honor, and said that their Messiah was now in heaven. Tad, who lived only a few years more, believed the same thing. When he stood beside the coffin in the White House, he asked:

"Is Father in heaven now? Yes? Then I am glad, for he was not really happy here."

Never again, since Abraham Lincoln lived and died, has an innocent man worn fetters in the United States. Since he lived, worked, and was slain, all men to whom God has given the gift of life are there born free.

INDEX

an intended victim of plot, 482; leaves Washington, 485; becomes President, 488

Grant, Mrs. Ulysses S., 468, 485

Great Britain, sympathies of, in the Civil War, 332, 358; the Trent affair, 358; on the point of recognizing the South, 371

Greeley, Horace, editor of *New York Tribune*, urges Douglas's reëlection to Senate, 188, 189; has interview with Lincoln, President elect, 239; Lincoln's understanding with, 297; blames Lincoln for lack of energy in Louisiana, 363; works against Lincoln, 408; forms cabal with Weed, 423

Greenback, originator of the, 449

Griffin, Charles, Union general, 468

Griffin, Mrs. Charles, Mrs. Lincoln's jealousy of, 468

Grigsby, Aaron, marries Lincoln's sister, 20, 21; turns up before Lincoln's election, 251

Grigsby, Mrs. Aaron (Lincoln's sister), 3–6; marriage, 20, 21; death, 21

Grigsby, Charles, Lincoln plays joke on, 22

Grigsby, Reuben, Lincoln plays joke on, 22

HAITI, independence of, recognized, 335

Hall, Squire, 251

Halleck, Henry W., Union general, 384; crusty epistle of Lincoln to, 384, 385

Hamilton, Alexander, attitude toward slavery, 41

Hamlin, Hannibal, Vice President, 251

Hampton Roads, *Merrimac* sinks Northern ships in, 339

Hanks, Dennis, cousin of Lincoln, joins the Lincolns in Indiana, 10; comes to Washington, 457

Hanks, Elizabeth. See SPARROW, MRS. THOMAS

Hanks, John, cousin of Lincoln, with Lincoln in Illinois, 26; with Lincoln in New Orleans, 32; causes name of Rail-splitter to be attached to Lincoln, 225, 226

Hanks, Lucy ("Aunt Sparrow"). See SPARROW, MRS. HENRY

Hanks, Nancy. See LINCOLN, MRS. THOMAS

Hardin, John J., in Congress, 104, 105

Harding, George F., extract from letter of Lincoln to, 223

Harper's Ferry, Va., captured by John Brown, 220

Harrisburg, Pa., journey of Lincoln from, to Washington, 257

Hay, John, secretary of Nicolay, 231; accompanies Lincoln on journey to Washington, 254

Henry, Dr., of Springfield, Ill., Lincoln's physician, 84, 212

Herndon, James, buy Offutt's shop and stock, 35; fails, 40

Herndon, William H., offends Mary Todd, 78, 79, 98; quoted on Lincoln's feeling for Mary Todd, 92; law partner of Lincoln, 94, 136, 147; Lincoln writes to, 109, 111; quoted on Lincoln as a story-teller, 129, 130; quoted on Lincoln's religious faith, 164, 165; an idealist, 167; in new Republican Party, 183, 189; mayor of Springfield, 183; disliked by Mrs. Lincoln, 217; quoted on Lincoln and Seward as candidates for presidential nomination, 224; works for Lincoln's nomination, 226; quoted on the composition of the first inaugural address, 252; conversation with Lincoln on day before the departure for Washington, 253; letter of Lincoln to, 320; welcomed by Lincoln to Washington, 321

Herold, David E., co-conspirator with Booth, 476, 483

Hill, Samuel, suitor of Ann Rutledge, 43, 44, 48

Hooker, Joseph, Union general, defeated at Chancellorsville, 394; letter of Lincoln to, 396

Hunter, David, Union officer, sent to advise Frémont, 309; reproved by Lincoln, 309; proclaims emancipation in Georgia, Florida, and South Carolina, 333; his action repudiated by Lincoln, 336

ILLINOIS, State Assembly of, 47; early capital of (Vandalia), 47; change of capital to Springfield, 53, 54, 56; a Northern and a Southern tradition in, 175; feeling in, 298; adopts XIIIth Amendment, 462

498 INDEX

Lincoln, Abraham : *Citizen,*—(*Continued*) 117–119; campaigns for Taylor, 119, 120

Fighter: seeks the office of Commissioner of the General Land Office at Washington unsuccessfully, 125–128; refuses secretaryship of Oregon, 128; on circuit, 128–132; methods in law practice, 132–137; life in Springfield, 137, 138; books he liked to read, 138; his fees, 139, 140; takes part in politics, 141; as a negotiator, 141; love for mankind, 142–144, 157, 163, 280; domestic life, 144–150; death of son, 146, 166; his firmness, 146; his moral purity, 149; assists father financially, 151; coldness toward father, 152, 153; dealings with John Johnston, 153–157; consideration for stepmother, 155–157; secures release of Johnston's son from prison, 157; his melancholy, 157–160; his irony, 160, 164; bodily peculiarities, 161; had no love of display, 162; his sense of justice and right, 162, 178; humorous epitaph written by, 163; religious faith, 163–166; his superstition, 166, 450, 451; view of "freedom of the will" and "predestination", 166–168; speaks against Kansas-Nebraska Bill and slavery, 175; letters to Speed's sister and Speed on slavery, 176, 177; views on capital and labor, 179, 280–282; advises revolution through the ballot box, 180; rescues a free slave from the South, 180; runs for Senate but is defeated, 180–182; takes leading part in Illinois in formation of Republican Party, 182, 183; receives votes for vice-presidential nomination at Philadelphia (1856), 182; refuses nomination for governorship of Illinois, 183; speech at Republican State Convention at Bloomington, Ill., 183, 184; takes Horace Greeley to task for urging Douglas for the Senate, 188, 189; some law cases of, 190–193; his "The Divided House" speech, 194–196; joint debates with Douglas, 196–209; celebrity of, 210–213; autobiographical data, 213–215; pecuniary affairs, 215, 216; issues Lincoln-Douglas debates, 217; cam-

paign speeches, 217–219; Cooper Institute speech, 220–222; spoken of in connection with the presidency, 222; political tactics of, 223, 224; the name, Rail-splitter attached to, 225, 226; nominated for presidency at Chicago, 226; receives delegation sent to announce nomination, 227; his letter of acceptance, 227, 228; results of his nomination, 228–230; his campaign, 230–233; election of, 233, 234; his way with visitors, 238, 239; opposes propositions for compromise, 239; his anxiety, 240–242; despondent over Buchanan's course, 242, 243; an omen of his end, 243–244; dependent on smuggled letters and secret messages for news, 246, 247; writes to Stephens, 248; his view of slavery as compared with that of Stephens, 248; forms Cabinet, 250, 251, 260; composes inaugural address, 252; leaves firm signboard hanging, 253; ropes his own trunks, 253, 254; departure from Springfield, 254; journey from Springfield to Washington, 255; arrives in Washington, 257, 258; replies to address of welcome, 259; inauguration, 261–264

Liberator: sends provisions to Fort Sumter, 275, 276; appeals for troops, 276; offers Lee commandership-in-chief, 278; calls for men and money, 279; discusses Constitution of Confederacy, 279, 280; his cabinet room, 283, 284; members of his Cabinet, 284–286; his management of the Cabinet, 287–291; his dealings with men, 291–294; beset by place hunters, 294–296, 329; as regards his management of foreign affairs, 296; understanding with Greeley, 297; management of the border States, 297–298; manner toward foreign envoys, 298–300; in conflict between needs and political considerations, 301, 302; discouragements of, 302, 303; his composure, 304; subordinates the slave issue for the preservation of the Union, 307; his handling of Frémont, 307–309; relations with McClellan, 310, 311; supports Cameron, 311, 312; overlooks

INDEX

503

injured, 477; visited by Lincoln, 478; attempted assassination of, 488

Seymour, Horatio, Governor of New York, 403

Sheridan, Philip H., at City Point, 467

Sherman, William T., Union general, his march to the sea, 406; under Grant, 416; secures Atlanta, 416, 430; his march through Georgia, 430, 458; takes Savannah, 457; at City Point, 467; receives surrender of Johnston, 477

Shields, James, State auditor of accounts, 90; lampoon on, 90, 91; proposed duel with Lincoln, 91, 92; becomes Senator, 121

Siam, King of, sends Lincoln tokens of esteem, 299

Sic semper tyrannis, used as signal in Winter Garden Theatre, 474, 475; Booth's cry after the assassination, 487

Slavery, seen by Lincoln at New Orleans, 25, 29; defenders of, 30, 31; attitude of the fathers of the country toward, 41; Jefferson quoted on, 5; beginnings of, in United States, 46; in the Constitution, 46; forbidden in Northwest Territory by Ordinance of 1787, 46; extent of, at foundation of Union, 46; extent of, defined by Missouri Compromise, 47; discussions on, 67; as connected with annexation of Texas, 102; Lincoln opposed to interference with, 102; in the District of Columbia, Bill to Abolish, drafted by Lincoln, 113, 114; and cotton, 168, 169; restriction, not abolition, of, the thing needed, 169; Lincoln speaks against, in Springfield, 175; letters of Lincoln on, 176, 177; contradiction between, and Declaration of Independence, 178, 179; love of ostentation a reason for defending, 179; Lincoln-Douglas debate on, 196–209; a Southern view of, 246; the difference between Lincoln's and Stephens's view of, 248; the corner-stone of the Confederacy, 249; transitional state of, 331, 332; abolition of, in District of Columbia, 335. *See also* SLAVES

Slaves, fugitive, proposal to arm, 332; idea that the Border States should propose the purchase of, by the Union, 333; fugitive, Army and Navy for-

bidden to aid in return of, 335, 347; Lincoln decides to emancipate, 344–346; and the ballot, 435. *See also* EMANCIPATION PROCLAMATION; NEGROES; SLAVES

Slidell, John. *See* MASON AND SLIDELL

Smith, Caleb B., Secretary of the Interior in Lincoln's Cabinet, 286

South, the, defenders of, 30, 31; threatens to secede from Union, 46; approves of Lincoln's protest against abolition doctrines, 67; supports Polk for presidency, 102; and the North, oppositions between, 168–170; rapid advance of movement tending towards secession in, 184, 220; the real reason for secession of, 245, 246; and the North, comparison of, 270–274; reasons for secession of, 272; opens the Civil War by firing on Fort Sumter, 276; blockaded, 394, 404, 405. *See also* CIVIL WAR; SLAVERY

South Carolina, nullifies tariff, 47; action of governor of, on receipt of information of Lincoln's election, 235; resignations of senators from, 235; secedes from the Union, 236; General Hunter declares emancipation in, 335

Sparrow, Henry, marries Lucy Hanks, 20

Sparrow, Mrs. Henry, 6, 7; her relationship to Lincoln, 20; marriage, 20

Sparrow, Mr. and Mrs., relatives of Lincoln, 10, 20; join the Lincolns in Indiana, 10

Sparrow, Thomas, marries Elizabeth Hanks, 20

Sparrow, Mrs. Thomas, 20

Speed, James, appointed Attorney General, 448

Speed, Joshua F., storekeeper, Springfield, Ill., 61, 62; his shop, 64; advises Lincoln in connection with Mary Todd, 81, 82; moves to mother's farm in Kentucky, 84; visited by Lincoln, 84; letters of Lincoln to, 85–88, 93, 107, 177; marriage, 85–89; letter of Lincoln to sister of, on slavery, 176; not a place hunter, 251; agent of Lincoln in Kentucky, 333

Speed, William, brother of Joshua F. Speed, 85